AAT

Qualifications and Credit Framework (QCF)

LEVEL 4 DIPLOMA IN ACCOUNTING

TEXT

Financial Performance

2011 Edition

First edition July 2010

Second edition June 2011

ISBN 9780 7517 9737 4 (previous ISBN 9780 7517 8566 1)

British Library Cataloguing-in-Publication Data
A catalogue record for this book is available from the British Library

Published by

BPP Learning Media Ltd
BPP House
Aldine Place
London
W12 8AA

www.bpp.com/learningmedia

Printed in the United Kingdom

CONTENTS

A NOTE ABOUT COPYRIGHT

INTRODUCTION

Since July 2010 the AAT's assessments have fallen within the **Qualifications and Credit Framework** and most papers are now assessed by way of an on demand **computer based assessment**. BPP Learning Media has invested heavily to produce new ground breaking market leading resources. In particular, our **suite of online resources** ensures that you are prepared for online testing by means of an online environment where tasks mimic the style of the AAT's assessment tasks.

The BPP range of resources comprises:

- **Texts**, covering all the knowledge and understanding needed by students, with numerous illustrations of 'how it works', practical examples and tasks for you to use to consolidate your learning. The majority of tasks within the texts have been written in an interactive style that reflects the style of the online tasks the AAT will set. Texts are available in our traditional paper format and, in addition, as ebooks which can be downloaded to your PC or laptop.

- **Question Banks**, including additional learning questions plus the AAT's practice assessment and a number of other full practice assessments. Full answers to all questions and assessments, prepared by BPP Learning Media Ltd, are included. Our question banks are provided free of charge in an online environment which mimics the AAT's testing environment. This enables you to familiarise yourself with the environment in which you will be tested.

- **Passcards**, which are handy pocket-sized revision tools designed to fit in a handbag or briefcase to enable you to revise anywhere at anytime. All major points are covered in the Passcards which have been designed to assist you in consolidating knowledge.

- **Workbooks**, which have been designed to cover the units that are assessed by way of project/case study. The workbooks contain many practical tasks to assist in the learning process and also a sample assessment or project to work through.

- **Lecturers' resources**, providing a further bank of tasks, answers and full practice assessments for classroom use, available separately only to lecturers whose colleges adopt BPP Learning Media material. The practice assessments within the lecturers' resources are available in both paper format and online in e format. What fantastic news: you can now give your students an online mock.

This Text for Financial Performance has been written specifically to ensure comprehensive yet concise coverage of the AAT's new learning outcomes and assessment criteria. It is fully up to date as at June 2011 and reflects both the AAT's unit guide and the practice assessment provided by the AAT.

Each chapter contains:

- Clear, step by step explanation of the topic

- Logical progression and linking from one chapter to the next

- Numerous illustrations of 'how it works'

- Interactive tasks within the text of the chapter itself, with answers at the back of the book. In general, these tasks have been written in the interactive form that students will see in their real assessments

- Test your learning questions of varying complexity, again with answers supplied at the back of the book. In general these test questions have been written in the interactive form that students will see in their real assessments

The emphasis in all tasks and test questions is on the practical application of the skills acquired.

If you have any comments about this book, please e-mail suedexter@bpp.com or write to Sue Dexter, Publishing Director, BPP Learning Media Ltd, BPP House, Aldine Place, London W12 8AA.

ASSESSMENT STRATEGY

The assessment will consist of two sections. Section 1 will consist of 8 questions covering the core topics of standard costing, forecasting, performance indicators, what if analysis and cost management techniques. Section 2 will consist of two written tasks one on variance analysis and one on performance analysis.

Learners will normally be assessed by computer-based assessment (CBA), which will include extended writing tasks, and will be required to demonstrate competence in both sections of the assessment. As this CBA will require both computer and human marking, results will normally be available approximately 6 weeks after the assessment.

Competency

Competency	For the purpose of assessment the competency level for AAT assessment is set at 70 per cent. The level descriptor below describes the ability and skills students at this level must successfully demonstrate to achieve competence.

QCF Level descriptor	Summary
	Achievement at level 4 reflects the ability to identify and use relevant understanding, methods and skills to address problems that are well defined but complex and non-routine. It includes taking responsibility for overall courses of action as well as exercising autonomy and judgement within fairly broad parameters. It also reflects understanding of different perspectives or approaches within an area of study or work.
	Knowledge and understanding
	<ul><li>Practical, theoretical or technical understanding to address problems that are well defined but complex and non routine</li><li>Analyse, interpret and evaluate relevant information and ideas</li><li>Be aware of the nature and approximate scope of the area of study or work</li><li>Have an informed awareness of different perspectives or approaches within the area of study or work</li></ul>
	Application and action
	<ul><li>Address problems that are complex and non-routine while normally fairly well defined</li><li>Identify, adapt and use appropriate methods and skills</li><li>Initiate and use appropriate investigation to inform actions</li><li>Review the effectiveness and appropriateness of methods, actions and results</li></ul>
	Autonomy and accountability
	<ul><li>Take responsibility for courses of action, including where relevant, responsibility for the work of others</li><li>Exercise autonomy and judgement within broad but generally well-defined parameters</li></ul>

AAT UNIT GUIDE

Financial Performance (FNPF)

Introduction

For the purpose of assessment both the Principles of Managing Financial Performance and the Measuring Financial Performance units will be combined and assessed together.

Purpose

The creation of these two core units at level four is recognition of the importance of calculating and measuring financial performance in every organisation. This builds on the basic costing concepts and techniques required at level three. However, an understanding and application of performance indicators and cost management extends costing into management accounting.

The "Principles of Managing Financial Performance (Knowledge)" unit is about understanding the principles of managing financial performance. Learners will have the knowledge to be able to use a range of techniques to analyse information on expenditure. They will be able to make judgements to support decision making, planning and control by managers.

The "Measuring Financial Performance (Skills)" unit is about measuring financial performance. Learners will have the skills to collect and analyse information, monitor performance, and present reports to management.

In order for learners to be successful in the two financial performance units they will need to be able to explain, define, describe, calculate and analyse a range of fundamental concepts and techniques. Many of the concepts and techniques are interrelated and learners will need to understand how the concepts and techniques interrelate. They may also be required to explain and describe these relationships.

Learners will need to have a detailed understanding of the fundamental management accounting concepts and techniques in order to demonstrate competence in the learning outcomes. Learners will also need to be able to define and explain the following fundamental concepts (for the knowledge standards) and apply their knowledge to questions which may require the calculation or application of one or more of these fundamental concepts or techniques (for the skills standards). The fundamental management accounting concepts and techniques which learners need to be able to explain, describe, identify, calculate and apply will be covered in the delivery guidance below.

1   Cost classification, cost recording, cost reporting and cost behaviour

Knowledge – Learning outcomes 1, 2 and 3 and Assessment criteria 1.3, 1.4, 2.1, 2.5

Skills outcomes 1 and 3 and Assessment criteria 1.1, 1.2, 1.3, 1.4, 1.5, 3.1, 3.2, 3.3

(a)   Production costing and the elements of direct and indirect costs, cost classification into materials, labour, and overhead,

(b)   Cost classification by behaviour (fixed, variable, stepped fixed and semi variable) relevant range for fixed costs.

(c)   Calculation of variable and fixed costs using the high low method of cost estimation

(d)   Prime cost, full production cost, marginal product cost,

(e)   High low method of fixed and variable cost estimation

(f)   Explain the types of cost centres, profit centres and investment centres

2   Marginal costing and Absorption costing

Knowledge – Learning outcomes 1, 2 and 3 and Assessment criteria 1.1, 1.3, 1.4, 2.3, 2.5

Skills – Learning outcomes 1 and 3 and Assessment criteria 1.1, 1.2, 1.3, 1.4, 1.5, 1.6

(a)   Absorption costing – definition, explanation and calculation of an overhead absorption rate, calculation of under and over absorption, explanation of the advantages and disadvantages of absorption costing – link with financial accounting requirements and price setting model.

(b)   Marginal costing – definition, explanation and calculation of the marginal cost, explanation of the advantages and disadvantages of marginal costing, marginal costing and decision making, see link with contribution theory below.

(c)   Marginal costing v Absorption costing – explain the differences between the treatment of costs, calculation of profit and effects of changing stock levels. Preparation of an absorption costing profit and loss account, a marginal costing profit and loss account, calculation of the changes in profit when stock levels change and a reconciliation between the marginal costing profit and the absorption costing profit.

(d)   Absorption costing v Marginal costing in decision making. Learners need to understand how absorption costing and marginal costing can be used in tasks which measure performance and which consider ways of enhancing value. Absorption costing may be relevant for measuring the performance of a business and it may also be appropriate to use absorption costing principles in enhancing value. A product may be re-engineered in order to reduce production costs and it would be perfectly appropriate to consider the full absorption cost of the redesigned product. Lifecycle costing needs to consider both fixed and variable costs. However, it may be inappropriate to use absorption costing in certain circumstances. For example, if the business is considering contracting out the manufacture of a product, selling surplus capacity or other limiting factor decisions, then marginal costing is the appropriate method as fixed costs will not change as a result of the decision. However, learners need to understand that certain fixed costs may well change and the marginal (incremental) cost may in these circumstances include both variable and fixed components.

(e) Practical limitations of cost classification, non linear behaviour

(f) Absorption costing v Marginal costing could feature in standard costing questions relating to performance measurement or as a stand alone

(g) Contribution analysis.

(h) Break even analysis and margin of safety.

3 **Standard Costing and Variance Analysis**

Knowledge – Learning outcomes 1, 2 and 3 and Assessment criteria 1.1, 1.2, 1.3, 1.4, 2.2, 2.3, 2.4, 2.5

Skills – Learning outcomes 1, 2 and 3 and Assessment criteria 1.1, 1.2, 1.3, 1.4, 1.5, 1.6, 1.7, 2.1, 2.2, 2.3

(a) Explain how standard costs can be established, the different types of standard (ideal, target, normal, basic) and how the type of standard can affect the behaviour of the budget holder and workforce.

(b) Explain the role of standard costing in the planning, decision making and control process. Standard costing variances aid budgetary control systems by breaking down the simple variance identified in a budgetary control system into components based upon an expected outcome. Standard costing is a method of analysing a variance from a budget when standard costs are used in creating the budget.

(c) Extract relevant data from the question in order to calculate various requirements. Learners may be required to calculate any of the following:

   (i)   Standard quantity of inputs (materials, labour, overheads)
   (ii)   Standard cost for given production volumes
   (iii) Actual quantity of inputs (materials, labour, overheads)
   (iv)   Actual costs for given production volumes

(d) Explain and calculate the following variances

    (i)   Raw materials total, price, usage
    (ii)   Labour total, rate, efficiency
    (iii) Labour idle time variance
    (iv) Fixed overhead expenditure variance
    (v)   Fixed overhead volume, capacity and efficiency

(e) Prepare an operating statement under both absorption costing principles and marginal costing principles.

(f) Prepare a reconciliation of the budgeted material cost with the actual material cost using the material cost variances

(g) Prepare a reconciliation of the budgeted labour cost with the actual labour cost using the labour cost variances

(h) Prepare a reconciliation of budgeted fixed overheads with actual fixed overheads using fixed overhead variances.

(i) Prepare journal entries for the posting of variances.

(j) Break down variances using index numbers to isolate controllable and non-controllable parts.

(k) Break down variances, using additional information, into controllable and non-controllable variances.

(l) Prepare reports giving possible reasons for the variances, showing an understanding of the interrelationship between the variances.

(m) Comment on additional information provided by the budget holder as to reasons for the variance. For example, the production manager may say that the quality of raw materials or the old, poorly maintained machines or unskilled staff have caused the adverse raw material usage variance, when the raw materials price variance was adverse, implying that the material was of better than expected quality. This may not be the case - it could be that the buyer bought an inferior material but still paid more than the standard. It may be that an independent assessment of the quality of the material needs to be made.

(n) Explain how standards are developed and appreciate the concepts of Ideal standard, attainable (expected) standard and basic standard. Explain how the chosen standard may affect the behaviour of managers and staff.

(o) Explain the difference between controllable and non-controllable variances, apply index numbers to variances in order to explain how general rising prices can cause variances, and adjust variances for changes in prices.

4   Performance indicators and "what if" analysis

Knowledge – Learning outcomes 1, 2 and 3 and Assessment criteria 1.1, 1.2, 1.3, 1.4, 3.1, 3.2, 3.3, 3.4, 3.5

Skills – Learning outcomes 1, 2 and 3 and Assessment criteria 1.1, 1.2, 1.3, 1.4, 1.5, 1.6, 2.5, 2.6, 2.7, 2.8, 2.9, 3.1, 3.2, 3.3

(a)   Calculate performance indicators

Learners will be asked to calculate a range of performance indicators. Some, such as the return on capital employed or the current ratio, are applicable to many organisations, whilst others might be unique to a particular type of organisation. For example, if the task relates to a hotel, learners might be given data and asked to calculate the cost per room night, the percentage occupancy and the average discount given to customers.

The following is a list of the type of performance indicators learners might be asked to calculate.

(1)   Financial (Profitability, Liquidity, Efficiency and Gearing)

   (a)   Gross profit margin, operating profit margin, administration costs as a percentage of turnover, any cost as a percentage of turnover.

   (b)   Current ratio, quick ratio.

   (c)   Trade cycles (debtor days, stock days, creditor days)

   (d)   Gearing ratio, debt to equity ratio

   (e)   Value added (turnover less the cost of materials used and bought in services)

(2)   Efficiency, Capacity and Activity ratios

   (a)   Labour efficiency ratio = standard hours for actual production/actual hours worked

   (b)   Capacity ratio = actual hours worked/ budgeted hours

   (c)   Labour activity ratio = standard hours for actual production/ budgeted hours, or actual output/budgeted output

(3)   Indicators to measure efficiency, effectiveness and productivity

   (a)   Measures of efficiency include ROCE, operating profit margin and efficiency ratio for labour.

   (b)   Effectiveness measures include percentage of production free from defects, delivery times to customer, number of coaches, buses or trains on time, percentage of learners passing exams first time, number of times a class is cancelled, percentage of parcels delivered within the agreed time. Average waiting times.

(c) Productivity measures are likely to be measured in units of output, or related to output in some way. Examples include number of, say, vehicles manufactured per week, operations undertaken per day, passengers transported per month, units produced per worker per day, rooms cleaned per hour or meals served per sitting.

(4) Indicators to measure quality of service and cost of quality

(a) The number of defects/units returned/warranty claims/customer complaints, the cost of inspection/repairs/re-working

(b) Prevention costs, appraisal costs, internal failure costs, external failure costs

(5) Learners may be asked to compare given indicators with performance indicators that they have calculated. They may have to undertake a benchmarking exercise and need to understand the purpose of benchmarking.

(6) Learners need to recognise that a business has to select key performance indicators and monitor these in order to manage the business. The balanced scorecard is an approach often used and learners need to understand the concept of a balanced scorecard and may be asked to prepare one from given performance indicators.

(7) Tasks may require the calculation of specific performance indicators. If this is the case the calculation of the indicator will either be obvious or the formula for the indicator will be provided. For example, if the task is based on a hotel the occupancy rate calculation should be obvious given the number of rooms sold in the month divided by the total number of room nights available in the month. If the indicator is more complicated the formula will be given.

(b) **Comment on the information generated from the calculation of the performance indicator**

Learners need to be able to explain what the ratios are designed to show and analyse the ratio.

(c) **Understand the interrelationships and limitations of the performance indicator**

Learners need to be able to explain and describe the limitations of the ratios and the interrelationships. Learners may also be required to apply their understanding of the interrelationship in order to make recommendations to management.

(d) Prepare estimates of capital investment projects using discounted cash flow techniques

Learners need to be able to explain, describe and calculate discounted cash flow calculations of net present value, net present cost and net terminal cost and make recommendations to management.

(e) "What if" analysis

After having prepared performance indicators, learners may be faced with taking or recommending action. They may be asked to do one or more of the following:

- Show what the results would have been if benchmark data had been achieved.

- Forecast the performance indicators for the next period based upon a set of assumptions.

- Re-calculate the performance indicators, taking account of given changes to the business, or perhaps select changes which will maximise given indicators.

- Work backwards through a ratio. For example, they may be asked, "What would the turnover need to have been for the asset turnover to be 3 times?", or "What would the operating profit need to have been for the ROCE to be 25%?". This is simple equation manipulation.

- Given several options, learners may be asked to evaluate and recommend a course of action. This could be to improve a key performance indicator like ROCE. They might also be asked to comment on options which cause an improvement in one indicator with a deterioration of another.

- Calculate indicators for 2 years and explain changes in performance.

- Compare 2 businesses and comment on their relative performance.

- Identify potential improvements and estimate the value of them.

- Suggest ways of improving the performance of a poorly performing business.

- Make recommendations.

- Make calculations and recommendations to management for any of the following scenarios

    - Make or buy decision – learners may be required to prepare workings and key ratios to aid the assessment of outsourcing manufacture

- Limiting factor decision making – learners may have to adjust figures and recalculate ratios if a resource constraint limits production.

- Break-even analysis and margin of safety – learners need to be able to calculate and comment on measures of risk, particularly where a business changes or proposes to change the fixed cost and variable costs of production.

- Closure of a business segment, transferring production overseas – learners may have to prepare calculations and make recommendations to management regarding the closure of a business segment.

- Mechanisation – learners may be required to provide calculations and make recommendations to management regarding changing the production process from a labour intensive one to a machine intensive one. They may also be required to bring in break-even analysis in order to demonstrate the changing risk in the business.

With scenario planning or "what if" analysis, learners have to understand how elements of the profit and loss account and balance sheet are linked. For example, a 10% increase in sales volume will lead to a 10% increase in variable costs as more units are produced but no increase in fixed costs, assuming that capacity exists (fixed costs are fixed over the relevant range). A 10% increase in sales price, however, will not lead to any changes in costs. The increase in sales will change the profit and, if no dividends are paid, this will increase the net assets of the business. The change in sales will therefore affect several ratios.

(f) **Key performance indicators and the behaviour of managers**

Learners need to understand that the way in which business unit managers are assessed can have a great influence on the decisions they make. The use of key performance indicators such as ROCE can lead to a lack of goal congruence where managers make decisions which improve performance in certain indicators but which may not be best for the organisation as a whole.

For example, a manager may not be prepared to invest in new machinery if the increase in the net asset position will reduce the ROCE, even though the investment may reduce other costs, lead to zero defects or increase customer satisfaction.

5 **Cost management**

Knowledge – Learning outcome 3 and Assessment criterion 3.6.

Skills – Learning outcomes 1, 2 and 3 and Assessment criteria 1.1, 1.2, 1.3, 1.4, 1.5, 2.2, 2.4, 2.8, 2.9, 3.1, 3.2, 3.3

(a) Life cycle costing and how it can be used to aid cost management. Learners may be required to calculate life cycle costs for different options. Life cycle cost calculations may require the use of discounted cash flow techniques.

(b) The concepts behind target costing (including value analysis/engineering). Learners may be required to explain target costing and prepare a target cost from information in the task. Learners may also have to analyse information provided from functional specialists like designers, engineers and marketing professionals.

(c) Activity based costing and how it can be applied to an organisation. Learners may be given information and asked to calculate the absorption rates under activity based costing and comment on its applicability.

(d) The principles of Total Quality Management. Learners may be provided with information about the various costs incurred to prevent faulty production and costs incurred to rectify faulty production and settle warranty claims. Learners may then be asked to calculate the cost of quality. Whilst the general theory is that organisations should plan to have zero defects, learners should be aware that there may be commercial justifications for allowing some defects, perhaps because of expensive quality assurance systems.

(e) Product lifecycle and how costs change throughout the life of a product. Concepts of economies of scale, mechanisation, a switch from variable to fixed costs may be assessed.

(f) Understanding of the planning, decision making and control stages in management accounting and how cost management techniques can aid the stages.

6 Basic statistical methods

Knowledge – Learning outcome 3 and Assessment criterion 3.4

Skills – Learning outcomes 1, 2 and 3 and Assessment criteria 2.1, 2.2, 2.3, 2.4

The learner must be able to explain the use and purpose of indexing, sampling and time series (e.g. moving averages, linear regression and seasonal trends).

Index numbers – learners must be able to calculate index numbers and use them to forecast costs and prices and also to subdivide variances. Learners must also be able to interpret indices and compare them with methods of securing contracts to reduce the risk of rising prices.

Moving averages – learners must be able to calculate moving averages and seasonal variations and use calculations to extrapolate a forecast of sales or costs.

Seasonal variations – learners need to understand types of variation from the trend and may be required to identify the seasonal variation or use the seasonal variation and a given trend to forecast sales volume, prices or cost information.

Regression analysis

Learners will **not** be required to derive the regression equation $y = a + bx$ but they may be given the equation and asked to use it to calculate a and b, given y and x, for several points, or to calculate y and x, given a and b. The equation could then be used to predict prices, demand and costs.

chapter 1:
COSTS

OVERVIEW OF A COSTING SYSTEM

One of the key concerns that the management of an organisation will have, will be how much the products that it produces, or the services that it provides, cost. This information will be vital for many purposes including the following:

- setting the selling price
- determining the quantities of production and sales
- continuing or discontinuing a product
- controlling costs
- controlling production processes
- appraising managers

Types of cost

Costs in both manufacturing and service industries are traditionally split between:

- material costs
- labour costs
- overheads (or expenses)

These costs in turn can be described as direct costs or indirect costs. This analysis depends upon whether the cost in question can be directly attributed to a unit of production or unit of service. The first stage in the cost allocation process then is to determine the cost units of the business.

In a manufacturing business the COST UNIT may be each unit of production or each batch of production. In a service business the identification of the cost unit may not be quite so straightforward but, for example, in a transport business the cost unit might be each lorry mile travelled or, in a restaurant, it might be each meal served.

Any material cost or labour cost or expense that can be directly related to the cost unit is a DIRECT COST of that cost unit. However many costs of the business cannot be directly attributed to a cost unit and these costs are initially taken to a cost centre.

A COST CENTRE is an area of the business, maybe a department such as the factory or canteen, for which costs are incurred that cannot be directly attributed to the cost units. These costs are known as INDIRECT COSTS or overheads and include, for example, the rent of the factory and the wages of the supervisor.

There are two types of cost centre – those that are directly involved in the production or provision of the cost unit, such as the factory, and these are known as PRODUCTION COST CENTRES. There are also cost centres that, while not actually producing the cost unit, do provide a service to the production cost centres, such as the canteen. These are known as SERVICE COST CENTRES.

Allocation and apportionment of overheads

The overheads of both the production and the service cost centres are part of the necessary cost of producing the cost units and therefore in some costing systems they are included in the overall cost of the cost unit. This is done by the following process:

- ALLOCATION of overheads that relate to just one cost centre, such as the depreciation of the factory machinery being allocated to the factory cost centre, or the food costs being allocated to the canteen.

- APPORTIONMENT of overheads that relate to a number of cost centres to each relevant cost centre on some fair basis, such as the apportionment of the rent of the building to each cost centre in the building on the basis of floor space occupied.

- RE-APPORTIONMENT of service cost centre costs to the production cost centres to ensure that all overheads are now included within the production cost centre costs.

- ABSORPTION of all of the overheads of each production cost centre into the cost of cost units on some fair basis, such as the number of labour hours or machine hours that each cost unit uses.

We can summarise this process in a diagram (this will be covered in more detail in Chapter 2):

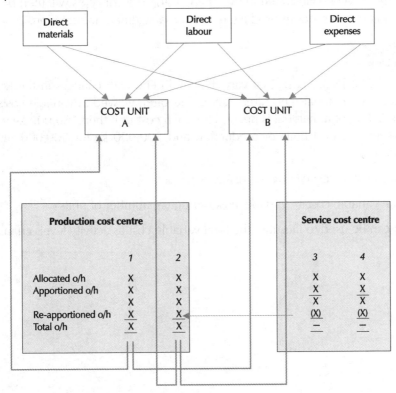

Cost centres, profit centres and investment centres

We have seen that a cost centre is an area or department of a business which incurs costs involved in the business operations. A PROFIT CENTRE is an area of the business which not only incurs costs but also earns revenue, for example a sales department in an organisation which earns revenue from sales but incurs costs such as a salesman's salary and commission. An INVESTMENT CENTRE is an area of the business which not only incurs costs and earns revenues but also accounts for its own capital investment. An example might be a separate division of the organisation which has a factory from which it produces goods, sells and despatches them.

CLASSIFICATION OF COSTS BY BEHAVIOUR

In order to be able to correctly deal with all of these different types of cost you must be able to recognise that different types of cost behave in different ways when the levels of activity in the organisation change. This is known as classification of costs by behaviour and the main classifications are:

- variable costs
- fixed costs
- stepped costs
- semi-variable costs

Each of these will be illustrated in this chapter and the concepts will then be used in later chapters in order to produce relevant management information.

Variable costs

VARIABLE COSTS are costs that vary directly in line with changes in the level of activity. Direct materials and direct labour are often viewed as variable costs. For example if 1 kg of a material is needed for each cost unit then 100,000 kg will be required for 100,000 units of production and 500,000 kg for 500,000 units of production.

The total variable cost can be expressed as:

Total variable cost = Variable cost per unit × number of units

A graph can be used to illustrate the total variable cost as activity levels change.

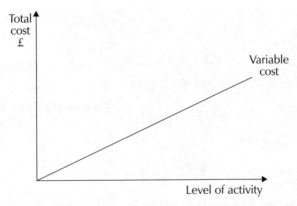

Direct costs such as materials costs may not always be true variable costs. For example, if a supplier offers a bulk purchasing discount for purchases above a certain quantity, then the cost per unit will fall if orders are placed for more than this quantity.

Fixed costs

A FIXED COST is one which does not change as activity levels alter. An example often used is that of the rent and rates of the factory. This will remain the same cost whether 100,000 units are produced or 500,000 units.

The behaviour of fixed costs can be shown graphically:

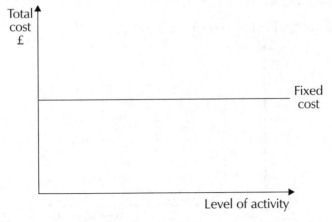

In practical terms fixed costs are only truly fixed over the RELEVANT RANGE. For example the rent of the factory will only remain constant provided that the level of activity is within the production capacity of the factory. If production levels increase above the capacity of the current factory then more factory space must be rented, thus increasing the rent cost for this level of production.

As the activity level increases the fixed cost remains fixed in total but the fixed cost per unit will fall as the total cost is spread over more units.

Task 1

A business incurs fixed costs of £100,000. Complete the table below showing the budgeted fixed cost per unit at each production level.

Production level	Budgeted fixed cost per unit £
20,000 units	5.00
40,000 units	2·50
80,000 units	1·25

Stepped costs

STEPPED COSTS are costs which are fixed over a relatively small range of activity but then increase in steps when certain levels of activity are reached. For example, if one production supervisor is required for each 30,000 units of a product that is made, then three supervisors are required for production of up to 90,000 units, four for production of up to 120,000 units, five for production up to 150,000 units and so on.

Stepped costs can be illustrated on a graph:

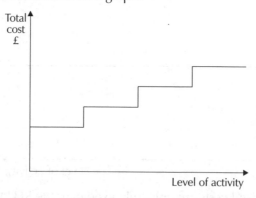

A stepped cost is really a fixed cost with a relatively short relevant range.

Task 2

Insert the missing term:

The | RELEVANT RANGE | of a cost is the activity levels over which the cost is fixed.

Semi-variable costs

SEMI-VARIABLE COSTS are costs which have a fixed element and also a variable element. For example, the telephone bill includes a fixed element being the fixed line rental for the period and a variable element which will increase as the number of calls increase.

The total of a semi-variable cost can be expressed as:

Total cost = Fixed element + (variable cost per unit × number of units)

A semi-variable cost can be illustrated on a graph as follows:

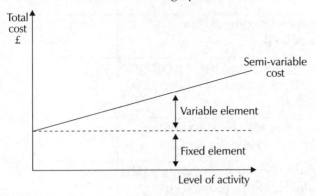

The calculation of the fixed and variable elements of a semi-variable cost will be considered in the next section of this chapter.

Task 3

Choose from the list below to show how each of the following costs would be classified according to their behaviour.

Cost	Behaviour
Stores department costs which include £5,000 of insurance premium and an average of £100 cost per materials receipt or issue	SEMI-VARIABLE
Machinery depreciation based upon machine hours used	VARIABLE
Salary costs of lecturers in a training college, where one lecturer is required for every 200 students enrolled	STEPPED
Buildings insurance for a building housing the stores, the factory and the canteen	FIXED
Wages of production workers who are paid per unit produced, with a guaranteed weekly minimum wage of £250	FIXED, THEN SEMI-VAR.

List

Variable

Fixed

Semi-variable

Fixed, then semi-variable

Stepped

HOW IT WORKS

The use of cost behaviour principles in product costing is illustrated in the following example.

Cameron Ltd produces one product which requires the following inputs:

Direct materials	1 kg @ £3.50 per kg
Direct labour	1 hour @ £6.00 per hour
Rent	£4,000 per quarter
Leased machines	£1,500 for every 4,000 units of production
Maintenance costs	£1,000 per quarter plus £1.00 per unit produced

Calculate the total cost of production and the cost per unit for each of the following production levels for the coming quarter:

- (a) 4,000 units
- (b) 10,000 units
- (c) 16,000 units

Direct materials – these are a variable cost with a constant amount per unit (1 kg × £3.50 = £3.50) therefore the total cost is found by multiplying the number of units by the unit cost:

£3.50 × 4,000 units	=	£14,000
£3.50 × 10,000 units	=	£35,000
£3.50 × 16,000 units	=	£56,000

Direct labour – another variable cost, with a unit cost of 1hr x £6 = £6:

£6.00 × 4,000 units	=	£24,000
£6.00 × 10,000 units	=	£60,000
£6.00 × 16,000 units	=	£96,000

Rent – this is a fixed cost and therefore provided we are still operating within the relevant range will remain at £4,000 whatever the production level.

Leased machines – this is a stepped cost and the number of machines leased will depend upon the quantity of production.

4,000 units	=	1 machine	=	£1,500
10,000 units	=	3 machines	=	£4,500
16,000 units	=	4 machines	=	£6,000

Maintenance costs – this is a semi-variable cost with a fixed element of £1,000 and a variable cost of £1 per unit. The total cost for each activity level is:

4,000 units	=	£1,000 + (4,000 × £1.00)	=	£5,000
10,000 units	=	£1,000 + (10,000 × £1.00)	=	£11,000
16,000 units	=	£1,000 + (16,000 × £1.00)	=	£17,000

Thus the total costs of production are:

	Production level – units		
	4,000	10,000	16,000
	£	£	£
Direct materials (variable)	14,000	35,000	56,000
Direct labour (variable)	24,000	60,000	96,000
Rent (fixed)	4,000	4,000	4,000
Leased machines (stepped)	1,500	4,500	6,000
Maintenance costs	5,000	11,000	17,000
Total cost	48,500	114,500	179,000
Number of units	4,000	10,000	16,000
Cost per unit	£12.13	£11.45	£11.19

The cost per unit is decreasing as the production quantity increases. This is because the fixed cost and the fixed element of the semi-variable cost are being spread over a larger number of units.

Variable costs with a discount

Suppose now that the supplier of the materials offers a bulk purchasing discount of 6% for all purchases if an order is placed for more than 8,000 kgs.

What is the direct materials cost in total and per unit at each level of production?

4,000 units

Total cost	4,000 × £3.50	=	£14,000
Cost per unit	£14,000/4,000	=	£3.50

10,000 units

Total cost	10,000 × (£3.50 × 94%)	=	£32,900
Cost per unit	£32,900/10,000	=	£3.29

16,000 units

| Total cost | 16,000 × (£3.50 × 94%) | = | £52,640 |
| Cost per unit | £52,640/16,000 | = | £3.29 |

The direct materials are now not a true variable cost as the cost per unit falls once production is in excess of 8,000 units.

Task 4

A salesperson receives a fixed salary of £800 per month plus commission of £20 for each sale confirmed in the month.

Complete the table to show the salesperson's monthly salary for the month, if confirmed sales are at each of the following levels.

Sales	Monthly salary £
4 sales	880
8 sales	960
15 sales	1100

Practical limitations of cost classifications

As we have seen in this chapter so far, it can be useful to classify costs according to their behaviour. However in order to have made these classifications we have assumed that the costs have a linear behaviour, that is they are a straight line when drawn on a graph. This may not always be the case in practice. For example we have seen that if a discount is given for purchases above a certain level, then the materials purchases cost will not be a true variable cost. Thus unit variable costs may fall as economies of scale are achieved. Similarly although the direct labour cost is often viewed as a variable cost, if activity levels reach a certain amount then overtime might be incurred and this will mean that the cost is no longer a straight-forward variable cost.

The assumption is normally that variable costs or the variable element of a semi-fixed cost will increase or decrease as activity levels in the form of units of output increase and fall. However the relevant level of activity may not always be units of output. For example an organisation's telephone bill is normally assumed to have a fixed element, the line rental, and a variable element, call costs, which increase as activity levels increase. In this case the relevant activity level causing the call cost to vary is the number of calls made. If we look at the call costs in relation to the level of output, in some organisations it may be the case that the call costs increase as the activity levels in terms of units of output fall, as the sales team will be trying to boost sales and therefore production.

Prime cost and full production cost

In the example above the costs were simply totalled, however for management accounting purposes it will sometimes be useful to categorise the costs in sub-totals.

The PRIME COST of a product is all the direct costs of producing that product.

The MARGINAL COST of a product is all the variable costs of producing that product (both direct eg materials and labour and indirect eg variable overheads).

The FULL PRODUCTION COST includes all the overheads or indirect costs of the production of the product, both fixed and variable.

HOW IT WORKS

Using the figures for the 4,000 units level of production from the previous example, we can now classify the costs as prime cost, marginal cost and full production cost.

	£
Direct materials	14,000
Direct labour	24,000
Prime cost	**38,000**
Variable element of maintenance costs	4,000
Marginal cost	**42,000**
Rent	4,000
Leased machines	1,500
Fixed element of maintenance costs	1,000
Full production cost	**48,500**

SEMI-VARIABLE COSTS

Semi-variable costs are more complex than variable and fixed costs as these costs have a fixed element which is not related to the level of activity, and a variable element which is related to the level of activity. For a semi-variable cost we need to be able to estimate, at any given level of activity, both the fixed element amount and the variable element rate.

Hi lo method of cost estimation

One method of estimating the fixed and variable elements of a semi-variable cost is to use the HI LO METHOD. Under this method historical data regarding the amount of the semi-variable cost at various activity levels is collected.

A comparison is then made between the costs at the highest level of activity and at the lowest level of activity, in order to isolate the variable rate of increase in the cost and then to find the fixed element of the cost. This method assumes that there is a linear relationship between the cost and output at the highest and lowest activity levels.

HOW IT WORKS

The costs of the factory maintenance department for Kilman Ltd appear to be partially dependent upon the number of machine hours operated each month. The machine hours and the maintenance department costs for the last six months are given below:

	Machine hours	Maintenance cost
		£
June	4,000	104,000
July	4,800	127,000
August	4,200	111,000
September	4,500	119,000
October	3,800	107,000
November	4,100	107,500

Step 1

Find the highest and lowest levels of activity (note that this is the activity level and is not necessarily the highest and lowest cost).

In this case the highest level is 4,800 hours in July and the lowest level is 3,800 hours in October.

Step 2

Compare the activity level and costs for each of these:

	Machine Hours	Cost £
Highest	4,800	127,000
Lowest	3,800	107,000
Increase	1,000	20,000

13

This shows that for an increase in 1,000 machine hours there has been an increase of £20,000 of costs. Therefore the variable cost per machine hour can be estimated as:

Variable rate of increase   =   £20,000/1,000 hours

                              =   £20 per machine hour

Step 3

We can now find the fixed element of the cost, by substituting the variable rate into either the highest or lowest activity level, with the fixed element appearing as the balancing figure. This will provide you with the same answer whether you use the highest or lowest level of activity.

Highest level

	£
Variable element 4,800 hours × £20	96,000
Fixed element (balancing figure)	31,000
Total cost	127,000

Lowest level

	£
Variable element 3,800 hours × £20	76,000
Fixed element (balancing figure)	31,000
Total cost	107,000

Therefore the fixed element of the maintenance department costs is £31,000 and the variable rate is £20 per machine hour.

Step 4

We can now use this analysis of the semi-variable cost to forecast figures for the maintenance department. The anticipated machine hours for the next three month period are as follows:

	Dec	Jan	Feb
Machine hours	4,000	4,500	5,000

The forecast maintenance department costs for these three months can be calculated:

Forecast maintenance department costs

	£
Dec (4,000 × £20) + £31,000	111,000
Jan (4,500 × £20) + £31,000	121,000
Feb (5,000 × £20) + £31,000	131,000

Interpolation and extrapolation

In the previous example we used our calculated figures about the cost movement in order to estimate the future costs of the maintenance department. In order to find the variable and fixed elements of the cost we looked at an activity range of 3,800 hours to 4,800 hours and estimated how the costs moved within that range.

For December and January the anticipated machine hour levels fall within this range, therefore it is likely that our estimates of cost will be fairly accurate (although they do not coincide with the historical costs associated with those levels – our model is not totally accurate as it is based on the assumption of a linear relationship which is unlikely to apply perfectly in practice). When the levels being forecast are within the range considered this is known as INTERPOLATION.

However for February the machine hours are estimated to be 5,000. This is outside the range that we considered and therefore our estimate of future cost is known as EXTRAPOLATION. Extrapolation may not be as accurate as interpolation, as the activity level is outside our historical data range and therefore we do not know how the costs will behave outside of the range.

Task 5

The production costs at various levels of production for a business are given below:

Production level	Production costs
units	£
24,000	169,000
20,000	143,000
28,000	191,000

The variable rate of production costs is

6·00 PER UNIT

The fixed amount of production costs is

23,000

CHAPTER OVERVIEW

- Direct costs are costs that can be related directly to a cost unit whereas indirect costs are initially allocated or apportioned to a cost centre, before being charged to cost units

- Costs are often classified according to their behaviour as activity levels change – the main classifications are variable costs, fixed costs, stepped costs and semi-variable costs

- Semi-variable costs include both a fixed element and a variable rate element – one method of calculating these two elements is to use the hi lo method

Keywords

Cost unit – the individual product or service for which costs are to be gathered

Direct costs – costs that can be directly attributed to cost units

Cost centre – an area of the business for which costs are to be gathered

Production cost centre – directly involved in the production of the cost unit

Service cost centre – provides a service to the production cost centres

Indirect costs – costs that cannot be attributed directly to a cost unit but are initially attributed to a cost centre

Allocation – overheads that relate to just one cost centre are charged directly to that cost centre

Apportionment – overheads that relate to a number of cost centres are shared between each relevant cost centre on some fair basis

Re-apportionment – sharing total service cost centre costs among the production cost centres to ensure that all overheads are now included within the production cost centre costs

Absorption – process of allocating overheads of each production cost centre into the cost of cost units on some fair basis.

Profit centre – an area of the business which incurs costs and earns revenues

Investment centre – an area of the business which incurs costs, earns revenues and is also responsible for its own capital investment

Variable costs – costs that increase/decrease directly in line with any changes in activity level

Fixed costs – costs that remain constant as activity levels change

Relevant range – the range of activity levels over which a fixed cost will not change

Stepped costs – costs which are fixed over a relatively small range and then increase in steps

Semi-variable costs – costs which have both a fixed element and variable element

Prime cost – all the direct costs of producing a product

Marginal cost – all the variable costs of producing a product (both direct eg materials and labour and indirect eg variable overheads)

Full production cost – all the costs of producing a product, including the overheads or indirect costs of production

Hi lo method – a method of estimating the fixed and variable elements of a semi-variable cost using historic data

Interpolation – estimation of a forecast figure within the range of activity levels considered

Extrapolation – estimation of a forecast figure outside the range of activity levels considered

TEST YOUR LEARNING

1 The direct materials cost for 10,000 units is estimated to be £43,600 and for 12,000 is estimated to be £52,320. This is a variable cost.

True or false? Tick the correct answer.

True ☑

False ☐

2 A business expects to incur fixed costs of £64,000 in the following month.

Complete the table below to show the total fixed cost and the fixed cost per unit at each of the following activity levels.

Activity level	Total fixed cost £	Fixed cost per unit £
3,000 units	64.000	21.33
10,000 units	64.000	6.40
16,000 units	64,000	4.00

3 A business makes 3,500 units per month with the following costs:

Direct materials £5 per unit

Direct labour £10 per unit

Rent £10,000 per month

Supervisor costs £7,500 per month for every 5,000 units of production

The marginal cost per month is

52500

The full production cost per month is

70.000

4 Given below are the activity levels and production costs for the latest six months for a factory:

	Activity level	Production cost
	units	£
July	103,000	469,000
August	110,000	502,000
September	126,000	547,000
October	113,000	517,000
November	101,000	472,000
December	118,000	533,000

(a) The variable element of the production cost is

> 3.00

The fixed element of the production cost is

> 169.000

(b) Complete the following table to show the estimated production costs at each of the levels of production.

Level of production	Production cost £
120,000 units	529.000
150,000 units	619.000

(c) Comment upon which of the two estimates of production costs calculated in (b) is likely to be most accurate and why.

The most accurate production cost is for 120,000 units as this falls within the range of activity levels previously experienced. This is a method known as interpolation.

The values for 150,000 units have been extrapolated and being outside the known range are not so readily relied upon.

chapter 2:
METHODS OF COSTING

chapter coverage 📖

In this chapter we will consider a variety of different methods of costing – absorption costing, marginal costing and activity based costing.

The topics that are to be covered are:

✍ Methods of costing

✍ Under- and over-absorption of overheads

✍ Activity based costing

METHODS OF COSTING

We have seen in outline how the cost of a cost unit is calculated. We will now move onto the different methods of calculating a cost per unit that a business may use. The method chosen will depend upon the type of business and the policy of management. There are three main methods of calculating a cost per unit:

- **ABSORPTION COSTING** – under this costing method a 'full' production cost per unit is calculated by including in the cost of the cost unit a proportion of the production overheads from each of the production and service cost centres. This is done by allocating, apportioning and absorbing the overheads.

- **VARIABLE OR MARGINAL COSTING** – under this method only the variable costs (or marginal costs) of production are included in the cost per cost unit. The fixed overheads are treated as period costs and not as part of the cost unit. The fixed overheads are charged to the income statement (profit and loss account) as an expense for the period.

- **ACTIVITY BASED COSTING** – this is a method of absorption costing which uses more sophisticated methods of allocating overheads to cost units than the normal methods of overhead allocation and apportionment. It does this by considering the activities that cause the overhead to be incurred and the factors that give rise to the costs (cost drivers).

HOW IT WORKS

Fenton Partners produce one product, the Fenton. The factory has two production departments, assembly and packing, and there is one service department, maintenance. 75% of the maintenance department's time is spent in the assembly department and the remainder in the packing department.

The expected costs of producing 100,000 units in the next quarter are as follows:

Direct materials	£24.00 per unit
Direct labour	2 hours assembly @ £7.00 per hour
	1 hour packing @ £6.00 per hour
Assembly overheads	£320,000
Packing overheads	£240,000
Maintenance overheads	£200,000

In each of the production and service departments it is estimated that 40% of the overheads are variable and the remainder are fixed. Overheads are absorbed on the basis of labour hours.

Calculate the cost per unit using the following costing methods:

(a) absorption costing

(b) marginal costing

Absorption costing

Production overheads

	Assembly	Packing	Maintenance
	£	£	£
Allocated and apportioned	320,000	240,000	200,000
Re-apportioned – maintenance (75%/25%)	150,000	50,000	(200,000)
Total overhead	470,000	290,000	–
Total hours 2 × 100,000	200,000		
1 × 100,000		100,000	
Absorption rate =	$\dfrac{470,000}{200,000}$	$\dfrac{290,000}{100,000}$	
=	£2.35 per labour hour	£2.90 per labour hour	

Interpretation:

For every one hour that the product is worked on in the assembly department, it is charged with a £2.35 share of the overheads incurred.

For every one hour that the product is worked on in the packing department, it is charged with a £2.90 share of the overheads incurred.

Unit cost

	£
Direct materials	24.00
Direct labour – assembly 2 hours × £7.00	14.00
Direct labour – packing 1 hour × £6.00	6.00
Prime cost	44.00
Overheads – assembly 2 hours × £2.35	4.70
– packing 1 hour × £2.90	2.90
Absorption cost per unit	51.60

23

Marginal costing

In this method only variable overheads are included in the cost per unit, so these must be ascertained:

		Assembly	*Packing*
Total overhead (as before)		£470,000	£290,000
Variable element (40%)		£188,000	£116,000
Labour hours (as before)		200,000	100,000
Absorption rate	=	$\dfrac{£188,000}{200,000}$	$\dfrac{£116,000}{100,000}$
	=	£0.94 per labour hour	£1.16 per labour hour

Unit cost

	£
Direct materials	24.00
Direct labour – assembly 2 hours × £7.00	14.00
Direct labour – packing 1 hour × £6.00	6.00
Prime cost	44.00
Variable overhead – assembly (2 hours × £0.94)	1.88
– packing (1 hour × £1.16)	1.16
Marginal cost per unit	47.04

Task 1

A business expects to produce 5,000 units of its single product in the next month, with the following costs being incurred:

	£
Direct materials	12,000
Direct labour	15,000
Variable overheads	23,000
Fixed overheads	25,000

Complete the following table to show the cost per unit under both absorption costing and marginal costing methods.

Costing method	Cost per unit £
Absorption costing	15.00
Marginal costing	10.00

Marginal and absorption costing, inventory (stock) levels and profit

As we have just seen, the unit cost is very different under marginal costing from that calculated under absorption costing.

Under absorption costing the fixed overhead is absorbed into the units produced in the period, and therefore the full production cost of the units actually sold in the period is charged to the income statement (profit and loss account) as part of cost of sales.

However under marginal costing a lower value is assigned to cost of sales, as the cost per unit only includes variable costs. The fixed costs are then charged to the income statement as a period cost.

This difference is also reflected in the valuation of inventory (stock). Under absorption costing, inventory is valued at the full production cost, which includes the absorbed fixed overhead. However under marginal costing a lower value is assigned to the value of inventory, as the cost per unit only includes variable costs.

If the opening inventory and closing inventory levels are the same (so that sales = production) then when we include revenue per unit and in total into our calculations, profit shown under both absorption costing and marginal costing will be the same. However if opening and closing inventory levels are different, ie there has been an increase or decrease in inventory levels, then absorption costing and marginal costing will not produce the same profit figure, because of the differences in the treatment of fixed overheads and the valuation of inventory.

An important difference in this context between absorption and marginal costing is that in the latter we calculate and focus on contribution per unit, which is revenue less variable costs per unit. We will look at the use of contribution for decision making in Chapter 3.

HOW IT WORKS

Spa Ltd makes a single product and produces management accounts including an income statement each month. In both May and June 100,000 units of the product were produced.

The production costs in both May and June were:

	£
Direct materials	200,000
Direct labour	300,000
Fixed overheads	300,000
Total costs	800,000

There were no opening inventories at the start of May and all of the production for May was sold. However in June only 75,000 units of production were sold, leaving 25,000 units in inventory.

Each unit is sold for £10.

(a) What is the cost per unit using:

(i) absorption costing
(ii) marginal costing?

(b) What is the profit for each month using:

(i) absorption costing
(ii) marginal costing?

(a) **Unit cost**

(i) Absorption costing:

£800,000/100,000 = £8 per unit

(ii) Marginal costing (ignore fixed overheads):

£500,000/100,000 = £5 per unit

(b) **Income statements**

    (i)   Absorption costing:

	May £	May £	June £	June £
Sales		1,000,000		750,000
Less: cost of sales				
Opening inventory	–		–	
Cost of production				
100,000 units × £8	800,000		800,000	
	800,000		800,000	
Less: closing inventory				
25,000 units × £8	–		(200,000)	
Cost of sales		800,000		600,000
Profit (absorption costing)		200,000		150,000

    (ii)   Marginal costing:

	May £	May £	June £	June £
Sales		1,000,000		750,000
Less: cost of sales				
Opening inventory	–			
Cost of production				
100,000 units × £5	500,000		500,000	
	500,000		500,000	
Less: closing inventory				
25,000 units × £5	–		(125,000)	
Marginal cost of sales		500,000		375,000
Contribution to fixed costs		500,000		375,000
Less: fixed costs		300,000		300,000
Profit (marginal costing)		200,000		75,000

In May the profit is the same under both costing methods, £200,000. This is because there is no movement in inventory during the period, since all of the production is sold.

In June however profit under absorption costing is £150,000, whereas it is only £75,000 under the marginal costing method. The reason for the £75,000 difference in profit is that the closing inventory under absorption costing includes £75,000 (£300,000/100,000 × 25,000 units) of fixed costs that are being carried forward to the next accounting period, whereas under marginal costing they were all written off in June.

The rules are that:

(1) **if inventory levels are rising, then absorption costing will give higher profits** as the fixed overheads are being carried forward into the next accounting period

(2) **if inventory levels are falling, then absorption costing will give a lower profit figure** as more fixed overheads from the previous period are charged to the income statement in this period

(3) **where inventory levels are constant** (provided that unit costs are constant), **then absorption costing and marginal costing will give the same level of profit**

A reconciliation of the profit figures can be prepared:

	May £	June £
Absorption cost profit	200,000	150,000
Change in inventory (sales = production)	0	
Increase in inventory (25,000 units – 0) × fixed cost per unit £3		(75,000)
Marginal cost profit	200,000	75,000

Task 2

A business operates an absorption costing system. At the start of last month the business had 2,500 units in inventory (stock). During the month it produced another 23,000 units and sold 24,000. The cost per unit of the product is as follows:

	£
Direct materials	10.00
Direct labour	14.00
Prime cost	24.00
Variable overheads	3.00
Fixed overheads	2.00
Absorption cost per unit	29.00

The business reported a profit of £504,000.

The profit if the business used marginal costing would have been
£ [   ]

UNDER- AND OVER-ABSORPTION OF OVERHEADS

As we have seen using absorption costing, the overhead cost of output is found using the budgeted overhead costs for the period and the budgeted activity level. However using budgeted figures means that the actual overhead cost is unlikely to be the same as the overheads absorbed into production, as we are relying on two estimates:

- overhead costs
- activity levels

These will inevitably differ from the actual values that are experienced during the period. Consequently, at the end of the period when the income statement (profit and loss account) is drawn up, the profit figure will be wrong as the overhead charge will be the absorbed amount rather than the actual amount. The error in the profit figure results from one of two possibilities:

(1) If more overheads are absorbed than have actually been incurred, this is known as OVER-ABSORPTION.

(2) If fewer overheads are absorbed than have actually been incurred, this is known as UNDER-ABSORPTION.

The amount over- or under-absorbed is adjusted for in the income statement after the production cost has been charged. Under-absorption means that too little overhead has been charged in the production cost, so a deduction is made from profit. Over-absorption means that too much overhead has been charged, so there is a compensating addition to profit.

Note that over- or under-absorption is not a problem in marginal costing, as the fixed overhead is treated as a period cost and not absorbed into units.

HOW IT WORKS

Cowslip Limited budgeted to make and sell 10,000 units of their product for each of the next three months (February – April). The units are sold for £20 each and direct costs per unit are £6. Budgeted overheads were £15,000 per month, and overheads are recovered using a rate per machine hour basis. Each unit requires 3 hours of machine time, the budgeted machine hours being 30,000.

The actual overheads incurred over the next three months were:

	£
February	15,000
March	14,000
April	16,000

All other actual costs, revenues and quantities were as budgeted (ie only the overheads incurred differ from budget).

The overhead absorption rate (based on the budget) will be

$$= \frac{\text{Overheads}}{\text{Machine hours}}$$

$$= \frac{£15,000}{10,000 \text{ units} \times 3h \text{ per unit}}$$

$$= £0.50 \text{ per machine hour}$$

or £1.50 per unit (3h @ £0.50)

In **February** a comparison of actual overheads and absorbed overheads will show that the two are the same:

	£
Actual overheads	15,000
Absorbed overheads	
(10,000 units × £1.50) or (30,000 hrs x £0.50)	15,000
Under-/over-absorption	Nil

In **March**, the production cost charged in the income statement will be the same as February, since 10,000 units were produced and the same number of machine hours were used. But we can't leave profit at the same level as before: the actual overheads are only £14,000, so we should have a profit of £1,000 more. By including 30,000 machine hours at a cost of £0.50 per hour in the income statement, we have absorbed more overheads than were actually incurred, which is an over-absorption.

	£
Actual overheads	14,000
Absorbed overheads (30,000h × £0.50)	15,000
Over-absorption	1,000

This over-absorption is credited to the income statement ie added back to profit.

In **April** actual overheads are £16,000

	£
Actual overheads	16,000
Absorbed overheads (30,000h × £0.50)	15,000
Under-absorption	1,000

Thus the overheads absorbed in April are less than the actual overhead incurred. The under-absorbed overheads will be debited to the income statement. Under-absorption means that not enough overheads have been charged against profits, so we deduct the under-absorption from profit to make up for this.

Note be very careful to calculate the under- or over-absorption based on actual versus absorbed costs; budgeted costs are not brought into this calculation. This is particularly relevant when the actual amounts of both overheads and activity are different from budget.

Let's say that in **May**, the number of units produced and sold by Cowslip Limited is 12,000 – actual machine hours amounted to 38,000 and overheads actually incurred amounted to £16,500. So this time both overheads and activity level are different from budget.

Calculate the overhead under- or over-absorbed as before, being careful to pick up the correct figures (highlighted).

	£
Actual overheads	**16,500**
Absorbed overheads (**38,000**h × £0.50)	19,000
Over-absorption	2,500

The profit calculation will take account of the over-absorption by adding £2,500 back to the profit for the period.

In summary, the under-/over-absorption is found by comparing:

	£
Actual overheads incurred for the period	X
Absorbed overheads:	
(actual units produced at absorption rate per unit) or	
(actual hours at absorption rate per hour)	X
Under-/over-absorption	X

Task 3

Tulip Limited planned to make 30,000 units, each of which was expected to require two hours of direct labour. Budgeted overheads were £54,000. Actual production was 28,000 units, requiring a total of 55,000 direct labour hours. Actual overheads were £47,000.

(a) The overhead absorption rate based on direct labour hours is
[   ]

(b) Complete the following sentence using the words in the list beneath:

The [   ] absorption of £[   ] should be
[   ] profit.

under-

over-

£2,500

£4,500

added to

deducted from

MARGINAL COSTING AND ABSORPTION COSTING COMPARED

Advantages of absorption costing:

- Fixed overheads have to be incurred to produce output so it is fair to charge each unit of product with a share of the fixed costs.

- Using full absorption cost to value inventory (stock) is consistent with the closing inventory value that is required by accounting standards (IAS2/SSAP9) for the external financial statements.

- In the long term an organisation needs to covers its fixed costs to be profitable so when setting selling prices, an organisation needs to be aware of the full cost of the product.

Advantages of marginal costing:

- Fixed costs are the same regardless of output and therefore it makes sense to charge them in full as a period cost.

- It does not require apportionment of fixed costs which can be arbitrary.

- By charging fixed costs as a period cost it avoids the under- or over-absorption of fixed overheads.

- It focuses on variable costs and contribution which can be more useful for decision making (see Chapter 3).

ACTIVITY BASED COSTING (ABC)

The final costing method to consider is that of activity based costing or ABC. This is a method of absorption costing which was developed in the 1970s and 1980s as an alternative to traditional absorption costing.

Under basic absorption costing, the production overheads of a cost centre are all absorbed on the same basis, usually labour hours or machine hours, no matter what the cause of the overhead. This could be viewed as quite an arbitrary approach to absorbing overheads, particularly as overheads now tend to form a very large part of product costs.

The principle of Activity Based Costing (ABC) is to breakdown the overheads into their constituent elements, for example costs incurred due to receiving materials, costs incurred due to issuing materials to production, costs incurred due to setting up machines for a production run (production setups), costs incurred due to quality control procedures etc.

Cost pools

Each of these elements that cause costs to be incurred are called ACTIVITIES and the costs associated with each activity are gathered together into COST POOLS.

For each cost pool what must then be identified is the factor that causes or drives these costs to change. This is known as the COST DRIVER.

The total of the cost pool is then divided by the number of times the cost driver takes place and this gives an overhead rate per cost driver. The overheads from the cost pool are then allocated to different products depending upon their particular usage of the cost driver.

For example, a product that required frequent purchases of materials and frequent production set-ups would have larger overheads allocated to it than a product that required few purchases and few production runs.

The diagram below illustrates in outline how ABC works:

Identify activities causing overheads	Activity 1	Activity 2
Gather all costs for each activity	Cost pool 1	Cost pool 2
Identify what causes the cost	Cost driver 1	Cost driver 2
Calculate cost driver rate	Cost pool 1 total ÷ No. of cost drivers	Cost pool 2 total ÷ No. of cost drivers
Apply to individual cost units	Use of cost driver 1 × cost driver 1 rate	Use of cost driver 2 × cost driver 2 rate

HOW IT WORKS

Caplan Ltd produces two products, the C and the P. The direct costs of the two products are given below:

	C	P
Direct materials	£3.50	£4.80
Direct labour	£2.00	£1.20

The budgeted production is for 120,000 units of C and 50,000 units of P.

The two main activities identified for the fairly simple production process are materials handling and production set-ups.

C requires only large production runs and large transfers of materials from stores. However P is a more complex product with a number of different types of materials required and shorter and more frequent production runs.

The budgeted overheads for Caplan are £800,000 and they are made up as follows:

	£
Materials handling cost pool	300,000
Production set-up cost pool	500,000
	800,000

The use of these activities for each product is:

	C	P	Total
Number of materials requisitions	200	800	1,000
Number of production set-ups	100	400	500

Calculate the total costs incurred and the unit cost of each product, using Activity Based Costing. Also calculate the direct (prime) cost and the overhead cost per unit.

Cost driver rate

Materials handling $\dfrac{£300,000}{1,000}$ = £300 per material requisition

Production set-ups $\dfrac{£500,000}{500}$ = £1,000 per production set-up

Total production costs and cost per unit

	C £	P £
Direct materials		
120,000 × £3.50	420,000	
50,000 × £4.80		240,000
Direct labour		
120,000 × £2.00	240,000	
50,000 × £1.20		60,000
Materials handling overhead		
200 × £300	60,000	
800 × £300		240,000

	C £	P £
Production set-up overhead		
100 × £1,000	100,000	
400 × £1,000		400,000
	820,000	940,000
Cost per unit	£820,000 / 120,000 units	£940,000 / 50,000 units
	£6.83 per unit	£18.80 per unit

Analysis of cost per unit

		C £	P £
Direct (or prime) costs	(3.50 + 2.00)	5.50	
	(4.80 + 1.20)		6.00
Materials handling overhead			
60,000/120,000		0.50	
240,000/50,000			4.80
Production set-up overhead			
100,000/120,000		0.83	
400,000/50,000			8.00
Unit cost		6.83	18.80

In this instance product C is charged with £1.33 of overhead, whereas the more activity intensive product P is charged with £12.80 of production overhead. Given that the direct labour cost of product P is only £1.20 compared to the £2.00 labour cost of product C, if the overheads had been apportioned according to labour hours, as with traditional absorption costing, then the picture would have been very different indeed.

Task 4

The costs of the quality control department of a manufacturing business are estimated to be £74,000 for the following quarter. During that period it is estimated that there will be 370 quality inspections of all the company's different products. Of these, Product A will require 25 inspections during the quarter and Product B will require 130 inspections.

(a)

Complete the table below using Activity Based Costing to show how much quality control overhead will be absorbed into Product A and Product B.

Overhead included in Product A	£
Overhead included in Product B	£

(b) It has been budgeted that 10,000 units of Product A will be produced in the period and 13,000 units of Product B.

Complete the table below to show the overhead cost per unit for Products A and B.

Product A overhead cost per unit	£
Product B overhead cost per unit	£

CHAPTER OVERVIEW

- Under absorption costing, all production overheads are allocated and apportioned to production cost centres and then absorbed into the cost of the products on some suitable basis

- Under marginal costing, the cost of the products is the variable cost of production with all fixed production costs being charged to the income statement (profit and loss account) as a period charge

- If inventory (stock) levels are constant then both absorption costing and marginal costing will report the same profit figure

- If inventory levels are increasing, absorption costing profit will be higher as **more** fixed overheads are carried forward to the following period in closing inventory than those brought forward in opening inventory

- If inventory levels are falling, marginal costing profit will be higher as **fewer** fixed overheads are carried forward under absorption costing in the closing inventory figure than those brought forward in opening inventory

- The difference in profit between absorption costing and marginal costing will be the fixed production overhead included in the increase/decrease in inventory levels under absorption costing

- Overhead absorption rates are based on budgeted values for activity levels and overheads incurred. In absorption costing, this results in under- or over-absorption of overheads which is adjusted for in the income statement (profit and loss account)

  - under-absorption is a deduction from profit in the income statement

  - over-absorption is an addition to profit in the income statement

- The under-/over-absorption is found by comparing the actual overhead incurred with the overhead absorbed in the period, where the overhead absorbed is calculated as:
  actual units produced at absorption rate per unit or actual hours at absorption rate per hour

- Activity based costing (ABC) considers the activities that cause overheads to be incurred and the factors that give rise to costs (cost drivers). It is a method of absorbing overheads into products on the basis of the amount of each activity that the particular product is expected to use in the period

Keywords

Absorption (full) costing – both variable and fixed production overheads are included in unit cost

Marginal (variable) costing – unit cost includes only variable production costs

Activity based costing (ABC) – a more complex approach to absorption of overheads, based upon an analysis of the detailed causes of the overheads

Contribution – sales value less variable cost of the goods sold

Overhead absorption rate – the rate at which overheads are charged to cost units calculated by dividing overheads by the level of activity

Over-absorption – more overheads are absorbed into production than have actually been incurred: add back to profit

Under-absorption – fewer overheads are absorbed into production than were actually incurred: deduct from profit

Activities – the elements of the overhead cost which cause costs to be incurred

Cost pools – costs that can be attributed to each activity

Cost driver – the factor that causes the costs for each cost pool

TEST YOUR LEARNING

1 Overheads apportioned to two production departments have been worked out, along with estimates for labour hours and machine hours expected in the coming budget period. P1 is a labour intensive department, while P2 is highly mechanised with relatively few machine operatives. The budgeted figures are as follows.

	P1	P2
Overheads apportioned	£50,000	£60,000
Machine hours	800	4,000
Labour hours	2,500	600

(a) The overhead absorption rate for department P1 is:

   A   £62.50
   B   £20.00
   C   £15.00
   D   £100.00

(b) The overhead absorption rate for department P2 is:

   A   £62.50
   B   £20.00
   C   £15.00
   D   £100.00

2 Complete the following table to show the amount of under- or over-absorption of overheads in each of the three cases below, and state whether this is an under- or an over-absorption and how this would be adjusted for in the income statement (profit and loss account).

	Amount of under-/over-absorption £	Under- or over-absorption	Add or subtract in income statement
An overhead absorption rate of £3 per unit, based on expected production levels of 500 units. Actual overheads turn out to be £1,600, and actual production is 650 units.			

2: Methods of costing

	Amount of under-/over- absorption £	Under- or over- absorption	Add or subtract in income statement
The budget is set at 1,000 units, with £9,000 overheads recovered on the basis of 600 direct labour hours. At the end of the period, overheads amounted to £8,600, production achieved was only 950 units and 590 direct labour hours had been worked.			

3   The budgeted overheads apportioned to a business's two production cost centres, X and Y, together with the budgeted labour hours and machine hours, are given below:

	X	Y
Overheads	£260,000	£380,000
Direct labour hours	20,000	120,000
Machine hours	100,000	10,000

Production cost centre X involves a highly mechanised process, with only a few machine workers. Production Y involves a highly labour intensive process.

(a) Complete the table to calculate separate departmental overhead absorption rates for each production cost centre using an appropriate basis.

Department	Overhead absorption rate
X	
Y	

(b) Each unit of Product A utilises the following hours in each production department.

	X	Y
Direct labour hours	1	4
Machine hours	5	2

The overhead to be included in the cost of each unit of product A is £ [_____]

4   Explain how fixed production overheads are treated in an absorption costing system and in a marginal costing system.

5   Given below is the budgeted information about the production of 60,000 units of a single product in a factory for the next quarter:

Direct materials   £12.50 per unit

Direct labour   – assembly   4 hours @ £8.40 per hour
                 – finishing   1 hour @ £6.60 per hour

Assembly production overheads   £336,000

Finishing production overheads   £84,000

It is estimated that 60% of the assembly overhead is variable and that 75% of the finishing overhead is variable.

Complete the table below to show the budgeted cost of the product using each method of costing.

Method of costing	Budgeted cost £
Absorption costing	
Marginal costing	

6   Given below are the budgeted figures for production and sales of a factory's single product for the months of November and December:

	November	December
Production	15,000 units	15,000 units
Sales	12,500 units	18,000 units
Direct materials	£12.00 per unit	£12.00 per unit
Direct labour	£8.00 per unit	£8.00 per unit
Variable production cost	£237,000	£237,000
Fixed production cost	£390,000	£390,000

Overheads are absorbed on the basis of budgeted production and the selling price of the product is £75.

There were 2,000 units of the product in inventory (stock) at the start of November.

(a) Prepare the budgeted income statements for each of the two months using:

    (i)   absorption costing

Absorption costing – income statement

	November		December	
	£	£	£	£
Sales				
Less: cost of sales				
Opening inventory				
Production costs				
	———		———	
Less: closing inventory				
	———		———	
		———		———
Profit		———		———

(ii) Marginal costing

Marginal costing – income statement

	November		December	
	£	£	£	£
Sales				
Less: cost of sales				
Opening inventory				
Production costs				
	_____		_____	
Less: closing inventory				
	_____			
			_____	
		_____		_____
Contribution		_____		_____
Less: fixed overheads		_____		_____
Profit		_____		_____

(b) Complete the table below to reconcile the absorption costing profit and the marginal costing profit for each of the two months.

	November	December
	£	£
Absorption costing profit		
Inventory changes		
Marginal costing profit		

7   A business produces two products, the LM and the NP. The direct costs
    of the two products are:

	LM	NP
Direct materials	£2.60	£3.90
Direct labour	£3.50	£2.70

The total overhead cost is made up as follows:

	£
Stores costs	140,000
Production set-up costs	280,000
Quality control inspection costs	180,000
	600,000

The budgeted production is for 50,000 units of LM and 20,000 units of
NP.

Each product is expected to make the following use of the service
activities:

	LM	NP	Total
Materials requisitions from stores	100	220	320
Production set-ups	80	200	280
Quality control inspections	30	60	90

Complete the following table to show the budgeted cost per unit for
each product using activity based costing and how much total budgeted
overhead is included in the unit cost for each product.

Product	Budgeted cost per unit £	Budgeted overhead per unit £
LM		
NP		

chapter 3:
DECISION MAKING

chapter coverage 📖

In this chapter we will look at a variety of ways in which costing information can be used for decision making purposes.

The topics that are to be covered are:

✎ Contribution and profit

✎ Cost-volume-profit analysis

✎ Limiting factor analysis

✎ More than one product

✎ Make or buy decisions

✎ Closure of a business segment

✎ Discounted cash flows

USE OF MARGINAL COSTING AND CONTRIBUTION FOR DECISION MAKING

In the chapter on methods of costing we defined CONTRIBUTION as sales revenue less variable costs. We can look at contribution in total, as we did in marginal costing, or at contribution per unit.

Provided that the selling price and variable costs remain constant at different levels of activity, then contribution per unit will also be a constant figure at each level of activity. When we consider fixed costs however, we can see that as activity levels increase, although the fixed costs themselves remain constant, the fixed cost per unit falls as the fixed costs are spread over more units. This means that even though contribution per unit will remain constant with increasing levels of activity, the full production cost (absorption cost) per unit will decrease and profit per unit will increase.

HOW IT WORKS

J R Grantham & Partners are considering expanding their business from its current production and sales of 100,000 units per annum. Market research suggests that it will almost certainly be possible to increase sales to 150,000 and possibly even to 180,000 units per annum.

The single product that the partnership produces sells for £20 and has variable costs of production of £15. The fixed costs are currently £400,000 per annum and are not expected to increase.

We will look at the contribution per unit, full production cost per unit and profit per unit at each activity level.

	100,000	150,000	180,000
	£	£	£
Sales	2,000,000	3,000,000	3,600,000
Variable costs	1,500,000	2,250,000	2,700,000
Contribution	500,000	750,000	900,000
Fixed costs	400,000	400,000	400,000
Profit	100,000	350,000	500,000
Contribution per unit	£5	£5	£5

Full production cost per unit
(variable + fixed)

	100,000	150,000	180,000
£15 + £400,000/100,000	£19		
£15 + £400,000/150,000		£17.67	
£15 + £400,000/180,000			£17.22
Profit per unit	£1	£2.33	£2.78

As we can see, there is a significant decrease in the full production cost per unit as the activity level rises, due to the fixed costs being spread over a larger number of units. This also therefore means that there is a significant increase in profit per unit as the activity level increases. However contribution per unit has remained constant.

This is one of the reasons why for decision making purposes contribution per unit is a much more meaningful figure than profit per unit, as the profit per unit figure is simply being affected by the spreading of the fixed costs.

HOW IT WORKS

A company produces a single product at a variable cost per unit of £20. During the year the company expects to make 100,000 units, all of which can be sold to existing customers for £30 per unit. The total fixed costs for the period are expected to be £4 per unit.

(i) How much profit will the company make?

(ii) A customer has offered to buy an extra 5,000 units as a one-off order at a price of £23. Should the company accept (assuming it has spare capacity)?

(iii) What would the profit be if the company only made and sold 80,000 units (ignore the one-off order for this purpose)?

We shall take each point in turn.

(i)   The full cost per unit is £20 + £4 = £24

The profit per unit is £30 - £24 = £6 per unit, so the total profit from 100,000 units is £600,000.

(ii)   The absorption cost of the product is £24 so on the face of it at a selling price of £23 the product would make a loss.

However we should consider the additional revenue and costs involved for the order:

	£
Sales (5,000 x £23)	115,000
Variable costs (5,000 x £20)	100,000
Contribution	15,000

Since the fixed costs for the period are being incurred anyway the company should accept the one-off order as it increases contribution and therefore profit by £15,000.

However the company would not want to accept £23 as the regular selling price as in the long term it needs to cover the fixed overheads for the period.

Note: It is possible that the company might incur additional fixed costs relating specifically to the additional order, in which case these would need to be taken into account in determining whether to accept.

(iii)   The profit from 80,000 units would not be 80,000 × £6 = £480,000 because if only 80,000 units are made the fixed overhead per unit would increase:

Total fixed costs were expected to be £4 × 100,000 units = £400,000.

Spread over 80,000 units this gives a fixed cost of £5 per unit and a new profit per unit of £30 – £25 = £5.

Hence total profit would be 80,000 × £5 = £400,000.

An alternative (and easier) calculation under marginal costing would be:

Contribution per unit = £30 – £20 = £10

Total contribution = 80,000 × £10 = £800,000, less fixed costs £400,000 = profit £400,000

Thus, for decision making purposes, you should always treat total profit as having two distinct elements:

1	Total contribution (= contribution/unit × units)	X
	Less:	
2	Fixed costs	(X)
		X

Element **1** (total contribution) varies proportionately with volume, while element **2** (fixed costs) is a lump-sum period deduction.

As fixed costs in total are assumed to be constant for the period, whatever volume of products is made, the most amount of profit will be achieved if the amount of contribution is maximised.

COST-VOLUME-PROFIT ANALYSIS

COST-VOLUME-PROFIT ANALYSIS is the general term for the analysis of the relationship between activity levels, costs and profit. One of the most common applications of this analysis is BREAK-EVEN ANALYSIS whereby the break-even point for a business is determined.

The BREAK-EVEN POINT is the level of activity where the sales revenue is equal to the total costs of the business, meaning that all costs are covered by sales revenue but no profit is made. This is obviously an important point for managers of a business to be aware of; if the activity level falls below the break-even point then losses will be made.

So the break-even point activity level can be expressed as the point where:

Sales revenue = Variable costs + Fixed costs

Alternatively

Sales revenue – Variable costs = Fixed costs

Remember that sales revenue minus variable costs is equal to contribution. So the relationship is that the break-even point is where:

Contribution = Fixed costs

Contribution per unit × break-even point (units) = Fixed costs

We saw in an earlier example in this chapter that provided selling price and variable costs remain constant at different levels of activity, contribution per unit will also remain constant. We can therefore use this to calculate the break-even point.

$$\text{Break-even point} = \frac{\text{Fixed costs}}{\text{Contribution per unit}}$$

HOW IT WORKS

Reardon Enterprises sells a single product with a selling price of £10 per unit. The variable costs of producing the product are £6 per unit and the fixed costs of the business are £200,000.

What is the break-even point in units?

$$\text{Break-even point} = \frac{£200,000}{£10 - £6}$$

$$= 50,000 \text{ units}$$

We can prove that this is the point where no profit or loss is made:

	£
Sales (50,000 × £10)	500,000
Variable costs (50,000 × £6)	(300,000)
Contribution (50,000 × £4)	200,000
Fixed costs	(200,000)
Profit	– 0

Therefore the management of Reardon Enterprises know they must ensure that sales volumes exceed 50,000 units per annum in order for the business to cover its total costs and make any profit.

Task 1

A business has a single product that it sells for £28. The variable costs of producing the product are £19 per unit and the fixed costs of the business are £360,000.

$28 - 19 = 9$

What is the break-even point in units?

$\frac{360,000}{9} = 40,000$

| 40,000 | units |

Target profit

It is also possible to extend the analysis using contribution per unit in order to determine the level of sales that is necessary in order not only to cover all of the costs but also to make a particular amount of profit, the target profit.

Thus we want:

Total contribution	X
Less: fixed costs	(X)
Target profit	X

Total contribution = contribution per unit x target number of units (activity level)

This needs to exactly cover fixed costs and generate the target profit.

Working back this gives us:

$$\text{Activity level} = \frac{\text{Fixed costs} + \text{target profit}}{\text{Contribution per unit}}$$

HOW IT WORKS

Returning to Reardon Enterprises the managing director, Anna Reardon, would like to ensure a profit of £100,000 for the coming year. What level of sales is required for this profit to be made?

$$\text{Activity level} = \frac{£200,000 + £100,000}{£10 - £6}$$

$$= 75,000 \text{ units}$$

Therefore if the business sells 75,000 units of the product a profit of £100,000 will be made. Again we can check this:

	£
Sales (75,000 × £10)	750,000
Variable costs (75,000 × £6)	(450,000)
Contribution	300,000
Fixed costs	(200,000)
Profit	100,000

Task 2

A business has fixed costs of £250,000. It sells just one product for a price of £80 and the variable costs of production are £60.

How many units of the product must be business sell in order to make a profit of £150,000?

$$\frac{250,000 + 150,000}{80 - 60} = \frac{400,000}{20} = 20,000$$

20,000	units

Margin of safety

Another figure that management might be interested in is the MARGIN OF SAFETY. This is the difference between the budgeted or forecast sales or actual current sales and the break-even sales level. This is usually expressed as a percentage of the budgeted, forecast or actual sales. (In the assessment, make sure you express the margin of safety as a percentage of the budgeted, forecast or actual sales, not as a percentage of break-even sales.)

HOW IT WORKS

Remember that Reardon Enterprise's break-even sales volume was 50,000 units. If the budgeted sales for the forthcoming year are 70,000 units, what is the margin of safety?

Margin of safety$\qquad = \qquad$ 70,000 units – 50,000 units

$\qquad\qquad\qquad = \qquad$ 20,000 units

This can be expressed as a percentage of budgeted sales, which should be used as the denominator in calculations.

$$\text{Margin of safety} = \frac{20,000}{70,000} \times 100$$

$$= 28.6\%$$

This tells management that sales can drop below the budgeted figure by 28.6% before losses start to be made.

Task 3

A business has budgeted to sell 75,000 units of its single product in the next year. The product sells for £32 and the variable costs of production are £24. The fixed overheads of the business are £480,000.

What is the margin of safety as a percentage?

20 %

(handwritten:) $\dfrac{480,000}{8} = 60,000$

$75000 - 60000 =$

$\dfrac{15000}{75000} \times 100 = 20\%$

Profit volume ratio

When we were calculating the break-even point above, the figure that was derived using contribution per unit and fixed costs was the number of units that had to be sold in order to break-even. However the break-even point can also be expressed in terms of the sales revenue required in order to break-even, by using the profit volume (P/V)ratio. This ratio can also be called the CONTRIBUTION TO SALES (C/S)RATIO.

$$\text{Profit volume ratio} = \frac{\text{Contribution}}{\text{Sales}} \times 100$$

Thus the P/V ratio measures contribution per £ sales revenue rather than per physical sales unit.

Thus, at break-even sales revenue

Total contribution (P/V ratio × break-even sales revenue)	X
Less: fixed costs	(X)
Profit	0

The break-even point in terms of sales revenue can then be found as:

$$\text{Break-even point (£)} = \frac{\text{Fixed costs}}{\text{Profit volume ratio}}$$

HOW IT WORKS

Reardon Enterprises sell their product for £10 and the variable costs are £6 per unit. Total fixed costs are £200,000.

$$\text{Profit volume ratio} = \frac{£10 - £6}{£10} \times 100$$

$$= 40\%$$

$$Break-even\ point\ (£) = \frac{200,000}{0.40}$$

$$= £500,000$$

(which corresponds to a unit activity level of $\frac{£500,000}{£10} = 50,000$, as before)

Task 4

A business has a single product that it sells for £36. The variable costs of producing the product are £27 per unit and the fixed costs of the business are £360,000.

$\frac{36-27}{36} \times 100 = 25\%$

What is the break-even point in terms of sales revenue?

$\frac{360,000}{.25} = 1,440,000$

£ 1,440,000

LIMITING FACTOR ANALYSIS

Obviously the managers of a business will wish to produce and sell more than the break-even number of units in order to cover fixed costs and make a profit. However, in practice, the quantity that they can produce and sell may be limited by one or more factors, the LIMITING FACTOR(S).

In many cases the limiting factor will be market demand, or the amount of units that customers are prepared to buy. However, in other instances the limiting factor might be the amount of materials that are available or the number of machine or labour hours that are available.

HOW IT WORKS

A business sells a single product for £35. The variable costs of the product are:

    Direct materials   3 kg per unit @ £3 per kg

    Direct labour   2 hours per unit @ £7.50 per hour

The fixed costs of the business are £800,000.

Materials as limiting factor

If the supply of materials is limited to 360,000 kg, how many units can the business produce and how much profit will be made?

Number of units that can be produced	= 360,000 kg/3 kg per unit
	= 120,000 units

	£
Sales (120,000 × £35)	4,200,000
Variable costs (120,000 × (£9 + £15))	2,880,000
Contribution	1,320,000
Fixed costs	800,000
Profit	520,000

Labour hours as limiting factor

If materials are now not restricted, but the business only has 280,000 labour hours available for production, how many units can be made and what is the profit at this production level?

Number of units that can be produced	= 280,000 hours/2 hours per unit
	= 140,000 units

	£
Sales (140,000 × £35)	4,900,000
Variable costs (140,000 × £24)	3,360,000
Contribution	1,540,000
Fixed costs	800,000
Profit	740,000

More than one product

We will now make the position a little more complicated by introducing a business that makes more than one product. If the availability of either materials or labour hours is the limiting factor, then it will be necessary to determine the optimum production mix.

In order to make a decision we must determine our criterion for the decision making process. In business the overriding criterion will normally be to make as much profit as possible (maximise profits). As fixed costs in total are assumed to be constant whatever combination of products is made, maximisation of profit will be achieved by maximising contribution.

If a business has more than one product, and one limiting factor, the technique to use in order to maximise contribution is to determine the contribution per unit of the limiting factor (or scarce resource) and concentrate upon the production of the product with the highest contribution per limiting factor unit.

HOW IT WORKS

Farnham Engineering makes three products A, B and C. The costs and selling prices of the three products are:

	A	B	C
	£	£	£
Direct materials @ £4 per kg	8	16	12
Direct labour @ £7 per hour	7	21	14
Variable overheads	3	9	6
Marginal cost	18	46	32
Selling price	22	54	39
Contribution	4	8	7

Sales demand for the coming period is expected to be as follows:

Product A	3,000 units
Product B	7,000 units
Product C	5,000 units

The supply of materials is limited to 50,000 kg during the period and the labour hours available are 28,000.

Step 1

We have to decide firstly if there is a limiting factor other than sales demand. Consider the materials usage for each product if the maximum sales demand is produced. (You are not given the actual usage of materials of each product but you can work it out – for example the materials cost for A is £8; as the materials are £4 per kg, product A must use 2 kg etc.)

	A	B	C	Total required
Materials (2/4/3kg)	6,000 kg	28,000 kg	15,000 kg	49,000 kg
Labour (1/3/2hrs)	3,000 hours	21,000 hours	10,000 hours	34,000 hours

As 50,000 kg of materials are available for the period and only 49,000 kg are required for the maximum production level, materials are not a limiting factor.

However, only 28,000 labour hours are available whereas 34,000 hours are required in order to produce the maximum demand. Therefore labour hours are the limiting factor.

Step 2

The next stage is to calculate the contribution per limiting factor unit – so in this case the contribution per labour hour – for each product. Then rank the products according to how high the contribution per labour hour is for each one.

	A	B	C
Contribution	£4	£8	£7
Labour hours per unit	1 hour	3 hours	2 hours
Contribution per labour hour:			
£4/1	£4.00		
£8/3		£2.67	
£7/2			£3.50
Ranking	1	3	2

A makes the most contribution per unit of limiting factor (labour hours) and therefore in order to maximise contribution, we must concentrate first on production of A up to its maximum sales demand, then on C, and finally, if there are any remaining hours available, on B.

The optimal production plan in order to maximise contribution is:

	Units produced	Labour hours required
A	3,000	3,000
C	5,000	10,000
B (balance)	5,000*	15,000
		(balancing figure)
		28,000

* **Working**: After making A and C there are 15,000 hours left. Each unit of B needs 3 hours so there is sufficient to make 15,000/3 = 5,000 units.

The contribution earned from this production plan is:

		£
A	(3,000 × £4)	12,000
B	(5,000 × £8)	40,000
C	(5,000 × £7)	35,000
Total contribution		87,000

Task 5

A business produces four products and the details are:

	P	Q	R	S
Contribution per unit	£12	£15	£9	£14
Materials per unit	3 kg	4 kg	1 kg	2 kg
Maximum demand (units)	2,000	6,000	1,000	4,000

Handwritten annotations:
- Under P: 6000 KGS, £4 KH, (3)
- Under Q: 24.000KG, £3.75KG, (4)
- Under R: 1000KG, £9 KG, (1)
- Under S: 8000KGS, £7KG, (2) = 39000 KG

Fixed costs amount to £30,000 each period, and the materials supply is limited to 30,000 kg.

(a) Complete the following table in order to determine the production plan that will maximise profit.

Product	Units produced
R	1000 *(1000 KGS)*
S	4000 *(8000 KGS)*
P	2000 *(6000 KG)*
Q	3750 *(15.000KGS)*

(b) The profit earned from this production plan will be

£ **115.250**

Handwritten calculation:
9000
56000
24.000
56250
145,250
30.000
115,250

MAKE OR BUY DECISIONS

A make or buy problem involves a decision by an organisation about whether it should make a product or whether it should pay another organisation to do so. Here are some examples of applications of make or buy decisions.

(a) Whether a company should manufacture its own components, or else buy the components from an outside supplier

(b) Whether a construction company should do some work with its own employees, or whether it should sub-contract the work to another company

(c) Whether a service should be carried out by an internal department or whether an external organisation should be employed

Essentially the choice is between whether to do something in-house - 'make', or contract it out - 'buy'. The 'make' option should give management more direct control over the work, but the 'buy' option often has the benefit that the external organisation has a specialist skill and expertise in the work. Make or buy decisions should certainly not be based exclusively on cost considerations.

If an organisation has the freedom of choice about whether to make internally or buy externally and has no scarce resources that put a restriction on what it can do itself, the relevant costs for the decision will be the differential costs between the two options.

HOW IT WORKS

Shellfish Co makes four components, W, X, Y and Z, for which costs in the forthcoming year are expected to be as follows.

	W	X	Y	Z
Production (units)	1,000	2,000	4,000	3,000
Unit marginal costs	£	£	£	£
Direct materials	4	5	2	4
Direct labour	8	9	4	6
Variable production overheads	2	3	1	2
	14	17	7	12

Directly attributable fixed costs per annum and committed fixed costs:

	£
Incurred as a direct consequence of making W	1,000
Incurred as a direct consequence of making X	5,000
Incurred as a direct consequence of making Y	6,000
Incurred as a direct consequence of making Z	8,000
Other fixed costs (committed)	30,000
	50,000

A sub-contractor has offered to supply units of W, X, Y and Z for £12, £21, £10 and £14 respectively. Should Shellfish Co make or buy the components?

(a) The relevant costs are the differential costs between making and buying, and they consist of differences in unit variable costs plus differences in directly attributable fixed costs. Sub-contracting will usually result in some directly attributable fixed costs being saved.

	W	X	Y	Z
	£	£	£	£
Unit variable cost of making	14	17	7	12
Unit variable cost of buying	12	21	10	14
Differential variable cost	(2)	4	3	2
Annual requirements (units)	1,000	2,000	4,000	3,000

	£	£	£	£
Extra variable cost/(saving) of buying (per annum)	(2,000)	8,000	12,000	6,000
Fixed costs saved by buying	(1,000)	(5,000)	(6,000)	(8,000)
Extra total cost/(saving) of buying	(3,000)	3,000	6,000	(2,000)

(b) The company would save £3,000 pa by sub-contracting component W (where the purchase cost would be less than the marginal cost per unit to make internally) and would save £2,000 pa by sub-contracting component Z (because of the saving in fixed costs of £8,000). Financially it would not appear to be viable to sub-contract component X and Y, since this would increase costs.

(c) In this example, relevant costs are the variable costs of in-house manufacture, the variable costs of sub-contracted units, and the saving in fixed costs. Normally relevant costs are only variable costs but in instances like this, the savings in fixed costs must be taken into consideration as incremental costs as well.

(d) **Further considerations**

   (i) If components W and Z are sub-contracted, the company will have spare capacity. How should that spare capacity be profitably used? Are there hidden benefits/costs to be obtained from sub-contracting? Would the company's workforce resent the loss of work to an outside sub-contractor, and might such a decision cause an industrial dispute? Alternatively can the spare capacity created be used for productive and profitable purposes?

   (ii) Would the sub-contractor be reliable with delivery times, and would it supply components of the same quality as those manufactured internally?

   (iii) Does the company wish to be flexible and maintain better control over operations by making everything itself?

   (iv) Are the estimates of fixed cost savings reliable? In the case of product W, buying is clearly cheaper than making in-house. In the case of product Z, the decision to buy rather than make would only be financially beneficial if it is feasible that the fixed cost savings of £8,000 will really be 'delivered' by management. All too often in practice, promised savings fail to materialise!

Task 6

A business produces three products with the following costs per unit:

	A	B	C
	£	£	£
Direct materials	1.60	2.00	0.80
Direct labour	3.20	3.60	1.60
Direct overheads	0.80	1.20	0.40
Fixed overheads	1.60	2.00	0.80

An external firm has offered to make these components and sell them to the company at the following prices:

A £5.50 5.60
B £8.40 6.80
C £4.00 2.80

On the basis of cost alone which if any products should be purchased from the external firm?

A A only ✓
B B only
C C only
D None of the products

CLOSURE OF A BUSINESS SEGMENT

Discontinuance or shutdown problems involve the following decisions:

(a) Whether or not to close down a product line, department or other activity, either because it is making losses or because it is too expensive to run.

(b) If the decision is to shut down, whether the closure should be permanent or temporary.

In practice, shutdown decisions may often involve longer-term considerations, and consideration of capital expenditures and revenues.

(a) A shutdown should result in savings in annual operating costs for a number of years into the future.

(b) Closure will probably release unwanted non-current (fixed) assets for sale. Some assets might have a small scrap value, but other assets, in particular property, might have a substantial sale value.

(c) Employees affected by the closure must be made redundant or relocated, perhaps after retraining, or else offered early retirement. There will be lump sum payments involved which must be taken into account in the financial arithmetic. For example, suppose that the closure of a regional office would result in annual savings of £100,000, non-current (fixed) assets could be sold off to earn income of £2 million, but redundancy payments would be £3 million. The shutdown decision would involve an assessment of the net capital cost of closure (£1 million) against the annual benefits (£100,000 pa).

It is possible, however, for shutdown problems to be simplified into short-run decisions, by making one of the following assumptions.

(a) Non-current asset sales and redundancy costs would be negligible.

(b) Income from non-current asset sales would match redundancy costs and so these capital items would be self-cancelling.

In such circumstances the financial aspect of shutdown decisions would be based on short-run relevant costs.

HOW IT WORKS

A company manufactures three products, Pawns, Rooks and Bishops. The present net annual income from these is as follows.

	Pawns £	Rooks £	Bishops £	Total £
Sales	50,000	40,000	60,000	150,000
Variable costs	30,000	25,000	35,000	90,000
Contribution	20,000	15,000	25,000	60,000
Fixed costs	17,000	18,000	20,000	55,000
Profit/loss	3,000	(3,000)	5,000	5,000

The company is concerned about its poor profit performance, and is considering whether or not to cease selling Rooks. It is felt that selling prices cannot be raised or lowered without adversely affecting net income. £5,000 of the fixed costs of Rooks are direct fixed costs which would be saved if production ceased (ie there are some attributable fixed costs). All other fixed costs, it is considered, would remain the same.

By stopping production of Rooks, the consequences would be a £10,000 fall in profits.

	£
Loss of contribution	(15,000)
Savings in fixed costs	5,000
Incremental loss	(10,000)

Suppose, however, it were possible to use the resources realised by stopping production of Rooks and switch to producing a new item, Crowners, which would sell for £50,000 and incur variable costs of £30,000 and extra direct fixed costs of £6,000. A new decision is now required.

	Rooks £	Crowners £
Sales	40,000	50,000
Less variable costs	25,000	30,000
	15,000	20,000
Less direct fixed costs	(5,000)	(6,000)
Contribution to shared fixed costs and profit	10,000	14,000

It would be more profitable to shut down production of Rooks and switch resources to making Crowners, in order to boost profits by £4,000 to £9,000 in total.

Timing of shutdown

An organisation may also need to consider the most appropriate timing for a shutdown. Some costs may be avoidable in the long run but not in the short run. For example, office space may have been rented and three months notice is required. This cost is therefore unavoidable for three months. In the same way supply contracts may require notice of cancellation. A month-by-month analysis of when notice should be given and when savings will be made will help the decision making process.

Qualitative factors

As usual the decision is not merely a matter of choosing the best financial option. Qualitative factors must once more be considered.

(a) What impact will a shutdown decision have on employee morale?

(b) What signal will the decision give to competitors? How will they react?

(c) How will customers react? Will they lose confidence in the company's products?

(d) How will suppliers be affected? If one supplier suffers disproportionately there may be a loss of goodwill and damage to future relations.

Transferring production overseas

In some cases management of an organisation may be considering shutting its UK operations and transferring its production operations overseas. This may be the case if key resources such as materials and labour are significantly cheaper in the foreign country. The quantitative and qualitative factors to be taken into account will tend to be very similar to those for a closure of a business segment. However there will also be other issues which are specific to setting up operations in a foreign country including:

- administrative/legal issues in setting up the operations

- the attitude of the host government to foreign investment

- the tax system in the country

- transportation issues involved in getting the products to their final destination.

Mechanisation decisions

In a similar way to decisions about closing a segment of the business, management may need information about changing the ways in which certain areas of the business operate. For example as technology plays a greater part in manufacturing, a business may be considering changing from a labour intensive production process to a machine intensive one.

There will be a number of aspects of costs that will need to be considered here:

- As with a closure of a business segment moving to a machine intensive production process will naturally mean a number of redundancy/early retirement costs

- However the reduction in the labour force will save on short term direct labour costs

- The investment in machinery will be very large and the methods of financing this investment should be considered

- In a machine based environment, it is likely that overheads in general will be much higher including machine maintenance, depreciation, power etc.

- Many of the additional overheads may be fixed overheads which may have an effect on the break-even point for the business. In order for the increased fixed overheads to be covered by contribution then more units may need to be sold. Break-even analysis may be needed to determine whether the business can sell enough products to cover the additional fixed costs.

- If the level of fixed costs in the business increases as a proportion of total cost, the profits of the business will become more sensitive to changes in sales volumes. This is because if the sales of a business fall and its costs are mainly variable, the reduction in sales will lead to a corresponding reduction in costs. However if a business has mainly fixed costs, when sales volumes fall, the cost base remains largely the same and as a result there is a bigger impact on profits.

- There will also be qualitative factors to take into consideration, including the effect on the morale of the remaining workforce and any environmental issues involved in the mechanisation process.

HOW IT WORKS

A business is considering the purchase of a machine which will cost £475,000 and be depreciated on a straight-line basis over its 10 year life with no residual value. The machine will allow the business to reduce the labour required to manufacture its product by 1.5 hours per unit. Currently the business makes and sells 4,000 units pa at £125 each and total annual fixed costs are £180,000.

The product's standard cost card shows the following variable costs:

		£
Direct material	3kg @ £5	15
Direct labour	6hrs @ £10	60
		75

Assuming the business continues to make and sell 4,000 units we will consider the impact the machine purchase will have on the break-even point, the margin of safety, the profit for the year and the ratio of fixed costs to total costs.

Currently:

Contribution per unit = £125 – £75 = £50

Break-even = £180,000/50 = 3,600 units.

Margin of safety = 4,000 – 3,600/4,000 = 10%

Profit = (4,000 x £50) – £180,000 = £20,000

Fixed costs/Total costs = 180,000/(180,000 + (4,000 @ £75)) = 37.5%

With machine:

Contribution per unit becomes (£125 – £15 – £45) = £65

Note that the labour cost is now 4.5 hours @ £10 = £45

Fixed costs increase by £47,500 to £227,500 pa due to depreciation

Break-even = £227,500/65 = 3,500 units.

Margin of safety = 4,000 – 3,500/4,000 = 12.5%

Profit = (4,000 x £65) – £227,500 = £32,500

Fixed costs/Total costs = 227,500/(227,500 + (4,000 @ £60)) = 48.7%

Here, the saving in direct labour (4,000 units at 1.5hrs x £10) £60,000 is greater than the increase in costs due to depreciation.

The break-even point is decreased and the margin of safety increased but the business becomes more risky due to the increased proportion of fixed costs. This is known as having higher operating gearing.

DISCOUNTED CASH FLOWS

In this final section of the chapter, we move to looking at longer term decision making rather than the short-term decision making considered so far in this chapter. The purpose of using discounted cash flows (DCF) is to deal with the problem of the time value of money.

If we are offered £100 now or £100 in one year's time we are not comparing like with like. If interest rates are, say, 10% per annum then if the £100 received now were invested it would earn interest for a year at 10%. After one year we would have:

£100 × 1.10 = £110

Therefore we would definitely prefer the £100 now because it offers us an investment opportunity to earn £110 in one year's time.

Another way of looking at it, would be that we would be indifferent between £100 now or £110 in one year's time. So we can say that the present value of £110 in one year's time is £100 now.

The present value of a future cash flow is calculated by applying a discount factor to the cash flow. The discount factor can be calculated as:

$$\frac{1}{(1+r)^n}$$

where: $r =$ the periodic interest rate or discount rate (expressed as a decimal)

$n =$ the number of periods before the cash flow occurs

Fortunately you do not need to remember the formula as there are present value tables which have calculated the discount factors for each time period and each discount rate. Note that the interest rate or discount rate is often referred to as the cost of capital.

HOW IT WORKS

A company is to invest in a project with an immediate cash outflow of £20,000. The receipts from this project are £10,000 in one year's time, £14,000 in two years' time and finally £6,000 in three years' time.

The interest rate applicable to the company is 8% and the discount factors at this rate are given below.

Period	Discount factor 8%
1	0.926
2	0.857
3	0.794

What is the present value of each of these cash flows?

Note that an immediate cash flow is taken as occurring at Time 0, a cash flow in one year's time as Time 1 etc. There is no need to apply a discount factor to a cash flow at Time 0.

Time	Cash flow	Discount factor @ 8%	Present value
	£		£
0	(20,000)	1.000	(20,000)
1	10,000	0.926	9,260
2	14,000	0.857	11,998
3	6,000	0.794	4,764

Discounted cash flow and project appraisal

The computation of a present value is a discounted cash flow technique. We are finding the discounted present value of each individual cash flow.

The cash flows that are relevant are the future incremental cashflows that will arise as a result of the project that is being considered.

Note that for decision making we use cash flow and not profits, since these are less subjective. As a result, if you are given the expected profits from a project you will need to add back any depreciation in order to estimate the cash flows.

If we are appraising a project, then the technique that we will use is to find the net present value of all of the cash flows of the project. We calculate the present value of each individual cash flow and then total them all, remembering that the initial cost of the project is still a cash outflow at Time 0. The total of the present values of the cash inflows minus the cash outflows is the project's NET PRESENT VALUE.

If the net present value (NPV) is positive, then the project should be accepted as this means that even after having taken account of the time value of money, the cash inflows from the project exceed the cash outflows. If however the net present value is a negative figure, then the project should be rejected.

HOW IT WORKS

Returning to our previous example:

A company is to invest in a project with an immediate cash outflow of £20,000. The receipts from this project are £10,000 in one year's time, £14,000 in two years' time and finally £6,000 in three years' time.

The interest rate applicable to the company is 8% and the discount factors at this rate are given below.

Period	Discount factor 8%
1	0.926
2	0.857
3	0.794

What is the net present value of this project and should the company invest in it?

Time	Cash flow	Discount factor	Present value
	£		£
0	(20,000)	1.000	(20,000)
1	10,000	0.926	9,260
2	14,000	0.857	11,998
3	6,000	0.794	4,764
Net present value			6,022

The project has a positive net present value and therefore the company should invest in it.

Net present cost

In some instances you may be required just to calculate the present value of the costs of an operation or decision. This is done in exactly the same way as above but simply deals with costs rather than revenues. This technique is often used to calculate the life cycle cost of a machine that is regularly used by a business.

HOW IT WORKS

A company is to invest in a machine with an immediate cash outflow of £100,000. The machine will have annual running costs of £20,000 for the next three years paid in arrears. At the end of its three year life the machine will have an estimated residual value of £30,000.

The interest rate applicable to the company is 8% and the discount factors at this rate are given below.

Period	Discount factor 8%
1	0.926
2	0.857
3	0.794

What is the net present cost (life cycle cost) of this machine?

Time	Cash flow	Discount factor @ 8%	Present value
	£		£
0	(100,000)	1.000	(100,000)
1	(20,000)	0.926	(18,520)
2	(20,000)	0.857	(17,140)
3 (30,000 – 20,000)	10,000	0.794	7,940
Net present cost			(127,720)

Net terminal value

Another method of looking at the cash flows of projects, although not as common as using net present values, is to calculate the NET TERMINAL VALUE of a project. This is the value at the end of the project's life.

The terminal value method considers each cash inflow as if it were an investment and the compound interest on this inflow until the end of the project is added to the value of the cash inflows.

For example suppose that £10,000 is received at Time 1 on a three period project with a discount rate of 10%.

The net terminal value of this receipt at Time 3 would be £10,000 x 1.10 x 1.10 = £12,100. In other words, i this receipt of £10,000 had been invested for the remainder of the project life then it would have had a final or terminal value of £12,100.

HOW IT WORKS

Returning to our previous example:

A company is to invest in a project with an immediate cash outflow of £20,000. The receipts from this project are £10,000 in one year's time, £14,000 in two years' time and finally £6,000 in three years' time.

The interest rate applicable to the company is 8%.

Calculate the net terminal value of the project.

This will involve calculating the terminal value (the value at Time 3) of each individual cash inflow and then deducting the terminal value of the cash outflow.

			Terminal value at Time 3
Cash inflow at Time 1	£10,000 × 1.08 × 1.08	=	£11,664
Cash inflow at Time 2	£14,000 × 1.08	=	£15,120
Cash inflow at Time 3		=	£6,000
Less: initial outflow (£20,000 × 1.08 × 1.08 × 1.08)			£32,784
			(£25,194)
Net terminal value			£7,590

Task 7

A business is considering replacing one of its current machines with a new machine.

Using the table below, calculate the discounted life cycle cost of purchasing the machine based upon the following:

- purchase price £400,000

- annual running costs of £45,000 for the next four years paid annually in arrears

- residual value of £150,000 at the end of the four years.

The discount factors at 5% are as follows:

Year 0   1.000

Year 1   0.952

Year 2   0.907

Year 3   0.864

Year 4   0.823

Year	0	1	2	3	4
Cash flow	(400,000)	(45,000)	(45,000)	(45,000)	105,000
Discount factor	1.000	0.952	0.907	0.864	0.823
Present value	(400,000)	(42,840)	(40,815)	(38,880)	86415
Net present cost	(436120)				

CHAPTER OVERVIEW

- Due to the nature of fixed costs, total unit cost will tend to decrease as activity levels increase, as the fixed costs are spread over more units of production – however if selling price and variable costs remain constant then contribution per unit will remain constant as activity levels change

- As fixed costs in total are assumed to be constant for the period, whatever volume of products is made, maximisation of profit will be achieved by maximising contribution

- Thus for decision making purposes we concentrate on marginal costing and contribution

- The break-even point in units is found by dividing the fixed costs by the contribution per unit

- If a target profit is required the unit sales to achieve this can be found by dividing the fixed costs plus target profit by the contribution per unit

- The difference between budgeted or actual sales and the break-even point is the margin of safety, which can be expressed as a percentage of budgeted or actual sales

- The profit volume ratio can be used to find the break-even point in terms of sales revenue

    Break-even point (£) = Fixed cost/Profit volume ratio

- Normally production of products is limited by sales demand however in some instances factors such as the availability of material, labour hours or machine hours is the limiting factor

- Where there is more than one product and a limiting factor, overall profit is maximised by concentrating production on the products with the highest contribution per limiting factor unit

- In a make or buy decision with no limiting factors, the relevant costs are the differential costs between the two options. Typically this includes any variable costs incurred/saved as a result of the decision and any savings in attributable fixed costs

- Shutdown/discontinuance problems can be simplified into short-run relevant cost decisions

- Whether or not to move from a labour intensive production process to a machine intensive production process will also have many short and some long term effects

- Discounted cash flows techniques are used in decision making to take account of the time value of money

- Time value of money recognises that £1 today is worth more than £1 at a future time, because money can be reinvested to earn more money over time

Keywords

Contribution – sales revenue or selling price per unit less variable costs

Cost-volume-profit analysis – analysis of the relationships between activity levels, costs and profits

Break-even analysis – calculations to determine the break-even point

Break-even point – level of sales whereby sales revenue is equal to total costs

Margin of safety – excess of budgeted or actual sales over the break-even point sales

Profit volume (P/V) ratio – ratio of contribution to sales

Contribution to sales (C/S) ratio – alternative name for the profit volume ratio

Limiting factor – a factor of production or sales that limits the amount of a product that can be produced or sold

Net present value – is the net total of the present value of a set of cash flows.

Net terminal value – the value of all cash flows as though invested until the end of the project less the original cash outflow

TEST YOUR LEARNING

1   If selling prices and variable costs remain constant at differing levels of activity, explain why unit cost will tend to fall as activity levels increase.
FIXED COSTS

2   A business has budgeted sales of its single product of 38,000 units. The selling price per unit is £57 and the variable costs of production are £45. The fixed costs of the business are £360,000.

The break-even point is [30,000] units $\frac{360,000}{57-45} = 30,000$

The margin of safety is [21] % $\frac{38,000 - 30,000}{38,000} \times 100 = 21\%$

3   A business has fixed costs of £910,000. It sells a single product at a selling price of £24 and the variable costs of production and sales are £17 per unit.

How many units of the product must the business sell in order to make a profit of £500,000? $\frac{910,000 + 500,000}{24 - 17} =$

A   71,428 units
B   82,941 units
C   130,000 units
(D)   201,429 units

4   A business sells its single product for £40. The variable costs of this product total £32. The fixed costs of the business are £100,000.

The sales revenue required in order to make a profit of £200,000 is

£ [1,500,000] $PV = \frac{40-32}{40} \times 100 = 20\%$ $\frac{100,000 + 200,000}{0.20}$

5   A business produces three products, the production and sales details of which are given below:

MAT
80,000
120,000
25,000
225,000 KGS ✓

LAB   *m/c*
20,000   *60,000*
80,000   *30,000*
5,000   *15,000* ✗
105,000 HRS ✓   *155,000 HRS*

	Product R	Product S	Product T
Direct materials @ £2 per kg	£16	£12	£10
Direct labour @ £9 per hour	£18	£36	£9
Selling price	£40	£60	£25
Machine hours per unit	6	4	3
Maximum sales demand	10,000 units	20,000 units	5,000 units

CONTRIB   £6   £12   £6
PER m/c Hour   £1   £3   £2

During the next period the supply of materials is limited to 250,000 kgs, the labour hours available are 120,000 and the machine hours available are also 120,000. Fixed costs are £50,000 per period.

(a) The limiting factor of production resources is ~~materials/labour hours~~/machine hours. Select the appropriate answer

(b) Complete the following table to show the production plan which will maximise profit.

Product	Units produced	
S	20,000	80000
T	5000	15.000
R	4166	25.000

(c) The profit that will be earned under this production plan is

£ 244.996

240.000   294.996
30.000   -50.000
24.996

244 996

6   A business has two products, X and Y, with the following costs per unit. 244 996

	X	Y
	Cost per unit £	Cost per unit £
Direct materials	2.50	3.00
Direct labour	8.00	6.00
Fixed overheads	3.00	1.50

The business could buy in X at £ 11 per unit, and Y at £10 per unit, but this would not save any amount of the fixed overheads.

On the basis of cost alone which if any products should be bought in?

A   Both X and Y
B   X only
C   Y only
D   Neither X nor Y

7   A business is considering investment in new machinery at a cost of £340,000 on 1 April 20X4. This machinery will be used to produce a new product which will give rise to the following net cash inflows:

31 March 20X5	£80,000
31 March 20X6	£70,000
31 March 20X7	£90,000
31 March 20X8	£120,000
31 March 20X9	£60,000

The new machinery is to be depreciated at 20% per annum on cost. The cost of capital is 7%.

Complete the table below to calculate the net present value of this project.

Year	Cash flows £	Discount factor at 7%	Present value £
0	(340,000)	1.000	(340,000)
1	80,000	0.935	74,800
2	70,000	0.873	61,110
3	90,000	0.816	73440
4	120,000	0.763	91560
5	60,000	0.713	42780
Net present value			3690

8   A business is considering investment in new plant and machinery on 1 January 20X6 at a cost of £90,000. The company has a cost of capital of 11%. The cash cost savings are estimated to be:

31 December 20X6	£23,000
31 December 20X7	£31,000
31 December 20X8	£40,000
31 December 20X9	£18,000

(a)   Complete the table below to determine the net present value of this project.

Year	Cash flows £	Discount factor at 11%	Present value £
0	(90,000)	1.000	(90,000)
1	23,000	0.901	20723
2	31,000	0.812	25172
3	40,000	0.731	29240
4	18,000	0.659	11862
Net present value			(3003)

(b)   Advise the business as to whether it should invest in the new plant and machinery and justify your advice.

        NO

chapter 4:
STATISTICAL METHODS

chapter coverage 📖

In this chapter we will look at some basic statistical methods that you may need to use for this Unit.

The topics that are to be covered are:

✍ Time series analysis

✍ Additive model

✍ Trend and seasonal variations

✍ Index numbers

✍ Linear regression

PREDICTING FUTURE COSTS AND REVENUES FROM HISTORIC DATA

A business may collect data about previous activities, costs and sales revenues and use it to help estimate future levels of activity, costs or sales. This chapter considers a number of statistical techniques that can be used in this way.

By studying the historic information it has captured, the business hopes to draw valid conclusions about the future. Sometimes this will require compromise, as the time and effort involved in examining all the data may outweigh the benefits and so a sample is selected. In order to provide a reasonable estimate, the sample of data on which such forecasts are made needs to be as representative as possible.

Techniques can be used to adjust the data for seasonal variations (time series) and also for changes in price levels (indexing).

TIME SERIES ANALYSIS

If we have collected cost or income data over a number of periods, such as sales revenue or production costs, this is known as a TIME SERIES. Such historic data may be used as a basis for forecasting future values. One of the key elements of information that management might require from a time series is an indication of the TREND. The trend is a feel for how the figure in question is changing over time – is it increasing rapidly, is it decreasing slightly?

The technique for determining the trend and other underlying components of a time series of figures is known as TIME SERIES ANALYSIS.

Elements of a time series

When considering results or costs over time there are four main elements that are likely to influence the figures:

- **Trend**

   The trend is the underlying movement of the figures over time. For example, sales may be erratic from month to month but in general terms are gradually rising.

- **Cyclical variations**

   Most economies will tend to have periods of growth and periods of recession. It is considered that such economic cycles typically take place over a seven to nine year period. Such long term economic cycles will cause alterations in the pattern of the actual results over time, known as CYCLICAL VARIATIONS. If the economy is growing then sales are likely to be increasing more rapidly but if the economy is in recession then sales growth may slow down or even reverse.

- **Seasonal variations**

  Most businesses will experience some sort of regular growth or reduction due to the seasonality of their business. This does not necessarily mean the actual seasons, summer, winter etc but some regular cycles for the particular business, repeated within a time frame of less than a year. These cycles are known as SEASONAL VARIATIONS. For example, a restaurant that is open 7 nights a week may generally experience peak numbers of customers on Friday and Saturday nights with lows on Monday and Tuesday.

- **Random variations**

  The actual results over time will also be influenced by random factors. For example in a manufacturing business if 30% of the workforce is affected by flu over a two week period then production will probably drop. These RANDOM VARIATIONS are totally unpredictable.

Task 1

What is the difference between a cyclical variation and a seasonal variation?

ADDITIVE MODEL

Under the additive model of time series analysis, it is assumed that the actual figure for each period of a time series is made up of the trend, the cyclical variation, the seasonal variation and any random variation added together. This can be expressed as follows:

Actual figure = T + C + S + R

where:

T	=	the trend
C	=	the cyclical variation
S	=	the seasonal variation
R	=	the random variation

You do not have to be concerned about calculations involving the cyclical variation or the random variation. Therefore we are left with the simpler expression:

Actual figure = T + S

We need only concern ourselves with the calculation of the trend and the seasonal variation.

There is also another model used in time series analysis, the multiplicative model, but this is not relevant for this syllabus.

TREND AND SEASONAL VARIATIONS

A simple way of detecting the trend from time series observations is to take averages over a certain period. If these averages change over time then there is evidence of a trend in the series.

Thus the technique that will be used is to take the actual figures from the time series and from these determine the trend using a technique of moving averages. Once the moving average (trend) has been identified it can be compared to the actual figure to ascertain the seasonal variation.

The expression above (Actual figure = T + S) can be altered slightly to read as follows:

Actual figure – T = S

Therefore by deducting the relevant trend figure from the actual figure the seasonal variation can be calculated.

We will consider first the calculation of the trend using moving averages.

Moving averages

The technique of calculating a MOVING AVERAGE is a key tool in time series analysis and is a method of finding averages for a number of consecutive periods. The number of periods of data to be included in the average is chosen such that a whole cycle of seasonal variations is included. Averaging these will thus smooth out seasonal variations. As each successive group of data is averaged, the underlying trend is highlighted.

HOW IT WORKS

Suppose that the sales figures for a business for the first six months of the year are as follows:

	£
January	33,000
February	39,000
March	36,000
April	44,000
May	35,000
June	49,000

It is felt that the sales cycle is on a quarterly basis – ie the seasonal variances repeat themselves every three months. What is required, therefore, is a three month moving average. This is done by firstly totalling the figures for January, February and March and then finding the average:

$$\frac{33,000 + 39,000 + 36,000}{3} = £36,000$$

Then we move on one month, and the average for February, March and April sales are calculated:

$$\frac{39,000 + 36,000 + 44,000}{3} = £39,667$$

Then the average for March, April and May:

$$\frac{36,000 + 44,000 + 35,000}{3} = £38,333$$

Then finally the average for April, May and June:

$$\frac{44,000 + 35,000 + 49,000}{3} = £42,667$$

Now we can show these moving averages together with the original figures – the convention is to show the moving average next to the middle month of those used to calculate the average.

	Actual data £	Moving average £
January	33,000	
February	39,000	36,000
March	36,000	39,667
April	44,000	38,333
May	35,000	42,667
June	49,000	

Task 2

Given below are the production costs for a factory for a six month period.

Complete the table to show the three month moving average for these figures.

Month	Actual £	Three month moving average £
March	226,500	—
April	251,600	238767
May	238,200	245800
June	247,600	242100
July	240,500	250.300
August	262,800	—

Centred moving averages

The trend for a time series is essentially the moving average for the time series. However, if the number of periods used in the moving average is an even number, such as the four quarters of the year, then there is a further calculation to make – the CENTRED MOVING AVERAGE. The reason for this is that if the moving average is based upon an even number of periods, then there is no central period to place the moving average against – a further average, the centred average, is required in order to find the trend.

HOW IT WORKS

The quarterly sales figures for Wrigley Partners for the last three years are given below:

		£
20X6	Quarter 1	88,900
	Quarter 2	100,300
	Quarter 3	63,800
	Quarter 4	75,200
20X7	Quarter 1	91,600
	Quarter 2	103,700
	Quarter 3	66,100
	Quarter 4	76,400
20X8	Quarter 1	95,400
	Quarter 2	106,000
	Quarter 3	68,800
	Quarter 4	77,100

By inspection, it would appear the sales figures exhibit seasonal variations over the four quarters of the year, for example Quarter 2 is always the highest and Quarter 3 the lowest. In order to find the trend of the time series a four quarterly centred moving average must first be calculated. Start with the four quarterly moving average:

First average:
$$\frac{88,900 + 100,300 + 63,800 + 75,200}{4} = 82,050$$

Second average:
$$\frac{100,300 + 63,800 + 75,200 + 91,600}{4} = 82,725$$

and so on.

		ACTUAL £	Moving average £
20X6	Quarter 1	88,900	
	Quarter 2	100,300	
			82,050
	Quarter 3	63,800	
			82,725
	Quarter 4	75,200	
			83,575
20X7	Quarter 1	91,600	
			84,150
	Quarter 2	103,700	
			84,450
	Quarter 3	66,100	
			85,400
	Quarter 4	76,400	
			85,975
20X8	Quarter 1	95,400	
			86,650
	Quarter 2	106,000	
			86,825
	Quarter 3	68,800	
	Quarter 4	77,100	

As the moving average being calculated is an even number, a four quarter moving average, then it is shown in between the second and third quarter each time – the middle of the four quarters.

Now in order to find the trend line the centred moving average must be calculated. This entails taking each consecutive pair of moving average figures and in turn averaging them and showing them against the third quarter.

First average: $\dfrac{82,050 + 82,725}{2} = 82,388$

Second average: $\dfrac{82,725 + 83,575}{2} = 83,150$

and so on.

		ACTUAL	Moving average	Centred moving average TREND
		£	£	£
20X6	Quarter 1	88,900		
	Quarter 2	100,300		
			82,050	
	Quarter 3	63,800		82,388
			82,725	
	Quarter 4	75,200		83,150
			83,575	
20X7	Quarter 1	91,600		83,863
			84,150	
	Quarter 2	103,700		84,300
			84,450	
	Quarter 3	66,100		84,925
			85,400	
	Quarter 4	76,400		85,688
			85,975	
20X8	Quarter 1	95,400		86,313
			86,650	
	Quarter 2	106,000		86,738
			86,825	
	Quarter 3	68,800		
	Quarter 4	77,100		

Calculating seasonal variations

We will now deal with identifying the seasonal variations. Remember the relationship between the actual figures, the trend and the seasonal variation in our simplified model:

Actual figure – trend = seasonal variation

We now include a final column on our table to show the seasonal variation for each quarter that can be directly compared to the trend.

For example, the centred moving average (the trend) for 20X6 quarter 3 is 82,388 but the actual observation for the same period is 63,800. The difference, which is due to seasonal variation, is – 18,588 (63,800 – 82,388), and is due to the seasonal variation.

		ACTUAL £	Moving average £	Centred moving average TREND £	Seasonal variation ACTUAL- TREND £
20X6	Quarter 1	88,900			
	Quarter 2	100,300			
			82,050		
	Quarter 3	63,800		82,388	–18,588
			82,725		
	Quarter 4	75,200		83,150	–7,950
			83,575		
20X7	Quarter 1	91,600		83,863	+7,737
			84,150		
	Quarter 2	103,700		84,300	+19,400
			84,450		
	Quarter 3	66,100		84,925	–18,825
			85,400		
	Quarter 4	76,400		85,688	–9,288
			85,975		
20X8	Quarter 1	95,400		86,313	+9,087
			86,650		
	Quarter 2	106,000		86,738	+19,262
			86,825		
	Quarter 3	68,800			
	Quarter 4	77,100			

The next stage is to find an average seasonal variation for each quarter, to get a representative seasonal variation for forecasting purposes. This is done by grouping the seasonal variations together, by quarter, in a table:

	Quarter 1	Quarter 2	Quarter 3	Quarter 4
20X6	–	–	–18,588	–7,950
20X7	+7,737	+19,400	–18,825	–9,288
20X8	+ 9,087	+ 19,262	–	–
Total	+ 16,824	+ 38,662	– 37,413	– 17,238
Average = total/2	+8,412	+19,331	–18,707	–8,619

The next stage is to ensure that the total seasonal variations total to zero:

$$+ 8,412 + 19,331 - 18,707 - 8,619 = +417$$

In this case they do not, therefore we must make minor adjustments to each of the seasonal variations by dividing the difference by 4:

$$417/4 = +104 \text{ (rounded)}$$

and then deducting this figure from each of the seasonal variations.

	Quarter 1 £	Quarter 2 £	Quarter 3 £	Quarter 4 £
Unadjusted seasonal variation	+8,412	+19,331	−18,707	−8,619
Add adjustment	−104	−104	−104	−105
Adjusted seasonal variation	+8,308	+19,227	−18,811	− 8,724

We now have seasonal variations that total to zero (because of rounding differences, the quarter 4 adjustment used was 105 rather than 104 to ensure this).

Task 3

Given below are the annual sales figures for a business for the last eight years. Complete the table to calculate a four year moving average and trend using the centred moving average.

	Actual £	Four year moving average £	Centred moving average = trend £
20X1	226,700		
20X2	236,500		
		236500	
20X3	240,300		238175
		239850	
20X4	242,500		240988
		242125	
20X5	240,100		243038
		243950	
20X6	245,600		244663
		245375	
20X7	247,600		
20X8	248,200		

Graphing the time series and trend

Let's return to our previous example. Wrigley Partners, at this stage it might be useful to draw the actual figures and the trend line onto a graph of the time series. When drawing a graph of a time series the time scale is always shown on the horizontal x axis and the figures on the vertical y axis.

Wrigley Partners – quarterly sales

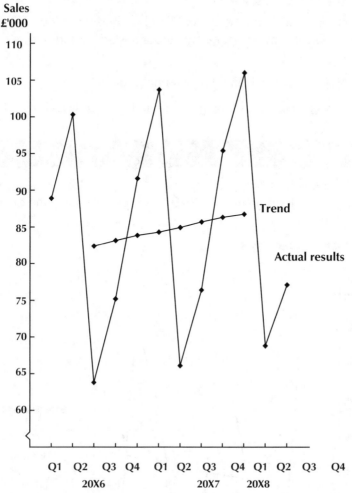

Using the trend

As you can see in the graph the sales of Wrigley Partners are irregular – quite high in quarters one and two, low in quarter three and higher again in Quarter 4. This is known as a seasonal business.

The trend line (taken from the centred moving averages) however smoothes out the seasonal elements and shows how the sales are generally increasing over the three years.

The trend line can then be extended and the likely trend of sales in future periods can be read off from the graph as estimates. This process of estimating a future figure from a line on a graph is known as EXTRAPOLATION.

Using the seasonal variations

Once the trend line has been extrapolated and a trend figure read off the graph for a future period the trend figure must be adjusted by the relevant seasonal adjustment.

Remember: Actual figure = Trend +/– Seasonal variation

This will then give an estimate of the future period's actual sales.

HOW IT WORKS

Returning to the graph of the quarterly sales of Wrigley Partners we will extend the trend line for the four quarters in 20X9 by simply extending the trend line by hand on the graph.

Wrigley Partners – quarterly sales

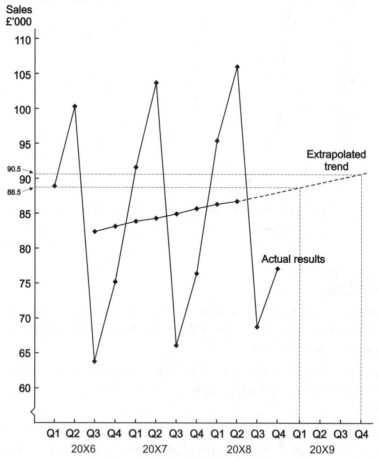

Once the trend line has been extended the estimated trend figures can then be read off from the graph (this will be easier if the graph is on graph paper):

20X9	Quarter 1	£88,500
	Quarter 2	£89,200
	Quarter 3	£89,900
	Quarter 4	£90,500

These figures however are not the expected sales for each quarter but the expected trend figure for each quarter. Quarters 1 and 2 are seasonally higher than the trend and Quarters 3 and 4 lower. Therefore we must apply the seasonal variation to the expected trend in order to find the anticipated sales figure.

		Trend	Seasonal variation	Forecast sales
		£	£	£
20X9	Quarter 1	88,500	+8,308	96,808
	Quarter 2	89,200	+19,227	108,427
	Quarter 3	89,900	−18,811	71,089
	Quarter 4	90,500	−8,724	81,776

Task 4

A manufacturing business has used its production costs for the last two years to identify a trend and monthly seasonal variations. Extrapolating the trend line has produced estimates of the trend in costs for the months of January to March 20X9 and time series analysis has provided monthly seasonal variations.

	Estimated trend	Seasonal variations
	£	£
January	205,600	+23,200
February	208,600	+9,230
March	209,200	−3,500

Complete the table to calculate the anticipated production costs for January to March 20X9

Month	Cost £
January	228,800
February	217,830
March	205,700

INDEX NUMBERS

We have seen how we can get a feel for how a time series is changing over time by plotting a trend line. Another simple and convenient method of doing this is to convert the actual figures to a series of INDEX NUMBERS.

Index numbers measure the change in value of a figure over time, by reference to its value at a fixed point.

This is done by determining firstly a BASE PERIOD which is the period for which the actual figure is equated to an index of 100. Each subsequent period's figure is converted to the equivalent index using the following formula:

$$\text{Index} = \frac{\text{Current period's figure}}{\text{Base period figure}} \times 100$$

HOW IT WORKS

The sales figures for a business for the first six months of the year are as follows:

	£
January	136,000
February	148,000
March	140,000
April	130,000
May	138,000
June	145,000

We will set the January figure as the base period, with an index of 100.

This means that the index for February is calculated as:

$$\frac{\text{Current period's figure}}{\text{Base period figure}} \times 100 = \frac{148,000}{136,000} \times 100 = 109$$

The index for March is:

$$\frac{140,000}{136,000} \times 100 = 103$$

The index for April is:

$$\frac{130,000}{136,000} \times 100 = 96$$

The index for May is:

$$\frac{138,000}{136,000} \times 100 = 101$$

The index for June is:

$$\frac{145,000}{136,000} \times 100 = 107$$

Interpreting an index

If the index for a period is greater than 100, this means that the current period figure is larger than the base period figure and if it is less than 100, the figure is lower than the base period figure. If the index is generally rising, then the figures are increasing over the base period but if the index is decreasing, the figures are decreasing compared to the base period.

Remember when interpreting an index that it represents the current period figure compared to the base period, not compared to the previous period.

HOW IT WORKS

We can show the actual sales together with the index for the previous example.

	£	Index
January	136,000	100
February	148,000	109
March	140,000	103
April	130,000	96
May	138,000	101
June	145,000	107

The index shows that although sales start to increase in February, they then fall again with April being lower than January. However by June the sales are again increasing, almost to the February level.

Task 5

The profit of a business for the last eight quarters is given below. Complete the table below to show the index for the profit figures using Quarter 1 20X7 as the base period.

		Profit £	Index
20X7	Quarter 1	86,700	100
	Quarter 2	88,200	101·7
	Quarter 3	93,400	107·7
	Quarter 4	90,500	104·4
20X8	Quarter 1	83,200	96·0
	Quarter 2	81,400	93·9
	Quarter 3	83,200	96·0
	Quarter 4	85,000	98·0

Retail price index

The Retail Price Index (RPI) is a measure of general price changes, which is published each month by the government.

A business can use the RPI to determine the extent to which its income and its costs have changed in line with general inflation.

HOW IT WORKS

A business has had the following sales for the last eight years:

	£
20X1	513,600
20X2	516,300
20X3	518,400
20X4	522,400
20X5	530,400
20X6	535,200
20X7	549,800
20X8	558,700

If we use 20X1 as the base year and then index the sales figures on that basis, the index will be as follows:

		Index
20X1	100.0	
20X2	516,300/513,600 × 100	100.5
20X3	518,400/513,600 × 100	100.9
20X4	522,400/513,600 × 100	101.7
20X5	530,400/513,600 × 100	103.3
20X6	535,200/513,600 × 100	104.2
20X7	549,800/513,600 × 100	107.0
20X8	558,700/513,600 × 100	108.8

This index shows a small but steady increase in sales revenue over the years. But is this due to an increase in sales volume, or simply the effects of inflation increasing the selling price?

We can consider the general increases in prices over the period by looking at the average Retail Price Index (RPI) for each of the years:

	RPI
20X1	140.7
20X2	144.1
20X3	149.1
20X4	152.7
20X5	157.5
20X6	162.9
20X7	165.4
20X8	170.2

We apply the RPI to the annual sales figures in order to show the RPI adjusted figures. This is done by using the following formula:

$$\text{Sales for current year} \times \frac{\text{RPI for year 1}}{\text{RPI for current year}}$$

20X1	Adjusted sales figure	$= 513,600 \times 140.7/140.7$	$= £513,600$
20X2	Adjusted sales figure	$= 516,300 \times 140.7/144.1$	$= £504,118$
20X3	Adjusted sales figure	$= 518,400 \times 140.7/149.1$	$= £489,194$

and so on:

	Sales £	Adjusted sales £
20X1	513,600	513,600
20X2	516,300	504,118
20X3	518,400	489,194
20X4	522,400	481,347
20X5	530,400	473,824
20X6	535,200	462,263
20X7	549,800	467,696
20X8	558,700	461,863

In 'real' terms, ie without inflationary effects, sales have fallen. This could be due to:

- falling sales volumes
- selling prices failing to keep up with general inflation

or a combination of these.

What has been done here is to turn each period's sales into 20X1 price terms to illustrate that, in terms of the prices then prevailing, the sales over time have decreased.

We can now calculate an index based upon these adjusted sales figure which shows a very different picture from the earlier index:

| 20X2 | Amended index | $= 504,118/513,600 \times 100$ | $= 98.2$ |

and so on:

	Sales £	Adjusted sales £	Index
20X1	513,600	513,600	100.0
20X2	516,300	504,118	98.2
20X3	518,400	489,194	95.2
20X4	522,400	481,347	93.7
20X5	530,400	473,824	92.3
20X6	535,200	462,263	90.0
20X7	549,800	467,696	91.1
20X8	558,700	461,863	89.9

This shows that the sales for the last eight years have in fact dramatically failed to keep up with the general rise in prices, as shown by the retail price index adjusted sales index.

Task 6

Given below are the monthly production costs for a business for the last year, together with the Retail Price Index for each month. Complete the table to show the adjusted production cost figures for the year based upon the Retail Price Index, in terms of June 20X7 prices.

		Costs	RPI	Restated costs
		£		£
20X7	June	133,100	171.1	133,100
	July	133,800	170.5	134,271
	Aug	133,600	170.8	133835
	Sept	134,600	171.7	134130
	Oct	135,800	171.6	135404
	Nov	135,100	172.1	134315
	Dec	135,600	172.1	134812
20X8	Jan	134,700	171.1	134700
	Feb	135,900	172.0	135189
	Mar	136,200	172.2	135330
	April	136,500	173.1	134923
	May	136,700	174.2	134267

Restating costs and income in current prices

In the previous example we took a series of sales figures and restated them in terms of prices prevailing in the earliest year of the time series. A further way of using the Retail Price Index is to restate earlier period's figures in terms of today's prices.

HOW IT WORKS

We will use the figures for sales which have been used earlier:

	£
20X1	513,600
20X2	516,300
20X3	518,400
20X4	522,400
20X5	530,400
20X6	535,200
20X7	549,800
20X8	558,700

The average Retail Price Index for each of these years was:

	RPI
20X1	140.7
20X2	144.1
20X3	149.1
20X4	152.7
20X5	157.5
20X6	162.9
20X7	165.4
20X8	170.2

In order to restate the sales in terms of year 20X8 prices the following formula is applied:

$$\text{Sales in current year} \times \frac{\text{RPI for 20X8}}{\text{RPI for the current year}}$$

The restated figures would appear as follows:

	Actual £	In year 20X8 prices £
20X1	513,600 × 170.2/140.7	621,284
20X2	516,300 × 170.2/144.1	609,814
20X3	518,400 × 170.2/149.1	591,762
20X4	522,400 × 170.2/152.7	582,269
20X5	530,400 × 170.2/157.5	573,169
20X6	535,200 × 170.2/162.9	559,184
20X7	549,800 × 170.2/165.4	565,756
20X8	558,700 × 170.2/170.2	558,700

We have now shown each year's sales in terms of year 20X8 prices. Again this shows that in real terms the sales have decreased over the period.

Task 7

Given below are the monthly production costs for a business for the last year, together with the Retail Price Index for each month. Complete the table to show the adjusted production cost figures for the year based upon the Retail Price Index, in terms of May 20X8 prices.

		Costs	RPI	Restated costs
		£		£
20X7	June	133,100	171.1	135,512
	July	133,800	170.5	136704
	Aug	133,600	170.8	136259
	Sept	134,600	171.7	136560
	Oct	135,800	171.6	137858
	Nov	135,100	172.1	136749
	Dec	135,600	172.1	137255
20X8	Jan	134,700	171.1	137141
	Feb	135,900	172.0	137638
	Mar	136,200	172.2	137782
	April	136,500	173.1	137367
	May	136,700	174.2	136700

LINEAR REGRESSION

There is a further technique that can be used in forecasting costs and income and also, in assessments, is sometimes used for forecasting sales volumes. This technique is known as LINEAR REGRESSION. Regression analysis involves the prediction of one variable eg cost, based on another variable eg volume of output, on the assumption that there is a linear relationship (straight line on a graph) between the two variables.

The equation of a straight line

Given below is a straight line drawn onto a graph

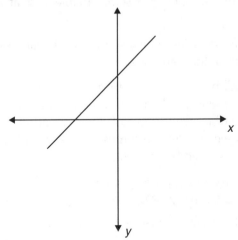

Any such straight line will have a defining equation in the following form:

$$y = a + bx$$

Both a and b are constants and represent specific figures:

- a is the point on the graph where the line intersects the y axis
- b represents the gradient of the line

We can now show a and b on the previous graph.

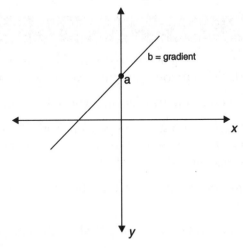

Using the equation of a straight line

The straight line drawn on the graphs above should remind you of two other straight line graphs that you have met earlier:

- the graph of a semi-variable cost
- the graph of a linear trend in a time series analysis

We can therefore use the equation for a straight line, or LINEAR REGRESSION EQUATION, in two possible ways in forecasting:

- to forecast the amount of a semi-variable cost at a given production level

- to forecast future sales volumes using the linear regression equation as the equation for the trend of sales.

In assessments you will not be required to derive the linear regression equation for a straight line. Either you will be given this equation and asked to find values of x and y, or you will be given values of x and y and asked to determine the values of a and b. However some care must be taken with what the variables x and y, and the constants a and b represent.

Dependent and independent variables

Given the equation of a straight line: $y = a + bx$:

- y is always the DEPENDENT VARIABLE

  (plotted on the vertical axis)

- x is always the INDEPENDENT VARIABLE

  (plotted on the horizontal axis).

The dependent variable y can be calculated using the linear regression equation, provided that a value is known for the independent variable x.

HOW IT WORKS

(a) A linear regression equation expresses the relationship between the costs of producing a product and the quantity of production.

Which is the dependent variable and which the independent variable?

The cost of production is the dependent variable as this will depend upon the quantity. Therefore x represents the quantity of production and y represents the costs of production.

(b) A linear regression equation expresses the trend line for a time series of sales volumes.

Which is the dependent variable and which the independent variable?

The volume of sales depends upon the time period in which the sales were made, so volume is represented by y and time is represented on the x axis (note, time is ALWAYS an independent variable!).

Task 8

A linear regression equation expresses the relationship between advertising costs and sales volume. Which is the dependent variable and which is the independent variable? *COSTS – INDEPENDENT VOLUME – DEPENDENT*

Determining a and b in a linear regression equation

We have seen that the linear regression equation is $y = a + bx$, where a is the point where the line intersects the y axis and b is the gradient of the line.

If we are considering the equation of a straight line depicting the relationship between cost (y) and output (x), say

$y = 10,500 + 5x$

then

$a = £10,500$, which represents the fixed costs (incurred even if output is zero)

and $b = £5$, which represents the variable costs per unit.

If you are given a number of figures for x and y, then it is possible to draw the linear regression line on a graph and determine the amounts represented by a and b.

HOW IT WORKS

A business has been monitoring its monthly production costs and has discovered the following:

- if production is 2,000 units then the cost of production is £7,000
- if production is 3,000 units then the cost of production is £9,000

If we assume that this relationship is linear, then the quantity of production will represent x and the cost of production will represent y. We can now plot these figures on a graph with the quantity of production on the x axis and the cost of production on the y axis.

- the first point to plot is where x = 2,000 units of production and y = production costs of £7,000
- the second point to plot is where x = 3,000 units of production and y = production costs of £9,000

Once these two points have been plotted, then a line can be joined between them.

Production cost £

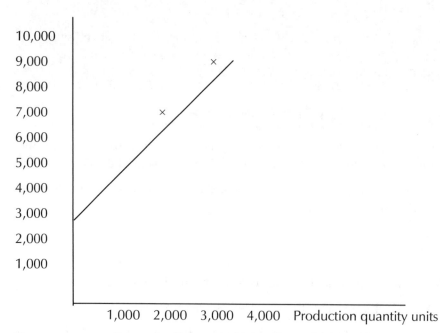

We can now easily read off the graph the figure for a in the linear regression equation. This is the point where the regression line meets the y axis, so in this case £3,000.

The figure for b requires a little more thought. This is the gradient of the line. We can see from our two points plotted that the cost of production increases by £2,000 (from £7,000 to £9,000) with a 1,000 unit increase in production (2,000 to 3,000). Therefore for every 1,000 increase in units there is £2,000 increase in costs giving a gradient of 2, therefore the figure for b is 2.

A graph does not have to be used to find a and b. Writing out the equation

$$y = a + bx$$

at each of the two activity levels gives:

$$£7,000 = a + (2,000 \times b)$$

$$£9,000 = a + (3,000 \times b)$$

Subtract these two equations to find b.

$$£(9,000 - 7,000) = (a + (3,000 \times b)) - (a - (2,000 \times b))$$

$$£2,000 = 1,000 \times b$$

Therefore b = £2,000/1,000 = 2.

Substituting b = 2 into either of the equations can be used to find a.

£7,000 = a + (2,000 x 2)

a = £7,000 - £4,000

a = £3,000

Therefore, the monthly production costs of the business can be described by the equation

y = £3,000 + 2x

Although this involves equations, in fact you have already been using this technique to determine semi-variable costs as this is similar to the hi lo technique that we used earlier in the Text. In that case, we took the highest and lowest levels of activity, and subtracted the costs to find first the variable cost element. We then used this with one of the levels of activity to find the fixed costs element. These are equivalent to b and a respectively in the linear regression equation.

Using the hi lo technique, we would have said:

Cost at activity level of 2,000 units is £7,000

Cost at activity level of 3,000 units is £9,000

Subtracting the two means that for 1,000 (3,000 – 2,000) extra units, we incur £(9,000 – 7,000) = £2,000 extra costs. So the variable costs are £2,000/1,000 = £2 per unit. This is b in the linear regression equation above.

Therefore, for 2,000 units, the cost of £7,000 is made up of variable costs of 2,000 units x £2 = £4,000. The fixed cost element must be £7,000 - £4,000 = £3,000. This is a in the linear regression equation above.

Forecasting semi-variable costs

If we are given the linear regression equation for a semi-variable cost (or we have calculated it through finding a and b), then provided that we know our forecast level of activity, x, we will be able to calculate the forecast level of cost, y.

HOW IT WORKS

The linear regression equation for the canteen costs (y) of a business for a month is as follows:

y = 20,000 + 45x

The variable x represents the number of employees using the canteen – the independent variable.

It is anticipated that the number of employees using the canteen in the next three months is as follows:

	Number of employees
January	840
February	900
March	875

What are the forecast canteen costs for each period?

		£
January	20,000 + (45 × 840)	57,800
February	20,000 + (45 × 900)	60,500
March	20,000 + (45 × 875)	59,375

Task 9

The linear regression equation for production costs (y) for a business is:

$$y = 63,000 + 3.20 x$$

If production is expected to be 44,000 units in the next quarter, what are the anticipated production costs?

£ 203,800

Forecasting sales

If we are given a linear regression equation which represents the trend for sales, then we can use this to estimate sales for future periods. The x variable is the time period and therefore this is normally given a sequential number starting with 1 for the first period of the time series. Given the trend equation we can then calculate the trend for sales for any future period. Note that this will only give meaningful results if the trend is observed to be approximately linear, ie a straight line, from its graph.

HOW IT WORKS

The trend for sales volume for one of Trinket Ltd's products is given:

$$y = 16.5 + 0.78 x$$

Where y is the volume of sales in thousands in any given time period and x is the time period.

The time series is based upon quarterly sales volumes starting in quarter 1 of 20X6.

The seasonal variations for each quarter are:

Quarter 1	−2,660
Quarter 2	+4,250
Quarter 3	+2,130
Quarter 4	−3,720

Estimate the sales volume for each quarter of 20X9.

Step 1

Find the values of x for the four quarters in 20X9.

Q1	20X6	x = 1
Q2	20X6	x = 2
Q3	20X6	x = 3
Q4	20X6	x = 4
Q1	20X7	x = 5

and so on until

Q1	20X9	x = 13

Step 2

Calculate the trend for each quarter before seasonal adjustments using the linear regression equation.

20X9	x value	$y = 16.5 + 0.78x$
		('000 units)
Q1	13	26.64
Q2	14	27.42
Q3	15	28.20
Q4	16	28.98

Step 3

Adjust the trend figures for the seasonal variations to find the seasonally adjusted sales volume.

Quarter	Trend ('000 units)	Seasonal adjustment volume (units)	Seasonally adjusted sales (units)
Q1	26.64	−2,660	23,980
Q2	27.42	+4,250	31,670
Q3	28.20	+2,130	30,330
Q4	28.98	−3,720	25,260

Interpolation and extrapolation

Again we have to consider that interpolation, an estimation within the historical range, is more reliable than extrapolation, an estimation beyond the historical range.

When using linear regression analysis to estimate future sales from a trend line, this is always extrapolation and this means that there is an underlying assumption that the current trend will continue into the future.

Task 10

The linear regression equation for the trend of sales in thousands of units based upon time series analysis of the monthly figures for the last two years is:

$$y = 4.8 + 1.2\,x$$

What is the estimated sales trend for each of the first three months of next year?

Month 1 $\boxed{34.800}$

Month 2 $\boxed{36.000}$

Month 3 $\boxed{37.200}$

CHAPTER OVERVIEW

- A series of cost or income data collected over a number of periods, such as sales revenue or production costs, is known as a time series. Such historic data may be used as a basis for forecasting future values.

- The four elements that make up the actual figures in a time series are the trend, cyclical variations, seasonal variations and random variations

- The additive model for time series is that the actual figure is made up of the trend plus the cyclical variation plus the seasonal variation plus the random variation – for this Unit only the trend and seasonal variation need be considered

- The trend is found by calculating a moving average for the actual figures – if the moving average is based upon an even number of periods, then the trend is actually found by calculating a centred moving average

- The seasonal variation for each period is calculated as the actual figure minus the trend – the average seasonal variation is then found for each period and adjustments are made to ensure that the total seasonal variation adds to zero

- The actual figures and the trend can be plotted on a time series graph with the time scale always shown on the horizontal axis

- Forecasts of future figures can be found by extending the trend line on the graph, reading off the estimated trend figure for the future period and then adjusting for the seasonal variation in that future period

- Another fairly simple method of showing whether income or expenditure has increased or decreased is to calculate an index – this is done by comparing each period's figures with those of the designated base period – the base period has an index of 100 and each period's index relates to that

- If the index for a period is above 100 then the income or expense is greater than the base period, but if it is below 100 then it is lower than in the base period – an increasing index shows a growth in the figures and vice versa

- The Retail Price Index can be used to determine whether income or costs have changed in line with general changes in inflation by adjusting each period's figures for changes in the RPI

- The RPI can be used either to turn the figures into prices based upon the earliest year or prices based upon the current year (or any year in between for that matter), however the resulting trend of figures will always be the same

- Regression analysis involves the prediction of one variable e.g. cost, based on another variable e.g. volume of output, on the assumption that there is a linear relationship between the two variables.

- Linear regression analysis can be used in order to estimate either semi-variable costs at a particular activity level or future sales volumes at a particular point in time, based on a linear trend
- The linear regression line, y = a + bx, will always be given to you in an assessment, you will not need to derive it, however care should be taken with the variables x and y: x is always the independent variable and y is the dependent variable

Keywords

Time series – a series of income or expense figures recorded for a number of consecutive periods

Trend – the underlying movements of the time series over the period

Time series analysis – a method of calculating the trend and other relevant figures from a time series

Cyclical variations – the effect on figures due to long term economic cycles

Seasonal variations – the regular short-term pattern of increases or decreases in figures that repeats due to the nature of the business

Random variations – the effects on the figures due to totally random events or circumstances

Moving average – the calculation of an average figure for the results of consecutive periods of time

Centred moving average – the average of two consecutive moving averages when the period for the moving average is an even number

Extrapolation – estimation of a future figure outside the range of data previously observed eg predicting future sales from a line on a graph

Index number – conversion of actual figures compared to a base period where the base year period is expressed as 100

Base period – the period for which the index is expressed as 100 and against which all other period figures are compared

Retail Price Index (RPI) – a measure of general price changes, which is published each month by the government.

Linear regression – a technique for forecasting semi-variable costs or future sales using the equation for a straight line

Linear regression equation – y = a + bx

where a is the point on the graph where the line intersects the y axis

b is the gradient of the line

Dependent variable – y is always the dependent variable

Independent variable – x is always in the independent variable

TEST YOUR LEARNING

1 Given below are the production cost figures for a business for the last year. Complete the table to calculate a three month moving average for these figures.

	Actual	Three month moving average
	£	£
July	397,500	
August	403,800	400,300
September	399,600	402,900
October	405,300	403667
November	406,100	406633
December	408,500	407500
January	407,900	408933
February	410,400	411433
March	416,000	413167
April	413,100	415533
May	417,500	417467
June	421,800	

2   Given below are the quarterly sales figures for a business for the last three and a half years. Complete the table to calculate a four quarter moving average, the trend using a centred moving average and the seasonal variations. Then adjust the seasonal variations as necessary.

		Actual	Four quarter moving average	Centred moving average = TREND	Seasonal variations
		£	£	£	£
20X5	Quarter 1	383,600			
	Quarter 2	387,600			
			365400		
	Quarter 3	361,800		365688	-3888
			365975		
	Quarter 4	328,600		366575	-37975
			367175		
20X6	Quarter 1	385,900		366013	19887
			364850		
	Quarter 2	392,400		366125	26275
			367400		
	Quarter 3	352,500		368225	-15725
			369050		
	Quarter 4	338,800		371288	-32488
			373525		
20X7	Quarter 1	392,500		375575	16925
			377625		
	Quarter 2	410,300		378325	31975
			379025		
	Quarter 3	368,900		379750	-10850
			380475		
	Quarter 4	344,400		382388	-37988
			384300		
20X8	Quarter 1	398,300			
	Quarter 2	425,600			

Seasonal variations:

	Quarter 1	Quarter 2	Quarter 3	Quarter 4
	£	£	£	£
20X5	—	—	−3888	−37975
20X6	19887	26275	−15725	−32488
20X7	16925	31975	−10850	−37988
Average	18406	+ 29125	−10154	−36150 = $\frac{1227}{4}$
Adjustment required				= 307

	Quarter 1	Quarter 2	Quarter 3	Quarter 4
	£	£	£	£
Unadjusted	18406	29125	−10154	−36150
Adjustment	−307	−307	−306	−307
Seasonal variation	+18099	+28818	−10460	−36457

3   Given below are the materials costs of a business for the last six months. Complete the table to calculate the index for each month's costs using January as the base month.

	Cost	Index
	£	
January	59,700	100
February	62,300	104.4
March	56,900	95.3
April	60,400	101.2
May	62,400	104.5
June	66,700	111.7

4 **(a)** Given below are the wages costs of a business for the last six months together with the Retail Price Index for those months. Complete the table to calculate the RPI adjusted wages cost figures for each of the six months, with all costs expressed in terms of June prices.

	Wages cost	RPI	Adjusted cost
	£		£
January	126,700	171.1	126848
February	129,700	172.0	129172
March	130,400	172.2	129718
April	131,600	173.0	130307
May	130,500	172.1	129893
June	131,600	171.3	131.600

(b) Using the adjusted RPI wages costs complete the table to calculate an index for the wages costs for each month with January as the base year.

	Adjusted cost	Index
	£	
January	126848	100
February	129172	101.8
March	129718	102.3
April	130307	102.7
May	129893	102.4
June	131600	103.7

5 The total production costs of a business are £15,000 if 1,000 units are produced, and £25,000 if 2,000 units are produced. The linear regression equation

$$y = a + bx$$

can be used to forecast the production costs where y is the total production cost and x is volume of production. Calculate a and b, and then the production costs if 1,400 units are produced.

6 The linear regression equation for costs of the stores department of a business is given as follows:

$$y = 13,000 + 0.8x$$

Where x is the number of units produced in a period.

The anticipated production levels for the next six months are given below. Complete the table to calculate the forecast stores department costs for the next six months.

	Production	Costs
	Units	£
January	5,400	17320
February	5,600	17480
March	5,700	17560
April	6,000	17800
May	5,500	17400
June	6,100	17880

7   A time series analysis of sales volumes each quarter for the last three years, 20X6 to 20X8, has revealed that the trend can be estimated by the equation:

$y = 2,200 + 45 x$

Where y is the sales volume and x is the time period.

The seasonal variations for each quarter have been calculated as:

Quarter 1	−200
Quarter 2	+500
Quarter 3	+350
Quarter 4	−650

Use the table below to estimate the sales volume for each quarter of 20X9.

	Value of x	Trend	Seasonal variation	Forecast sales
Quarter 1 20X9	13	2785	−200	2585
Quarter 2 20X9	14	2830	+500	3330
Quarter 3 20X9	15	2875	+350	3225
Quarter 4 20X9	16	2920	−650	2270

chapter 5:
STANDARD COSTING

── **chapter coverage** 📖 ──

In this chapter we will introduce the important concept of standard costing. We will look at how standards are developed and their uses in a management control system. We will then move on to the calculation of all of the basic variances, before considering further aspects of calculating variances in the next chapter.

The topics that are to be covered are:

✎ Introduction to standard costing systems

✎ How standard costs are set

✎ Types of standard

✎ Direct materials variances

✎ Direct labour variances

✎ Fixed overhead variances

✎ Fixed overhead efficiency and capacity variances

✎ Fixed overhead variances – absorption costing

✎ Reconciliation of total standard cost to total actual cost

✎ Marginal costing variances

✎ Standard cost bookkeeping

INTRODUCTION TO STANDARD COSTING SYSTEMS

A STANDARD COSTING SYSTEM is one in which the expected cost of each unit of production is set out in a standard cost card and the actual cost of the units actually produced is compared in detail to this standard cost card. VARIANCES, the difference between the actual costs of the production and the standard costs, are then calculated and are used by management in running the business efficiently.

There are several areas involved in a standard costing system:

- setting the standards – see below

- calculating the variances – we will concentrate on this aspect in this chapter

- interpreting the variances – this will be considered in the next chapter

- reporting variances to management and management action – again this will be considered in the next chapter.

Uses of a standard costing system

Many manufacturing organisations and some service industries make use of standard costing systems, as they can be advantageous to management in a variety of different ways and can provide management with information to aid their three principal tasks of planning, decision making and control.

- the standard quantities of materials and labour required for production can be useful when planning future operations and setting budgets

- the standard costs of production can be useful for decision making – for example in comparing the costs of two similar products or setting selling prices

- Standard costing variances aid control by breaking down the overall variance into its individual components. The variances calculated by comparing actual costs to standard costs can provide management with information about areas of the business which require monitoring or some action to be taken.

Variances to be calculated

The variances to be calculated for this Unit are set out in the diagram below:

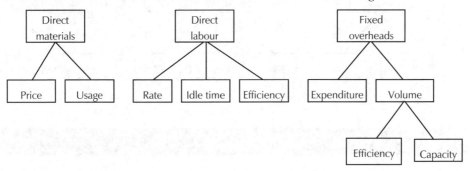

Absorption costing

You will remember from Chapter 2, that under a system of absorption costing the overheads of the business are absorbed into the cost units on the basis of a pre-determined overhead absorption rate. This means that the cost of the unit of production is a 'full' cost including its share of production overheads.

For this Unit, the only overheads that are to be considered are the fixed overheads. The diagram above illustrates the fixed overhead variances that will need to be calculated – the total variance is split into an expenditure variance and a volume variance and the volume variance in turn can be analysed into an efficiency variance and a capacity variance.

Marginal costing

Again you should remember from Chapter 2 that under a marginal costing accounting system the cost of cost units is made up of their variable costs only. The fixed overheads are treated as period costs and are written off to the income statement as an expense of the period, rather than being included in the cost of the cost units.

For the purposes of this Unit, the direct materials and direct labour will be treated as variable costs. The fixed overheads are not absorbed into the cost units or included on the standard cost card for the products. Therefore the fixed overhead variances to be calculated for marginal costing are reduced to just the fixed overhead expenditure variance, with no further analysis required.

Therefore the diagram summarising the variances required under a marginal standard costing system will be rather simpler than the earlier diagram:

Variances summary

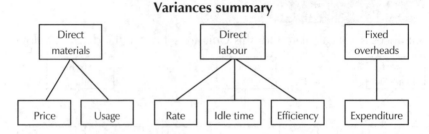

HOW STANDARD COSTS ARE SET

Standard costs

A standard cost is the planned unit cost of a product or service. This is usually documented in a standard cost card. Standard costing is a method of analysing a difference between actual performance and budget (known as a variance), when standard costs have been used to create the budget.

A standard cost card shows full details of the standard cost of each product.

The standard cost of product 1234 is set out below.

STANDARD COST CARD – PRODUCT 1234

	£	£
Direct materials		
Material X – 3 kg at £4 per kg	12	
Material Y – 9 litres at £2 per litre	18	
		30
Direct labour		
Grade A – 6 hours at £7 per hour	42	
Grade B – 8 hours at £8 per hour	64	
		106
Standard prime cost		136
Fixed production overhead – 14 hours at £4.50 per hour		63
Standard full production cost		199

Notice how the total standard cost is built up from standards for each cost element: standard quantities of materials at standard prices, standard quantities of labour time at standard rates and so on. It is therefore determined by management's estimates of the following.

- The expected prices of materials, labour and expenses
- Efficiency levels in the use of materials and labour
- Budgeted overhead costs and budgeted volumes of activity

We will now think about how each of the standard costs on the standard cost card are set.

Direct materials standard cost

The standard cost for the direct materials in a product is made up of two elements:

- the amount of material expected to be used in one unit
- the price of the material per kg, litre etc

The amount of material required for each unit of a product can be found from the original product specification – the amount originally considered necessary for each unit.

This figure may however be amended over time as the actual amount used in production is monitored.

The basic price of the material can be found from suppliers' quotations or invoices. However when setting the standard, the following should also be taken into account:

- general inflation rates

- any foreseen increases in the price of this particular material

- any seasonality in the price

- any discounts available for bulk purchases

- any anticipated scarcity of the material which may mean paying a higher price

Direct labour standard cost

The standard cost of the direct labour for a product will be made up of:

- the amount of time being spent on each unit of the product
- the hourly wage rate for the employees working on the product

The information for the amount of labour time for each unit may come from time sheets, clock cards, computerised recording systems on the machines being used or from formal observations of the operations, known as work study or more commonly a 'time and motion' study. Factors that should be taken into account when setting the standard for the amount of labour time include:

- the level of skill or training of the labour used on the product
- any anticipated changes in the grade of labour used on the product
- any anticipated changes in work methods or productivity levels
- the effect on productivity of any bonus scheme to be introduced

The hourly rate for the direct labour used on the product can be found from the payroll records. However consideration should be given to:

- anticipated pay rises

- any anticipated changes of the grade of labour to be used

- the effect of any bonus scheme on the labour rate
- whether any overtime is anticipated and whether the premium should be built into the hourly rate

Fixed overhead standard cost

The fixed overhead standard cost will be based on the total of the budgeted costs for each of the elements of the fixed overhead. Under marginal costing there is no further calculation to be done.

Under absorption costing the total budgeted fixed overhead must then be used to calculate the standard overhead absorption rate. This is found by dividing the total budgeted fixed overhead by the budgeted activity level, which may be measured in terms of:

- number of units produced
- direct labour hours
- machine hours

The information for determining the total budgeted fixed overhead will come from bills or invoices for past periods plus any anticipated price changes, either based upon specific indices or a general measure of inflation such as the Retail Price Index.

TYPES OF STANDARD

As you will have seen above when we looked at how standards are set, there are various bases that can be used, for example, are expected price rises included in the standard, are the effects of changes in work practices included in the standard etc?

There are therefore a number of different figures that can be calculated as the standard cost.

Ideal standards

IDEAL STANDARDS are standard costs that are set on the basis that ideal working conditions applying. Therefore there is no allowance for wastage, inefficiencies or idle time when setting the materials and labour cost standards.

There are two main problems with ideal standards:

Planning – if ideal standards are used for planning purposes, it is likely that the results will be inaccurate, as the standard does not reflect the reality of the working conditions. Therefore if a labour cost standard is set with no allowance for any inefficiency or idle time in the operations, the reality is that the operations will take longer or will require more employees than that which has been planned for.

Control – if ideal standards are compared to actual costs then this will always result in adverse variances as the reality is that there will be some inefficiencies and wastage. This can demotivate managers and employees who will feel that in reality these standards can never be met and therefore they may stop trying to meet them. A further problem with these adverse variances is that they will be viewed as the norm and be ignored, meaning that any corrective action that might be required is not taken.

Attainable standards

ATTAINABLE STANDARDS are ones which better reflect the reality of the workplace and which allows for small amounts of normal wastage and inefficiency. An attainable standard is one that is achievable; however, it will only be met if the operations are carried out efficiently and cost-effectively.

If attainable standards are well set, then the variances that result will tend to be a mixture of favourable and adverse variances as sometimes the standard will be exceeded and sometimes it will not quite be met. Attainable standards are often viewed as motivational to managers and employees, as they are not out of reach in the way that ideal standards are but they can be met if all goes to plan.

Current standards

CURRENT STANDARDS are based on **current working conditions** (current wastage, current inefficiencies). The disadvantage of current standards is that they do not attempt to improve on current levels of efficiency. Standards set are on a short term basis and frequent revisions may be necessary.

Basic standards

BASIC STANDARDS are the historical standard costs, probably the ones set when the product was first produced. As such, they are likely to be out of date, as they will not have taken account of inflation or any changes in working practices.

If basic standards are used to compare to actual costs, then this will tend to result in large variances, both adverse and favourable, depending upon how out of date the basic standard is. These variances will therefore be little more than meaningless. For this reason basic standards are rarely used for variance analysis but may still be kept as historical information alongside other more up-to-date standards.

Task 1

What are the potential problems of using ideal standards to calculate variances?

DIRECT MATERIALS VARIANCES

The TOTAL MATERIALS VARIANCE is the difference between the actual cost of the materials used in the production and the standard cost for the actual level of production.

Note that we are using the standard cost for the actual level of production as our comparison for the actual costs of production even if the actual level of production is different from that which was budgeted. This is an example of flexing a budget.

For example suppose that 1,000 units were budgeted to be produced with a total standard material cost of £1,000. If 1,500 units were produced with a total material cost of £1,400 it would be meaningless to compare £1,400 to £1,000 as they are for different numbers of units. Only by flexing the budget, to show the standard cost of the actual production of 1,500 units at £1,500, can a meaningful comparison be made.

The total direct material variance can be either favourable or adverse. If the actual cost of the materials is more than the standard cost for that level of production then there will be an ADVERSE VARIANCE (also known as unfavourable), as the production has cost more than anticipated. However if the actual cost of the materials is less than the standard cost for that level of production then the variance will be a FAVOURABLE VARIANCE. In our earlier illustration, as the standard material cost for 1,500 units of production is £1,500 and the actual cost was £1,400 this is a favourable variance of £100.

The total direct material variance can then be split into the MATERIALS PRICE VARIANCE and the MATERIALS USAGE VARIANCE.

Direct materials price variance

This variance is calculated to show the difference between the standard price due to be paid for the materials actually used and the actual price paid.

As we are comparing the standard price to the actual price, we must base this upon the same quantities. The quantity to be used for the price variance is the actual quantity used. The price variance can therefore be expressed as follows:

	£
Actual quantity at standard price	X
Actual quantity at actual price	X
Direct materials price variance	X

If the actual price is more than the standard price, the variance will appear as a negative figure indicating an adverse variance. If the actual price is less than the standard price, the variance will be a positive figure indicating a favourable variance. However when determining whether a variance is adverse or favourable it is normally advisable to consider the logic of the situation – is the actual price more or less than the standard price?

Direct materials usage variance

This variance will indicate whether the amount of materials actually used in the production is more or less than the standard usage for that level of production. In this case we are comparing the actual quantity to the standard quantity for the actual level of production and therefore when valuing these quantities, the same price must be used – this is the standard price of the materials.

The price variance can be expressed as:

	£
Standard quantity of material for actual production at the standard price	X
Actual quantity of material for actual production at the standard price	X
Direct materials usage variance	X

Again if the actual quantity is more than the standard quantity, the variance will be adverse but if the actual quantity is less than the standard quantity, the variance will be favourable.

HOW IT WORKS

The standard cost card for one of Lawson Ltd's products, the George, is shown below:

	£
Direct materials 4 kg @ £2.00 per kg	8.00
Direct labour 2 hours @ £7.00 per hour	14.00
Fixed overheads 2 hours @ £3.00 per hour	6.00
Total standard absorption cost	28.00

The budgeted level of production for July was 20,000 units but in fact only 18,000 units were produced.

The actual quantity of materials used in July was 68,000 kg and the total cost of the materials was £142,800.

We will now determine the direct materials cost variances.

Total materials cost variance

	£
Standard materials cost for actual production 18,000 units × 4 kg × £2.00	144,000
Actual materials cost	142,800
Total materials cost variance	1,200 Fav

As the actual cost is less than the total standard cost (based on the flexed budget) the variance is favourable.

Materials price variance

	£
Actual quantity at standard price 68,000kg × £2.00	136,000
Actual quantity at actual price	142,800
Materials price variance	6,800 Adv

As the actual price is more than the standard, the variance is adverse.

The 68,000 kg were actually purchased for a price of £142,800 which is £2.10 per kg (£142,800/68,000) whereas the standard price is only £2.00 per kg.

Materials usage variance

	£
Standard quantity for actual production at standard price 18,000 × 4 kg × £2.00	144,000
Actual quantity for actual production at standard price 68,000 kg × £2.00	136,000
Materials usage variance	8,000 Fav

As the actual quantity total is less than the standard quantity total, then the variance is favourable.

For the production of 18,000 units the requirement should have been for 72,000 kg (18,000 × 4 kg), whereas the production level was achieved using only 68,000 kg.

We can finally just check our calculations by ensuring that the sum of the price and usage variances equals the total materials variance:

Materials price variance	6,800 Adv
Materials usage variance	8,000 Fav
Total materials cost variance	1,200 Fav

Task 2

A product has a standard usage of 12 litres of material, at a standard price of £20.50 per litre. The production of the product during the last month was 24,000 units, for which 312,000 litres were used at a total cost of £6,240,000.

(a) What is the total materials cost variance?

Total materials cost variance £ `336,000` (A)

(b) What is the materials price variance?

Materials price variance £ `156,000` (F)

(c) What is the materials usage variance?

Materials usage variance £ `492,000` (A)

Material inventory (stock)

Sometimes a business will purchase more material than it uses in production for the period which results in material inventory (stock). In this situation the material price variance is based on the quantity of material purchased whereas the usage variance is based on the quantity actually used in production.

HOW IT WORKS

Studley Ltd makes a product that requires 3kg of material at £5 per kg. During March 4,000 kgs of material were purchased at a price of £19,200. In the period 1,200 units of product were made using 3,800 kgs of the material.

We will now determine the direct materials cost variances.

Materials price variance

	£
Actual quantity purchased at standard price	20,000
4,000 kg × £5.00	
Actual quantity purchased at actual price	19,200
Materials price variance	800 Fav

As the actual price is less than the standard, the variance is favourable.

Materials usage variance

	£
Standard quantity for actual production at standard price 1,200 × 3 kg × £5.00	18,000
Actual quantity used for actual production at standard price 3,800 kg × £5.00	19,000
Materials usage variance	1,000 Adv

As the actual quantity total is more than the standard quantity total, then the variance is adverse.

Note: The difference between the actual quantity purchased and used is an increase in inventory (stock) of 200 kgs (4,000 - 3,800).

Task 3

A company manufactures a product that requires 5 kg of material at £10 per kg. During June 8,000 kgs of material were purchased at a price of £75,000. In the period 1,500 units of product were made using 7,700 kgs of the material.

(a) What is the materials price variance?

Materials price variance £ [5000] F

(b) What is the materials usage variance?

Materials usage variance £ [2000] A

DIRECT LABOUR VARIANCES

The TOTAL LABOUR VARIANCE is the difference between the actual cost of labour for the period and the standard cost of labour for the actual production in the period. Note again, that as with the materials cost, we are comparing the actual cost to the standard cost for the actual quantity of production (the flexed budget).

The total direct labour cost variance can then be split into the LABOUR RATE VARIANCE and the LABOUR EFFICIENCY VARIANCE. The rate variance is very similar to the materials price variance and the efficiency variance mirrors the materials usage variance, and therefore the calculations of these variances are the same as for the equivalent materials variance.

Labour rate variance

The labour rate variance shows the difference between the actual cost of the labour for the hours worked and the standard cost for those hours worked. As the actual rate of pay and the standard rate of pay are being compared, then the hours used must remain constant – the actual hours paid.

The variance can be expressed as:

	£
Actual hours at standard rate	X
Actual hours at actual rate	X
Labour rate variance	X

If the actual rate is greater than the standard rate, the variance is adverse and if the actual cost is less than the standard the variance is favourable.

Labour efficiency variance

The labour efficiency variance, just like the materials usage variance, is used to calculate whether the hours actually worked in order to produce the actual quantity of output are more or less than the standard hours needed for the actual quantity of production – did the labour force work efficiently or not?

As the standard hours are being compared to the actual hours, they must be valued at the same hourly rate – the standard rate of pay.

This can be expressed as:

	£
Standard hours for actual production at the standard rate	X
Actual hours for actual production at the standard rate	X
Labour efficiency variance	X

If the actual hours are more than the standard hours for the actual level of production, then the workforce has been inefficient and the variance will be adverse. If the actual hours are less than the standard hours, then the employees have worked efficiently and the variance is favourable.

HOW IT WORKS

The standard cost card for the George is given again below:

	£
Direct materials 4 kg @ £2.00 per kg	8.00
Direct labour 2 hours @ £7.00 per hour	14.00
Fixed overheads 2 hours @ £3.00 per hour	6.00
Total standard absorption cost	28.00

Remember that the actual production was 18,000 units, rather than the 20,000 units originally budgeted for.

The total cost of the labour for the month was £254,600 for 38,000 hours.

Total direct labour cost variance

	£
Standard labour cost for actual production	
18,000 × 2 hours × £7.00	252,000
Actual labour cost	254,600
Total labour cost variance	2,600 Adv

As the actual cost is greater than the standard total cost, the variance is adverse.

Labour rate variance

	£
Actual hours at standard rate 38,000 hours × £7.00	266,000
Actual hours at actual rate	254,600
Labour rate variance	11,400 Fav

The actual rate is less than the standard rate, therefore the variance is favourable.

The actual labour rate per hour that was paid was £6.70 per hour (£254,600/38,000) compared to the standard rate of £7.00 per hour.

Labour efficiency variance

	£
Standard hours for actual production at standard rate	
18,000 × 2 hours × £7.00	252,000
Actual hours for actual production at standard rate	
38,000 hours × £7.00	266,000
Labour efficiency variance	14,000 Adv

As the actual hours are greater than the standard hours, the variance is adverse.

Production of 18,000 units should have taken 36,000 hours (18,000 × 2) whereas in fact the production was inefficient and took 38,000 hours.

Finally, a check to ensure that the sub-variances total back to the total labour cost variance.

	£
Labour rate variance	11,400 Fav
Labour efficiency variance	14,000 Adv
Total labour variance	2,600 Adv

Task 4

A product has a standard requirement of 4 hours of direct labour per unit at a standard hourly rate of £6.50. During the last month production was 12,000 units using 45,000 hours at a total cost of £306,000.

$12,000 \times 4 \times 6.50$
$= 312,000$
$= 306,000$

(a) What is the total direct labour cost variance?

Total direct labour cost variance £ ___6000___ F

(b) What is the labour rate variance?

Labour rate variance £ ___13,500___ A

$45,000 @ 6.50 = 292,500$
$= 306,000$

(c) What is the labour efficiency variance?

Labour efficiency variance £ ___19,500___ F

$4 \times 12000 \times 6.50 = 312,000$
$45,000 \times 6.50 \quad 292,500$

Idle time variance

A company may operate a costing system in which any idle time is recorded. Idle time may be caused by machine breakdowns or not having work to give to employees, perhaps because of bottlenecks in production or a shortage of orders from customers. When idle time occurs, the labour force is still paid wages for time at work, but no actual work is done. Time paid for without any work being done is unproductive and therefore inefficient. In variance analysis, idle time is always an adverse efficiency variance.

When idle time is recorded separately, it is helpful to provide control information which identifies the cost of idle time separately, and in variance analysis, there will be an idle time variance as a separate part of the total labour efficiency variance. The remaining efficiency variance will then relate only to the productivity of the labour force during the hours spent actively working.

HOW IT WORKS

The standard direct labour cost of product X is as follows.

2 hours of grade Z labour at £5 per hour = £10 per unit of product X.

During the period, 1,500 units of product X were made and the cost of grade Z labour was £17,500 for 3,080 hours. However, there was a shortage of customer orders and 100 hours were recorded as idle time.

Calculate the following variances.

(a) The direct labour total variance
(b) The direct labour rate variance
(c) The idle time variance
(d) The direct labour efficiency variance

Variances

(a) **The direct labour total variance**

	£
1,500 units of product X should have cost £10 per unit	15,000
(standard labour cost for actual production)	
Actual labour cost for actual production	17,500
Direct labour total variance	2,500 (A)

Actual cost is greater than standard cost. The variance is therefore adverse.

(b) **The direct labour rate variance**

The rate variance is a comparison of what the hours paid should have cost and what they did cost.

	£
3,080 hours of grade Z labour should have cost £5 per hour	15,400
(actual hours at standard rate)	
but did actually cost (actual hours at actual rate)	17,500
Direct labour rate variance	2,100 (A)

Actual cost is greater than standard cost. The variance is therefore adverse.

(c) **The idle time variance**

The idle time variance is the hours of idle time, valued at the standard rate per hour.

Idle time variance = 100 hours (A) × £5 = £500 (A)

Idle time is always an adverse variance.

(d) **The direct labour efficiency variance**

The efficiency variance considers the hours actively worked (the difference between hours paid for and idle time hours). In our example, there were (3,080 − 100) = 2,980 hours when the labour force was not idle. The variance is calculated by taking the amount of output produced (1,500 units of product X) and comparing the time it should have taken to make them, with the actual time spent actively making them (2,980 hours). Once again, the variance in hours is valued at the standard rate per labour hour.

1,500 units of product X should take 2hrs each	3,000 hrs
(standard hours for actual production)	
but did take (3,080 − 100)	2,980 hrs
Direct labour efficiency variance in hours	20 hrs (F)
× standard rate per hour	× £5
Direct labour efficiency variance in £	100 (F)

(e) **Summary**

Direct labour rate variance	2,100 (A)
Idle time variance	500 (A)
Direct labour efficiency variance	100 (F)
Direct labour total variance	2,500 (A)

FIXED OVERHEAD VARIANCES

Under an absorption costing system fixed overheads are absorbed into the actual units of production on the basis of a pre-determined overhead absorption rate. This standard absorption rate may be expressed as an amount per unit or as an amount per direct labour hour or direct machine hour.

However the absorption rate is expressed, the following figures will always be compared:

Fixed overheads incurred	v	Fixed overheads absorbed

If the total fixed overheads incurred are exactly as budgeted and the units of production or hours worked are also exactly as budgeted then these two figures will be equal.

However in practice it is likely that one of three situations may occur:

(a) the fixed overheads are greater or smaller than the budgeted amount

(b) the actual production or the hours worked are more or less than budgeted; or

(c) there is a combination of both of the first two situations.

When any of these occur then the fixed overheads incurred and the fixed overheads absorbed. will be different. There will either be an UNDER-ABSORPTION OF OVERHEADS or an OVER-ABSORPTION OF OVERHEADS. This under- or over-absorption is the TOTAL FIXED OVERHEAD VARIANCE.

As we have seen any under- or over-absorption of overheads will be due to either the amount incurred being different to the budgeted figure or the amount absorbed being different to budget. The total fixed overhead variance can therefore be analysed into these two possible causes by calculating the FIXED OVERHEAD EXPENDITURE VARIANCE and the FIXED OVERHEAD VOLUME VARIANCE.

Fixed overhead expenditure variance

Remember that fixed overheads are, by definition, not expected to alter if the level of production is different to that which is budgeted. Therefore any difference between the budgeted fixed overhead and the actual fixed overhead must be caused by unexpected changes in prices of one or more of the elements of cost in the total fixed overhead.

The fixed overhead expenditure variance is therefore simply:

	£
Budgeted fixed overhead	X
Actual fixed overhead	X
Fixed overhead expenditure variance	X

If the actual overhead is greater than the budgeted overhead, this is an adverse variance but if the actual overhead is less than the budgeted figure, this is a favourable variance.

Fixed overhead volume variance

In Chapter 2 we saw that when using absorption costing, the standard absorption rate per unit of output is found using the budgeted overhead costs for the period and the budgeted activity level. However using budgeted figures means that the actual overhead cost is unlikely to be the same as the overheads absorbed into production, as we are relying on two estimates:

- overhead costs
- activity levels

The fixed overhead expenditure variance measures the difference between actual and budgeted fixed overhead.

The fixed overhead volume variance measures the fact that if the actual level of activity differs from the budget, more or less fixed overhead will be absorbed than was budgeted for.

Together the two variances equal the over- or under-absorption of fixed overhead that we calculated in Chapter 2.

The calculation of the fixed overhead volume variance will depend upon the absorption rate that is used for fixed overheads.

If fixed overheads are absorbed on the basis of units of production then the calculation is:

	£
Actual production at standard absorption rate per unit	
(= Fixed OH absorbed)	X
Budgeted production at standard absorption rate per unit	
(= Budgeted fixed OH)	X
Fixed overhead volume variance	X

If the actual production is greater than the budgeted production then this is a favourable outcome and therefore a favourable volume variance. If actual production is less than budgeted then this is not so good and the volume variance will be adverse.

Note that these variances do not represent an actual cost saving or overrun – this is dealt with by the expenditure variance. They show the necessary adjustments arising from over/under-absorption of fixed overheads due to differences in the level of activity compared to the budget. For example, if actual production is greater than budgeted, this will lead to a fixed overhead over-absorption, ie cost of production will be charged with too much fixed overhead, which will ultimately go through to profit. To compensate for this a favourable fixed overhead volume variance (one that increases profits again) is added back.

Again think through the logic of the outcome in order to determine whether the variances are favourable or adverse rather than relying on getting the formula the right way round.

If the fixed overheads are absorbed on the basis of labour hours or machine hours it is important that you use the standard hours for the actual production and not the actual hours. Under this basis of absorption the fixed overhead volume variance would be calculated as:

	£
Standard hours for actual production at the standard absorption rate per hour	X
Standard hours for budgeted production at the standard absorption rate per hour	X
Fixed overhead volume variance	X

Again if the actual production expressed in standard hours is greater than budgeted the variance is favourable, but if the actual production is less than budgeted the variance is adverse.

HOW IT WORKS

Using our example of Lawson Ltd's production of the George for the month of July it can be seen that the same results will be obtained whichever method of absorption is used.

The standard cost card for the George is given below:

	£
Direct materials 4 kg @ £2.00 per kg	8.00
Direct labour 2 hours @ £7.00 per hour	14.00
Fixed overheads 2 hours @ £3.00 per hour	6.00
Total standard absorption cost	28.00

The actual production was 18,000 units rather than the budgeted figure of 20,000 and this production took a total of 38,000 labour hours.

The actual fixed overhead incurred in the period was £115,000.

Fixed overhead variances – absorption basis – per unit

The fixed overhead absorption basis will initially be taken to be per unit. From the standard cost card we can see that the standard absorption rate is £6.00 per unit.

In order to find the total fixed overhead variance we need to find the under- or over-absorbed overhead.

Total fixed overhead variance

	£
Fixed overhead incurred	115,000
Fixed overhead absorbed (18,000 units × £6.00)	108,000
Overhead under-absorbed	7,000 Adv

As there is an under-absorption of overhead this is an adverse variance as more fixed overhead needs to be charged to the income statement (profit and loss account).

Fixed overhead expenditure variance

In order to find the fixed overhead expenditure variance, the budgeted fixed overhead is required. By returning to the standard cost card and the budgeted production information we can deduce this figure.

The standard cost card shows the standard fixed overhead absorption rate to be £6.00 per unit. This was based upon planned production of 20,000 units therefore the budgeted fixed overhead must have been:

20,000 units × £6.00 per unit = £120,000

The fixed overhead expenditure variance is therefore:

	£
Budgeted fixed overhead	120,000
Actual fixed overhead	115,000
Fixed overhead expenditure variance	5,000 Fav

As the actual fixed overhead is less than the budgeted figure, this is a favourable variance.

Fixed overhead volume variance

As the fixed overheads are being absorbed on a unit basis the calculation is:

	£
Actual production at standard absorption rate 18,000 units × £6.00 per unit	108,000
Budgeted production at standard absorption rate 20,000 units × £6.00 per unit	120,000
Fixed overhead volume variance	12,000 Adv

The variance is adverse, as actual production is less than budgeted production, and has therefore absorbed less than it should have done. The shortfall is made up by this adverse variance being charged to the income statement (profit and loss account).

We will now check that the fixed overhead expenditure and volume variances add back to the fixed overhead total variance:

	£
Fixed overhead expenditure variance	5,000 Fav
Fixed overhead volume variance	12,000 Adv
Fixed overhead total variance	7,000 Adv

Fixed overhead variances – absorption basis – labour hours

If the fixed overheads were to be absorbed on a labour hour basis, we can see from the standard cost card that the standard absorption rate is £3.00 per direct labour hour.

Total fixed overhead variance

To find the total fixed overhead variance, that is the under- or over-absorbed fixed overhead, the fixed overhead incurred is compared to the fixed overhead absorbed. The fixed overhead is absorbed not on the basis of the actual labour hours worked (38,000) but on the basis of the standard labour hours for the actual production which in this case would be 18,000 units × 2 hours = 36,000 hours.

	£
Fixed overhead incurred	115,000
Fixed overhead absorbed (36,000 hours × £3.00 per hour)	108,000
Overhead under-absorbed	7,000 Adv

As there is an under-absorption of overhead this is an adverse variance, as more fixed overhead needs to be charged to the income statement (profit and loss account).

Fixed overhead expenditure variance

As this variance has nothing to do with overhead absorption, then the figures are exactly the same as before.

The fixed overhead expenditure variance is therefore:

	£
Budgeted fixed overhead	120,000
Actual fixed overhead	115,000
Fixed overhead expenditure variance	5,000 Fav

As the actual fixed overhead is less than the budgeted figure, this is a favourable variance.

Fixed overhead volume variance

As the fixed overheads are being absorbed on a direct labour hour basis then again the actual absorption is based upon the standard labour hours for the actual production. The calculation is:

	£
Standard hours for actual production at standard absorption rate	
36,000 hours × £3.00 per hour	108,000
Budgeted production hours at standard absorption rate	
20,000 units × 2hrs x £3.00 per hour	120,000
Fixed overhead volume variance	12,000 Adv

The variance is adverse as standard hours for actual production are less than budgeted production hours.

As you can see the variances are exactly the same whichever basis of absorption is used, but if the absorption basis is labour hours or machine hours then the absorption must be based upon the standard hours for the actual production not the actual labour hours worked or the machine hours worked.

Task 5

During the month of September a business incurred fixed overheads of £26,000. The actual production of the business's single product was 2,500 units, taking 5,500 direct labour hours. Budgeted production had been for 2,400 units each requiring two standard direct labour hours. Fixed overheads are absorbed on the basis of £5.00 per direct labour hour.

Calculate the following figures:

(a) the budgeted fixed overhead

Budgeted fixed overhead £ [   ]

(b) the total fixed overhead variance

Total fixed overhead variance £ [   ]

(c) the fixed overhead expenditure variance

Fixed overhead expenditure variance £ [2000 A]

(d) the fixed overhead volume variance

Fixed overhead volume variance £ [1000 F]

2 × 2500 × 5
4800 × 5
26.000
24,000

FIXED OVERHEAD EFFICIENCY AND CAPACITY VARIANCES

If the fixed overheads are absorbed on a unit basis then the only fixed overhead variances that can be calculated are the expenditure and volume variances. However, if the overheads are absorbed on an hourly basis then the fixed overhead volume variance can be analysed further into a FIXED OVERHEAD EFFICIENCY VARIANCE and a FIXED OVERHEAD CAPACITY VARIANCE.

This analysis of the fixed overhead volume variance helps to explain the causes of the volume variance:

- was the volume variance due to the workforce working more or less efficiently than budgeted? – the efficiency variance

- was the volume variance due to the workforce working for more or fewer total hours than budgeted? – the capacity variance.

Fixed overhead efficiency variance

This variance considers how efficiently the workforce produced the goods by comparing the time the actual production should have taken to the time it actually took, all valued at the hourly absorption rate. It is calculated in a similar way to the labour efficiency variance.

The calculation is:

	£
Standard hours for actual production at standard absorption rate	X
Actual hours for actual production at standard absorption rate	X
Fixed overhead efficiency variance	X

If the actual hours are greater than the standard hours then the workforce has been inefficient and the variance is adverse. However if the actual hours are less than the standard hours, the workforce have worked efficiently and the variance is favourable.

Fixed overhead capacity variance

The capacity variance measures whether all of the available hours were used or indeed if more hours were worked than were budgeted for. These hours are all valued at the standard hourly absorption rate.

The calculation is:

	£
Actual hours worked at standard absorption rate	X
Budgeted hours at standard absorption rate	X
Fixed overhead capacity variance	X

If the actual hours worked are greater than the budgeted hours then this is good for the business and is therefore a favourable variance. If the actual hours worked are less than those that were budgeted for, the variance is adverse.

HOW IT WORKS

Let's return to Lawson Ltd and the July production of the George.

The standard cost card is again shown:

	£
Direct materials 4 kg @ £2.00 per kg	8.00
Direct labour 2 hours @ £7.00 per hour	14.00
Fixed overheads 2 hours @ £3.00 per hour	6.00
Total standard absorption cost	28.00

Budgeted production was 20,000 units and actual production was 18,000 units taking 38,000 hours. The fixed overhead incurred in the month was £115,000.

The fixed overhead variances calculated so far are:

	£
Fixed overhead expenditure variance	5,000 Fav
Fixed overhead volume variance	12,000 Adv
Total fixed overhead variance	7,000 Adv

We will now analyse the fixed overhead volume variance into its constituent elements.

Fixed overhead efficiency variance

	£
Standard hours for actual production at standard absorption rate	
18,000 units × 2 × £3.00 per hour	108,000
Actual hours for actual production at standard absorption rate	
38,000 hours × £3.00 per hour	114,000
Fixed overhead efficiency variance	6,000 Adv

As the actual production took more hours than the standard hours for that level of production then this is an adverse efficiency variance.

Fixed overhead capacity variance

For this calculation, the total budgeted hours must be deduced from the standard cost card. The budgeted production was for 20,000 units and each unit has standard hours of two direct labour hours, therefore the budgeted labour hours were 40,000.

	£
Actual hours worked at standard absorption rate	
38,000 hours × £3.00 per hour	114,000
Budgeted hours at standard absorption rate	
40,000 hours × £3.00 per hour	120,000
Fixed overhead capacity variance	6,000 Adv

Only 38,000 hours were worked although 40,000 hours had been budgeted for, therefore this is an adverse capacity variance, since not all the productive capacity has been used.

Now we can check that the efficiency and capacity variances total back to the volume variance:

	£
Fixed overhead efficiency variance	6,000 Adv
Fixed overhead capacity variance	6,000 Adv
Fixed overhead volume variance	12,000 Adv

The total fixed overhead variances can be presented as follows:

	£	£
Fixed overhead expenditure		5,000 Fav
Fixed overhead efficiency	6,000 Adv	
Fixed overhead capacity	6,000 Adv	
Fixed overhead volume		12,000 Adv
Total fixed overhead variance		7,000 Adv

Task 6

During the month of September a business incurred fixed overheads of £25,000. The actual production of the business's single product was 2,500 units taking 5,500 direct labour hours. Budgeted production had been for 2,400 units each requiring two standard direct labour hours. Fixed overheads are absorbed on the basis of £5.00 per direct labour hour.

Calculate the following figures:

(a) the budgeted direct labour hours for the month 2400×2

   Budgeted direct labour hours $\boxed{4800}$ hours

(b) the fixed overhead efficiency variance $2 \times 2500 \times 5 = 25000$

   Fixed overhead efficiency variance £ $\boxed{2500 \quad A}$ $5500 \times 5 = 27.500$

(c) the fixed overhead capacity variance $5500 \times 5 = 27.500$

   Fixed overhead capacity variance £ $\boxed{3500 \quad F}$ $4800 \times 5 = 24.000$

   3500

FIXED OVERHEADS VARIANCES – ABSORPTION COSTING

We can now summarise the fixed overhead variances that can be calculated under an absorption costing system using the figures from Lawson Ltd.

Remember that it is only when fixed overheads are absorbed on an hourly basis that we can analyse the volume variance further, into efficiency and capacity variances.

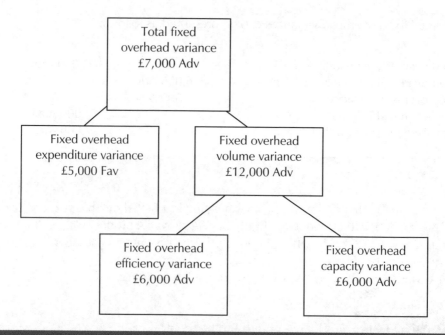

RECONCILIATION OF TOTAL STANDARD COST TO TOTAL ACTUAL COST

Once all of the cost variances have been calculated, it is then useful to summarise the total standard cost, variances and total actual cost using a RECONCILIATION STATEMENT (sometimes called an OPERATING STATEMENT).

It is common practice to start with the total standard cost for the actual production, then adjust this for the variances calculated in order to finish with the total actual cost of production. This can be illustrated as follows:

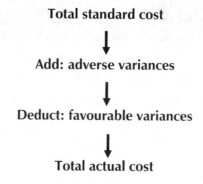

When preparing the operating statement or reconciliation, think about the addition and subtraction of variances. Adverse variances are added to the total standard cost, as this means that the actual cost is higher than the standard cost (or amount absorbed in the case of fixed overheads). Favourable variances are deducted from the standard cost, as this means that the actual cost is less than the standard/absorbed cost.

HOW IT WORKS

We will now summarise all of the variances calculated for Lawson Ltd.

	£
Materials price variance	6,800 Adv
Materials usage variance	8,000 Fav
Total materials cost variance	1,200 Fav

	£
Labour rate variance	11,400 Fav
Labour efficiency variance	14,000 Adv
Total labour cost variance	2,600 Adv

	£	£
Fixed overhead expenditure variance		5,000 Fav
Fixed overhead efficiency variance	6,000 Adv	
Fixed overhead capacity variance	6,000 Adv	
Fixed overhead volume variance		12,000 Adv
Fixed overhead total variance		7,000 Adv

We will also need the standard cost card for the George:

	£
Direct materials 4 kg @ £2.00 per kg	8.00
Direct labour 2 hours @ £7.00 per hour	14.00
Fixed overheads 2 hours @ £3.00 per hour	6.00
Total standard absorption cost	28.00

Remember that the actual production costs for July were:

	£
Direct materials	142,800
Direct labour	254,600
Fixed overhead	115,000

We will now produce the reconciliation or operating statement.

Firstly we must calculate the total standard cost of the actual production of 18,000 units:

	£
Direct materials 18,000 × £8.00	144,000
Direct labour 18,000 × £14.00	252,000
Fixed overhead 18,000 × £6.00	108,000
Total standard production cost	504,000

Alternatively this figure for total standard cost of production can be calculated as 18,000 × £28 which is the total standard cost of each product from the standard cost card.

We need to reconcile this figure to the total actual production cost:

	£
Direct materials	142,800
Direct labour	254,600
Fixed overhead	115,000
Total actual production cost	512,400

Reconciliation statement – July

	Variances		
	Adverse	Favourable	
	£	£	£
Total standard cost			504,000
Variances:			
Materials price	6,800		
Materials usage		8,000	
Labour rate		11,400	
Labour efficiency	14,000		
Fixed overhead expenditure		5,000	
Fixed overhead efficiency	6,000		
Fixed overhead capacity	6,000		
	32,800	24,400	
Add: adverse variances			32,800
Less: favourable variances			(24,400)
Total actual cost			512,400

Task 7

If you are producing a reconciliation statement which reconciles the standard cost of production to the actual cost, explain whether favourable cost variances are added or subtracted and why.

MARGINAL COSTING

In a standard marginal costing system the standard cost card will only include the variable costs of production as the fixed overheads are not included in the cost of the cost units, but are written off as a period cost.

The calculations of the materials and labour variances are exactly the same as in an absorption costing system. The only difference is that there is only one fixed overhead variance – the expenditure variance – as all of the other fixed overhead variances are due to absorption which does not take place under marginal costing.

HOW IT WORKS

If Lawson Ltd operated a marginal costing system then the standard cost card for the George would appear as follows:

	£
Direct materials 4 kg @ £2.00 per kg	8.00
Direct labour 2 hours @ £7.00 per hour	14.00
	22.00

The actual production was 18,000 compared to budgeted production of 20,000 units. The budgeted fixed overhead was £120,000 and the fixed overhead incurred was £115,000.

The materials and labour variances would be calculated in exactly the same manner as before, giving the same figures:

	£
Materials price variance	6,800 Adv
Materials usage variance	8,000 Fav
Total materials cost variance	1,200 Fav

	£
Labour rate variance	11,400 Fav
Labour efficiency variance	14,000 Adv
Total labour cost variance	2,600 Adv

The fixed overhead expenditure variance is, as before, the difference between the budgeted and actual fixed overhead: £5,000 favourable (£120,000 – £115,000).

A reconciliation or operating statement can now be prepared between the standard marginal cost of production and the actual cost of production.

First we must calculate the standard production cost under marginal costing:

	£
Direct materials 18,000 × £8.00	144,000
Direct labour 18,000 × £14.00	252,000
Marginal cost of production (18,000 x £22)	396,000
Fixed overheads	120,000
Total cost under marginal costing	516,000

As before, the actual cost of production was £512,400.

Reconciliation statement – July

	Variances		
	Adverse	Favourable	
	£	£	£
Total standard cost			516,000
Variances:			
Materials price	6,800		
Materials usage		8,000	
Labour rate		11,400	
Labour efficiency	14,000		
Fixed overhead expenditure		5,000	
	20,800	24,400	
Add: adverse variances			20,800
Less: favourable variances			(24,400)
Total actual production cost			512,400

STANDARD COST BOOKKEEPING

When an organisation runs a standard costing system, the variances need to be included in the ledger accounts. This is known as standard cost bookkeeping.

In a standard costing bookkeeping system variances are recorded as follows:

- the materials price variance is recorded in the stores control account

- the labour rate variance is recorded in the wages control account

- the following variances are recorded in the work in progress control account:

   - materials usage variance
   - labour efficiency variance
   - idle time variance

- the production overhead expenditure variance will be recorded in the production overhead control account

- the production overhead volume variance will be recorded either in the production overhead control account or in the work in progress control account

- the balance of variances in the variance accounts will be written off to the income statement (profit and loss account).

Adverse variances are debited to the variance account as an expense and favourable variances are credited to the variance account.

HOW IT WORKS

Zed Co operates an integrated accounting system and a standard absorption costing system and prepares its accounts monthly.

The following variances have been calculated for the month of October.

Direct material price variance	£40 Fav
Direct material usage variance	£80 Adv
Direct labour rate variance	£45 Adv
Direct labour efficiency variance	£360 Fav
Fixed overhead expenditure variance	£100 Fav
Fixed overhead volume variance	£50 Adv

The Journal entries to record these variances are as follows:

Direct material price variance

Debit	Stores control account	£40	
Credit	Variance account		£40

Direct material usage variance

Debit	Variance account	£80	
Credit	Work in progress control account		£80

Direct labour rate variance

Debit	Variance account	£45	
Credit	Wages control account		£45

Direct labour efficiency variance

Debit	Work in progress control account	£360	
Credit	Variance account		£360

Fixed overhead expenditure variance

Debit	Production overhead control account	£100	
Credit	Variance account		£100

Fixed overhead volume variance

Debit	Variance account	£50	
Credit	Production overhead control account		£50

In some accounting systems there is a separate account for each type of variance rather than a single variance account.

Task 8

A firm uses standard costing and an integrated accounting system. The double entry for an adverse material usage variance is

A   DR stores control account

       CR work-in-progress control account

B   DR material usage variance account

       CR stores control account

C   DR work-in-progress control account

       CR material usage variance account

D   DR material usage variance account

       CR work-in-progress control account

CHAPTER OVERVIEW

- The direct materials standard cost is set by determining the estimated quantity of material to be used per unit and the estimated price of that material

- The direct labour standard cost is set by determining the estimated labour time per unit and the estimated rate per hour

- The fixed overhead standard cost is determined by finding a realistic estimate of each of the elements of the fixed overhead

- The standards that can be set include ideal standards, attainable standards and basic standards

- A standard costing system allows the standard cost of production to be compared to the actual costs and variances calculated. This can help management perform their three main roles of decision making, planning and control

- For this Unit materials, labour and fixed overhead variances must be calculated and reconciliations of standard cost to actual cost prepared in both a standard absorption costing system and a standard marginal costing system

- The total direct materials cost variance can be split into a materials price variance and a materials usage variance.

- The total direct labour cost variance can be split in a similar manner into the labour rate variance and the labour efficiency variance

- The total fixed overhead cost variance in an absorption costing system is the amount of fixed overhead that has been under- or over-absorbed in the period

- The total fixed overhead variance can then be analysed into the fixed overhead expenditure variance and fixed overhead volume variance

- If fixed overheads are absorbed on an hourly basis then care must be taken when calculating the volume variance as the standard hours for the actual production should be used rather than the actual hours worked

- Only if fixed overheads are absorbed on an hourly basis can the fixed overhead volume variance be further analysed into an efficiency variance and a capacity variance

- A reconciliation of the standard cost for the actual production to the actual cost of production can be performed by adding the adverse variances to the standard cost and deducting the favourable variances. This is also sometimes called an operating statement.

- CHAPTER OVERVIEW cont'd

- In a standard marginal costing system the materials and labour variances are calculated in exactly the same manner as in an absorption costing system – however there is only one fixed overhead variance, the fixed overhead expenditure variance

- In a standard cost bookkeeping system, the variances are recorded as follows:

  - The material price variance is recorded in the stores control account.

  - The labour rate variance is recorded in the wages control account.

  - The following variances are recorded in the work in progress account.

    - Material usage variance
    - Idle time variance
    - Labour efficiency variance

  - The production overhead expenditure variance will be recorded in the production overhead control account.

  - The production overhead volume variance may be recorded in the fixed production overhead account. (Note. Alternatively, you may find the volume variance recorded in the work in progress account.)

  - The balance of variances in the variance accounts at the end of a period may be written off to the income statement.

- Adverse variances are debited to the relevant variance account; favourable variances are credited in the relevant variance account.

Keywords

Standard costing system – the expected costs of each unit of production is set out in a standard cost card and the actual cost of the unit actually produced is compared in detail to this standard cost card

Standard cost card – document detailing the estimated cost of a unit of a product

Variances – the difference between the actual costs of production and the standard costs

Ideal standards – standards set on the basis of perfect working conditions

Attainable standards – realistically achievable standards into which are built elements of normal wastage and inefficiency

Current standards – standards based on current working conditions

Basic standards – historical standards that are normally set when the product is initially produced

Standard costing system – a system which assigns standard costs to each cost unit and allows a comparison of standard costs to actual costs and the calculation of variances

Variances – the difference between the standard costs and the actual costs for a period

Total material variance – the difference between the standard materials cost for the actual production and the actual cost

Adverse variance – where the actual cost is greater than the standard cost

Favourable variance – where the actual cost is less than the standard cost

Materials price variance – the difference between the standard price of the materials purchased and their actual cost

Materials usage variance – the difference between the standard quantity of material for the actual production and the actual quantity, valued at the standard price of material

Total labour variance – the difference between the standard labour cost for the actual production and the actual cost

Labour rate variance – the difference between the standard rate of pay for the actual hours and the actual cost

Labour efficiency variance – the difference between the standard hours for the actual production and the actual hours, valued at the standard labour rate per hour

Labour idle time variance – an adverse efficiency variance – the difference between the actual hours paid for and the actual hours of productive labour, valued at the standard labour rate per hour

Under-absorption of overheads – where the amount of fixed overhead absorbed into cost units for the period is less than the overhead incurred

Over-absorption of overheads – where the amount of fixed overhead absorbed into cost units for the period is more than the overhead incurred

Total fixed overhead variance – the under or over absorbed fixed overhead for the period

Fixed overhead expenditure variance – the difference between the budgeted fixed overhead and the actual fixed overhead

Fixed overhead volume variance – the difference between actual production level and budgeted production level, valued at the standard absorption rate per unit

Fixed overhead efficiency variance – the difference between the standard hours for the actual production and the actual hours, valued at the standard labour hour absorption rate

Fixed overhead capacity variance – the difference between the actual hours worked and the hours budgeted to be worked, valued at the standard labour hour absorption rate

Reconciliation or operating statement – a statement which uses the variances for the period to reconcile the standard cost for the actual production to the actual cost

TEST YOUR LEARNING

1 Explain where the information for setting the direct labour cost standard would be found and what factors should be taken into consideration when setting it.

2 Explain where the information for setting the direct material cost standard would be found and what factors should be taken into consideration when setting it.

3 Explain the difference between ideal standards, attainable standards and basic standards.

4 A business budgeted to produce 1,600 units of one of its products, the YG, during the month of October. The YG uses 7 kg of raw material with a standard cost of £6.00 per kg. During the month the actual production was 1,800 units of YG using 12,000 kg of raw materials costing £70,800.

Calculate the following figures:

(a) the total materials cost variance

Total materials cost variance £ ⬚

(b) the materials price variance

Materials price variance £ ⬚

(c) the materials usage variance

Materials usage variance £ ⬚

5 Production of product FFD for the month of December in a manufacturing business was 15,400 units using 41,000 hours of direct labour costing £265,200. The standard cost card shows that the standard input for a unit of FFD is 2.5 hours at a rate of £6.80 per hour.

Calculate the following figures:

(a) the total labour cost variance

Total labour cost variance £ ⬚

(b) the labour rate variance

Labour rate variance £ ⬚

(c) the labour efficiency variance

Labour efficiency variance £ ⬚

6 A business incurred fixed overheads of £56,000 in the month of May. The fixed overheads are absorbed into units of production at the rate of £2.50 per direct labour hour. The actual production during the month was 6,400 units although the budget had been for 7,000 units. The standard labour cost for the production is 3 hours per unit at an hourly rate of £7.20. During the month 20,000 labour hours were worked at a total cost of £148,600.

Calculate the following figures:

(a) the budgeted fixed overhead for the month

Budgeted fixed overhead £ ⬚

(b) the fixed overhead expenditure variance

Fixed overhead expenditure variance £ ⬚

(c) the fixed overhead volume variance

Fixed overhead volume variance £ ⬚

(d) the fixed overhead efficiency variance

Fixed overhead efficiency variance £ ⬚

(e) the fixed overhead capacity variance

Fixed overhead capacity variance £ ⬚

7 The standard cost card for a business's product, the MU, is shown below:

	£
Direct materials 4.2 kg at £3.60 per kg	15.12
Direct labour 1.5 hours at £7.80 per hour	11.70
Fixed overheads 1.5 hours at £2.80 per hour	4.20
	31.02

The budgeted production was for 1,800 units of MU. The actual costs during the month of June for the production of 1,750 units of the MU were as follows:

	£
Direct materials 7,500 kg	25,900
Direct labour 2,580 hours	20,600
Fixed overheads	8,100

You are to:

(a) calculate the materials price and usage variances

Materials price variance £ ⬚

Materials usage variance £ ⬚

(b) calculate the labour rate and efficiency variances

Labour rate variance £ [   ]

Labour efficiency variance £ [   ]

(c) calculate the fixed overhead expenditure, efficiency and capacity variances

Fixed overhead expenditure variance £ [   ]

Fixed overhead efficiency variance £ [   ]

Fixed overhead capacity variance £ [   ]

(d) complete the table to prepare a reconciliation statement reconciling the standard cost of the production to the total cost

Reconciliation statement

	Adverse variances	Favourable variances	
	£	£	£
Standard cost of production			
Variances			
Materials price			
Materials usage			
Labour rate			
Labour efficiency			
Fixed overhead expenditure			
Fixed overhead efficiency			
Fixed overhead capacity			
Add: adverse variances			
Less: favourable variances			
Actual cost of production			

8 A business operates a marginal standard costing system and the cost card for its single product is given below:

	£
Direct materials 12 kg @ £4.80	57.60
Direct labour 3 hours @ £8.00	24.00
	81.60

The budgeted output for the period was 2,100 units and the budgeted fixed overhead was £95,000.

The actual production in the period was 2,400 units and the actual costs were as follows:

	£
Direct materials 29,600 kg	145,000
Direct labour 6,900 hours	56,200
Fixed overhead	92,000

You are to:

(a) calculate the total direct materials cost variance and the materials price and usage variances

Direct materials cost variance £ [ ]

Materials price variance £ [ ]

Materials usage variance £ [ ]

(b) calculate the total direct labour cost variance and the labour rate and efficiency variances

Direct labour cost variance £ [ ]

Labour rate variance £ [ ]

Labour efficiency variance £ [ ]

(c) calculate any relevant fixed overhead variances

Fixed overhead expenditure variance £ [ ]

(d) complete the table to produce a reconciliation statement reconciling the standard cost of the production to the actual cost.

	Adverse variances	Favourable variances	
	£	£	£
Standard cost of actual production			
Variances			
Materials price			
Materials usage			
Labour rate			
Labour efficiency			
Fixed overhead expenditure			
Add adverse variances			
Less: favourable variances			
Total actual cost			

9 Which three of the following variances are recorded in the work-in-progress control account in a standard cost bookkeeping system?

- Material price variance
- Material usage variance
- Labour rate variance
- Variable overhead efficiency variance
- Idle time variance

chapter 6:
STANDARD COSTING – FURTHER ASPECTS

──────── **chapter coverage** 📖 ────────

We will now take standard costing a little further and look at the reasons for variances and how to break down some variances further to determine their causes and in particular those causes that are controllable and those that are not.

The topics that are to be covered are:

✍ Reasons for variances

✍ Interdependence of variances

✍ Further analysis of variances into controllable and non-controllable parts

REASONS FOR VARIANCES

When reporting variances to management a simple operating (reconciliation) report as illustrated in the last chapter is a useful starting point. However management will also wish to know the reasons for the variances. Before we look at a specific example we will consider some of the possible reasons for each type of variance:

Materials price variance – adverse

- an unexpected price increase from a supplier
- loss of a previous trade or bulk buying discount from a supplier
- purchase of a higher grade of materials

Materials price variance – favourable

- negotiation of a better price from a supplier
- negotiation of a trade or bulk purchase discount from a supplier
- purchase of a lower grade of materials

Materials usage variance – adverse

- greater wastage due to a lower grade of material
- greater wastage due to use of a lower grade of labour
- problems with machinery

Materials usage variance – favourable

- use of a higher grade of material which led to less wastage
- use of more skilled labour leading to less wastage than normal
- new machinery which provides greater efficiency

Labour rate variance – adverse

- unexpected increase in labour costs
- use of a higher grade of labour than anticipated
- unexpectedly high levels of overtime

Labour rate variance – favourable

- use of a lower grade of labour than budgeted for
- less overtime than budgeted for

Labour efficiency variance – adverse

- use of a less skilled grade of labour
- use of a lower grade of material which takes longer to work on
- more idle time than budgeted
- poor supervision of the workforce
- problems with machinery

Labour efficiency variance – favourable

- use of a more skilled grade of labour
- use of a higher grade of material which takes less time to work on
- less idle time than budgeted
- use of new more efficient machinery

Fixed overhead expenditure variance – adverse or favourable

- an unexpected increase or decrease in the cost of any element of fixed overheads

Fixed overhead volume variance – adverse or favourable

- an unexpected increase or decrease in production volume. If absorption is done on the basis of labour or machine hours, analysis of the volume variance into the efficiency and capacity variances can help to find reasons for the volume variance.

Fixed overhead efficiency variance – adverse or favourable

- if the absorption basis is that of labour hours then the fixed overhead efficiency variance will be due to the same causes as the labour efficiency variance
- if the absorption basis is that of machine hours then the fixed overhead efficiency variance will reflect how efficiently the machinery has been used to produce the cost units

Fixed overhead capacity variance – adverse or favourable

- if the absorption basis is that of labour hours, this variance measures whether more or less hours were worked than originally budgeted
- if the absorption basis is that of machine hours, the capacity variance measures whether more or less machine hours were operated than originally budgeted

Task 1

If a business has a favourable labour rate variance of £2,500, which of the following might have been the cause of this?

- A   more overtime paid than budgeted
- B   use of a lower grade of material which takes longer to work on
- C   more idle time than budgeted
- D   use of a lower grade of labour than anticipated

INTERDEPENDENCE OF VARIANCES

You may have noticed from some of the possible causes of variances given above, that many of these are likely to be inter-related. This is known as the INTERDEPENDENCE OF VARIANCES.

For example, a favourable material price variance that is caused by purchasing a lower grade of material may lead directly to an adverse materials usage variance, as the lower grade of material means that there is greater wastage.

A further example might be the use of a lower grade of labour on a job than budgeted, leading to a favourable labour rate variance but an adverse materials usage variance, as the less skilled labour cause more materials wastage.

Responsibility for variances

Investigating the causes of variances and determining any interdependence between the variances is an important aspect of management control, as in a system of responsibility accounting the managers responsible for various elements of the business will be held accountable for the relevant variances.

Take the example of a favourable material price variance caused by purchasing a lower grade of material which leads directly to an adverse materials usage variance. The initial reaction might be to praise the purchasing manager for the favourable variance and to lay blame for the adverse usage variance on the production manager. However, the true picture is that, in the absence of any further reasons for the variance, the responsibility for both variances lies with the purchasing manager.

When asked to explain a variance, the budget holder may provide information that is inaccurate or ignores any interdependence. In this case, the holder of the materials budget, the purchasing manager, may suggest that the favourable material price variance is due to better price negotiations with the supplier. However an independent assessment of quality by the production manager may lead to the true cause of the variance (the lower grade of material) and its impact elsewhere in the business in terms of adverse usage, being revealed

Other reasons for variances

As well as the reasons suggested so far for variances that might occur, one fundamental reason for a variance, particularly one that recurs each period, may be that the standard is out of date. If the standard does not reflect the reality of the cost or usage of materials, labour or overheads then this will be a significant cause of any variances.

Standards should be regularly reviewed, at least annually, and kept up-to-date in terms of the costs of materials, labour and fixed overheads and in terms of the usage of materials and labour hours required for each product.

Further causes of variances may be one-off events such as a power cut, breakdown of machinery or annual staff holidays.

Alteration of standard costs

The decision to alter a standard cost should be not be taken lightly and should only be done when there is a long term or permanent change in the cost of the resource or the usage.

For example, suppose a material price variance has been caused by a change of supplier due to the fact that the normal supplier was out of supplies. Purchases will continue to be made from the normal supplier in future. In this case the standard should not be changed. However if there is a general price increase for the material in question, no matter which supplier is used, then the standard direct materials cost should be revised.

HOW IT WORKS

Given below is the absorption cost reconciliation or operating statement for Lawson Ltd for the production of the George in July 20X8, showing all of the variances calculated in the previous chapter.

Reconciliation or operating statement – July

	Variances		
	Adverse	Favourable	
	£	£	£
Total standard cost			504,000
Variances:			
Materials price	6,800		
Materials usage		8,000	
Labour rate		11,400	
Labour efficiency	14,000		
Fixed overhead expenditure		5,000	
Fixed overhead efficiency	6,000		
Fixed overhead capacity	6,000		
	32,800	24,400	
Add: adverse variances			32,800
Less: favourable variances			(24,400)
Total actual cost			512,400

Upon investigation of the variances, the following is discovered:

- the supplier of the materials has permanently increased its prices but has also significantly improved the quality of the material

- some of the workforce used in the period were of a lower grade than normal and they were not as familiar with the production process as the normal labour force

- during the period there was a machine breakdown which caused a significant amount of idle time when the workforce was not actually able to make the product

- due to the machine breakdown, the power costs for the period were lower than anticipated

- Lawson Ltd has recently reduced the amount of factory space that it rents but the standard rental cost has not been adjusted.

You are to write a report to the Operations Manager identifying possible causes of the variances and making any suggestions for action that should be taken.

REPORT

To: Operations Manager, Lawson Ltd
From: An Accountant
Date: August 20X8
Subject: Variances

The direct materials, direct labour and fixed overhead variances for the period have been calculated.

There is an adverse materials price variance, caused by the supplier of the materials permanently increasing his prices. However, the quality of the material has also been improved, which will have played a part in the favourable materials usage variance. We should consider other suppliers for the supply of our materials, but if their prices are the same as our supplier's, or the material quality is not as good, then the standard cost of the materials should be altered. If it can be shown that the higher quality material has caused the favourable usage variance then consideration should also be given to alteration of the direct materials usage per unit on the standard cost card.

The favourable labour rate variance will be due to the use of lower grade labour than normal for some of the period and this may also have partly caused the adverse labour efficiency variance. The labour efficiency variance is also partly due to the machine breakdown during the period, which has meant that labour hours have been paid for when no productive work was achieved (idle time). The machine breakdown is a one-off event which should not be built into the standard costs. However, if it is anticipated that the lower grade of labour will now normally be used for the production, then the standard labour rate and hours should be changed.

The fixed overhead expenditure variance was favourable due to lower power costs, due to the machine breakdown and also a reduction in factory rental. The reduction in rent is a permanent reduction and therefore the budgeted fixed overhead should be altered to reflect this in future periods.

The fixed overhead efficiency variance is due to the adverse labour efficiency variance and the factors that caused it, as discussed above. The adverse capacity variance shows that not all the available labour hours in the original budget were worked and the reasons for this should be investigated. One possible explanation may be that there are not enough employees who are skilled enough to produce the George.

161

Task 2

A business has recently taken on a new contract which required it to hire new workers. In its first period the results for the contract showed a favourable labour rate variance of £2,500, but an adverse labour efficiency variance of £6,250 and an adverse material usage variance of £5,750.

The manager responsible for hiring labour has suggested that the favourable labour rate variance was due to them managing to agree a lower rate per hour with the workforce.

What other possible explanations could there be for the favourable labour rate variance which might also explain the adverse labour efficiency and materials usage variances? What action could be taken to ascertain the true picture?

FURTHER ANALYSIS OF VARIANCES

In assigning responsibility for variances, managers should only be held accountable for factors that are within their control. Variances are caused by two basic factors:

- planning factors – when setting standards and formulating budgets for how much will be produced, we are engaged in planning. A great deal of planning is actually (well-informed) guesswork, and it is useful to try to separate out a variance caused by a guess that turns out to be wrong (and therefore to an extent uncontrollable), from variances caused by other decisions

- control factors – as the production period goes on, managers must make a great many control decisions, such as buying material of a lower grade than planned, or taking advantage of a discount offered, which had not been anticipated at the planning stage. It is therefore useful to separate out variances caused by control decisions from those caused by planning assumptions

It is sometimes the case that a variance can be split into two parts:

- the part that is caused by some particular factor that is known, such as actual change in materials prices (sometimes called a planning or uncontrollable variance since it is attributable to a failure in planning, rather than an operational decision)

- the part that is caused by other factors that we do not specifically know about (sometimes called a control variance, since it is attributable to factors experienced in actual operations)

Examples of variances that might be split into planning and control variances include the following:

- materials price variance – analysed between the element due to a specific price change (planning) and that due to other factors (control)

- materials price variance – analysed between the element due to a seasonal change in price of the material (planning) and that due to other factors (control)

- materials usage variance – analysed between the element due to the learning process for the workforce (planning) and that due to other factors (control)

- labour rate variance – analysed between the element due to specific wage increases (planning) and that due to other factors (control)

- labour efficiency variance – analysed between the element due to the learning process or training period (planning) and that due to other elements (control)

Materials price changes

The standard materials cost will often be set based upon the anticipated materials price during the period. However the actual price of the materials may have been materially different during the period, meaning that the materials price variance may not show the true picture of what is happening.

The materials price variance is calculated as follows:

	£
Standard price for actual quantity used	X
Actual cost of materials	X
Materials price variance	X

This can then be analysed into:

Price variance due to known price change (planning variance)		Price variance due to other factors (control variance)	
	£		£
Standard price for actual quantity used	X	Price-adjusted cost for actual quantity used	X
Price-adjusted cost for actual quantity used	X	Actual cost	X
	X		X

HOW IT WORKS

The standard direct materials cost for a business's product is:

4 kg @ £5.00 per kg = £20.00

During the month of October production was 12,000 units of the product and the actual materials cost was £248,000 for 45,600 kg. The market price of the materials has been unexpectedly increased to £5.50 per kg for the whole month, due to shortages.

Calculate the total materials price variance and then show how it can be analysed between the planning element (caused by the price increase) and the control element (caused by other factors).

Total materials price variance

	£
Standard price for actual quantity 45,600 kg × £5.00	228,000
Actual quantity at actual price	248,000
	20,000 Adv

Planning variance due to price increase

	£
Standard price for actual quantity 45,600 kg × £5.00	228,000
Adjusted price for actual quantity 45,600 kg × £5.50	250,800
	22,800 Adv

Control variance due to other factors

	£
Adjusted price for actual quantity 45,600 × £5.50	250,800
Actual quantity at actual price	248,000
	2,800 Fav

Total materials price variance £20,000 Adv

Planning variance due to price increase £22,800 Adv

Control variance due to other factors £2,800 Fav

The total materials price variance shows an adverse price variance of £20,000. However when we analyse the price variance, we can see that all of that was caused by the new higher price (the planning variance) and that indeed the control variance caused by other factors was in fact favourable. Therefore the purchasing manager should be praised for the favourable control variance and not blamed for the uncontrollable adverse planning variance.

Task 3

A business's product has a standard direct material cost of £24.60 (3 kg @ £8.20 per kg). During the month of September the total production of the product was 1,500 units using 4,600 kg of materials at a total cost of £40,800. During the month the price was unexpectedly increased due to a shortage of the material to £9.00 per kg.

(a) The total materials price variance was £ [   ]

(b) The planning variance due to the price increase was
£ [   ]

The control variance due to other factors was
£ [   ]

Seasonal variations in price

In some businesses, material prices will tend to be different at different times of the year, due to availability or other factors. When considering the materials price variance, it may be useful to analyse this into the planning price variance due to the season and the control price variance due to any other factors.

HOW IT WORKS

A business makes a product which uses a raw material which has a standard price of £20.00 per kg. Each unit of the product requires 3 kg of this material. The price of the materials for the last 6 years has been subjected to a time series analysis and the following seasonal variations have been seen to occur.

Jan – Mar	–£2.00
Apr – Jun	+£1.00
Jul – Aug	+£3.00
Sep – Dec	–£2.00

During February 10,000 units of the product were made and the price paid for the 32,000 kg of material was £560,000.

What is the total materials price variance and how can this be analysed to show the planning variance due to the season and the control variance due to other factors?

Total materials price variance

	£
Standard cost for actual quantity 32,000 kg × £20	640,000
Actual quantity at actual price	560,000
	80,000 Fav

Planning variance due to seasonality

	£
Standard cost for actual quantity 32,000 kg × £20	640,000
Adjusted price for actual quantity 32,000 kg × (£20 –£2.00)	576,000
	64,000 Fav

Control variance due to other factors

	£
Adjusted price for actual quantity 32,000 kg × (£20 –£2.00)	576,000
Actual quantity at actual price	560,000
	16,000 Fav

Total materials price variance £80,000 Fav

Planning variance due to seasonality £64,000 Fav

Control variance due to other factors £16,000 Fav

The total favourable price variance of £80,000 can now be seen to be due only partly to the seasonal factors. There is also £16,000 of favourable control variance due to other factors.

Task 4

The standard cost of direct materials for a product is made up of 5 kg of material at an average standard cost of £6.00 per kg. It has been noted over the years that the cost of the material fluctuates on a seasonal basis around the average standard cost as follows:

Jan – June   –£0.90

July – Dec   +£0.90

In the month of October the actual production was 2,000 units and 10,300 kg of material were used at a cost of £69,500.

(a)   The total materials price variance was £ [   ]

(b)   The planning variance due to the seasonal price change was £[   ]

The control variance due to other factors was £ [   ]

Labour efficiency variances

It is often the case that a labour force will have to learn how to produce a product, so their level of production will be lower in the early days of production and should increase in later periods. If the productivity of the workforce is affected by still being in this learning or training period, then the total labour efficiency variance may be misleading.

In exactly the same way as we did for the materials price variance, we can analyse the labour efficiency variance into the element that has been caused by the learning process (and which should be anticipated at the planning stage) and the element caused by other controllable factors.

HOW IT WORKS

A business has just started production of a new product, with a long-run standard labour cost of 4 hours per unit at an hourly rate of £8.00.

However, in this first learning period of production, it is anticipated that each unit will take 20% longer to make than the long-run standard time.

The production in the first period was 2,000 units and the actual hours worked were 10,000 at a cost of £75,000.

What is the total labour efficiency variance, the planning variance caused by the learning process and the control variance caused by other factors?

Total labour efficiency variance

	£
Standard hours for actual production at standard rate 2,000 × 4 hours × £8.00	64,000
Actual hours at standard rate 10,000 × £8.00	80,000
	16,000 Adv

Planning variance due to learning process

	£
Standard hours for actual production at standard rate 2,000 × 4 hours × £8.00	64,000
Adjusted hours for actual production at standard rate 2,000 × (4 hours × 1.20) × £8.00	76,800
	12,800 Adv

Control variance due to other factors

	£
Adjusted hours for actual production at standard rate 2,000 × (4 hours × 1.20) × £8.00	76,800
Actual hours at standard rate 10,000 × £8.00	80,000
	3,200 Adv

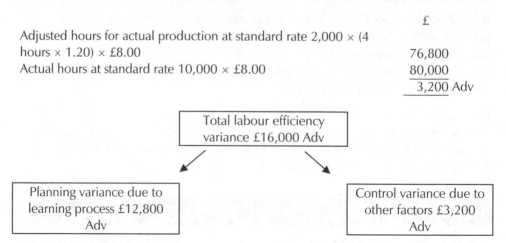

The total adverse efficiency variance is made up of only £12,800 that relates to the learning process – the remaining £3,200 of adverse variance is due to other control factors.

Task 5

A business has just had its first month of production of a new product. During the period 12,000 units were produced in 48,000 hours costing £288,000 in direct labour. The standard labour cost has been set at 3.5 hours for each unit of production at a rate of £6.20 per labour hour. However it is anticipated that the first month's production will take 25% longer than the standard hours.

(a) The total labour efficiency variance was £ [   ]

(b) The planning variance due to the early production problems was

£ [   ]

The control variance due to other factors was £ [   ]

Using indices to update standard costs

In some instances you may be given information about indices, either specific indices relating to the materials the business uses or indices regarding the labour rates. These index numbers can then be used to update an old standard cost.

HOW IT WORKS

A business has the following standard direct materials cost for its product:

    10 kg @ £3.40 per kg = £34.00

The standard cost of the material was set when the price index for the material stood at 170. During the month of July, 4,000 units of the product were made, using 38,000 kg, at a total cost of £135,000. For July, the price index for the material was 185.

Calculate the total materials price variance and analyse it into the planning variance that relates to the price increase and the control variance that is related to other factors.

Total materials price variance

	£
Standard price of actual materials 38,000 kg × £3.40	129,200
Actual quantity at actual price	135,000
	5,800 Adv

Planning variance relating to price increase

	£
Standard price of actual materials 38,000 kg × £3.40	129,200
Adjusted price for actual materials 38,000 kg × (£3.40 × 185/170)	140,600
	11,400 Adv

Control variance relating to other factors

	£
Adjusted price for actual materials 38,000 × (£3.40 × 185/170)	140,600
Actual quantity at actual price	135,000
	5,600 Fav

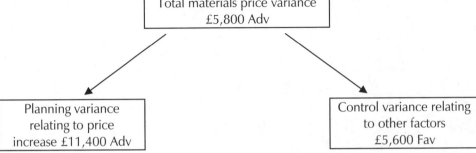

Although the price variance is only £5,800 adverse, this is due to the fact that there is a favourable control variance due to other factors of £5,600, which has been netted off against the £11,400 adverse planning variance caused by the price increase.

Task 6

A business has a direct labour standard cost of 4 hours per product at a standard hourly rate of £7.50. This standard labour rate was set when the relevant labour index stood at 120. The labour rate index is now 130. During the period the actual production was 5,000 products using 21,000 hours costing £160,000.

(a)   The total labour rate variance was £ [   ]

(b)   The planning variance due to the specific index of labour rate increases
       was   £ [   ]

       The control variance due to other factors was   £ [   ]

CHAPTER OVERVIEW

- Each type of variance can have a variety of causes – often the variances are interdependent, meaning that a factor that caused one variance is also the factor that causes other variances

- Once the reasons for the variances have been discovered, then responsibility for the variances, both favourable as well as adverse, can be assigned to the relevant managers

- A business may need to carry out an independent investigation of the reasons for a variance, in order to ascertain whether the explanation of the variance provided by the budget holder is reasonable. This may help them decide whether there is any interdependence and assess who should be held responsible.

- Some variances may be due to the setting of the standard and therefore be uncontrollable by the relevant manager – in some circumstances the standard will need to be altered if there has been a long term or permanent change in the cost or usage of the resources

- If the actual price of materials is significantly different to standard price, due to a problem with the standard, then this can have an effect on materials price variance that can appear misleading – the materials price variance can then be analysed into the planning variance caused by the price increase (uncontrollable) and the control variance caused by other factors

- The materials price variance can also be affected by any seasonality of materials prices – again the total price variance can be analysed into the planning variance which is due to the seasonal element of the price and the control variance caused by other factors

- There may be occasions when the labour efficiency variance does not give a true picture of the situation, particularly in the early stages of production when the workforce are still learning how to make the product – in such cases the labour efficiency variance can be analysed into the planning variance caused by the learning process and the control variance caused by other factors

- If a standard cost is based upon an index for a particular material or labour price then the standard cost can be updated using the current value of the index in order to analyse the materials price or labour rate variance into planning and control variances

Keywords

Interdependence of variances – this is where the factor which causes one variance can also be the cause of another variance

System of responsibility accounting – where the managers responsible for various elements of the business will be held accountable for the variances within their control.

Planning variances – the part of the variance that is due to the standard cost used at the planning stage being wrong. This variance is often considered uncontrollable.

Control variances – the part of the variance that is due to other controllable operational factors or decisions

TEST YOUR LEARNING

1   Given below is the operating statement for one of the factories of a business for the month of November, reconciling the total standard cost to the total actual cost for the month.

Operating statement – November

	Variances Adverse £	Variances Favourable £	£
Total standard cost			634,200
Variances:			
Materials price	9,200		
Materials usage	14,600		
Labour rate		15,400	
Labour efficiency	13,200		
Fixed overhead expenditure	7,200		
Fixed overhead efficiency	11,500		
Fixed overhead capacity		6,000	
	55,700	21,400	
Add: adverse variances			55,700
Less: favourable variances			(21,400)
Total actual cost			668,500

You also discover the following information:

- due to staff shortages a more junior grade of labour than normal, from one of the other factories, had to be used in the production process, giving rise to inefficiencies and additional wastage

- the material price has been increased by all suppliers and it is doubtful that the materials can be purchased more cheaply than this in future

- due to its inventory (stock)-holding policy the factory has had to rent some additional space but this has not been recognised in the standard fixed overhead cost

- due to the inefficiencies of labour, more hours had to be worked than normal in the month

Write a report to the Managing Director explaining the possible reasons for the variances for the month and making any suggestions about future actions that should be taken.

2   What possible effect will the following scenarios have on variances?

Scenarios	Possible effects
A business replaces machinery with new equipment	
A company has supply issues with a raw material	

3   The standard direct materials cost for a product is:

12 litres @ £2.40 per litre = £28.80

During week 23, the total production was 1,200 units of the product which used 14,000 litres of material. The price of the material has suddenly increased to £2.80 per litre and the business paid £38,500 during the month for materials.

(a)   The total materials price variance was £ [   ]

(b)   The planning variance due to the price increase was
£ [   ]

The control variance caused by other factors was
£ [   ]

4   A business makes a product that requires 6.5 kg of material input, which has been assigned a standard cost of £8.00 per kg. However the price of the material fluctuates throughout the year and the seasonal variations have been monitored over a number of years using time series analysis. The seasonal variations in price are:

Jan – Mar	−£1.84
Apr – June	−£0.40
July – Sept	+£0.64
Oct – Dec	+£1.60

During June the output was 1,800 units of finished product using 12,300 kg of material. The total material cost was £95,200.

(a)   The total materials price variance was £ [   ]

(b)   The planning variance due to the seasonal variation was
£ [   ]

The control variance due to other factors was
£ [   ]

5   A business has just started to produce a new product which it is anticipated will require 11 direct labour hours per unit for the first month of production. However as the employees become used to making the product it is thought that the labour time per unit will reduce to 9 hours, which is the figure which has been used for the standard cost of the direct labour together with a labour rate of £6.80 per hour.

During the first month of production 2,400 units were produced, taking 27,000 hours to produce and the labour cost was £182,600.

(a)   The total labour efficiency variance was £ [   ]

(b)   The planning variance due to the learning process in production was £ [   ]

The   control   variance   due   to   other   factors   was £ [   ]

6   A business set the standard cost for its materials at 7 kg per unit at a price of £6.50 per kg when the index for those particular material prices stood at 130. During the month of November 14,000 units of the product were produced using 100,000 kg of materials and the total cost was £670,000. In November the index for the materials price stood at 138.

(a)   The total materials price variance was £ [   ]

(b)   The   planning   variance   due   to   the   price   increase   was £ [   ]

The   control   variance   due   to   other   factors   was £ [   ]

chapter 7:
PERFORMANCE INDICATORS

PERFORMANCE INDICATORS

In the previous two chapters we considered standard costing as a method of providing information for management to allow them to control costs and hence performance. In this chapter we will consider other methods of summarising both financial and non-financial information about a business, for the purposes of management's control of costs and enhancement of value. This information for management will be provided by calculating a variety of performance indicators.

PERFORMANCE INDICATORS are methods of summarising the performance of all or parts of the organisation for a period. Performance indicators are ways of summarising performance using a formula. Some of the performance indicators will be expressed as absolute figures, such as inventory (stock) turnover period in days, whereas others will be expressed as relative figures or percentages, for example, a gross profit percentage where gross profit is expressed as a percentage of sales.

Financial and non-financial data

Some of the performance indicators will be based upon financial data. For example, a gross profit margin is calculated using figures for gross profit and sales, both taken from the income statement (profit and loss account). However other performance indicators will be based upon non-financial data, such as calculation of the number of units produced per hour.

Using the performance indicators

The performance indicators that we will consider in this chapter are vital tools of management as they serve as summaries of the performance of the business during the period. For example, if the production director is informed that productivity is 50 units per hour for the month then this has summarised information about the number of units produced and the number of hours worked, without the need for management to have these detailed figures.

However none of these performance indicators is of much significance on their own. They are only useful if they are being compared to other figures. The comparisons that are useful are:

- comparison to previous period's performance measures
- comparison to budgeted performance measures or target measures
- comparison to industry average performance measures
- comparison to other similar organisations' measures

The latter three comparisons are all forms of BENCHMARKING.

Comparability

If the performance indicators are to be used in comparison with another measure then it is important that we are comparing like with like. In general, performance indicators are a good method of providing consistent information; provided the same formula is used in each period, the performance indicators can be compared over time in order to discover the trend of performance.

However, care must be taken to ensure that the figures used are strictly comparable. For example, if the performance indicators of a business are being compared with those of another business and the businesses have different accounting policies regarding, say, depreciation, then the resulting comparison may be distorted.

A further problem may be when figures are being compared over a period of time during which there has been an increase in prices. In such instances, before the performance indicators are calculated the figures should be made comparable by using an appropriate index (this was considered in detail in Chapter 4).

PRODUCTIVITY

PRODUCTIVITY is a measure of how hard the employees are working or how productive they are being in their hours at work and is likely to be measured in terms of units of output.

As with many performance indicators, productivity can be measured in different ways but the basic calculation is to discover how many units of product or service are being produced either each hour or by each employee.

HOW IT WORKS

Harris Engineering has two factories which each make single and similar products. The production figures for the two factories for the month of June are given below:

	Factory A	Factory B
Units produced	285,000	146,000
Number of production workers	30	16
Hours worked	4,800	2,600

The productivity of the two factories could be expressed in two ways: productivity per hour or productivity per employee.

Method 1 – Productivity per labour hour

$$\text{Productivity per labour hour} = \frac{\text{Output in the period}}{\text{Hours worked in the period}}$$

	Factory A	Factory B
$=$	$\dfrac{285,000\,\text{units}}{4,800\,\text{hours}}$	$\dfrac{146,000\,\text{units}}{2,600\,\text{hours}}$
$=$	59.4 units per hour	56.2 units per hour

Obviously the productivity of the two factories can be compared (provided that the units produced are similar) and these figures indicate that productivity per labour hour is slightly higher in Factory A than in Factory B.

This productivity level could also then be compared with that in previous months and with budgeted figures.

Suppose that the budgeted figures for the month for Factory A were 250,000 units of production in 4,400 labour hours.

$$\text{Budgeted productivity} = \frac{250,000\,\text{units}}{4,400\,\text{hours}}$$

$$= 56.8 \text{ units per labour hour}$$

In this case, the actual productivity during June is high compared to the standard or budgeted productivity.

Increase in productivity

An increase in productivity means that more units can be produced in one hour or by one employee. This will normally mean a reduction in costs, as the same number of units can be produced in fewer hours and therefore with reduced labour costs, machine costs and overheads.

HOW IT WORKS

Returning to Harris Engineering, in Factory B 146,000 units were produced in 2,600 hours in June resulting in productivity of 56.2 units produced per hour. Labour is paid at a rate of £10 per hour. If the productivity of Factory B could be increased to 59 units per hour (as in Factory A) what effect would this have on the labour cost of Factory B?

Suppose that 146,000 units are to be produced next month. If productivity increases to 59 units per hour then this production will take:

$$\frac{146,000}{59} = \text{approx } 2,475 \text{ hours}$$

Time saving 2,600 – 2,475   =   125 hours

Cost saving 125 × £10   =   £1,250

This increase in productivity therefore could bring about a labour cost saving of £1,250.

Method 2 – Productivity per employee

$$\text{Productivity per employee} = \frac{\text{Output in the period}}{\text{No of employees working on output}}$$

	Factory A	Factory B
$=$	$\dfrac{285,000}{30}$	$\dfrac{146,000}{16}$
$=$	9,500 units per employee	9,125 units per employee

Again comparison can be made between the two factories, to productivity in previous periods or to budgeted productivity levels.

Which method to use?

In a manufacturing situation, the most useful method of measuring productivity is normally method 1, productivity per labour hour, as on the factory floor each employee will be likely to be doing different tasks. It is probably not the case, in the previous example, that each of the 30 production workers in Factory A actually produced 9,500 units.

However method 2, the productivity per employee, is most appropriate in a situation where each employee is doing an identical job and the job in question can take a varied amount of time.

HOW IT WORKS

Harris Engineering has a sales department which processes all orders for goods. In June the six members of the telephone sales team processed 1,240 orders.

$$\text{Productivity per employee} = \frac{\text{Output} = \text{number of orders}}{\text{Number of employees}}$$

$$= \frac{1,240 \text{ orders}}{6 \text{ employees}}$$

$$= 207 \text{ orders per employee}$$

Task 1

An advertising company has produced 216 advertisements in the current quarter using 26 advertising executives. In the previous quarter only 188 advertisements were produced when there were 22 executives.

What is the productivity of the company for this quarter and the previous quarter?

Current quarter 8.3

Previous quarter 8.5

Value added

A further method of measuring productivity is to calculate the VALUE ADDED per employee.

When a business buys raw materials and services from suppliers, it is buying them at their value to the supplier. The business will then process or work on these raw materials, incorporating any bought-in services, and will aim to sell the final goods for more than the materials and services cost, in order to make a profit.

Value added is the difference between the value of the inputs in a business and the value of the outputs. The inputs are the cost of materials and bought in services and the value of the outputs is the sales revenue of the business.

Value added = Sales revenue – (cost of materials and bought in services)

The value added therefore is the extra value that the employees of the business have added to the materials and services in order to bring them to the value of their selling price. Value added can therefore be used as a measure of overall company performance and often the value added per employee is a performance indicator used by management in order to measure productivity.

HOW IT WORKS

You are given the following information about a small manufacturing business for the year ending 30 June 20X8.

Sales revenue	£835,400
Cost of materials used	£466,700
Cost of bought in services	£265,000
Number of employees	12

What is the total value added and the value added per employee?

Value added	=	Sales revenue – (cost of materials and bought in services)
	=	£835,400 – (466,700 + 265,000)
	=	£103,700
Value added per employee	=	£103,700/12
	=	£8,642

Note: No deduction is made for the wages paid to the employees

CONTROL RATIOS: EFFICIENCY, CAPACITY AND ACTIVITY

A further method of measuring the productivity of the workforce is to calculate what are generally known as the CONTROL RATIOS of efficiency, capacity and activity.

Remember from an earlier chapter that the labour efficiency variance was calculated to determine whether the workforce had been more or less efficient than the standard efficiency. This was calculated by comparing:

- the standard hours for the actual production, and
- the actual hours worked

These three ratios of efficiency, capacity and activity are calculated using these same two figures, together with the budgeted total hours.

Efficiency ratio

As the name implies the EFFICIENCY RATIO is a measure of how efficiently the workforce has operated during a period and is expressed as a percentage. It is calculated as:

$$\text{Efficiency ratio} = \frac{\text{Standard hours for actual production}}{\text{Actual hours worked}} \times 100$$

If the ratio is 100% this means that the workforce has worked as efficiently as the standard that was set. If the ratio is more than 100% then they have worked more efficiently and if it is less than 100%, less efficiently.

Capacity ratio

The CAPACITY RATIO measures whether the workforce has worked to full planned capacity or not. This is done by comparing the actual hours worked to the hours that were budgeted for and is expressed as a percentage.

$$\text{Capacity ratio} = \frac{\text{Actual hours worked}}{\text{Budgeted hours}} \times 100$$

If the ratio is less than 100% then the workforce have not worked for as long as was budgeted for and if it is more than 100%, they have worked for longer.

Activity ratio

The ACTIVITY RATIO is an indicator of how the actual output compares to the budgeted output. It is calculated as:

$$\text{Activity ratio} = \frac{\text{Standard hours for actual production}}{\text{Budgeted hours}} \times 100$$

This ratio can also be calculated from actual and budgeted output levels, in which case it is known as the production volume ratio.

$$\text{Production volume ratio} = \frac{\text{Actual output}}{\text{Budgeted output}} \times 100$$

HOW IT WORKS

Harris Engineering has a third factory, Factory C, which produces a product made from the components produced by Factories A and B. The production figures for June for this factory are as follows:

	Factory C
Budgeted production in units	4,800
Actual production in units	4,500
Labour hours worked	10,000
Standard hours for each unit	2

Efficiency ratio

$$\text{Efficiency ratio} = \frac{\text{Standard hours for actual production}}{\text{Actual hours worked}} \times 100$$

$$= \frac{4{,}500 \text{ units} \times 2 \text{ hours per unit}}{10{,}000} \times 100$$

$$= \frac{9{,}000}{10{,}000} \times 100$$

$$= 90\%$$

The workforce has worked well below standard levels, taking 10,000 hours to produce output that should have taken only 9,000 hours.

Capacity ratio

$$\text{Capacity ratio} = \frac{\text{Actual hours worked}}{\text{Budgeted hours}} \times 100$$

$$= \frac{10,000}{4,800 \text{ units} \times 2 \text{ hours}} \times 100$$

$$= \frac{10,000}{9,600} \times 100$$

$$= 104.17\%$$

The capacity ratio shows that more hours have been worked than were budgeted. The workforce has exceeded the budgeted capacity level.

Activity ratio

$$\text{Activity ratio} = \frac{\text{Standard hours for actual production}}{\text{Budgeted hours}} \times 100$$

$$= \frac{4,500 \text{ units} \times 2 \text{ hours}}{4,800 \text{ units} \times 2 \text{ hours}} \times 100$$

$$= \frac{9,000}{9,600} \times 100$$

$$= 93.75\%$$

This shows that actual output was only 93.75% of the budgeted output.

This could also be calculated as the production volume ratio:

$$\textbf{Production volume ratio} = \frac{\text{Actual output}}{\text{Budgeted output}} \times 100$$

$$= \frac{4,500 \text{ units}}{4,800 \text{ units}} \times 100$$

$$= 93.75\%$$

Relationship between the control ratios

The three control ratios are related to each other as follows:

Efficiency ratio		Capacity ratio		Activity ratio
	$\times$		$=$	

This means that we can explain the activity ratio by referring to the other two ratios.

HOW IT WORKS

Using the figures for Factory C, remember that the three control ratios were calculated as:

Efficiency ratio	90%
Capacity ratio	104.17%
Activity ratio	93.75%

These are related as follows:

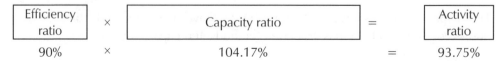

Efficiency ratio	×	Capacity ratio	=	Activity ratio
90%	×	104.17%	=	93.75%

The activity ratio shows production was only 93.75% of the budgeted level. We can now explain that this was due to the significantly lower level of efficiency than budgeted for, despite the workforce working for more hours than budgeted for.

Task 2

A manufacturing organisation had a budgeted output planned for the month of October of 288,000 units. 268,000 units were in fact produced. The standard production time for each unit is 3 hours.

What is the activity ratio for the month?

☐ %

EFFECTIVENESS

In addition to considering productivity and efficiency, an organisation may want to measure effectiveness. This considers the extent to which the objectives of the organisation are being met.

The measure used will depend on the nature of the organisation:

Organisation	Measure of effectiveness
Parts manufacturer	% of production free from defects
Furniture retailer	% of goods delivered to customer within 10 days of ordering
Training college	% of students passing exams first time
Parcel delivery company	% of parcels delivered on time
Train service provider	% of trains run to timetable

Task 3

A hospital wants to monitor the performance of its out-patients department.

Suggest appropriate effectiveness measures that could be used to assess:

    (i)   the booking of appointments
    (ii)   the service received by the patient

PROFITABILITY MEASURES

The aim of most businesses is to make a profit, therefore management will be interested in profitability performance measures. The profitability measures could also be described as efficiency indicators, as they are measuring the efficiency with which the business has used its assets to earn profits.

Gross profit margin

The GROSS PROFIT of a business is the sales for the period less the cost of those sales. In a manufacturing business, the cost of sales figure will be the manufacturing cost of goods sold, and in a retail business, the cost of sales will be the cost of the products that were actually sold during the period. The cost of sales is calculated as follows:

Cost of sales	£
Opening inventory (stock)	X
Add: Purchases/Production cost	X
	X
Less: closing inventory (stock)	(X)
	X

For a service organisation the sales for the period will be the amount of revenue that is billed to customers for the service provided. However, the cost of sales figure will not be based upon physical goods, as rather than selling goods, a service organisation trades in providing the service, for example an accountancy firm. The cost of sales figure in such an organisation is likely to be made up of the direct salaries of those employees providing the service, together with any other direct costs of providing the service.

The GROSS PROFIT MARGIN is calculated by showing the gross profit as a percentage of the sales figure for the period:

$$\text{Gross profit margin} = \frac{\text{Gross profit}}{\text{Sales}} \times 100$$

Operating profit margin

The OPERATING PROFIT of a business is the gross profit less the selling, distribution and administration costs. This is also the same as the profit before any interest payable or any tax.

The OPERATING PROFIT MARGIN is calculated by showing the operating profit as a percentage of the sales figure for the period:

$$\text{Operating profit margin} = \frac{\text{Operating profit}}{\text{Sales}} \times 100$$

Net profit margin

The NET PROFIT of a business is the profit shown in the income statement (profit and loss account) after deduction of all of the expenses, usually including interest and tax for the period. The NET PROFIT MARGIN is calculated by showing the net profit as a percentage of the sales figure for the period:

$$\text{Net profit margin} = \frac{\text{Net profit}}{\text{Sales}} \times 100$$

Expenses

It is also sometimes useful to express individual items of expenses as a percentage of the sales figure, in order to determine how these expenses have changed. This is done by the following calculation:

$$\text{Expense percentage} = \frac{\text{Expense}}{\text{Sales}} \times 100$$

If this percentage is being compared over time, when sales and production levels are changing, it is important to be aware of the difference between variable expenses and fixed expenses. If sales and production are increasing then we would also expect to see:

- similar increases in variable expenses therefore the expense percentage should remain fairly constant

- fixed expenses should be remaining reasonably constant thereby giving a decrease in the expense percentage

HOW IT WORKS

The income statement (profit and loss account) for Hampton Manufacturing for the year ending 30 September 20X8 is given below:

Hampton Manufacturing – income statement for the year ended 30 September 20X8

	£	£
Revenue*		1,350,400
Cost of sales		
Opening inventory (stock)	144,300	
Purchases	49,200	
	993,500	
Less: closing inventory (stock)	156,300	
		837,200
Gross profit		513,200
Less: expenses		
Selling and distribution costs	168,400	
Administration expenses	105,600	
		274,000
Operating profit		239,200

* Note that the term "revenue" in the income statement is just the technical accounting name for sales.

What is the gross profit margin, the operating profit margin and the expense percentage for each category of expense?

Gross profit margin	$=$	$\dfrac{£513,200}{£1,350,400} \times 100$
	$=$	38.0%
Operating profit margin	$=$	$\dfrac{\text{Operating profit}}{\text{Sales}} \times 100$
	$=$	$\dfrac{£239,200}{£1,350,400} \times 100$
	$=$	17.7%
Selling costs percentage	$=$	$\dfrac{\text{Selling cost}}{\text{Sales}} \times 100$

$$= \quad \frac{£168,400}{£1,350,400} \times 100$$

$$= \quad 12.5\%$$

$$\text{Administration costs percentage} \quad = \quad \frac{\text{Administration cost}}{\text{Sales}} \times 100$$

$$= \quad \frac{£105,600}{£1,350,400} \times 100$$

$$= \quad 7.8\%$$

If the expenses were being compared over a number of periods in which sales were rising, we would probably expect to see the selling costs percentage remain fairly stable, as this is a variable cost, and the administration costs percentage fall, as most administration costs are likely to be fixed.

Comparison of gross profit margin and operating profit margin

It has already been noted that when performance indicators are calculated it will normally be for the purposes of comparison either with previous periods, budgeted figures or those of another organisation or an industry average.

If the gross profit margin is compared over time, any changes or differences are likely to be due to:

- changes in the selling price of the goods
- changes in the sales mix of the goods
- changes in the production costs or price of the goods
- a combination of these factors

Any movement in the operating profit margin will be explained in part by changes in the gross profit margin. If the operating profit does not move in line with the gross profit margin, then this will be due to changes in the expense percentages which may be due to the expenses being either variable or fixed.

Task 4

A business has a gross profit of £58,700 and net profit of £22,500 for the month of November, after deducting interest of £2,500 and tax of £4,750. The sales for the month were £133,400.

What is the gross profit margin, the operating profit margin and the net profit margin?

Gross profit margin   44   %

Operating profit margin   22.3 %

Net profit margin   16.9 %

Improvement of gross profit margin

If the gross profit margin for a business can be increased by raising selling prices or reducing cost of sales, then the overall profitability of the business can be increased.

HOW IT WORKS

Hampton Manufacturing has a gross profit margin of 38% (calculated above) on sales of £1,350,000. However other firms in the same line of business have a gross profit margin of 40%. If Hampton were to improve its gross profit margin to 40%, it would make additional profit for the year.

	£
Current gross profit	513,200
Gross profit @ 40% margin (£1,350,400 × 40%)	540,160
Additional profit	26,960

Based on the current year's sales level, if the gross profit margin can be increased by 2 percentage points, the profits can be increased by almost £27,000.

Note that one way in which the gross profit margin can be increased is by an increase in selling price. This will have no effect on any costs, either variable or fixed, so will feed through to an increase in profit provided that sales volume is maintained. However from a commercial point of view, an increase in selling price may render the company's products uncompetitive. Another method of increasing total profit is to increase sales volume. This will have no effect on the gross profit margin as any increase in volume will be matched by increased variable costs (cost of sales). However this could lead to an increase in operating and net profit margin, as many expenses are fixed and will not lead to an increase if volume increases.

Return on capital employed

The RETURN ON CAPITAL EMPLOYED is sometimes known as the primary ratio as it is of great importance to the business. It is calculated as:

$$\text{Return on capital employed (ROCE)} = \frac{\text{Profit}}{\text{Capital employed}} \times 100$$

As such it is relating the profit that has been earned for the period to the capital from the statement of financial position (balance sheet) to determine what return has been made on the owners' investment in the business. As the capital figure is made up of the assets minus the liabilities then the ROCE can also be seen to be showing the profit that has been generated from the net assets of the business and is therefore sometimes known as 'return on net assets'.

ROCE can be calculated in different ways. Both the return element (the profit), and the capital can be calculated in different ways and it is important to ensure that the return being used matches with the capital figure used.

HOW IT WORKS

Given below is the full income statement for Hampton Manufacturing for the year ending 30 September 20X8 and the statement of financial position at that date.

Hampton Manufacturing – income statement for the year ended 30 September 20X8

	£	£
Revenue		1,350,400
Cost of sales		
Opening inventory	144,300	
Purchases	849,200	
	993,500	
Less: closing inventory	156,300	
		837,200
Gross profit		513,200
Less: expenses		
Selling and distribution costs	168,400	
Administration expenses	105,600	
		274,000
Operating profit		239,200
Interest payable		50,000
Profit after interest payable		189,200
Tax		56,000
Profit after tax		133,200

Hampton Manufacturing – statement of financial position as at 30 September 20X8

	£	£
Non-current (fixed) assets		2,428,300
Current assets:		
Inventory (stock)	156,300	
Receivables (debtors)	225,000	
Bank	10,200	
	391,500	
Payables (creditors)	(169,800)	
Net current assets		221,700
		2,650,000
Less: Long term loan		400,000
		2,250,000
Capital		1,500,000
Reserves		200,000
Retained earnings		550,000
		2,250,000

What is the return on capital employed?

Method 1

The most common method of calculating ROCE is to compare the operating profit (before interest and tax), to the capital provided by all the providers of funds. This is not only the shareholders, whose funds are the capital plus all reserves including the retained earnings, but also any long term capital within the business such as long term loans. The reason for this is that we are looking at the profits that are available for all of the providers of funds for the business.

This capital employed figure can be calculated in one of two ways:

From the capital side of the statement of financial position:

	£
Capital	1,500,000
Reserves	200,000
Retained earnings	550,000
Long term loan	400,000
Capital employed	2,650,000

From the assets side of the statement of financial position:

	£
Non-current (fixed) assets	2,428,300
Current assets	391,500
Less: current liabilities	(169,800)
Capital employed	2,650,000

As you can see the same figure is reached under each method.

Return on Capital Employed is the operating profit as a percentage of this capital employed:

$$\text{ROCE} = \frac{\text{Operating profit}}{\text{Share and loan capital} + \text{reserves} = \text{capital employed}}$$

$$= \frac{239,200}{2,650,000} \times 100$$

$$= 9.0\%$$

It is **recommended** that you use this method of calculating ROCE in assessments.

Method 2

A less common method of calculating a return is to use as the capital figure just the capital relating to the shareholders – capital, reserves and the retained earnings. This is then matched with the profit available for the shareholders, which is the profit after interest payable (and tax). Technically the ratio is known as the RETURN ON SHAREHOLDERS' FUNDS .

$$\text{Return on shareholders' funds} = \frac{\text{Profit after tax}}{\text{Shareholders' funds}} \times 100\%$$

$$= \frac{£133,200}{£2,250,000}$$

$$= 5.9\%$$

Task 5

A business has made an operating profit of £365,800 for the year. The statement of financial position shows that shareholders' funds total £1,700,000 and that there is a long term loan outstanding of £600,000, upon which annual interest of 12% is paid.

What is the return on capital employed using each of the methods above?

Method 1 [   ] %

Method 2 [   ] %

RESOURCE UTILISATION

Performance measures relating to RESOURCE UTILISATION show how efficiently and effectively an organisation is using the various resources at its disposal.

These measures concentrate on the statement of financial position (balance sheet) but also relate the statement of financial position figures to sales and cost of sales in the income statement. We will start with measures that consider the overall assets and liabilities of the business and then consider the more detailed elements of the working capital of the business.

Asset turnover

ASSET TURNOVER is a performance indicator which compares the sales or revenue of the business to the capital employed. The measure is calculated as follows:

$$\text{Asset turnover} = \frac{\text{Revenue}}{\text{Capital employed}}$$

Remember that total capital from the statement of financial position is equal to the assets of the organisation less the current liabilities, or alternatively shareholders' funds + long term loans.

You will note that asset turnover is an absolute figure and not a percentage. What this figure is showing is the amount of sales revenue that is being earned by every £1 of capital or every £1 of investment in assets and liabilities.

Asset turnover and return on capital employed

Asset turnover is an important indicator in its own right, as it shows how effectively the assets and liabilities of the business have been used to create revenue during the period. It is also an important figure as it is one of the elements that makes up ROCE as can be seen below:

$$\boxed{\text{ROCE}} \quad = \quad \boxed{\text{Asset turnover}} \quad \times \quad \boxed{\begin{array}{c}\text{Operating profit} \\ \text{margin}\end{array}}$$

If we look at how each of these figures is calculated you will see how this works:

$$\frac{\text{Operating profit}}{\text{Capital employed}} \quad = \quad \frac{\text{Revenue}}{\text{Capital employed}} \quad \times \quad \frac{\text{Operating profit}}{\text{Revenue}}$$

The importance of this relationship is that we can then explain any change in ROCE by changes in asset turnover and changes in operating profit margin.

HOW IT WORKS

Given below is a summary of these three performance indicators for Jason Enterprises for the last two years:

	20X6	20X5
Operating profit margin	13%	15%
Asset turnover	1.40	1.44
Return on capital employed	18.2%	21.6%

The return on capital employed has been significantly reduced over the period, and by looking at its component elements we can see that the reduction is due not only to a decrease in the operating profit margin of 2% but also a fall in asset turnover from the assets earning £1.44 for every £1 invested in 20X5, to only earning £1.40 per £1 invested in 20X6.

This combination of factors has caused the fall in return on capital employed.

Non-current (fixed) asset turnover

Another useful indicator to management of how effectively the organisation is using its resources is a measure of how much the non-current assets, the major long term assets of the business, are earning.

NON-CURRENT (FIXED) ASSET TURNOVER is measured as an absolute figure rather than a percentage, and shows the amount of revenue earned for each £1 invested in non-current assets:

$$\text{Non-current asset turnover} = \frac{\text{Revenue}}{\text{Net book value of non-current assets}}$$

HOW IT WORKS

We will now return to the statement of financial position of Hampton Manufacturing:

Hampton Manufacturing – statement of financial position as at 30 September 20X8

	£	£
Non-current (fixed) assets		2,428,300
Current assets:		
Inventory (stock)	156,300	
Receivables (debtors)	225,000	
Bank	10,200	
	391,500	
Payables (creditors)	(169,800)	
Net current assets		221,700
		2,650,000
Less: Long term loan		400,000
		2,250,000
Capital		1,500,000
Reserves		200,000
Retained earnings		550,000
		2,250,000

Remember that revenue for the year was £1,350,400, the operating profit margin was 17.7% and ROCE was 9.0%. We can now calculate the asset turnover and non-current asset turnover and show how the ROCE is made up.

$$\text{Asset turnover} = \frac{\text{Revenue}}{\text{Capital employed}}$$

$$= \frac{£1,350,400}{£2,650,000}$$

$$= 0.51 \text{ times}$$

This tells us that for every £1 invested in the assets and liabilities, or the capital of the business, 51 pence of sales revenue has been earned.

We can now relate the ROCE to the net profit margin and asset turnover:

ROCE	=	Asset turnover	×	Operating profit margin
9.0%	=	0.51	×	17.7%

Finally we can calculate the non-current asset turnover:

$$\text{Non-current asset turnover} = \frac{\text{Revenue}}{\text{Net book value of non-current assets}}$$

$$= \frac{£1,350,400}{£2,428,300}$$

$$= 0.56$$

For every £1 invested in the non-current assets, 56 pence of sales revenue is being earned. This figure can be used in comparison with previous periods' non-current asset turnover or with that of a similar organisation.

Working backwards through a ratio

In the computer based test you may be given a certain amount of information about a ratio and from this information be expected to work backwards to calculate a figure from the income statement or the statement of financial position.

HOW IT WORKS

A business has an asset turnover of 2 times and capital employed of £450,000. What is the revenue of the business?

$$\text{Asset turnover} = \frac{\text{Revenue}}{\text{Capital employed}}$$

$$2 = \frac{\text{Revenue}}{£450,000}$$

$$\text{Revenue} = 2 \times £450,000 = £900,000$$

Task 6

An accountancy firm has asset turnover of 1.2 in the month of June and the capital of the firm totals £350,000.

What is the revenue for the month?   1.2 × 350,000

£ 420,000

WORKING CAPITAL RATIOS

Continuing with the calculation of ratios indicating the resource utilisation of a business, we will now consider the WORKING CAPITAL of the business in more detail.

Working capital is the total of the current assets of the business less the current liabilities. It is the amount of money invested in inventory (stock) and receivables (debtors) less the credit allowed from payables (creditors) and it is a necessary part of most business's investment.

The component elements of working capital are constantly changing as the diagram below illustrates:

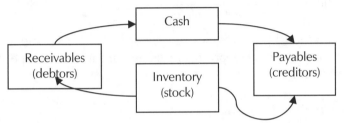

- inventory is turned into receivables when it is sold
- inventory is purchased on credit which means we have payables
- receivables will eventually be turned into cash
- cash will be used to pay payables

We will consider the overall working capital situation first and then look at the individual elements of inventory, receivables and payables.

The overall working capital performance indicators are a measure of the LIQUIDITY of the business. Liquidity is a measure of how safe the business is in terms of its cash availability. Even if a business is profitable, it must still have enough cash to be able to pay its payables when they fall due.

The current ratio

The CURRENT RATIO relates the total current assets to the total current liabilities:

$$\text{Current ratio} = \frac{\text{Current assets}}{\text{Current liabilities}}$$

This is normally expressed as a ratio, for example 2.4 : 1. It shows how many times the current liabilities are covered by the current assets.

It is often said that a current ratio of 2 : 1 is 'safe'. However although this can be used as a benchmark figure, care should be taken with the type of business that you are dealing with. For example, supermarkets will tend to have much lower current ratios than this, as they have few, if any, receivables, rapid inventory movements and large amounts of payables.

Quick ratio

One problem with using the current ratio as a measure of liquidity is that the inventory of a business, although a current asset, is not a particularly liquid asset. For inventory to be turned into cash, it must first be processed or manufactured, then it must be sold and turned into receivables and only finally will it become cash when the customers pay.

Due to the lack of liquidity of inventory, a further ratio, the QUICK RATIO (sometimes known as the acid test ratio), is calculated which excludes inventory from the current assets figure.

$$\text{Quick ratio} = \frac{\text{Current assets} - \text{inventory}}{\text{Current liabilities}}$$

Again it is often thought that a quick ratio of at least 1 : 1 is 'safe' and this can certainly be used as a benchmark figure. However, again, the type of business must be considered.

Inventory (stock)

We shall now move on to the individual elements of working capital, starting with inventory. It is useful for management to have an indication of how long inventories are being held. In some businesses inventory must be sold - or 'turned over' - quickly, for example if the inventory is made up of perishable foods. However in other businesses inventory may be held for some considerable period before it is sold (eg in the construction industry).

A business needs to control how long inventory is being held, as capital is being tied up in the inventory, while it is waiting to be sold. Therefore an INVENTORY DAYS ratio can be calculated to show the length of time that inventory is held in the business.

$$\text{Inventory days} = \frac{\text{Average inventory}}{\text{Cost of sales}} \times 365$$

This will indicate the number of days on average that the inventory is being held before sale. You will note that 'average inventory' has been used here. This is calculated as:

Average inventory =

$$\frac{\text{Opening inventory} + \text{closing inventory}}{2}$$

In some tests you may not have information about the opening inventory and therefore the closing inventory figure can be used in the calculation rather than average inventory. However if the opening inventory figure is available, then use average inventory in your calculation.

Rather than being expressed in terms of the number of days for which inventory is held, inventory turnover can also be expressed as the number of times a year that the inventory is turned over:

$$\text{Inventory turnover} = \frac{\text{Cost of sales}}{\text{Average/closing inventory}}$$

A high inventory turnover figure calculated on this basis indicates that inventory is moving in and out of the business quickly, whereas a low figure indicates that inventory is in the business for some time before it is sold.

Receivables' collection period

The RECEIVABLES' (DEBTORS') COLLECTION PERIOD, also known as receivables' days, is a measure that shows how long it is taking for the credit customers of the business to pay.

$$\text{Receivables' collection period} = \frac{\text{Trade receivables}}{\text{Credit sales}} \times 365 \text{ days}$$

There are a number of potential problems with this calculation. Firstly a separate figure for credit sales may not be available, in which case total sales must be used. However if the total sales include a large proportion of cash sales this will distort the picture shown. A further problem may be with the use of year end receivables. These may not be representative of the average amounts owing throughout the year. Therefore if possible, use the average of opening and closing receivables but in tests it is rare for this information to be available.

The receivables collection period can be compared over time in order to assess how well receivables are being managed. It can also be compared to the stated credit terms, for example if invoices are due to be paid within 60 days we would not wish to see receivables days being much more than this figure. Finally a business would try, if possible to match its receivables and payables (creditors) days, so that it is not giving away more credit than it is receiving from suppliers.

Payables' payment period

Management may also wish to know how long we take to pay our credit suppliers. This is calculated by the PAYABLES' (CREDITORS') PAYMENT PERIOD, or payables' days.

$$\text{Payables' payment period} = \frac{\text{Trade payables}}{\text{Credit purchases}} \times 365 \text{ days}$$

As with sales, we may not have a separate figure for credit purchases, therefore total purchases will need to be used. In some cases there will not even be a separate figure for purchases, in which case cost of sales must be used even though this is not so appropriate. In many tests only cost of sales will be available, so use this figure. If the average of opening and closing payables is available this is again a better figure than just the closing figure but normally only the closing statement of financial position figure will be available.

The payables' payment period can be compared over time to determine the trend in payment times. It can also be compared to the receivables' collection period. If customers are taking 75 days on average to pay, then we would not wish to have a payables' payment period of just 15 days, as this means that money is being paid out of the business much more rapidly than it is being received.

HOW IT WORKS

Given below are the income statement and statement of financial position for Hampton Manufacturing again:

Hampton Manufacturing – income statement for the year ended 30 September 20X8

	£	£
Revenue		1,350,400
Cost of sales		
Opening inventory	144,300	
Purchases	849,200	
	993,500	
Less: closing inventory	156,300	
		837,200
Gross profit		513,200
Less: expenses		
Selling and distribution costs	168,400	
Administration expenses	105,600	
		274,000
Operating profit		239,200
Interest payable		50,000
Profit after interest payable		189,200
Tax		56,000
Profit after tax		133,200

Hampton Manufacturing – statement of financial position as at 30 September 20X8

	£	£
Non-current assets		2,428,300
Current assets:		
Inventory	156,300	
Receivables	225,000	
Bank	10,200	
	391,500	
Payables	(169,800)	
Net current assets		221,700
		2,650,000
Less: Long term loan		400,000
		2,250,000
Capital		1,500,000
Reserves		200,000
Retained earnings		550,000
		2,250,000

We will now calculate all of the working capital ratios.

$$\text{Current ratio} = \frac{\text{Current assets}}{\text{Current liabilities}}$$

$$= \frac{£391,500}{£169,800}$$

$$= 2.3 : 1$$

$$\text{Quick ratio} = \frac{\text{Current assets} - \text{inventory}}{\text{Current liabilities}}$$

$$= \frac{£391,500 - £156,300}{£169,800}$$

$$= 1.4 : 1$$

$$\text{Average inventory} = \frac{£144,300 + £156,300}{2}$$

$$= £150,300$$

Inventory days	$=$	$\dfrac{\text{Average inventory}}{\text{Cost of sales}} \times 365$
	$=$	$\dfrac{£150,300}{£837,200} \times 365$
	$=$	66 days
Inventory turnover (times)	$=$	$\dfrac{\text{Cost of sales}}{\text{Average inventory}}$
		$\dfrac{£837,200}{£150,300}$
	$=$	5.6 times
Receivables' collection period	$=$	$\dfrac{\text{Trade receivables}}{\text{Credit sales}} \times 365$
	$=$	$\dfrac{£225,000}{£1,350,400} \times 365$
	$=$	61 days
Payables' payment period	$=$	$\dfrac{\text{Trade payables}}{\text{Credit purchases}} \times 365$
	$=$	$\dfrac{£169,800}{£849,200} \times 365$
	$=$	73 days

Task 7

A business has opening inventory of £13,500 and closing inventory of £17,000. Purchases during the year were £99,000.

What is the inventory turnover in days?

[58] days

(handwritten annotations:)
$13.500 + 99.000 - 17,000$
$\text{cost of sales} = 95,500$
$\dfrac{15250}{95.500} \times 365$
$\dfrac{13.500 + 17.000}{2} = 15250$

Improvement in working capital management

As we saw at the start of this section, the components of working capital are constantly changing but will eventually become cash receipts and cash payments. We have seen how performance indicators for individual elements of working capital – inventory, receivables and payables – can be calculated.

If the management of working capital can be improved, for example by shortening inventory turnover days or receivables' collection period, or by extending the payables' payment period, then this will mean that the business will have additional cash available.

HOW IT WORKS

The performance indicators for Hampton Manufacturing show the following:

Inventory turnover days	66 days
Receivables' collection period	61 days
Payables' payment period	73 days

The industry average figures for working capital are:

Inventory turnover days	50 days
Receivables' collection period	48 days
Payables' payment period	80 days

If Hampton were to improve its working capital practices in order to be in line with the industry average figures, what effect would this have on the cash balance?

Reduction in inventory turnover period (66 days – 50 days) = 16 days

The value of 16 days of inventory is:

$$\frac{\text{Cost of sales}}{365} \times 16 \quad = \quad \frac{837,200}{365} \times 16$$

$$= \quad £36,699$$

Reduction in receivables' collection period (61 days – 48 days) = 13 days

The value of 13 days of receivables is:

$$\frac{\text{Credit sales}}{365} \times 13 \quad = \quad \frac{1,350,400}{365} \times 13$$

$$= \quad £48,096$$

Increase in payables' payment period (80 days – 73 days) = 7 days

The value of 7 days of payables is:

$$\frac{\text{Credit purchases}}{365} \times 7 \quad = \quad \frac{849,200}{365} \times 7$$

$$= \quad £16,286$$

If all three improvements were made there would be an improvement in the cash balance of £101,081 (£36,699 + 48,096 + 16,286).

Months not days

In the assessment you may be asked to calculate inventory turnover, receivables' collection period or payables' payment period in months rather than in days. In these situations simply substitute 12 months for 365 days in the formula and the answer will automatically be expressed in months.

HOW IT WORKS

A business has payables of £24,000 and purchases during the year were £101,000. What is the payables' payment period in months?

$$\text{Payables' payment period} = \frac{\text{Payables}}{\text{Purchases}} \times 12$$

$$= \frac{£24,000}{£101,000} \times 12$$

$$= 2.9 \text{ months}$$

GEARING

Some companies are not only financed by share capital from the shareholders but also by long term loans, for example from banks. These long term loans are shown separately as such in a company's statement of financial position.

When long term loans are taken out this produces additional commitments for a company:

- the company needs to be able to pay the annual interest on the loan
- the company needs to be able to pay off the loan when it falls due.

These additional commitments mean that companies with long term loan capital are often viewed as more risky than those companies without any long term loans or with smaller amounts of loan capital. For this reason there are two main performance indicators that measure the effect of long term loan capital on a company.

Interest cover

INTEREST COVER is a measure of how easily the company can make its interest payments out of annual profits. It is measured as:

$$\text{Interest cover} = \frac{\text{Profit before interest charges}}{\text{Interest charges}}$$

This will give an indication of how safe the annual interest payments are in terms of the profit that the company is making.

Gearing ratio

The GEARING RATIO is a measure of the amount of long term loan capital that a company has compared to the other sources of long term finance, being the share capital and reserves of the company.

The gearing ratio can be measured in one of two ways:

$$\text{Method 1} \quad \text{Gearing ratio} = \frac{\text{Long term loan finance}}{\text{Shareholders' funds}} \times 100$$

This is sometimes known as the debt:equity ratio

$$\text{Method 2} \quad \text{Gearing ratio} = \frac{\text{Long term loan finance}}{\text{Shareholders' funds} + \text{long term finance}} \times 100$$

HOW IT WORKS

Returning to Hampton Manufacturing:

Hampton Manufacturing – income statement for the year ended 30 September 20X8

	£	£
Revenue		1,350,400
Cost of sales		
Opening inventory	144,300	
Purchases	849,200	
	993,500	
Less: closing inventory	156,300	
		837,200
Gross profit		513,200
Less: expenses		
Selling and distribution expenses	168,400	
Administration expenses	105,600	
		274,000
Operating profit		239,200
Interest payable		50,000
Profit after interest payable		189,200
Tax		56,000
Profit after tax		133,200

Hampton Manufacturing – statement of financial position as at 30 September 20X8

	£	£
Non-current assets		2,428,300
Current assets:		
Inventory	156,300	
Receivables	225,000	
Bank	10,200	
	391,500	
Payables	(169,800)	
Net current assets		221,700
		2,650,000
Less: Long term loan		400,000
		2,250,000
Capital		1,500,000
Reserves		200,000
Retained earnings		550,000
		2,250,000

$$\text{Interest cover} = \frac{\text{Profit before interest charges}}{\text{Interest charges}}$$

$$\text{Interest cover} = \frac{£239,200}{£50,000}$$

$$= 4.78$$

This indicates that the interest payments due for the year are just over one fifth of the profits made during the year. This would tend to indicate that the interest payments are quite safe unless there is a large fall in profits.

The gearing ratio can be measured in one of two ways:

Method 1 $\dfrac{\text{Gearing}}{\text{ratio}} = \dfrac{\text{Long term loan finance}}{\text{Shareholders' funds}} \times 100$

$\dfrac{\text{Gearing}}{\text{ratio}} = \dfrac{£400,000}{£2,250,000} \times 100$

$= 17.8\%$

Method 2 $\dfrac{\text{Gearing}}{\text{ratio}} = \dfrac{\text{Long term loan finance}}{\text{Shareholders' funds} + \text{long term finance}} \times 100$

$\dfrac{\text{Gearing}}{\text{ratio}} = \dfrac{£400,000}{£2,250,000 + £400,000} \times 100$

$= 15.1\%$

Whichever method is used, this indicates that the gearing ratio of the company is quite low. Compared to either the shareholders' funds or the total capital the amount of loan capital is relatively low.

RATIO ANALYSIS

As well as being able to calculate the performance indicators considered in this chapter, you will also need to be able to interpret the indicators and to comment intelligently on them. The performance indicators that you will have calculated will be compared either over time within the organisation, with target or budgeted figures, with another similar organisation or with industry average figures.

Interpreting the performance indicators

In the next example we will bring together many of the performance indicators covered in this chapter and not only calculate them but also comment on their significance to explain what they reveal about the organisation.

HOW IT WORKS

Jamboree Ltd is a manufacturing organisation which produces a range of small plastic tricycles for children. You are given below summarised income statements for the years ended 31 October 20X7 and 31 October 20X8 and summarised statements of financial position at those dates.

Summarised income statements

	Y/e 31 Oct 20X8	Y/e 31 Oct 20X7
	£'000	£'000
Revenue	420	320
Cost of sales	256	180
Gross profit	164	140
Expenses	100	89
Operating profit	64	51
Interest payable	10	10
Profit before tax	54	41
Tax	16	12
Profit after tax	38	29

Summarised statements of financial position

	31 Oct 20X8		31 Oct 20X7	
	£'000	£'000	£'000	£'000
Non-current assets		394		369
Current assets:				
Inventory	50		30	
Receivables	69		44	
Cash	2		12	
	121		86	
Payables	52		30	
Net current assets		69		56
		463		425
Long term loan		100		100
		363		325
Capital		250		250
Retained earnings		113		75
		363		325

You are required to calculate the following ratios and then to comment on the performance of the company over the last two years in the light of these ratios:

(a) gross profit margin
(b) operating profit margin
(c) expenses to sales
(d) return on capital employed
(e) asset turnover
(f) non-current asset turnover
(g) current ratio
(h) quick ratio
(i) inventory turnover in days
(j) receivables' collection period
(k) payables' payment period
(l) interest cover
(m) gearing ratio (loans/shareholders' funds)

Calculate the ratios first and tabulate them so that they are easy to compare.

		20X8	20X7
(a)	Gross profit margin		
	164/420 × 100	39.0%	
	140/320 × 100		43.8%
(b)	Operating profit margin		
	64/420 × 100	15.2%	
	51/320 × 100		15.9%
(c)	Expenses to sales		
	100/420 × 100	23.8%	
	89/320 × 100		27.8%
(d)	Return on capital employed		
	64/463 × 100	13.8%	
	51/425 × 100		12.0%
(e)	Asset turnover		
	420/463	0.91	
	320/425		0.75
(f)	Non-current asset turnover		
	420/394	1.07	
	320/369		0.87
(g)	Current ratio		
	121/52	2.3 : 1	
	86/30		2.9 : 1

		20X8	20X7
(h)	Quick ratio		
	71/52	1.4 : 1	
	56/30		1.9 : 1
(i)	Inventory turnover in days		
	50/256 × 365	71 days	
	30/180 × 365		61 days
(j)	Receivables' collection period		
	69/420 × 365	60 days	
	44/320 × 365		50 days
(k)	Payables' payment period		
	52/256 × 365	74 days	
	30/180 × 365		61 days
(l)	Interest cover		
	64/10	6.4	
	51/10		5.1
(m)	Gearing ratio (loans/shareholders' funds)		
	100/363	27.5%	
	100/325		30.8%

Now consider the whole picture – look at the movement in each ratio and decide why it might have changed and how all the movements in the ratios piece together. The main points to make are given below – you may find it useful to consider profitability, resource utilisation and working capital in separate sections. Remember that as well as summarising the movement you need to try and explain why this might have arisen.

Profitability

- Revenue has increased by 31% ($\frac{(420-320)}{320} \times 100\%$)

- Gross profit margin has decreased – this may be due to a lowering of prices in order to increase the revenue and market share

- Operating profit margin has decreased slightly but not as much as the gross profit margin, as the percentage of expenses to sales has decreased – this may be due to the fact that some of the expenses were fixed costs and have therefore not increased with revenue

- Return on capital employed has increased despite the fall in profit margins, due to a significant improvement in asset turnover and non-current asset turnover

Resource utilisation

- Asset turnover has increased significantly as has non-current asset turnover

- There has obviously been investment in non-current assets during 20X8 as the non-current asset total has increased despite this year's depreciation having been charged

- Therefore the increase in asset and non-current asset turnover may be due to efficiencies as a result of the new non-current assets

Working capital

- In overall terms both the current ratio and the quick ratio have fallen, although they are still at healthy levels – the main reasons for this are the reduction in cash and the significant increase in payables

- Investment in inventory has increased with inventory now being held for 71 days rather than 61 – there is no obvious reason for this although it could be due to the company stocking a wider range of tricycles

- Receivables' collection period has also increased by 10 days to 60 days, which may be due to offering longer credit periods to attract new customers

- Payables' payment period has increased by 13 days to 74 days which may be due to the lack of cash, evidenced by the significantly reduced level of cash at the year-end

Gearing

Gearing is relatively low and interest cover quite high. Therefore the company looks quite safe in this area.

Task 8

A business had a gross profit margin of 38.7% for the year ending 30 June 20X7 and a gross profit margin of 35.2% for the year ending 30 June 20X8.

Suggest reasons for the change in gross profit margin.

DECREASE IN SELLING PRICE.

INCREASE IN PURCHASES or PRODUCTION COSTS

LARGE WRITE OFF OF INVENTORIES

213

LIMITATIONS OF RATIO ANALYSIS

It has been noted throughout this chapter that care must be taken when using ratios in order to draw conclusions about an organisation for a variety of reasons. These limitations of ratio analysis are now summarised below:

Comparing like with like – if ratios are to be compared then they must have been calculated in the same way and using comparable figures. When comparing ratios over time in an organisation, if there has been any change in accounting policies over the period then this may impact upon the ratios. If comparing the accounts of two different companies it is likely that they will have different accounting policies and strict adjustments should be made to bring the accounting policies in line before calculating the ratios.

Inflation – if ratios are being compared over time on the basis of historical cost accounting figures then adjustments must be made using an appropriate index in order to restate all the figures in terms of one particular price.

Representative figures – in many cases we are using year end statement of financial position amounts to calculate ratios and these may not necessarily be representative of the value throughout the year.

Accounting adjustments – as year end figures are used for the ratios, just one significant accounting adjustment or transaction before the year end can alter the position shown by the statement of financial position and the resulting ratios. For example if a large cash payment were made to suppliers just before the year end, this would significantly improve the payables' payment period.

Age of non-current assets – if we are comparing one company to another using ratio analysis, the figures may not be entirely comparable unless the non-current assets are of similar age.

Key performance indicators and the behaviour of managers – the way in which managers are assessed on their performance can have a major influence on the decisions that they make. If key performance indicators such as ROCE are used to assess a manager then there is the possibility of a lack of goal congruence in decision making. For example a new piece of machinery may benefit the business as a whole as it will reduce costs and improve quality but the manager in charge of that department may be reluctant to invest if it will reduce his department's ROCE on which he is assessed.

THE BALANCED SCORECARD

So far in this chapter we have considered a variety of performance indicators, both financial and non-financial, which can be used to provide information to management to help them to control costs and enhance value.

The BALANCED SCORECARD is a framework that can be used to determine which performance indicators are important to a business. The balanced scorecard approach is to recognise that there is not just one perspective – the financial one – but four different perspectives of a business, all of which must be monitored.

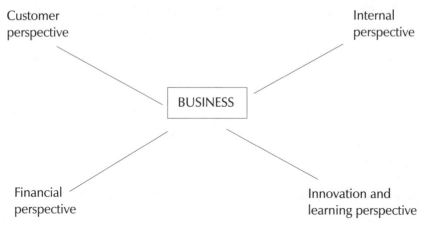

We will now consider the types of performance indicator that might be calculated to measure these four perspectives.

Perspective	Concerned with:	Possible performance indicators
Customer	Customer satisfaction and loyalty therefore quality, delivery, after-sales service	▪ number of repeat orders ▪ average delivery period ▪ number of complaints
Internal	Internal processes and technical excellence	▪ value added ▪ number of units rejected in quality inspections
Financial	Profits and satisfying the needs of shareholders or owners	▪ ROCE ▪ gross, operating and net profit margins
Innovation and learning	Improvement of existing products and development of new products	▪ training costs per employee ▪ percentage of sales from new products

HOW IT WORKS

Lampoon Productions has in the past produced just one fairly successful product. Recently, however, a new version of this product has been launched. Development work continues to add a related product to the product range. Given below are some details of the activities during the month of November.

Units produced	—	existing product	25,000
	—	new product	5,000
Cost of units produced	—	existing product	£375,000
	—	new product	£70,000
Sales revenue	—	existing product	£550,000
	—	new product	£125,000
Hours worked	—	existing product	5,000
	—	new product	1,250
Development costs			£47,000

Suggest and calculate performance indicators that could be used for each of the four perspectives on the balanced scorecard.

Customer

■ Percentage of sales represented by new products

$$= \frac{£125,000}{£550,000+£125,000} \times 100$$

$$= 18.5\%$$

Internal

■ Productivity — existing product $= \dfrac{25,000 \text{ units}}{5,000 \text{ hours}}$

$= 5$ units per hour

— new product $= \dfrac{5,000 \text{ units}}{1,250 \text{ hours}}$

$= 4$ units per hour

■ Unit cost — existing product $= \dfrac{£375,000}{25,000 \text{ units}}$

$= £15$ per unit

— new product $= \dfrac{£70,000}{5,000 \text{ units}}$

$= £14$ per unit

Financial

- Gross profit   – existing product $= \dfrac{£550,000 - 375,000}{£550,000}$

       $= 32\%$

       – new product $= \dfrac{£125,000 - 70,000}{£125,000}$

       $= 44\%$

Innovation and learning

- Development costs as % of sales $= \dfrac{£47,000}{£675,000}$

       $= 7\%$

SERVICE ORGANISATIONS

So far in this chapter we have concentrated on performance indicators for manufacturing organisations. Performance indicators obviously also have to be calculated for organisations that provide a service rather than a tangible product, such as accountancy firms, a transport provider, a hotel or a college of education.

Many of the performance indicators considered in this chapter will be relevant to service industries, although they will need to be expressed slightly differently. For example, the cost per unit in a manufacturing industry might become the cost per chargeable hour in an accountancy firm or the cost per passenger mile in a transport provider.

Productivity will also be assessed in service organisations, adapted to suit their circumstances – in an accountancy firm it might be measured as the percentage of chargeable hours to total hours; in a college of education the number of students enrolled per lecturer; in a transport company the number of passengers transported per month.

Service organisations will normally expect to make a profit and therefore most of the financial performance indicators will be relevant to service organisations.

It should be noted, however, that often the main revenue-generating assets of a service business are its employees. As the 'worth' of employees is not generally reflected on the statement of financial position, measures such as ROCE, asset turnover and non-current asset turnover are perhaps not as relevant or significant in the service sector.

The main difference between manufacturing and service organisations however is that the service organisations will probably be more interested in non-financial performance indicators. For example, an accountancy firm will monitor the number of clients that leave the firm for another firm, a transport provider will be concerned about delays on routes, a college of education will take particular note of the students' assessments of the lecturers.

Service organisations are sometimes the scenario in an assessment for a number of tasks. Use the information in the scenario and the techniques that you have learnt in this chapter to adapt performance indicators to the requirements of the organisation being considered. However the AAT have made it clear that if the formula for performance indicator is not obvious then it will be given.

WHAT IF? ANALYSIS

Throughout the chapter we have covered a variety of performance indicators. In an assessment, in addition to calculating and comparing performance indicators you may be required to conduct 'WHAT IF?' ANALYSIS, which is a technique that assesses the impact of potential changes before they are actually made.

- Forecast performance indicators based on the assumptions you are given

- Recalculate performance indicators to take account of changes to a business eg the purchase of new machinery

- Use performance indicators to evaluate and recommend the best course of action in a given situation

- Show what the results of the business would have looked like if certain performance targets (benchmarks) had been achieved

CHAPTER OVERVIEW

- Performance indicators can be calculated to summarise productivity, profitability and resource utilisation – some of the performance indicators will be financial measures and some will be non-financial measures

- Productivity can be measured as units produced per hour or units produced per employee – productivity can also be measured by considering the value added per employee

- A further method of measuring productivity is to use the three control ratios – efficiency, capacity and activity

- The gross profit margin measures the profitability of the trading element of the organisation and the operating and net profit margins give a measure of profitability after deduction of expenses

- The return on capital employed relates the operating profit to the amount of capital invested in the business to give an overall return to the providers of that capital – the return on capital employed is made up of the asset turnover multiplied by the operating profit margin

- Measures of resource utilisation include asset turnover and non-current asset turnover which show the amount of revenue earned for each £1 investment

- Working capital overall can be monitored by calculation of the current ratio and the quick ratio – individual elements of the working capital can be controlled by monitoring of inventory turnover, receivables' collection period and payables' payment period

- The gearing level (amount of debt finance) can be measured using either interest cover or the gearing ratio

- Not only must the performance indicators be calculated but they must also be interpreted using ratio analysis. In order to do this comparative figures (or benchmarks) are required.

- The balanced scorecard is an approach to monitoring performance indicators which recognises that there are four distinct perspectives to the business – the customer perspective, internal perspective, the financial perspective and the innovation and learning perspective

- Service organisations will also require performance indicators but they may be slightly different from those for manufacturing or retail organisations due to the nature of the organisation.

- "What if?" analysis involves forecasting performance indicators or results given certain assumptions about a business or recalculating these to take account of given changes to the business in order to assess the impact of different courses of action.

Keywords

Performance indicators – ways of summarising elements of performance using a formula

Benchmarking – comparison of actual figures to a pre-determined target or industry best practice

Productivity – a measure of how hard the employees are working

Value added – sales value less the cost of materials and bought in services

Control ratios – the productivity measures of efficiency, capacity and activity

Efficiency ratio – a measure of how efficiently the employees have worked compared to standard efficiency

Capacity ratio – a measure indicating whether the employees have worked to full capacity

Activity ratio – an indicator of how the actual output compares to budgeted output

Effectiveness – a measure of the extent to which the objectives of the organisation are being met.

Gross profit – sales value minus cost of sales

Gross profit margin – gross profit as a percentage of sales

Operating profit – profit after deduction of cost of sales, selling, administration and distribution expenses (or profit before interest and tax)

Operating profit margin – operating profit as a percentage of sales

Net profit – profit after deduction of expenses, interest and tax

Net profit margin – net profit as a percentage of sales

Return on capital employed – operating profit as a percentage of total capital

Return on shareholders' funds – net profit as a percentage of shareholders' funds

Resource utilisation – how productively and effectively an organisation uses its resources

Asset turnover – the amount of sales revenue earned for each £1 invested in the capital of the business

Non-current asset turnover – the amount of sales revenue earned for each £1 invested in non-current assets

Working capital – current assets less current liabilities

Liquidity – how much cash the business can access

Current ratio – ratio of current assets to current liabilities

Quick ratio – ratio of current assets less inventory to current liabilities

Inventory turnover – number of days inventory is held or the number of times a year inventory is turned over

Receivables' collection period – the number of days it takes customers to pay

Payables' payment period – the number of days before suppliers are paid

Interest cover – is the number of times that the annual interest charge is covered by the annual profit.

Gearing ratio – is a measure of the percentage of long term loan capital in the capital structure

Balanced scorecard – a framework for performance indicators which recognises that there are four perspectives of a business (customer, internal, financial and innovation & learning)

What if? analysis – a technique that is used to assess the impact of potential changes before they are actually made

TEST YOUR LEARNING

1 Given below are the production figures for a factory for the last four months.

	August	September	October	November
Output in units	257,300	251,400	262,300	258,600
Budgeted output	250,000	255,000	260,000	260,000
Hours worked	24,400	24,600	26,700	25,600

The standard time for each unit of production is 6 minutes.

Complete the table below showing the performance indicators for each of the four months:

	Aug	Sept	Oct	Nov
Productivity per labour hour	10.5 units	10.2	9.8	10.1
Efficiency ratio	105.5%	102.2	98.2	101.0
Capacity ratio	97.6%	96.5	102.7	98.5
Activity ratio	102.9%	98.6	100.9	99.5

2 Given below are the production figures for a factory for the last three months.

	April	May	June
Production costs	£418,300	£424,500	£430,500
Production wages	£83,700	£86,000	£86,300
Output in units	121,700	123,500	128,000
Hours worked	11,200	11,500	11,500
Budgeted output	120,000	125,000	125,000
Sales revenue	£625,000	£634,000	£656,000
Number of employees	81	83	83

Production costs are made up of the materials for production and the bought in services required in the month. It is estimated that 11 units should be produced each hour.

Complete the table to calculate the following performance indicators for each of the last three months and for the three months in total:

(a) (i) productivity per labour hour

(ii) efficiency ratio

(iii) capacity ratio

(iv) activity ratio

(v) value added per employee

	April	May	June	Total AV.
Productivity per labour hour	10.9.	10.7	11.1	10.9
Efficiency ratio	93.8%	97.6%	101.2%	99.2%
Capacity ratio	102.7%	101.2%	101.2%	101.7%
Activity ratio	101.4%	98.8%	102.4%	100.9%
Value added per employee	2552	2524	2717	2598

(b) The labour rate is £7.50 per hour. Production for July will be the same as in June. If productivity can be increased to 11.5 units per hour, what is the cost saving in production wages?

£ [2767.50]

$$\frac{128\,000}{11.5} = 11,131\ \text{HOURS}$$

$$\begin{array}{r} 11.500 \\ -11.131 \\ \hline 369 \times 7.50 = \end{array}$$

3 A travel firm employs five sales representatives. Sales of holidays are seasonal and you are provided with the following figures for the last year:

	July – Sept	Oct – Dec	Jan – March	April – June
Holidays sold	6,200	4,100	7,700	5,900
Total costs	£113,200	£115,400	£125,500	£120,400

(a) For each quarter of the year complete the following table to calculate:

(i) the productivity per sales representative
(ii) the cost per holiday sold

	July – Sept	Oct – Dec	Jan – Mar	Apr – June	
Productivity	1240	820	1540	1180	
Cost per holiday	18.26	28.15	16.30	20.41	

(b) Comment upon why you think the cost per holiday sold fluctuates so much.

4 Given below is a summary of a business's performance for the last six months:

	Jan	Feb	Mar	April	May	June
	£000	£000	£000	£000	£000	£000
Revenue	400	480	450	510	560	540
Cost of sales	210	270	260	320	340	330
Expenses	140	144	141	136	157	152
Interest	–	–	–	3	3	3
Shareholders' funds	240	290	319	353	406	434
Loan	–	–	–	40	40	40

For each month of the year you are to complete the table calculate the following performance indicators:

(a) gross profit margin
(b) operating profit margin
(c) percentage of expenses to revenue
(d) return on capital employed
(e) asset turnover

Comment on what the performance measures indicate about the business activities for the last six months.

	Jan	Feb	Mar	April	May	June
Gross profit margin	47.5%	43.8%	42.2%	37.3%	39.3%	38.9%
Net profit margin	12.5%	13.8%	10.9%	10.6%	11.3%	10.7%
% expenses to revenue	35%	30%	31.3%	26.7%	28%	28.1%
Return on capital employed	20.8%	22.8%	15.4%	13.7%	14.1%	12.2%
Asset turnover	1.67	1.66	1.41	1.30	1.26	1.14

5   Given below is a summary of the performance of a business for the last three years:

	20X6	20X7	20X8
	£000	£000	£000
Revenue	820	850	900
Cost of sales	440	445	500
Expenses	290	305	315
Interest	—	3	3
Capital and reserves	500	560	620
Long term loan	—	50	50
Non-current assets	385	453	498
Receivables	85	112	128
Inventory	50	55	67
Payables	30	34	41
Bank balance	10	24	18

For each of the three years complete the table to calculate the following performance measures and comment on what the measures indicate about the performance of the business over the period:

(a)   gross profit margin
(b)   operating profit margin
(c)   return on capital employed
(d)   asset turnover
(e)   non-current asset turnover
(f)   current ratio
(g)   quick ratio
(h)   receivables' collection period
(i)   inventory turnover in days
(j)   payables' payment period
(k)   interest cover
(l)   gearing ratio

	20X6	20X7	20X8
Gross profit margin	46.3%	47.6%	44.4%
Operating profit margin	11.0%	11.8%	9.4%
Return on capital employed	18%	16.4%	12.7%
Asset turnover	1.64	1.40	1.34
Non-current asset turnover	2.13	1.88	1.81
Current ratio	4.83	5.62	5.20
Quick ratio	3.2	4.0	3.6
Receivables' collection period	38 DAYS	48	52
Inventory days	42	45	49
Payables' payment period	25	28	30
Interest cover	—	33.3	28.3
Gearing ratio	—	8.9%	8.1%

6   A retail business has three small department stores in Flimwell, Hartfield
and Groombridge. The figures for the first six months of 20X8 are given
below:

	Flimwell	Hartfield	Groombridge
Financial details	£	£	£
Revenue	540,000	370,000	480,000
Opening inventory	51,000 AV	45,000 AV	30,000 AV
Closing inventory	56,000	50,000	32,000
Purchases	210,000 − 5000	165,000 −5000	192,000 − 2000
Expenses	270,000	175,000	225,000
Capital	550,000	410,000	510,000
Payables	25,800	27,500	30,500
Non-financial details			
Floor area	2,400 sq m	1,700 sq m	2,000 sq m
Employees	28	13	26
Hours worked	30,500	14,100	28,300

(a) Complete the table to calculate the following performance indicators for each store:

    (i)   gross profit margin
    (ii)   operating profit margin
    (iii) return on capital employed
    (iv) asset turnover
    (v)   inventory turnover in days
    (vi) payables' payment period
    (vii) sales per square metre of floor area
    (viii) sales per employee
    (ix) sales per hour worked.

	Flimwell	Hartfield	Groombridge
Gross profit margin	62.0%	56.8%	60.4%
Operating profit margin	12.0%	9.5%	13.5%.
Return on capital employed	11.8%	8.5%	12.7%
Asset turnover	0.98	0.90	0.94
Inventory turnover days	95	108	60
Payables' payment period	45	61	58
Sales per sq m	225	218	240
Sales per employee	19286	28462	18462
Sales per hour worked	17.70	26.24	16.96

(b) Use the performance indicators calculated in (a) to write a report to the sales director of the chain comparing the performances of the three stores for the six month period. In the report explain the effect on the cash balance if the payables payment period in Flimwell were increased to that of Hartfield.

7   (a) A business operates on a gross profit margin of 44% and sales for the period were £106,500. What is the gross profit?

£ | 46 860 | 106.500 x 44%

(b) A business operates on a gross profit margin of 37.5% and the gross profit made in the period was £105,000. What was the figure for revenue for the period?

105,000

£ | 280,000 | $\frac{105,000}{.375}$

(c) A business had revenue of £256,000 in a month, with a gross profit margin of 41% and an operating profit margin of 13.5%. What were the expenses for the month?

256.000 x ·41 = 104960

£ | 70 400 | 256.000 x ·135 = 34560

EXPENSE =   70 400

(d) A business has a return on capital employed of 12.8% and made an operating profit for the period of £50,000. What is the capital employed?

50,000

£ | 390 625 | $\frac{50,000}{.128}$

(e) A business has an operating profit percentage of 10% and a return on capital employed of 15%. What is the asset turnover of the business?

| 1·5 | times $\frac{15}{10} = 1.5$

(f) A business has opening inventory and closing inventory of £118,000 and £104,000 respectively and made purchases during the year totalling £465,000. How many times did inventory turn over during the year?

$\frac{118+104}{2} = 11$

| 4·3 | times   465.000 + 118,000- 102 = 111,000

(g) A business has a receivables' collection period of 64 days and the closing receivables figure is £64,000. What is the figure for revenue for the year?

£ | 365.000 | $\frac{64,000 \times 365}{64}$

8   Given below is the summarised income statement and statement of financial position of a manufacturing company for the year ended 30 September 20X8:

Income statement

	£000	£000
Revenue		372
Opening inventory of finished goods	19	
Materials	28	
Labour	40	
Production overheads	14	
	101	
Closing inventory of finished goods	21	
Cost of sales		80
Gross profit		292
Administration costs	184	
Interest payable	6	
Training costs	9	
Research costs	25	
		224

OP·PROFIT 74 68 +

NET PROFIT

Statement of financial position

	£000	£000
Non-current assets		232
Current assets:		
Inventory of finished goods	21	
Receivables	62	
Cash	9	
	92	
Payables	24	
Net current assets		68
		300
Long term loan		(100)
		200
Capital and reserves		200

You are to complete the table to calculate the following performance indicators and for each one to identify which balanced scorecard perspective is being measured.

(a) Operating profit margin
(b) Return on capital employed
(c) Inventory turnover in days
(d) Asset turnover
(e) Research costs as a percentage of production costs
(f) Training costs as a percentage of the labour cost

		Balanced scorecard perspective
Operating profit margin	19.9%	FINANCIAL
Return on capital employed	24.7%	FINANCIAL
Inventory turnover	91 DAYS	CUSTOMER
Asset turnover	1.24	INTERNAL
Research costs as % of production costs	31.25%	INNOVATION AND LEARNING
Training costs as a % of labour cost	22.5%	INTERNAL

chapter 8:
COST MANAGEMENT

---

chapter coverage 📖

In this chapter we will look at a variety of final aspects of financial performance – largely the topics of quality and target costing.

The topics we shall cover are:

- ✎ What is quality?
- ✎ Costs of quality
- ✎ Performance indicators for quality
- ✎ Total Quality Management
- ✎ Target costing
- ✎ Product life cycle

WHAT IS QUALITY?

So far in this Text we have been considering the production of products and the provision of services, from the point of view of the maker of the product or the provider of the service. Here we move onto considerations of quality, which means that we must now consider the product or service from the customer's perspective.

Quality and value

QUALITY could be described as the 'degree of excellence of the product or service' or 'how well the product or service serves its purpose'.

Quality is therefore judged by the customer. The product or service will only be perceived as having quality if it satisfies the customer. To do this the product or service must have two main elements:

- it must be fit for the purpose for which it has been acquired
- it must represent value for money to the customer.

This does not mean that products or services need to be made more expensive by using better materials or more highly skilled staff. Provided that the product or service does what it is meant to do and is viewed as value for money by the customer, then this product or service will have quality.

HOW IT WORKS

Let us consider travelling by aeroplane from London to Zurich. The basic requirements of this service to a customer are:

- the customer reaches his destination safely
- the flight departs and arrives on time.

Provided that these requirements are met, then the service will be fit for its purpose.

The price that the customer will pay for the flight however will depend upon the customer's perspective of value. One customer may choose a low cost 'no frills' flight which includes no food or refreshment and probably less leg-room in the seats. This will represent value to that customer.

Alternatively another customer may choose a first class seat on a scheduled flight as their perception of value is the luxury of the first class lounge, additional space, more comfortable seats and the provision of refreshments.

Both services will have quality if they serve their purpose and are perceived as value for money by the customer.

Enhancement of value

As value is important in judging whether a product or service has quality, then it is important to consider what the customer expects from the product or service.

Many industries are now highly competitive, with many businesses providing the same type of goods or service and competing for customers. In these situations, value can be enhanced by considering what the customer requires and improving the perceived value of the product or service.

HOW IT WORKS

If we consider the banking system, there are many High Street banks and building societies that provide the same basic services of current and deposit accounts, cheque books and debit cards. In order to compete for customers, many of these banks have attempted to enhance the value of the service that they provide, by offering additional services that are thought to enhance the value of the basic service to the customer, with no additional cost to the customer. Therefore many banks now try to compete by offering services such as telephone banking, internet banking and text messaging banking.

Managing for quality

Returning now to the perspective of the producer of goods or the provider of a service, it is obviously essential that the goods or services are fit for their purpose. In order to ensure this quality of the goods or services management needs to embrace the principle of GETTING IT RIGHT FIRST TIME.

This means accepting that the cost of prevention of defective goods should be recognised as less than the cost of correction when faulty goods are sold to customers. We will return to this principle of getting it right first time later in the chapter.

COSTS OF QUALITY

The COSTS OF QUALITY are the costs of ensuring and assuring quality and also any losses incurred when quality is not achieved.

There are generally thought to be four main areas of quality related costs and for computer based assessments these are the terms that you need to be able to define. The four types of quality costs are:

- prevention costs
- appraisal costs
- internal failure costs
- external failure costs

Prevention costs

PREVENTION COSTS are the costs incurred prior to, or during, production in order to investigate, prevent or reduce defects in products or mistakes in services.

These costs might include any of the following:

- improvements in product design or specification to reduce defective products
- improvements in systems designed to reduce mistakes in the provision of services
- design, development and maintenance of quality control equipment
- administration of quality control
- provision of training for quality control

Appraisal costs

APPRAISAL COSTS are the costs incurred in initially ascertaining how the product or service conforms to quality requirements. They are all of the costs associated with assessing the level of quality achieved.

These costs will include:

- design, development and maintenance of inspection equipment
- inspection of goods and raw materials received
- inspection of production processes and work in progress
- inspection or performance testing of finished goods
- appraisal of the quality of services provided
- sample testing of finished production, perhaps to the point of destruction

Internal failure costs

INTERNAL FAILURE COSTS are the costs arising from inadequate quality before the goods or services are sold to the customer. Therefore they are costs arising within the organisation due to the failure to achieve the required level of quality.

Internal failure costs will include:

- investigation and analysis of failed units
- re-work costs
- re-inspection costs
- lost contribution on defective units scrapped or sold at a lower price than normal
- losses due to faults in raw materials purchased

- costs of reviewing product design or specification after finding defective units
- costs of production delays

External failure costs

EXTERNAL FAILURE COSTS are costs arising from inadequate quality discovered after the goods or services have been sold to the customer.

These costs might include:

- costs of running a customer service department
- costs of administering customer complaints
- product liability costs
- costs of replacing or repairing goods returned from customers
- loss of future custom from dissatisfied customers

Task 1

Categorise the following examples in terms of the four different types of quality costs

(a) improvements in product design or specification to reduce defective products   PREVENTION

(b) loss of future custom from dissatisfied customers   EXTERNAL

(c) lost contribution on defective units scrapped or sold at a lower price than normal   INTERNAL

(d) sample testing of finished production   APPRAISAL

HOW IT WORKS

Smithson Ltd is a manufacturer of small electrical items of kitchen equipment such as toasters, food processors, microwave ovens etc.

A number of events that occurred recently are given below.

(a) One line of microwave ovens has had to be recalled due to a few isolated incidents where the oven has caught fire. It is highly likely that the company may have to pay damages to the customers involved in the fires. It is unlikely that any of the owners of the recalled products will buy Smithson goods again.

(b) The company engineers have designed a new motor for one of the food processors which should ensure far fewer breakdowns and a longer life of the machine.

(c)   It has been discovered that the external surface of one of the toasters, which has been made with a new material from a new supplier, gets scratched in the production process and all of these toasters can only be sold at a lower price as seconds.

(d)   The company has introduced more detailed inspection procedures for microwave ovens following the recall incident.

(e)   The company produces a range of different food mixers and it has been discovered that one particular line fails more often than others and the cause is to be investigated and put right.

We will now analyse each of these events and determine what effects they are likely to have on the various categories of quality costs – prevention, appraisal, internal failure and external failure.

(a)   **Recall of microwaves**

Prevention costs – these will increase as the fault must be eliminated which may require redesign of the product

Appraisal costs – these will probably increase as this microwave will require closer monitoring in future to ensure that the problem has been eliminated

Internal failure costs – these will increase due to investigation of the failure, repairs to any ovens in stock which may cause disruption to the production process and re-inspection costs

External failure costs – the costs of repairing the microwaves, any damages claims received from customers and the loss of these customers for future sales

(b)   **Design of new motor**

Prevention costs – these would be the cost of the design and its implementation

Internal failure costs – these should be reduced as the product is more reliable

External failure costs – these should be reduced as the product is more reliable and has a longer lifespan

(c)   **Scratched toasters**

Prevention costs – new design or finding a new supplier

Internal failure costs – the lost contribution from having to sell the toasters at a lower price

(d)   **Inspection procedures for microwaves**

Appraisal costs – these will increase with the costs of inspection procedures

Internal failure costs – these should reduce as the benefits of the inspection are felt

External failure costs – these should reduce as fewer defective products will be sold to customers

(e) **Food mixers**

Prevention costs – these will be incurred in the re-design of the product once the cause has been identified

Internal failure costs – these will increase due to investigation of the problem

External failure costs – these should reduce as fewer defective products are sold to customers

Task 2

A car manufacturer recalls a particular make of car due to the fact that the handbrake fails if the car door is slammed shut.

Complete the table to show what effect will this have on the different categories of quality cost.

Cost of quality	Effect
Prevention costs	INCREASE – MODIFY PRODUCT DESIGN
Appraisal costs	MAY INCREASE IF PRODUCTION MORE CLOSELY MONITORED
Internal costs	INCREASE – REDESIGN, REPAIRS + INSPECTION
External costs	INCREASE – REPAIRS, CLAIMS LOSS OF GOODWILL

Measuring the costs of quality

Now we have been able to analyse the costs of quality into their constituent elements we will need to consider how we can measure these costs.

Normally the cost accounting system of an organisation will have to be adapted in order to be able to find the costs of quality.

For example, in a traditional cost accounting system, normal losses will be allowed for in the production costs. Therefore, the costs of wasted materials, scrapping of defective products and reworking of products with faults are all included in the production cost and are not separately identifiable or highlighted for management attention. Similarly costs of inspections will be included in production overheads without being separately identified.

Therefore if the costs of quality are to be measured, the cost accounting system must be amended in order that the various relevant costs can be separately identified.

Explicit and implicit costs of quality

The costs of quality that can be quantified from the cost accounting records are known as EXPLICIT COSTS. However, there are other types of cost which are not recorded in the accounting records and which can only be estimated – these are known as IMPLICIT COSTS.

Implicit costs might include:

- the opportunity cost of lost sales to existing customers who are dissatisfied due to faulty goods and will not purchase from the organisation again

- loss of goodwill or reputation due to factors such as the widespread recall of one of an organisation's products, affecting potential customers

- costs of production disruption due to reworking of faulty products – these costs will be included in the production costs but cannot be separately identified

- costs incurred due to the practice of holding higher levels of inventory (stock) of raw materials in order to allow faulty materials to be replaced without disruption to production.

HOW IT WORKS

Given below is a summary of the costs of quality identified earlier for Smithson Ltd. Now we will decide which are explicit costs and which are implicit costs.

	Explicit	Implicit
(a) **Recall of microwaves**		
Prevention costs – redesign costs	x	
Appraisal costs – inspection costs	x	
Internal failure costs –		
investigation of the failure	x	
disruption of production process from reworking		x
re-inspection costs	x	
External failure costs –		
cost of repairs to the microwaves	x	
damages claims		x
loss of customers		x

		Explicit	Implicit
(b)	**Design of new motor**		
	Prevention costs –		
	cost of the design/implementation	✘	
	Internal failure costs – reduced due to design		✘
	External failure costs – reduced due to design		✘
(c)	**Scratched toasters**		
	Prevention costs –		
	new design	✘	
	finding a new supplier		✘
	Internal failure costs – lost contribution	✘	
(d)	**Inspection procedures for microwaves**		
	Appraisal costs – costs of inspection procedures	✘	
	Internal failure costs – reduced due to inspections		✘
	External failure costs – reduced as fewer defective products will be sold		✘
(e)	**Food mixers**		
	Prevention costs – re-design of the product	✘	
	Internal failure costs – investigation of the problem	✘	
	External failure costs –		
	reduced as fewer defective products are sold to customers		✘

This analysis of the costs of quality highlights a few areas:

- the explicit costs should all be available from the accounting records

- some of the implicit costs can also be estimated, such as the amount of likely claims for damages from customers of the microwaves

- other implicit costs may not be possible to estimate such as the lost microwave customers or the disruption to the production process from repairs and reworking

- some of the implicit elements are not costs but reductions of quality costs such as the reduction of external quality costs as less defective products are sold – it will not often be possible to put a value to these.

Task 3

Give two examples of explicit quality costs and two examples of implicit quality costs.

Explicit quality costs

    (1)

    (2)

Implicit quality costs

    (1)

    (2)

Calculating the costs of quality

As we have just seen, in practice determining the costs of quality is a complicated business. However in tests the situation will be simplified and you may be required to identify and total the costs of quality.

HOW IT WORKS

Scooby Products estimates that two out of every 1,000 of its products that are sold are defective in some way. When the goods are returned they are replaced free of charge. It is estimated that every customer who buys a faulty product will return it and will not buy Scooby Products' goods again. Each unit costs £30 to manufacture and is sold at a price of £40.

Due to quality inspections it is also estimated that 10,000 defective units a year are discovered before they are sold and these can then be sold as 'seconds' at a price of £25. The quality inspections cost £450,000 each year.

The unit sales of the product are 20 million each year.

We will analyse and calculate the explicit costs of quality:

If unit sales are 20 million and two out of every 1,000 units sold are defective then the number of defective units is $20,000,000/1,000 \times 2 = 40,000$ units.

	£
Appraisal costs – inspection costs	450,000
Internal failure costs – lost contribution on seconds (10,000 units × (£40 – £25))	150,000
External failure costs – cost of replacement products (40,000 × £30)	1,200,000
	1,800,000

There is also the implicit cost of the loss of 40,000 customers each year who will not buy Scooby Products' items again.

Task 4

A manufacturing business estimates that it has to sell 3,000 defective units of its product at a 'seconds' price of £12 per unit. The normal selling price is £25 per unit and the inspection procedure that identifies these defective units costs £20,000.

What is the total cost of quality and what type of quality costs has the business incurred?   3000 × 13 = 39.000
                                                                                        20.000

£ [59.000]

Type of quality costs [APPRAISAL + INTERNAL FAILURE]

PERFORMANCE INDICATORS FOR QUALITY

In just the same way as performance indicators are produced to summarise the production operations for a business so performance indicators can be produced to value the quality of the organisation's products or services. Most of these performance indicators will be measures of customer satisfaction.

If we start by thinking about performance indicators for the quality of physical goods these can be a mixture of financial and non-financial performance indicators.

Financial indicators

Financial indicators to assess customer satisfaction with the products and therefore their quality might include the following:

- cost per customer of the customer service department
- cost per customer of after-sales service
- the percentage of the sales value of returned goods to total sales value
- unit cost of returned goods
- unit cost of repair of returned goods
- cost of reworking defective goods as a percentage of total production cost

Non-financial indicators

- number of goods returned
- percentage of number of goods returned to number of goods sold
- number of warranty claims as a percentage of total units sold
- number of customer complaints as a percentage of total number of sales

Quality control and inspections

At this stage a distinction should be drawn between quality control (prevention - before the event) and quality inspections (detection – after the event). Quality control is about prevention of defective products or mistakes in provision of a service. Quality inspections are to do with detection and identification of defective products or mistakes in provision of a service. Whilst ideally an organisation would plan to have zero defects, the costs of the quality assurance needed to guarantee this may be so high as to be prohibitive and so some defects may be tolerated.

Quality inspections

If a manufacturing business carries out quality inspections, this will often be done by taking a sample of the production and testing this for defective products. Quality inspections normally take place at three points in the production process:

- receiving inspections when raw materials and components are received from suppliers

- production floor or process inspections for work in progress

- final inspection of finished goods

From these inspections, and using the sample results, further performance indicators can be established such as:

- percentage of defective materials compared to total materials
- number of anticipated defective units
- percentage of defective units to total of units produced

Measuring quality of services

Finding performance indicators for quality for manufactured goods is much more straightforward than finding performance indicators for the quality of services.

Measuring the quality of a service again involves measuring customer satisfaction, therefore the first stage is to ensure that the organisation knows what it is that the customer expects from the service.

Some of the performance indicators for quality of a service may be qualitative, such as surveys of customer opinion. A further method of assessing the quality of a service may be by inspection, either by an internal or an external body, such as government inspections of schools.

There can also be quantitative, although normally non-financial, performance indicators for a service, such as average waiting times for hospital operations or the percentage of train journeys that did not run on time.

Task 5

What type of quality performance indicators might a taxi firm consider?

TOTAL QUALITY MANAGEMENT

TOTAL QUALITY MANAGEMENT (TQM) is a quality management system in an organisation that involves all areas of the organisation not just the production element. The philosophy behind quality management must be applied in all the activities of the business – design, production, marketing, administration, purchasing, sales and even the finance function.

TQM can be defined as a continuous improvement in quality, productivity and effectiveness obtained by establishing management responsibility for processes as well as output. In this system every process has an identified process owner and every person in an entity operates within a process and contributes to its improvement (Chartered Institute of Management Accountant's (CIMA) *Official Terminology*).

Principles of TQM

As we have seen, defective products or mistakes in production or provision of a service are costly. These costs include:

- materials wastage
- idle time
- reworking costs
- production disruption costs
- re-inspection costs
- costs of dealing with complaints
- costs of replacing faulty goods
- costs of loss of customer goodwill

The basic principle behind TQM is that of continuous improvement. This can be described as the concept of 'getting it right first time' and 'getting it even more right next time'. By getting it right first time the costs outlined above will be reduced to the point where they should not occur at all. Costs of prevention are less than the costs of correction.

TQM seeks to ensure that the goods produced or the services supplied are of the highest quality.

Training

In order for TQM to work in all areas of an organisation, training and motivation of staff is vital in order for each individual to have the attitude of constantly seeking improvement in what they do. All staff within the organisation must be taught that they have customers. These may be external customers of the business or internal customers in the form of colleagues in the business that use an individual's work. Each individual should endeavour to ensure that they get it right first time and therefore that their excellent work is passed on in the chain.

Quality circles

Another important concept behind TQM is that every employee is involved and anyone with an idea should be allowed to put this forward. This is often done by groups of employees being formed within the organisation known as QUALITY CIRCLES.

These quality circles normally consist of about ten employees with a range of skills, roles and seniority who meet regularly to discuss problems of quality and quality control and to perhaps suggest ways of improving processes and output. This means that there is input from all levels within the organisation and from different disciplines such as marketing, design, engineering, information technology and office administration as well as production.

TARGET COSTING

If the selling price of a product is fixed by market forces, then the product must be made at a cost that is lower than the market selling price, in order for the business to make a profit. The TARGET COST is determined by taking the fixed selling price and deducting the required profit margin. Be careful in tasks to see whether you are given a required profit margin (profit as a percentage of sales price) or a required mark-up (cost as a percentage of sales price) when determining target costs.

Once determined, this target cost is then presented to the product designers for them to achieve. This may be done by the use of value analysis.

Task 6

A car manufacturer wants to calculate a target cost for a new car, the price of which will be set at £27,950. The company requires an 8% profit margin.

The target cost is £ [25,714] $27\,950 \times 8\% = 2236$

$$\begin{array}{r} 27950 \\ \underline{2236} \\ 25714 \end{array}$$

Value analysis

The aim behind VALUE ANALYSIS is to reduce the cost of a product or service without any reduction in the value to the customer. Value analysis is where every aspect of a product or service is analysed to determine whether it does provide value to the customer and whether its function can be achieved in any other way at a lower cost.

Value engineering

Technically, value analysis is applied to products or services already being produced or provided. If this process takes place during the design stage of a product or in the planning stage of a service then it is known as VALUE ENGINEERING.

Specialists in design, engineering, work methods and technology, amongst others, will be involved in this process. When designing a product or planning a service each element of the product or service must be considered to determine whether it does add value to the product or service for the consumer and then to ensure that this is included in the product or service at the lowest possible cost.

Cost reduction

The aim of value analysis is cost reduction; however, care must be taken to ensure that short term cost reduction does not affect long term profitability. For example, costs could be reduced by cutting back on staff training. However, this could lead to inefficiencies, wastage, low morale or high labour turnover.

The aim should be long term cost reduction by improving productivity and the efficiency with which all of the resources of the organisation are used.

Assessment of cost reductions

A variety of methods can be used to assess whether cost reductions are possible including:

- work study
- organisation and method study
- variety reduction

Work study

Work study can be used in manufacturing processes to determine factors such as:

- the most efficient layout of the factory and the stores function
- the most efficient usage of materials, labour and machinery to reduce wastage and idle time
- the most efficient work methods and procedures

Organisation and method study

This is similar to work study but it is used in the administrative functions of the business in order to improve office procedures and determine factors such as:

- maximising the benefits from computerisation
- determining the most efficient office layout, work flows and communications

- elimination of unnecessary or duplicated office procedures
- minimising the amount of paperwork

Variety reduction

The aim of variety reduction is to reduce either the number of products produced, or the number of types of components used, in order to reduce costs.

By reducing the range of products that are produced and concentrating on just a small number of products, this can increase economies of scale of production, but this must be balanced with value to the customer. If consumers require a wide range of choices of a product then such cost cutting will not be of benefit due to lost sales and goodwill.

Often a more effective way of cutting costs is to standardise the components used in the products. If the same basic components are used in many of the products, then cost savings can be made by bulk buying from suppliers and a smaller variety of inventories (stock) being held.

Benefits of value analysis

If value analysis and cost reduction procedures are successfully carried out in an organisation this can have a number of benefits for both the organisation and the customer:

- reduced costs for the organisation and potentially reduced prices for the customer with no loss of value
- continuous improvement in the design and manufacture of products
- improvement of customer service due to the use of standard components
- design of products and services with customer value always considered

Value analysis and value engineering can help an organisation to reduce costs while still maintaining the quality of the product or service that it provides.

PRODUCT LIFE CYCLE

Most products have a limited PRODUCT LIFE CYCLE which will show different sales and profitability patterns at different stages of the life cycle.

The product life cycle is generally thought to split naturally into five separate stages:

- development
- launch (or introduction)
- growth
- maturity
- decline

Development and launch stages

During this period of the product's life there are large outgoings in terms of development expenditure, purchase of non-current (fixed) assets necessary for production, the building up of inventory (stock) levels and advertising and promotion expenses. Costs are incurred but no revenue is generated.

Launch/introduction stage

The product is introduced to the market. It is likely that even after the launch sales will be quite low and the product will be making a loss at this stage. Further amounts will need to be spent on advertising to make potential customers aware of the product.

Growth stage

If the launch of the product is successful then during the growth stage there will be fairly rapid increases in sales and a move to profitability as the costs of the earlier stages are covered. These sales increases however are not likely to continue indefinitely.

Maturity stage

In the maturity stage of the product life cycle, the growth in demand for the product will probably start to slow down and sales volumes will become more constant. It will continue to be profitable. In many cases this is the stage where the product is modified or improved, in order to sustain demand, and this may then result in a small surge in sales.

Decline stage

At some point in a product's life, unless it is a consumable item such as chocolate bars, the product will reach the end of its sale life. The market will have bought enough of the product and it will reach saturation point where sales will decline. This is the point where the business should consider no longer producing the product.

The level of sales and profits earned over a life cycle can be illustrated diagrammatically as follows.

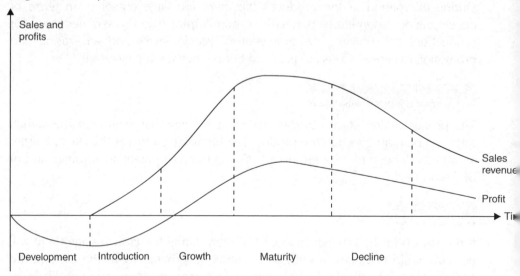

The horizontal axis measures the duration of the life cycle, which can last from, say, 18 months to several hundred years. Children's crazes or fad products have very short lives while some products, such as binoculars (invented in the eighteenth century) can last a very long time.

Market considerations

It is also important to consider the overall market for a particular product. Is the market a new, emerging market for a new product, an established market for a long-standing product or a declining market for a product which is no longer of great interest to consumers?

For example no matter how technologically advanced a VHS video recorder is, DVD players mean that demand for video recorders is in terminal decline.

Life cycle costing

Under traditional costing methods the costs of a product are only recorded and analysed once production of the product has begun. However, a product's life cycle costs are incurred from its design stage through development to market launch, production and sales, and finally to its eventual withdrawal from the market. It is recognised that in reality a large proportion of the costs of a product are incurred before production has started in the early stages of the product life cycle.

Life cycle costing recognises all of these pre-production costs of the product such as:

- design costs
- prototyping

- programming
- process design
- equipment acquisition

Traditional cost accumulation systems are based on the financial accounting year and tend to dissect a product's life cycle into a series of 12-month periods. This means that traditional management accounting systems do not accumulate costs over a product's entire life cycle and do not therefore assess a product's profitability over its entire life. Instead they do it on a periodic basis.

The aim of life cycle costing is to ensure that all the costs of the product are accumulated over the whole of its life cycle in order to ensure that all costs are covered by revenue from the product. It may be necessary to use the discounted cash flow techniques that we considered earlier in this Text (to calculate net present values) when calculating life cycle costs.

Task 7

A manufacturer is developing a new high-technology product which is expected to sell rapidly once launched. However, the product will have a very short life cycle, as competitors develop new innovations and this product becomes obsolete.

The development of the product will require purchase of specialist equipment for £100,000 in December 20X4. This equipment will have scrap value of £20,000 in December 20X8.

Development staff costs of £200,000 will be incurred in 20X5. Assume these costs occur at the end of the year.

In December 20X5, the company will pay a PR agency £30,000 to begin designing and delivering an advertising campaign. Sales of the product are then expected as follows, with profit margin of 40%. Assume sales are received and the costs of production are incurred at the end of each year.

	Sales (£)
20X6	800,000
20X7	2,000,000
20X8	200,000

The company will cease making and selling the product by December 20X8.

(a) Calculate the total life cycle costs and total profit over the life cycle of this product, ignoring the time value of money.

(b) Calculate the net present value of the project at December 20X4, assuming the company's cost of capital is 10% so the discount factors are:

Year	Discount factor @ 10%
0	1.000
1	0.909
2	0.826
3	0.751
4	0.683

(c) Using your answers, advise the company whether it should undertake this project.

CHAPTER OVERVIEW

- Quality of a product or service is what is perceived from the customer's perspective – is the product/service fit for its purpose and value for money?

- An aspect of a product has value if the customer perceives it as being worth paying money for

- Costs of quality are of four types – prevention costs, appraisal costs, internal failure costs and external failure costs

- In order to measure the costs of quality the cost accounting system may have to be modified in order to highlight the relevant figures – figures that can be taken from the accounting records are explicit costs of quality but there may also be other implicit costs of quality which cannot be found from the accounting records

- An organisation can monitor its quality levels and costs of quality by a variety of financial and non-financial performance indicators – for an organisation which provides a service some of the performance indicators will tend to be qualitative rather than quantitative

- Total quality management is an ethos whereby every person in an organisation strives for continuous improvement by trying to get it right first time

- Target costing involves setting a target for the cost of a product or service by deducting the desired profit margin from the market selling price. The target cost represents the maximum amount of cost that the organisation can incur and still make the desired level of profit.

- Value analysis is a method of analysing the constituent elements of a product or service in order to try to reduce the cost with no loss in value to the customer

- Most products have a limited life cycle which involves the stages of development and launch, growth, maturity and decline. The position of the product within its life cycle will affect sales and profitability patterns and be an important factor in cost management

- The aim of life cycle costing is to ensure that all the costs of a product (including development costs) are accumulated over the whole of its life cycle, with or without discounting, in order to ensure that all costs are covered by revenue from the product.

Keywords

Quality – the degree of excellence of a product/service and how well it serves its purpose

Getting it right first time – the basic concept behind total quality management – the costs of prevention are less than the costs of correction

Costs of quality – costs of ensuring quality and any losses incurred when quality is not achieved

Prevention costs – costs incurred to investigate, prevent and reduce defects or mistakes

Appraisal costs – costs associated with assessing the level of quality achieved

Internal failure costs – costs arising within the organisation due to the failure to achieve quality, eg reworking

External failure costs – costs arising from inadequate quality discovered after the goods/services have been sold, eg repairs

Explicit costs – costs that can be found within the accounting records

Implicit costs – costs not recorded in the accounting records

Total quality management – a system of continuous improvement in quality, productivity and effectiveness

Quality circles – groups of employees who meet regularly to discuss quality issues

Target cost – the desired cost of a product which the designers must achieve, based on deducting the desirable profit margin from the market selling price

Value analysis – analysis of every aspect of existing products/services in order to reduce the cost with no reduction in value to the customer

Value engineering – value analysis in the design stage of a product or planning stage of a service

Product life cycle – model to show different sales and profitability patterns at different stages of a product's life

Life cycle costing – accumulation of all costs including pre-production costs

TEST YOUR LEARNING

1   For each of the following, state which type of cost of quality it is (prevention, appraisal, internal failure or external failure):

Type of cost of quality

(a)	products scrapped due to faulty raw materials
(b)	training for quality control staff
(c)	costs of customer after sales service department
(d)	lost contribution on defective products sold as seconds
(e)	costs of inspection of raw materials
(f)	maintenance of quality control equipment
(g)	cost of replacing faulty products returned by customers
(h)	costs of production delays due to re-working defective products discovered in quality inspection
(i)	claims from customers relating to defective products
(j)	performance testing of finished goods

2   A business estimates that one in 3,000 of its products are found to be faulty after sale. Of these it is estimated that 60% are returned by customers and can be repaired at a cost of £20 per product. It is felt that the customers who do not return the products will not buy the company's products again and the cost of advertising for replacement customers is £40,000 per annum.

Total sales of the product are 5,000,000 units each year.

Complete the table to list all of the costs of quality and the amount of that cost where possible. State into which category of cost of quality each cost falls.

Cost of quality	Amount £	Category of cost

3 A manufacturing organisation carries out quality inspections on product A. In the last year 2,000 defective units were discovered and had to be sold as seconds at a price of £45, compared with the normal selling price of £80. The costs of the quality inspections totalled £60,000 for the year.

Sales of product A are 1 million units each year and it is estimated that a further 1 in every 1,000 sales will be defective. Of these it is expected that 75% will be returned by customers and will be replaced at no cost to the customer. The cost of producing a unit of product A is £50. The customers who do not return their products are unlikely to buy the company's products again.

Complete the table to list all of the costs of quality incurred by the business and the amount of each cost if possible. State which type of cost of quality each cost is and whether it is an explicit cost or an implicit cost.

Cost of quality	Amount £	Category of cost	Explicit or implicit

4 A manufacturing business has the following details for the period just ended:

Total sales	£1,500,000
Cost of customer after sales service department	£280,000
Total sales returns (sales value)	£120,000
Costs of repairs of returned products	£40,000
Number of after sales service customers	60,000
Total units sold	50,000 units
Number of units returned	4,000
Number of customer complaints	3,000

Complete the table calculating the performance indicators for quality from the information provided.

Cost per after sales service customer	
Sales returns as a % of sales	
Repair cost per returned units	
Complaints as a % of unit sales	

5 Explain what is meant by Total Quality Management.

6 Explain the stages of a product life cycle including the likely effect of each stage on sales quantity and profitability.

ANSWERS TO CHAPTER TASKS

CHAPTER 1 Costs

1   Fixed cost per unit:

Production level	Budgeted fixed cost per unit £
20,000 units	5.00
40,000 units	2.50
80,000 units	1.25

Working

Production level			Cost £
20,000 units	£100,000/20,000	=	£5.00 per unit
40,000 units	£100,000/40,000	=	£2.50 per unit
80,000 units	£100,000/80,000	=	£1.25 per unit

2   The **relevant range** of a cost is the activity levels over which the cost is fixed.

3

Cost	Behaviour
Stores department costs which include £5,000 of insurance premium and an average of £100 cost per materials receipt or issue	Semi-variable
Machinery depreciation based upon machine hours used	Variable
Salary costs of lecturers in a training college where one lecturer is required for every 200 students enrolled	Stepped
Buildings insurance for a building housing the stores, the factory and the canteen	Fixed
Wages of production workers who are paid per unit produced, with a guaranteed weekly minimum wage of £250	Fixed then semi-variable

4

Sales	Monthly salary £
4 sales	880
8 sales	960
15 sales	1,100

Working

Sales		Monthly salary £
4 sales £800 + (4 × £20)	=	£880
8 sales £800 + (8 × £20)	=	£960
15 sales £800 + (15 × £20)	=	£1,100

5

The variable rate of production costs is

£6 per unit

The fixed amount of production costs is

£23,000

Workings

	Activity level – units	Cost – £
Highest	28,000	191,000
Lowest	20,000	143,000
Increase	8,000	48,000
Variable rate = £48,000/8,000	=	£6 per unit

Fixed amount using highest level:

Variable cost 28,000 units × £6	£168,000
Total cost	£191,000
Fixed cost	£23,000

CHAPTER 2 Methods of costing

1

Costing method	Cost per unit £
Absorption costing	15.00
Marginal costing	10.00

Workings

Cost per unit – absorption costing

	£
Direct materials	12,000
Direct labour	15,000
Variable overheads	23,000
Fixed overheads	25,000
Total cost	75,000

Cost per unit   = £75,000/5,000

                         =   £15 per unit

Cost per unit – marginal costing

	£
Direct materials	12,000
Direct labour	15,000
Variable overheads	23,000
Total cost	50,000

Cost per unit   =   £50,000/5,000

                         =   £10 per unit

2

	£
Absorption cost profit	504,000
Change in inventory:	
Decrease in inventory 2,500 – 1,500 = 1,000 units × fixed cost per unit £2	2,000
Marginal cost profit	506,000

3

(a) The overhead absorption rate based on direct labour hours is £0.90 per direct labour hour.

(b) The **over**-absorption of £**2,500** should be **added to** profit.

Workings

(a) Overhead absorption rate $= \dfrac{£54,000}{60,000h}$ (budgeted direct labour hours)

$= £0.90$ per direct labour hour

(b)

	£
Actual overheads	47,000
Absorbed overheads (55,000h × £0.90 per h)	49,500
Over-absorption	2,500

The amount over-absorbed will be an addition to profit.

4

(a)

Overhead included in Product A	£5,000
Overhead included in Product B	£26,000

Workings

Cost per inspection	=	£74,000/370
	=	£200 per inspection
Overhead included in A's cost	=	£200 × 25
	=	£5,000
Overhead included in B's cost	=	£200 × 130
	=	£26,000

(b)

Product A overhead cost per unit	£0.50
Product B overhead cost per unit	£2.00

Product A   £5,000/10,000 units = £0.50

Product B   £26,000/13,000 units = £2.00

CHAPTER 3 Decision making

1 Break-even point $= \dfrac{£360,000}{£28 - £19}$

$= 40,000$ units

2 Target profit output $= \dfrac{£250,000 + £150,000}{£80 - £60}$

$= 20,000$ units

3 Break-even point $= \dfrac{£480,000}{£32 - £24}$

$= 60,000$ units

Margin of safety $= \dfrac{£75,000 - 60,000}{75,000} \times 100$

$= 20\%$

4 Profit volume ratio $= \dfrac{£36 - £27}{£36} \times 100$

$= 25\%$

Break-even point $= \dfrac{£360,000}{0.25}$

$= £1,440,000$

5

(a)

Product	Units produced
R	1,000
S	4,000
P	2,000
Q	3,750

Workings

	P	Q	R	S
Contribution per kg	£4.00	£3.75	£9.00	£7.00
Ranking	3	4	1	2

Production plan

	Units produced	Kgs used
R	1,000	1,000
S	4,000	8,000
P	2,000	6,000
Q (balance = 15000/4)	3,750	15,000
		30,000

(b) The profit earned from this production plan will be £115,250

Working

Profit £

P (2,000 × £12)	24,000
Q (3,750 × £15)	56,250
R (1,000 × £9)	9,000
S (4,000 × £14)	56,000
Contribution	145,250
Less: fixed costs	30,000
Profit	115,250

6   A

	A	B	C
	£	£	£
Direct materials	1.60	2.00	0.80
Direct labour	3.20	3.60	1.60
Direct overheads	0.80	1.20	0.40
Variable cost of production	5.60	6.80	2.80
External price	5.50	8.40	4.00

On the basis of costs alone only product A should be purchased externally as it is cheaper to buy than to make.

7

Year	0	1	2	3	4
Cash flow	-400,000	-45,000	-45,000	-45,000	105,000
Discount factor	1.000	0.952	0.907	0.864	0.823
Present value	-400,000	-42,840	-40,815	-38,880	86,415
Net present cost	-436,120				

CHAPTER 4 Statistical methods

1 A cyclical variation in a time series is due to the long term fluctuations of the economy as a whole. A seasonal variation is a regular variation in the results due to the nature of the business, and will repeat itself within a short-term period, eg a week, quarter, year.

2

Month	Actual	Three month moving average
	£	£
March	226,500	
April	251,600	238,767
May	238,200	245,800
June	247,600	242,100
July	240,500	250,300
August	262,800	

3

	Actual	Four year moving average	Centred moving average = trend
	£	£	£
20X1	226,700		
20X2	236,500		
		236,500	
20X3	240,300		238,175
		239,850	
20X4	242,500		240,988
		242,125	
20X5	240,100		243,038
		243,950	
20X6	245,600		244,663
		245,375	
20X7	247,600		
20X8	248,200		

4

Month	Cost £
January	228,800
February	217,830
March	205,700

Workings

January	£205,600 + 23,200	=	£228,800
February	£208,600 + 9,230	=	£217,830
March	£209,200 – 3,500	=	£205,700

5

		Profit £	Index
20X7	Quarter 1	86,700	100.0
	Quarter 2	88,200	101.7
	Quarter 3	93,400	107.7
	Quarter 4	90,500	104.4
20X8	Quarter 1	83,200	96.0
	Quarter 2	81,400	93.9
	Quarter 3	83,200	96.0
	Quarter 4	85,000	98.0

Workings

20X7	Quarter 1	86,700	100.0
	Quarter 2	88,200/86,700 × 100	101.7
	Quarter 3	93,400/86,700 × 100	107.7
	Quarter 4	90,500/86,700 × 100	104.4
20X8	Quarter 1	83,200/86,700 × 100	96.0
	Quarter 2	81,400/86,700 × 100	93.9
	Quarter 3	83,200/86,700 × 100	96.0
	Quarter 4	85,000/86,700 × 100	98.0

6

		Costs	RPI	Restated costs
		£		£
20X7	June	133,100	171.1	133,100
	July	133,800	170.5	134,271
	Aug	133,600	170.8	133,835
	Sept	134,600	171.7	134,130
	Oct	135,800	171.6	135,404
	Nov	135,100	172.1	134,315
	Dec	135,600	172.1	134,812
20X8	Jan	134,700	171.1	134,700
	Feb	135,900	172.0	135,189
	Mar	136,200	172.2	135,330
	April	136,500	173.1	134,923
	May	136,700	174.2	134,267

Workings

		£	£
20X7	June	133,100 × 171.1/171.1	133,100
	July	133,800 × 171.1/170.5	134,271
	Aug	133,600 × 171.1/170.8	133,835
	Sept	134,600 × 171.1/171.7	134,130
	Oct	135,800 × 171.1/171.6	135,404
	Nov	135,100 × 171.1/172.1	134,315
	Dec	135,600 × 171.1/172.1	134,812
20X8	Jan	134,700 × 171.1/171.1	134,700
	Feb	135,900 × 171.1/172.0	135,189
	Mar	136,200 × 171.1/172.2	135,330
	Apr	136,500 × 171.1/173.1	134,923
	May	136,700 × 171.1/174.2	134,267

7

		Costs	RPI	Restated costs
		£		£
20X7	June	133,100	171.1	135,512
	July	133,800	170.5	136,704
	Aug	133,600	170.8	136,259
	Sept	134,600	171.7	136,560
	Oct	135,800	171.6	137,858
	Nov	135,100	172.1	136,749
	Dec	135,600	172.1	137,255
20X8	Jan	134,700	171.1	137,141
	Feb	135,900	172.0	137,638
	Mar	136,200	172.2	137,782
	April	136,500	173.1	137,367
	May	136,700	174.2	136,700

Workings

Adjusted figures

		£	£
20X7	June	133,100 × 174.2/171.1	135,512
	July	133,800 × 174.2/170.5	136,704
	Aug	133,600 × 174.2/170.8	136,259
	Sept	134,600 × 174.2/171.7	136,560
	Oct	135,800 × 174.2/171.6	137,858
	Nov	135,100 × 174.2/172.1	136,749
	Dec	135,600 × 174.2/172.1	137,255
20X8	Jan	134,700 × 174.2/171.1	137,141
	Feb	135,900 × 174.2/172.0	137,638
	Mar	136,200 × 174.2/172.2	137,782
	Apr	136,500 × 174.2/173.1	137,367
	May	136,700 × 174.2/174.2	136,700

8 It is generally assumed that the level of sales will depend on the advertising undertaken, so:

- Dependent variable – sales volume
- Independent variable – advertising costs

9 Production costs   = $63,000 + (3.2 \times 44,000)$
              = £203,800

10 $y = 4.8 + 1.2 x$

The first two years account for $x = 1$ to $x = 24$

Thus the x values in which we are interested are $x = 25, 26, 27$

Month 1 $x = 25 : y = 4.8 + 1.2(25)$ $= 34.8$ ie £34,800

Month 2 $x = 26 : y = 4.8 + 1.2(26)$ $= 36.0$ ie £36,000

Month 3 $x = 27 : y = 4.8 + 1.2(27)$ $= 37.2$ ie £37,200

CHAPTER 5 Standard costing

1 If ideal standards are used to calculate variances, then the result will be adverse variances. This will tend to mean that these adverse variances become the norm and are accepted without questioning. Ideal standards will also tend to demotivate managers and employees, as they cannot hope to meet the standards.

2 (a) Total materials cost variance   £

         Standard cost for actual production

             $24,000 \times 12 \times £20.50$ 5,904,000

         Actual cost   6,240,000

                                             336,000 Adv

     (b) Materials price variance

         Actual quantity at standard price

             $312,000 \times £20.50$ 6,396,000

         Actual quantity and actual price   6,240,000

                                             156,000 Fav

     (c) Materials usage variance

         Standard quantity for actual production at standard price

             $24,000 \times 12 \times £20.50$ 5,904,000

         Actual quantity at standard price

             $312,000 \times £20.50$ 6,396,000

                                             492,000 Adv

3

(a)   Materials price variance £5,000 favourable

(b)   Materials usage variance £2,000 adverse

Workings

(a)

Actual quantity purchased at standard price	80,000
8,000kg × £10.00	
Actual quantity purchased at actual price	75,000
Materials price variance	5,000 Fav

(b)

	£
Standard quantity for actual production at standard price	75,000
1,500 × 5 kg × £10.00	
Actual quantity used for actual production at standard price	77,000
7,700 kg × £10.00	
Materials usage variance	2,000 Adv

4   (a)   Total direct labour cost variance

	£
Standard cost for actual production	
12,000 × 4 × £6.50	312,000
Actual cost	306,000
	6,000 Fav

(b)   Labour rate variance

Actual hours at standard rate	
45,000 × £6.50	292,500
Actual hours at actual rate	306,000
	13,500 Adv

(c)   Labour efficiency variance

Standard hours for actual production at standard rate	
12,000 × 4 × £6.50	312,000
Actual hours for actual production at standard rate	
45,000 × £6.50	292,500
	19,500 Fav

5   (a)   Budgeted fixed overhead   =   2,400 units × 2 hours × £5.00

                                               =   £24,000

     (b)   Total fixed overhead variance

	£
Fixed overhead incurred	26,000
Fixed overhead absorbed	
2,500 × 2 × £5.00	25,000
	1,000 Adv

     (c)   Fixed overhead expenditure variance

Budgeted fixed overhead	24,000
Actual fixed overhead	26,000
	2,000 Adv

     (d)   Fixed overhead volume variance

Actual production at standard absorption rate	
2,500 × 2 × £5.00	25,000
Budgeted production at standard absorption rate	
2,400 × 2 × £5.00	24,000
	1,000 Fav

6   (a)   Budgeted direct labour hours   =   2,400 × 2

                                               =   4,800 hours

     (b)   Fixed overhead efficiency variance

	£
Standard hours for actual production at standard absorption rate	
2,500 × 2 × £5.00	25,000
Actual hours for actual production at standard absorption rate	
5,500 × £5.00	27,500
	2,500 Adv

     (c)   Fixed overhead capacity variance

Actual hours at standard absorption rate	
5,500 × £5.00	27,500
Budgeted hours at standard absorption rate	
4,800 × £5.00	24,000
	3,500 Fav

7   If the starting point for the reconciliation is the standard cost of the actual production and there is a favourable variance this means that the actual cost was less than the standard cost and therefore the favourable variance is deducted.

8   D

CHAPTER 6 Standard costing – further aspects

1   D

2   The favourable labour rate variance could be due to the manager responsible for hiring labour taking on a lower grade of worker, hence the lower rate of pay per hour.

The less skilled workers may have taken longer to do the job and been more inefficient in their usage of material, causing the adverse labour efficiency and materials usage variances.

An independent investigation would need to be carried out into the grade of labour hired and the normal hourly rate for such labour. Other independent factors that may have caused material wastage (e.g. poor quality material) or labour inefficiency (machine breakdowns) should also be investigated.

Note: since this is the first period for the new contract it is possible that the manager responsible for hiring workers has provided valid information and that the other variances are caused by the fact that the standards set were inaccurate or that there was some learning process involved

3   (a)   The total materials price variance was £3,080 adverse

(b)   The planning variance due to the price increase was £3,680 adverse

The control variance due to other factors was £600 favourable

Workings

Total materials price variance	£
Standard price of actual quantity	
4,600 kg × £8.20	37,720
Actual quantity and actual price	40,800
	3,080 Adv
Planning variance due to the price increase	
Standard price of actual quantity	
4,600 kg × £8.20	37,720
Adjusted price for actual quantity	
4,600 kg × £9.00	41,400
	3,680 Adv

Control variance due to other causes	£
Adjusted price for actual quantity	
4,600 kg × £9.00	41,400
Actual quantity at actual price	40,800
	600 Fav

4 (a)　The total materials price variance was £7,700 adverse

　　(b)　The planning variance due to the seasonal price change was £9,270 adverse

　　　　The control variance due to other factors was £1,570 favourable

Workings

Total materials price variance	£
Standard price of actual quantity	
10,300 kg × £6.00	61,800
Actual quantity at actual price	69,500
	7,700 Adv

Planning variance due to seasonal price	
Standard price of actual quantity	
10,300 kg × £6.00	61,800
Adjusted price for actual quantity	
10,300 kg × (£6.00 + £0.90)	71,070
	9,270 Adv

Control variance due to other factors	
Adjusted price for actual quantity	
10,300 kg × (£6.00 + £0.90)	71,070
Actual quantity at actual price	69,500
	1,570 Fav

5 (a)　The total labour efficiency variance was £37,200 adverse

　　(b)　The planning variance due to early production problems was £65,100 adverse

　　　　The control variance due to other causes was £27,900 favourable

Workings

Total labour efficiency variance   £

Standard hours for actual quantity at standard rate

12,000 × 3.5 × £6.20	260,400

Actual hours at standard rate

48,000 × £6.20	297,600
	37,200 Adv

Planning variance due to early production problems

Standard hours for actual quantity at standard rate

12,000 × 3.5 × £6.20	260,400

Adjusted hours for actual quantity at standard rate

12,000 × (3.5 × 1.25) × £6.20	325,500
	65,100 Adv

Control variance due to other causes   £

Adjusted hours for actual quantity at standard rate

12,000 × (3.5 × 1.25) × £6.20	325,500

Actual hours at standard rate

48,000 × £6.20	297,600
	27,900 Fav

6   (a)   The total labour rate variance was £2,500 adverse

(b)   The planning variance due to the labour rate increase was £13,125 adverse

The control variance due to other causes was £10,625 favourable

Total labour rate variance   £

Standard rate for actual hours

21,000 × £7.50	157,500

Actual hours at actual rate

	160,000
	2,500 Adv

Planning variance due to rate increase

Standard rate for actual hours

21,000 × £7.50	157,500

Adjusted price for actual hours

21,000 × (£7.50 × 130/120)	170,625
	13,125 Adv

Control variance due to other causes

Adjusted price for actual hours

21,000 × (£7.50 × 130/120)	170,625
Actual hours at actual rate	160,000
	10,625 Fav

CHAPTER 7 Performance indicators

1   Current quarter   Previous quarter

Productivity

216/26   8.3 per executive

188/22   8.5 per executive

2   Activity ratio $= \dfrac{\text{Standard hours for actual production}}{\text{Budgeted hours}} \times 100$

$$= \dfrac{268,000 \times 3}{288,000 \times 3} \times 100$$

$$= \quad 93.1\%$$

3   Possible effectiveness measures might include:

     (i)   Booking system:

            % of patients offered an appointment within a week

            % of appointments cancelled

     (ii)   Service:

            % of patients seen on time

            Average waiting times

            % of patients requiring a second visit (measures effectiveness of treatment)

4   Gross profit margin $= \dfrac{£58,700}{£133,400} \times 100$

$$= \quad 44.0\%$$

Operating profit = Profit before interest and tax

$$= 22,500 + 2,500 + 4,750$$

$$= 29,750$$

Operating profit margin $= \dfrac{£29,750}{£133,400} \times 100$

$$= 22.3\%$$

Net profit margin $= \dfrac{£22,500}{£133,400} \times 100$

$= 16.9\%$

5 $\text{ROCE} = \dfrac{£365,800}{£1,700,000 + £600,000} \times 100 \qquad = 15.9\% \qquad \text{(Method 1)}$

or

$\text{ROCE} = \dfrac{£365,800 - 12\% \times (£600,000)}{£1,700,000} \times 100 = 17.3\% \qquad \text{(Method 2)}$

6 Asset turnover, 1.2 $= \dfrac{\text{Revenue}}{£350,000}$

Revenue $= 1.2 \times £350,000$

$= £420,000$

7 Average inventory $= \dfrac{£13,500 + £17,000}{2}$

$= £15,250$

Cost of sales $= £13,500 + 99,000 - 17,000$

$= £95,500$

Inventory days $= \dfrac{£15,250}{£95,500} \times 365$

$= 58$ days

8 Possible reasons for a decrease in gross profit margin include:

- decrease in selling price
- increase in purchases or production costs
- large write off of inventories

CHAPTER 8 Cost management

1

(a) Improvements in product design or specification to reduce defective products = prevention cost

(b) Loss of future custom from dissatisfied customers = external failure cost

(c) Lost contribution on defective units scrapped or sold at a lower price than normal = internal failure cost

(d) Sample testing of finished production = appraisal cost

2

Cost of quality	Effect
Prevention costs	Increase as product design must be modified to eliminate the problem in future
Appraisal costs	There may be none, although could increase if this product line has to be more closely monitored in future
Internal costs	Increase due to investigation of problem, review of product design, repairs and re-inspection
External costs	Increase due to cost of repairs, any claims relating to the failure and loss of customer goodwill

3   Explicit quality costs

- costs of quality inspections
- costs of repairs to faulty products returned
- costs of replacing faulty products
- costs of design review to ensure quality

Implicit quality costs –

- loss of customer goodwill
- disruption of production process due to repairs/reworking
- potential claims from customers

(Note: Only two examples of each were required)

4

	£
Inspection costs – Appraisal cost	20,000
Lost contribution on seconds – Internal failure cost	
3,000 units × (£25 – £12)	39,000
Total quality cost	59,000

5   Quality performance indicators for a taxi firm:

- percentage of taxis arriving on time compared to total taxi journeys
- percentage of repeat customers compared to total customers
- survey results of customer satisfaction
- number of customer complaints

6 The target cost is £25,714

Working

Profit required = 8% × £27,950 = £2,236

Target cost = £ 27,950 - £2,236 = £25,714

7 (a) The profit over the life cycle of the product is £890,000.

Workings

	£
Sales (800,000 + 2,000,000 + 200,000)	3,000,000
Cost of sales (balancing figure)	(1,800,000)
Profit = 40% x sales =	1,200,000
Loss on specialist equipment (100,000 – 20,000)	(80,000)
Development staff costs	(200,000)
PR agency costs	(30,000)
Profit	890,000

(b) The net present value of the project is £624,350

Workings

Time (end of year)	Cash inflows/(outflows)	Discount factor @ 10%	PV
0 (20X4)	(100,000)	1.000	(100,000)
1 (20X5)	(200,000 + 30,000) = (230,000)	0.909	(209,070)
2 (20X6)	800,000 x 40% = 320,000	0.826	264,320
3 (20X7)	2,000,000 x 40% = 800,000	0.751	600,800
4 (20X8)	20,000 + 200,000 x 40% = 100,000	0.683	68,300
Total net present value			624,350

(c) A profit is generated over the product's life cycle, and the net present value of the project is also positive, and so this project should be undertaken.

TEST YOUR LEARNING
– ANSWERS

CHAPTER 1 Costs

1

True | ✓ |

| 10,000 units | Cost per unit £43,600/10,000 | = | £4.36 |
| 12,000 units | Cost per unit £52,320/12,000 | = | £4.36 |

As the cost per unit is the same at each level of production this would appear to be a purely variable cost.

2

Activity level	Total fixed cost £	Fixed cost per unit £
3,000 units	64,000	21.33
10,000 units	64,000	6.40
16,000 units	64,000	4.00

Working

3,000 units	£64,000/3,000 = £21.33
10,000 units	£64,000/10,000 = £6.40
16,000 units	£64,000/16,000 = £4.00

3   The marginal cost per month is

| £52,500 |

The full production cost per month is

| £70,000 |

Workings

	Production cost £
Direct material costs (£5 × 3,500)	17,500
Direct labour costs (£10 × 3,500)	35,000
Marginal cost	52,500
Rent	10,000
Supervisor cost	7,500
Full production cost	70,000

4 (a) The variable element of the production cost is

£3 per unit

The fixed element of the production cost is

£169,000

(b)

Level of production	Production cost £
120,000 units	529,000
150,000 units	619,000

Workings

(a)

		£
Highest level	126,000	547,000
Lowest level	101,000	472,000
Increase	25,000	75,000

$$\text{Variable rate} = \frac{£75,000}{25,000} = £3 \text{ per unit}$$

Using highest level:

	£
Variable cost 126,000 × £3	378,000
Fixed costs (balancing figure)	169,000
Total cost	547,000

(b)	(i)	120,000 units	£
		Variable cost 120,000 × £3	360,000
		Fixed cost	169,000
		Total forecast cost	529,000

	(ii)	150,000 units	£
		Variable cost 150,000 × £3	450,000
		Fixed cost	169,000
		Total forecast cost	619,000

(c) The estimate of costs for 120,000 units is likely to be more accurate than that for 150,000 units. This is due to the fact that 120,000 is within the range of activity levels used to calculate the variable costs and fixed costs (interpolation) whereas 150,000 units is outside that range (extrapolation). We cannot be sure that the costs will still behave in the same manner at an activity level of 150,000 units.

CHAPTER 2 Methods of costing

1 (a) B

(b) C

Workings

$$\text{Department P1} = \frac{£50,000}{2,500 \text{ h}}$$

$$= £20 \text{ per direct labour hour}$$

$$\text{Department P2} = \frac{£60,000}{4,000 \text{ h}}$$

$$= £15 \text{ per machine hour}$$

2

	Amount of under-/over- absorption £	Under- or over- absorption	Add or subtract in income statement
An overhead absorption rate of £3 per unit, based on expected production levels of 500 units. Actual overheads turn out to be £1,600, and actual production is 650 units.	350.00	Over-	Add
The budget is set at 1,000 units, with £9,000 overheads recovered on the basis of 600 direct labour hours. At the end of the period, overheads amounted to £8,600, production achieved was only 950 units and 590 direct labour hours had been worked.	250.00	Over-	Add

Workings

(a)

	£
Actual overheads	1,600
Absorbed overheads (650 units @ £3 per unit)	1,950
Over-absorption	350

The over-absorption of £350 would be added to profit in the income statement.

(b)

	£
Actual overheads	8,600
Absorbed overheads (590h × £15* per h)	8,850
Over-absorption	250

$$* \text{ Overhead absorption rate} = \frac{£9,000}{600 \text{ direct labour hours}} = £15 \text{ per direct labour hour}$$

The over-absorption of £250 would be added to profit in the income statement.

3 (a)

Department	Overhead absorption rate
X	£2.60 per machine hour
Y	£3.17 per direct labour hour

Workings

$$X = \frac{£260,000}{100,000}$$

= £2.60 per machine hour

as X is a highly mechanised department most of the overhead will relate to the machinery therefore machine hours have been used to absorb the overhead.

$$Y = \frac{£380,000}{120,000}$$

= £3.17 per direct labour hour

as Y is a highly labour intensive department most of the overhead will relate to the hours that are worked by the labour force therefore labour hours are used to absorb the overhead.

(b)   The overhead to be included in the cost of product A is £25.68

Working

Product A – department X overhead	£2.60 × 5	= £13.00
Product A – department Y overhead	£3.17 × 4	= £12.68
		£25.68

4 In an absorption costing system all fixed production overheads are absorbed into the cost of the products and are included in unit cost. In a marginal costing system the fixed production overheads are written off in the income statement (profit and loss account) as a period cost.

5

Method of costing	Budgeted cost £
Absorption costing	59.70
Marginal costing	57.11

Workings

Absorption costing – unit cost

	£
Direct materials	12.50
Direct labour assembly (4 × £8.40)	33.60
Finishing (1 × £6.60)	6.60
Assembly overheads (£336,000/60,000)	5.60
Finishing overheads (£84,000/60,000)	1.40
	59.70

Marginal costing – unit cost

		£
Direct materials		12.50
Direct labour assembly (4 × £8.40)		33.60
Finishing (1 × £6.60)		6.60
Assembly overheads	$\dfrac{£336,000 \times 60\%}{60,000}$	3.36
Finishing overheads	$\dfrac{£84,000 \times 75\%}{60,000}$	1.05
		57.11

6 Unit cost

	£
Direct materials	12.00
Direct labour	8.00
Variable overhead (£237,000/15,000)	15.80
Marginal costing unit cost	35.80
Fixed overhead (£390,000/15,000)	26.00
Absorption costing unit cost	61.80

(a)   (i)   **Absorption costing – income statement**

	November		December	
	£	£	£	£
Sales		937,500		1,350,000
(12,500/18,000 × £75)				
Less: cost of sales				
Opening inventory				
(2,000 × £61.80)	123,600			
(4,500 × £61.80)			278,100	
Production costs				
(15,000 × £61.80)	927,000		927,000	
	1,050,600		1,205,100	
Less: closing inventory				
(4,500 × £61.80)	278,100			
(1,500 × £61.80)			92,700	
		772,500		1,112,400
Profit		165,000		237,600

(ii) **Marginal costing – income statement**

	November £	£	December £	£
Sales		937,500		1,350,000
(12,500/18,000 × £75)				
Less: cost of sales				
Opening inventory				
(2,000 × £35.80)	71,600			
(4,500 × £35.80)			161,100	
Production costs				
(15,000 × £35.80)	537,000		537,000	
	608,600		698,100	
Less: closing inventory				
(4,500 × £35.80)	161,100			
(1,500 × £35.80)			53,700	
		447,500		644,400
Contribution		490,000		705,600
Less: fixed overheads		390,000		390,000
Profit		100,000		315,600

(b)

	November £	December £
Absorption costing profit	165,000	237,600
Inventory changes	(65,000)	78,000
Marginal costing profit	100,000	315,600

Working

	November £	December £
Increase in inventory × fixed cost per unit		
((4,500 − 2,000) × £26)	(65,000)	
Decrease in inventory × fixed cost per unit		
((4,500 − 1,500) × £26)		78,000

7

Product	Budgeted cost per unit £	Budgeted overhead per unit £
LM	9.78	3.68
NP	27.41	20.81

Workings

Stores cost $= \dfrac{£140,000}{320}$

$= £437.50$ per materials requisition

Production set-up costs $= \dfrac{£280,000}{280}$

$= £1,000$ per set-up

Quality control costs $= \dfrac{£180,000}{90}$

$= £2,000$ per inspection

Product costs

		LM £	NP £
Direct materials	50,000 × £2.60	130,000	
	20,000 × £3.90		78,000
Direct labour	50,000 × £3.50	175,000	
	20,000 × £2.70		54,000
Stores costs	100 × £437.50	43,750	
	220 × £437.50		96,250
Production set-up costs	80 × £1,000	80,000	
	200 × £1,000		200,000
Quality control costs	30 × £2,000	60,000	
	60 × £2,000		120,000
Total cost		488,750	548,250

		LM	NP
Cost per unit		$\dfrac{488,750}{50,000}$	$\dfrac{548,250}{20,000}$
		= £9.78	= £27.41

Analysis of total unit cost

		LM	NP
Direct costs	(2.60 + 3.50)	6.10	
	(3.90 + 2.70)		6.60
Overheads	$\dfrac{(43,750+80,000+60,000)}{50,000}$	3.68	
	$\dfrac{(96,250+200,000+120,000)}{20,000}$		20.81
		9.78	27.41

CHAPTER 3 Decision making

1   As activity levels increase, the total fixed costs will be split amongst more units, and the amount of fixed costs absorbed into the cost of a unit will get smaller. With no change in selling cost or variable cost, the total unit cost will decrease.

2   The break-even point is **30,000** units

The margin of safety is **21%**

Workings

$$\text{Break-even point} \quad = \quad \frac{£360,000}{£57 - £45}$$

$$= \quad 30,000 \text{ units}$$

$$\text{Margin of safety} \quad = \quad \frac{38,000 - 30,000}{38,000}$$

$$= \quad 21\%$$

3   D

$$\text{Target profit sales} \quad = \quad \frac{£910,000 + £500,000}{£24 - £17}$$

$$= \quad 201,429 \text{ units}$$

4   The sales revenue required in order to make a profit of £200,000 is **£1,500,000**

Workings

$$\text{Profit volume ratio} \quad = \quad \frac{£(40 - 32)}{£40} \times 100$$

$$= \quad 20\%$$

$$\text{Target profit sales revenue} \quad = \quad \frac{£100,000 + £200,000}{0.20}$$

$$= \quad £1,500,000$$

Alternatively: Units required to make £200,000 profit = £300,000/8 = 37,500 units

Total revenue required = 37,500 x £40 = £1,500,000

5 (a) The limiting factor of production resources is materials/labour hours/**machine hours**.

Working

Resource requirements for maximum demand

	R	S	T	Total
Materials	80,000 kg	120,000 kg	25,000 kg	225,000 kg
Labour hours	20,000 hours	80,000 hours	5,000 hours	105,000 hours
Machine hours	60,000 hours	80,000 hours	15,000 hours	155,000 hours

Therefore the machine hours available are the limiting factor.

(b)

Product	Units produced
S	20,000
T	5,000
R	4,166

Workings

Contribution per machine hour

	R	S	T
Contribution	£6	£12	£6
Machine hours	6	4	3
Contribution/machine hour	£1.00	£3.00	£2.00
Ranking	3	1	2

Production plan

Product	Units produced	Machine hours used
S	20,000	80,000
T	5,000	15,000
R (balance 25,000 / 6 = 4,166.67 = 4,166 complete units))	4,166	24,996
		119,996

(c) The profit that will be earned under this production plan is £244,996

Workings

Product contribution:	£
R (4,166 × £6)	24,996
S (20,000 × £12)	240,000
T (5,000 × £6)	30,000
Total contribution	294,996
Less: fixed costs	(50,000)
Profit	244,996

6 D

	X	Y
	£	£
Direct materials	2.50	3.00
Direct labour	8.00	6.00
Variable cost of production	10.50	9.00
External price	11.00	10.00

On the basis of costs alone neither products should be purchased externally as they are cheaper to make.

7

Year	Cash flows £	Discount factor at 7%	Present value £
0	(340,000)	1.000	(340,000)
1	80,000	0.935	74,800
2	70,000	0.873	61,110
3	90,000	0.816	73,440
4	120,000	0.763	91,560
5	60,000	0.713	42,780
Net present value			**3,690**

Remember that depreciation is not a cash flow and is therefore excluded from the net present value calculations.

8

(a)

Year	Cash flows £	Discount factor at 11%	Present value £
0	(90,000)	1.000	(90,000)
1	23,000	0.901	20,723
2	31,000	0.812	25,172
3	40,000	0.731	29,240
4	18,000	0.659	11,862
Net present value			(3,003)

(b) As the investment in the new plant and machinery has a negative net present value at the cost of capital of 11%, then the investment should not take place.

CHAPTER 4 Statistical methods

1

	Actual £	Three month moving average £
July	397,500	
August	403,800	400,300
September	399,600	402,900
October	405,300	403,667
November	406,100	406,633
December	408,500	407,500
January	407,900	408,933
February	410,400	411,433
March	416,000	413,167
April	413,100	415,533
May	417,500	417,467
June	421,800	

2

		Actual	Four quarter moving average	Centred moving average = TREND	Seasonal variations
		£	£	£	£
20X5	Quarter 1	383,600			
	Quarter 2	387,600			
			365,400		
	Quarter 3	361,800		365,688	-3,888
			365,975		
	Quarter 4	328,600		366,575	-37,975
			367,175		
20X6	Quarter 1	385,900		366,013	+19,887
			364,850		
	Quarter 2	392,400		366,125	+26,275
			367,400		
	Quarter 3	352,500		368,225	-15,725
			369,050		
	Quarter 4	338,800		371,288	-32,488
			373,525		
20X7	Quarter 1	392,500		375,575	+16,925
			377,625		
	Quarter 2	410,300		378,325	+31,975
			379,025		
	Quarter 3	368,900		379,750	-10,850
			380,475		
	Quarter 4	344,400		382,388	-37,988
			384,300		
20X8	Quarter 1	398,300			
	Quarter 2	425,600			

Working

Seasonal variations:

	Quarter 1	Quarter 2	Quarter 3	Quarter 4
	£	£	£	£
20X5	–	–	–3,888	–37,975
20X6	+19,887	+26,275	–15,725	–32,488
20X7	+16,925	+31,975	–10,850	–37,988
	+36,812	+58,250	–30,463	–108,451
Average	+ 18,406	+ 29,125	–10,154	–36,150

Total of seasonal variations 18,406 + 29,125 – 10,154 – 36,152 = 1,227

Adjustment required = 1,227/4

= 307

	Quarter 1	Quarter 2	Quarter 3	Quarter 4
	£	£	£	£
Unadjusted	+18,406	+29,125	–10,154	–36,150
Adjustment	–307	–307	–306	–307
Seasonal variation	+18,099	+28,818	–10,460	–36,457

3

	Cost	Index
	£	
January	59,700	100.0
February	62,300	104.4
March	56,900	95.3
April	60,400	101.2
May	62,400	104.5
June	66,700	111.7

Workings

January	59,700/59,700 = 100.0
February	62,300/59,700 = 104.4
March	56,900/59,700 = 95.3
April	60,400/59,700 = 101.2
May	62,400/59,700 = 104.5
June	66,700/59,700 = 111.7

4 (a)

	Wages cost	RPI	Adjusted cost
	£		£
January	126,700	171.1	126,848
February	129,700	172.0	129,172
March	130,400	172.2	129,718
April	131,600	173.0	130,307
May	130,500	172.1	129,893
June	131,600	171.3	131,600

Workings

(a)

	Wages cost	Adjusted cost
	£	£
January	126,700 × 171.3/171.1	126,848
February	129,700 × 171.3/172.0	129,172
March	130,400 × 171.3/172.2	129,718
April	131,600 × 171.3/173.0	130,307
May	130,500 × 171.3/172.1	129,893
June	131,600 × 171.3/171.3	131,600

(b)

	Adjusted cost	Working	Index
	£		
January	126,848	126,848/126,848	100.0
February	129,172	129,172/126,848	101.8
March	129,718	129,718/126,848	102.3
April	130,307	130,307/126,848	102.7
May	129,893	129,893/126,848	102.4
June	131,600	131,600/126,848	103.7

5    $y = 5,000 + 10 b$

Production cost of 1,400 units = £19,000

Workings

£15,000 = a + (1,000 x b)

£25,000 = a + (2,000 x b)

£(25,000 – 15,000) = (a + (1,000 x b)) – (a – (2,000 x b))

£10,000 = 1,000 x b

b = £10,000/1,000 = £10

£15,000 = a + 1,000 x 10

a = £15,000 - £10,000

a = £5,000

so the regression line is $y = 5,000 + 10 b$

Production cost of 1,400 units = 5,000 + (10 x 1,400) = £19,000

6

	Production	Costs
	Units	£
January	5,400	17,320
February	5,600	17,480
March	5,700	17,560
April	6,000	17,800
May	5,500	17,400
June	6,100	17,880

Workings

Stores costs:

January	$13,000 + (0.8 \times 5,400)$	17,320
February	$13,000 + (0.8 \times 5,600)$	17,480
March	$13,000 + (0.8 \times 5,700)$	17,560
April	$13,000 + (0.8 \times 6,000)$	17,800
May	$13,000 + (0.8 \times 5,500)$	17,400
June	$13,000 + (0.8 \times 6,100)$	17,880

7

	Value of x	Trend	Seasonal variation	Forecast sales
Quarter 1 20X9	13	2,785	– 200	2,585
Quarter 2 20X9	14	2,830	+ 500	3,330
Quarter 3 20X9	15	2,875	+ 350	3,225
Quarter 4 20X9	16	2,920	– 650	2,270

Workings

Value of x for Quarter 1, 20X9

Quarter 1 20X6 $\quad = \quad 1$

Add: 3 years of 4 quarters $\quad = \quad \dfrac{12}{13}$

Trend for Quarter 1, 20X9: $2,200 + (45 \times 13) = 2,785$

Trend for Quarter 2, 20X9: $2,200 + (45 \times 14) = 2,830$

Trend for Quarter 3, 20X9: $2,200 + (45 \times 15) = 2,875$

Trend for Quarter 4, 20X9: $2,200 + (45 \times 16) = 2,920$

CHAPTER 5 Standard costing

1   The information for the amount of labour time for each cost unit would come from payroll records such as time sheets or from physical observations such as time and motion studies. Factors that should be taken into account include:

- the level of skill or training of the labour grade to be used on the product

- any anticipated changes on the grade of labour used on the product

- any anticipated changes in work methods or productivity levels

- the effect of any bonus scheme on productivity

The hourly rate for the direct labour can be found from payroll records but the following factors should be considered:

- anticipated pay rises
- anticipated changes in grade of labour
- effect of any bonus scheme on the labour rate
- whether any anticipated overtime is built into the hourly rate.

2   The information for the amount of material required for each unit of a product can be found from the original product specification – the amount originally considered necessary for each unit. Factors that should be taken into account include:

- the level of skill of the labour to be used on the product

- any anticipated changes to the quality of material sourced

- any anticipated changes in work methods/equipment used to work the material.

This figure may however be amended over time as the actual amount used in production is monitored.

The basic price of the material can be found from suppliers' quotations or invoices. However when setting the standard, the following should also be taken into account:

- general inflation rates

- any foreseen increases in the price of this particular material

- any seasonality in the price

- any discounts available for bulk purchases

- any anticipated scarcity of the material which may mean paying a higher price

3   Ideal standards are set on the basis of perfect working conditions. No allowance is made for normal wastage or inefficiencies. Attainable standards are standards that are set on the basis of normal working conditions by building in some element to reflect normal wastage or inefficiencies. Attainable standards are capable of being met by efficient operations. Basic standards are the original historical standards based upon the original expectations of cost for the product.

4   (a)   Total materials cost variance

		£
Standard cost of actual production		
1,800 × 7 kg × £6.00		75,600
Actual cost of actual production		70,800
		4,800 Fav

(b)   Materials price variance

		£
Actual usage at standard cost		
12,000 × £6.00		72,000
Actual cost of actual production		70,800
		1,200 Fav

(c)   Materials usage variance

Standard usage for actual production at standard cost		
1,800 × 7 kg × £6.00		75,600
Actual usage at standard cost		
12,000 × £6.00		72,000
		3,600 Fav

5   (a)   Total labour cost variance

		£
Standard cost of actual production		
15,400 × 2.5 hours × £6.80		261,800
Actual cost of actual production		265,200
		3,400 Adv

    (b) Labour rate variance

        Actual hours at standard rate

41,000 × £6.80	278,800
Actual hours at actual rate	265,200
	13,600 Fav

    (c) Labour efficiency variance

        Standard hours for actual production at standard rate

15,400 × 2.5 × £6.80	261,800
Actual hours at standard rate	
41,000 × £6.80	278,800
	17,000 Adv

6   (a) Budgeted fixed overhead   =   7,000 units × 3 hours × £2.50

                                          =   £52,500

    (b) Fixed overhead expenditure variance

	£
Budgeted fixed overhead	52,500
Actual fixed overhead	56,000
	3,500 Adv

    (c) Fixed overhead volume variance

        Actual product at standard absorption rate

6,400 units × 3 hours × £2.50	48,000
Budgeted production at standard absorption rate	
7,000 units × 3 hours × £2.50	52,500
	4,500 Adv

    (d) Fixed overhead efficiency variance

        Standard hours for actual production at standard absorption rate

6,400 units × 3 × £2.50	48,000
Actual hours at standard absorption rate	
20,000 × £2.50	50,000
	2,000 Adv

(e) Fixed overhead capacity variance

Actual hours at standard absorption rate

20,000 × £2.50   50,000

Budgeted hours at standard absorption rate

7,000 × 3 × £2.50   52,500

                                                        2,500 Adv

7 (a) Materials price variance   £

Actual quantity at standard price

7,500 × £3.60   27,000

Actual quantity at actual price   25,900

                                                        1,100 Fav

Materials usage variance

Standard usage for actual production at standard   £
price

1,750 × 4.2 × £3.60   26,460

Actual usage at standard price

7,500 × £3.60   27,000

                                                        540 Adv

(b) Labour rate variance

Actual hours at standard rate

2,580 × £7.80   20,124

Actual hours at actual rate   20,600

                                                        476 Adv

Labour efficiency variance

Standard hours for actual production at standard rate

1,750 × 1.5 × £7.80   20,475

Actual hours at standard rate

2,580 × £7.80   20,124

                                                        351 Fav

(c) Fixed overhead expenditure variance

Actual fixed overhead	8,100
Budgeted fixed overhead	
1,800 × 1.5 × £2.80	7,560
	540 Adv

Fixed overhead efficiency variance

Standard hours for actual production at standard absorption rate

1,750 × 1.5 × £2.80	7,350
Actual hours at standard absorption rate	
2,580 × £2.80	7,224
	126 Fav

Fixed overhead capacity variance

Actual hours at standard absorption rate	£
2,580 × £2.80	7,224
Budgeted hours at standard absorption rate	
1,800 × 1.5 × £2.80	7,560
	336 Adv

(d) Standard cost of actual production

Direct materials 1,750 × 4.2 × £3.60	26,460
Direct labour 1,750 × 1.5 × £7.80	20,475
Fixed overhead 1,750 × 1.5 × £2.80	7,350
Total cost 1,750 × £31.02	54,285

Reconciliation statement

	Adverse variances	Favourable variances	
	£	£	
Standard cost of production			54,285
Variances :			
Materials price		1,100	
Materials usage	540		
Labour rate	476		
Labour efficiency		351	
Fixed overhead expenditure	540		
Fixed overhead efficiency		126	
Fixed overhead capacity	336	——	
	1,892	1,577	
Add: adverse variances			1,892
Less: favourable variances			(1,577)
Actual cost of production			54,600

8 (a) Total direct materials cost variance   £

Standard cost of actual production

     2,400 × 12 × £4.80   138,240

Actual cost of actual production   145,000

     6,760 Adv

Materials price variance

Actual quantity at standard price

     29,600 × £4.80   142,080

Actual quantity and actual price   145,000

     2,920 Adv

Materials usage variance

Standard quantity for actual production at standard price

2,400 × 12 × £4.80	138,240
Actual quantity at standard price	
29,600 × £4.80	142,080
	3,840 Adv

(b) Total direct labour variance

Standard cost of actual production

2,400 × 3 × £8.00	57,600
Actual cost of actual production	56,200
	1,400 Fav

Labour rate variance

Actual hours at standard rate

6,900 × £8.00	55,200
Actual hours at actual rate	56,200
	1,000 Adv

Labour efficiency variance

Standard hours for actual production at standard rate

2,400 × 3 × £8.00	57,600
Actual hours at standard rate	
6,900 × £8.00	55,200
	2,400 Fav

(c) Fixed overhead expenditure variance

Actual fixed overhead	92,000
Budgeted fixed overhead	95,000
	3,000 Fav

(d) Standard cost of production   £

	£
Direct materials 2,400 × 12 × £4.80	138,240
Direct labour 2,400 × 3 × £8.00	57,600
Variable cost (2400 x 81.60)	195,840
Fixed overheads	95,000
Total standard cost	290,840

	Adverse variances	Favourable variances	
	£	£	£
Standard cost of actual production			290,840
Variances			
Materials price	2,920		
Materials usage	3,840		
Labour rate	1,000		
Labour efficiency		2,400	
Fixed overhead expenditure	___	3,000	
	7,760	5,400	
Add adverse variances			7,760
Less: favourable variances			(5,400)
Total actual cost			**293,200**

9   Material usage variance, variable overhead efficiency variance and idle time variance. The material price variance is recorded in the stores control account. The labour rate variance is recorded in the wages control account.

CHAPTER 6 Standard costing – further aspects

1 **REPORT**

To: Managing Director
From: Accountant
Date: xx.xx.xx
Subject: November production cost variances

The November production cost is 5% more than the standard cost for the actual production, due to a number of fairly significant adverse variances.

The main cause appears to have been the labour that was used in production for the month which was a more junior grade than normal due to staff shortages. Although this has given a favourable labour rate variance, it has also caused adverse labour efficiency and materials usage variances due to inefficiencies and wastage from the staff. This inefficiency in labour hours has also led to the fixed overhead efficiency adverse variance.

For future months we should either ensure that we have enough of the normal grade of labour for production of this product or train the junior staff in the production process.

There is also an adverse materials price variance which has been due to an increase in the price of our materials. As it is believed that this is a permanent price increase by all suppliers, we should consider altering the direct materials standard cost to reflect this, otherwise each month we will have adverse materials price variances.

The factory now has an additional rent cost which has presumably caused the adverse fixed overhead expenditure variance. If the additional inventory requirement and hence the additional rent is a permanent change then this should be built into the budgeted fixed overhead figure.

Due to the labour inefficiency, more hours have been worked than were budgeted for, leading to the favourable capacity variance. This indicates that the factory has more capacity than we have been making use of which, if the inefficiencies are sorted out, could be used to increase monthly production if required.

2

Scenario	Possible effects
A business replaces machinery with new equipment	• Favourable materials usage variance, if new machinery leads to less waste. • Alternatively, adverse materials usage variance, if workers have to adapt to using new machinery • Adverse fixed overheads expenditure variance (higher depreciation charged, although overheads may decrease leading to favourable variance if more power-efficient). • Favourable labour efficiency if workers can work faster (and so favourable overhead efficiency variance)
A company has supply issues with a raw material	• Adverse materials price variance • Possible adverse materials usage variance, if can only source inferior material • Adverse labour efficiency variance (idle time) if no material for production • Possible adverse labour rate efficiency, if must use overtime to catch up, when material does become available.

3 (a) The total materials price variance was £4,900 adverse

(b) The planning variance due to the price increase was £5,600 adverse

The control variance due to other factors was £700 favourable

Workings

Total materials price variance

	£
Standard price for actual quantity used	
14,000 × £2.40	33,600
Actual quantity at actual price	38,500
	4,900 Adv

Planning variance due to price increase

	£
Standard price of actual quantity used	
14,000 × £2.40	33,600
Adjusted price for actual quantity	
14,000 × £2.80	39,200
	5,600 Adv

Control variance due to other causes

	£
Adjusted price for actual quantity	
14,000 × £2.80	39,200
Actual quantity at actual price	38,500
	700 Fav

4   (a)   The total materials price variance is £3,200 favourable

      (b)   The planning variance due to the seasonal variation is £4,920 favourable

          The control variance due to other factors is £1,720 adverse

Workings

Total materials price variance

	£
Standard price for actual quantity used	
12,300 × £8.00	98,400
Actual quantity at actual price	95,200
	3,200 Fav

Planning variance due to seasonal variation

Standard price for actual quantity used

12,300 × £8.00	98,400

Adjusted price for actual quantity

12,300 × (£8.00 - £0.40)	93,480
	4,920 Fav

Control variance due to other factors

	£
Adjusted price for actual quantity	
12,300 × (£8.00 - £0.40)	93,480
Actual quantity at actual price	95,200
	1,720 Adv

5 (a) The total labour efficiency variance was £36,720 adverse

(b) The planning variance due to the learning process was £32,640 adverse

The control variance due to other factors was £4,080 adverse

Workings

Total labour efficiency variance

	£
Standard hours for actual production at standard rate	
2,400 × 9 × £6.80	146,880
Actual hours at standard rate	
27,000 × £6.80	183,600
	36,720 Adv

Planning variance due to learning process

Standard hours for actual production at standard rate	
2,400 × 9 × £6.80	146,880
Adjusted hours for actual production at standard rate	
2,400 × 11 × £6.80	179,520
	32,640 Adv

Control variance due to other causes

Adjusted hours for actual production at standard cost

2,400 × 11 × £6.80	179,520
Actual hours at standard rate	183,600
	4,080 Adv

6 (a) The total materials price variance was £20,000 adverse

(b) The planning variance due to price changes was £40,000 adverse

The control variance due to other factors was £20,000 favourable

Workings

Total materials price variance

	£
Standard price for actual quantity used	
100,000 × £6.50	650,000
Actual quantity at actual price	670,000
	20,000 Adv

Planning variance due to price change

Standard price for actual quantity used	
100,000 × £6.50	650,000
Adjusted price for actual quantity	
100,000 × (£6.50 × 138/130)	690,000
	40,000 Adv

Control variance due to other causes

Adjusted price for actual quantity	
100,000 × (£6.50 × 138/130)	690,000
Actual quantity at actual price	670,000
	20,000 Fav

CHAPTER 7 Performance indicators

1

	Aug	Sept	Oct	Nov
Productivity per labour hour	10.5 units	10.2 units	9.8 units	10.1 units
Efficiency ratio	105.5%	102.2%	98.2%	101.0%
Capacity ratio	97.6%	96.5%	102.7%	98.5%
Activity ratio	102.9%	98.6%	100.9%	99.5%

Workings

		August	*September*	*October*	*November*
(a)	Productivity per labour hour	$\dfrac{257,300}{24,400}$	$\dfrac{251,400}{24,600}$	$\dfrac{262,300}{26,700}$	$\dfrac{258,600}{25,600}$
		= 10.5 units	= 10.2 units	= 9.8 units	= 10.1 units
(b)	Standard hours for actual	$\dfrac{257,300}{10}$	$\dfrac{251,400}{10}$	$\dfrac{262,300}{10}$	$\dfrac{258,600}{10}$
		= 25,730	= 25,140	= 26,230	= 25,860
	Efficiency ratio	$\dfrac{25,730}{24,400} \times 100$	$\dfrac{25,140}{24,600} \times 100$	$\dfrac{26,230}{26,700} \times 100$	$\dfrac{25,860}{25,600} \times 100$
		= 105.5%	= 102.2%	= 98.2%	= 101.0%
(c)	Budgeted hours	$\dfrac{250,000}{10}$	$\dfrac{255,000}{10}$	$\dfrac{260,000}{10}$	$\dfrac{260,000}{10}$
		= 25,000	= 25,500	= 26,000	= 26,000
	Capacity ratio	$\dfrac{24,400}{25,000} \times 100$	$\dfrac{24,600}{25,500} \times 100$	$\dfrac{26,700}{26,000} \times 100$	$\dfrac{25,600}{26,000} \times 100$
		= 97.6%	= 96.5%	= 102.7%	= 98.5%
(d)	Activity ratio	$\dfrac{25,730}{25,000} \times 100$	$\dfrac{25,140}{25,500} \times 100$	$\dfrac{26,230}{26,000} \times 100$	$\dfrac{25,860}{26,000} \times 100$
		= 102.9%	= 98.6%	= 100.9%	= 99.5%

2

	April	May	June	Total
Productivity per labour hour	10.9 units	10.7 units	11.1 units	10.9 units
Efficiency ratio	98.8%	97.6%	101.2%	99.2%
Capacity ratio	102.7%	101.2%	101.2%	101.7%
Activity ratio	101.4%	98.8%	102.4%	100.9%
Value added per employee	£2,552	£2,524	£2,717	£2,598

Workings

(a)

		April	May	June	Total
(i)	Productivity per labour hour	$\dfrac{121,700}{11,200}$	$\dfrac{123,500}{11,500}$	$\dfrac{128,000}{11,500}$	$\dfrac{373,200}{34,200}$
		= 10.9 units	= 10.7 units	= 11.1 units	= 10.9 units
(ii)	Standard hours for actual production	$\dfrac{121,700}{11}$	$\dfrac{123,500}{11}$	$\dfrac{128,000}{11}$	$\dfrac{373,200}{11}$
		= 11,064	= 11,227	= 11,636	= 33,927
	Efficiency ratio	$\dfrac{11,064}{11,200} \times 100$	$\dfrac{11,227}{11,500} \times 100$	$\dfrac{11,636}{11,500} \times 100$	$\dfrac{33,927}{34,200} \times 100$
		= 98.8%	= 97.6%	= 101.2%	= 99.2%
(iii)	Budgeted hours	$\dfrac{120,000}{11}$	$\dfrac{125,000}{11}$	$\dfrac{125,000}{11}$	$\dfrac{370,000}{11}$
		= 10,909	= 11,364	= 11,363	= 33,636
	Capacity ratio	$\dfrac{11,200}{10,909} \times 100$	$\dfrac{11,500}{11,364} \times 100$	$\dfrac{11,500}{11,363} \times 100$	$\dfrac{34,200}{33,636} \times 100$
		= 102.7%	= 101.2%	= 101.2%	= 101.7%
(iv)	Activity ratio	$\dfrac{11,064}{10,909} \times 100$	$\dfrac{11,227}{11,364} \times 100$	$\dfrac{11,636}{11,363} \times 100$	$\dfrac{33,927}{33,636} \times 100$
		= 101.4%	= 98.8%	= 102.4%	= 100.9%

(v) Value added

£625,000 –	£206,700			
£418,300				
£634,000 –		£209,500		
£424,500				
£656,000 –				
£430,500			£225,500	£641,700
Value added	206,700	209,500	225,500	641,700
per employee	81	83	83	247
	= £2,552	= £2,524	= £2,717	= £2,598

The value added per employee for the total three months could also have been calculated as the value added over the three month period divided by the 82 employees, the average for the three months, giving £641,700/82 = £7,826.

(b) £2,767.50

Hours at increased productivity level	=	$\dfrac{128,000 \text{ units}}{11.5}$
	=	11,131 hours
June hours		11,500
Saving in hours		369

Cost saving 369 @ £7.50 = £2,767.50

3 (a)

	July – Sept	Oct – Dec	Jan – Mar	Apr – June	
Productivity	1,240	820	1,540	1,180	
Cost per holiday	£18.26	£28.15	£16.30	£20.41	

Workings

		July – Sept	Oct – Dec	Jan – Mar	Apr – June
(i)	Productivity	$\dfrac{6,200}{5}$	$\dfrac{4,100}{5}$	$\dfrac{7,700}{5}$	$\dfrac{5,900}{5}$
		= 1,240	= 820	= 1,540	= 1,180
(ii)	Cost per holiday	$\dfrac{113,200}{6,200}$	$\dfrac{115,400}{4,100}$	$\dfrac{125,500}{7,700}$	$\dfrac{120,400}{5,900}$
		= £18.26	= £28.15	= £16.30	= £20.41

(b) The cost per holiday booking fluctuates from £16.30 to £28.15 depending upon the quarter in question. This is due to the fact that the large majority of the costs appear to be fixed costs with similar total costs each quarter. However, as the output (the holiday bookings) change, these fixed costs will remain the same and will simply be spread over more or fewer holiday bookings depending upon the quarter. For example in October to December the costs are similar to those of the other quarters but they are only being spread over 4,100 holiday bookings.

4

	Jan	Feb	Mar	April	May	June
Gross profit margin	47.5%	43.8%	42.2%	37.3%	39.3%	38.9%
Net profit margin	12.5%	13.8%	10.9%	10.6%	11.3%	10.7%
% expenses to revenue	35.0%	30.0%	31.3%	26.7%	28.0%	28.1%
Return on capital employed	20.8%	22.8%	15.4%	15.3%	15.5%	13.4%
Asset turnover	1.67	1.66	1.41	1.30	1.26	1.14

Workings

		Jan	Feb	Mar	Apr	May	June
(a)	Gross profit margin	$\frac{190}{400}$	$\frac{210}{480}$	$\frac{190}{450}$	$\frac{190}{510}$	$\frac{220}{560}$	$\frac{210}{540}$
		47.5%	43.8%	42.2%	37.3%	39.3%	38.9%
(b)	Operating profit margin	$\frac{50}{400}$	$\frac{66}{480}$	$\frac{49}{450}$	$\frac{54}{510}$	$\frac{63}{560}$	$\frac{58}{540}$
		12.5%	13.8%	10.9%	10.6%	11.3%	10.7%

(c)	Expenses to revenue	$\dfrac{140}{400}$	$\dfrac{144}{480}$	$\dfrac{141}{450}$	$\dfrac{136}{510}$	$\dfrac{157}{560}$	$\dfrac{152}{540}$
		35.0%	30.0%	31.3%	26.7%	28.0%	28.1%
(d)	Return on capital employed	$\dfrac{50}{240}$	$\dfrac{66}{290}$	$\dfrac{49}{319}$	$\dfrac{54}{393}$	$\dfrac{63}{446}$	$\dfrac{58}{474}$
		20.8%	22.8%	15.4%	13.7%	14.1%	12.2%
(e)	Asset turnover	$\dfrac{400}{240}$	$\dfrac{480}{290}$	$\dfrac{450}{319}$	$\dfrac{510}{393}$	$\dfrac{560}{446}$	$\dfrac{540}{474}$
		1.67	1.66	1.41	1.30	1.26	1.14

There has been a rapid rise in revenue of 35% over the six-month period which has been partly funded by additional loan capital in April. This increase in revenue however has not yet been matched by increases in profits.

The gross profit margin has reduced over the period and at its lowest was almost 10% below the margin for January. The operating profit margin has been steadily decreasing but not as dramatically as the gross profit margin due to the fact that expenses appear to be being well controlled. The decrease in the expenses to sales percentage indicates that many of the expenses are fixed and are therefore not rising in line with the increase in turnover.

Return on capital employed has also declined over the period partly due to the decrease in operating profit margin but also due to a significantly worsening asset turnover. This may be due to the fact that the new assets that have been funded by the loan have not yet become fully functional and we will see an improvement in asset turnover when the benefit of these new assets starts to be seen.

5

	20X6	20X7	20X8
Gross profit margin	46.3%	47.6%	44.4%
Operating profit margin	11.0%	11.8%	9.4%
Return on capital employed	18.0%	16.4%	12.7%
Asset turnover	1.64	1.39	1.34
Non-current asset turnover	2.13	1.88	1.81
Current ratio	4.8:1	5.6:1	5.2:1
Quick ratio	3.2: 1	4.0:1	3.6:1
Receivables' collection period	38 days	48 days	52 days
Inventory days	41 days	45 days	49 days
Payables' payment period	25 days	28 days	30 days
Interest cover	N/a	33.3	28.3
Gearing ratio	N/a	8.9%	8.1%

Workings

		20X6	20X7	20X8
(a)	Gross profit margin	$\frac{380}{820} \times 100$	$\frac{405}{850} \times 100$	$\frac{400}{900} \times 100$
		46.3%	47.6%	44.4%
(b)	Operating profit margin	$\frac{90}{820} \times 100$	$\frac{100}{850} \times 100$	$\frac{85}{900} \times 100$
		11.0%	11.8%	9.4%
(c)	Return on capital employed	$\frac{90}{500} \times 100$	$\frac{100}{610} \times 100$	$\frac{85}{670} \times 100$
		18.0%	16.4%	12.7%
(d)	Asset turnover	$\frac{820}{500}$	$\frac{850}{610}$	$\frac{900}{670}$
		1.64	1.39	1.34
(e)	Non-current asset turnover	$\frac{820}{385}$	$\frac{850}{453}$	$\frac{900}{498}$
		2.13	1.88	1.81
(f)	Current ratio	$\frac{145}{30}$	$\frac{191}{34}$	$\frac{213}{41}$
		4.8 : 1	5.6 : 1	5.2 : 1
(g)	Quick ratio	$\frac{95}{30}$	$\frac{136}{34}$	$\frac{146}{41}$
		3.2 : 1	4.0 : 1	3.6 : 1
(h)	Receivables' collection period	$\frac{85}{820} \times 365$	$\frac{112}{850} \times 365$	$\frac{128}{900} \times 365$
		38 days	48 days	52 days
(i)	Inventory days	$\frac{50}{440} \times 365$	$\frac{55}{445} \times 365$	$\frac{67}{500} \times 365$
		41 days	45 days	49 days
(j)	Payables' payment period	$\frac{30}{440} \times 365$	$\frac{34}{445} \times 365$	$\frac{41}{500} \times 365$
		25 days	28 days	30 days
(k)	Interest cover	n/a	100/3	85/3
			= 33.3	= 28.3
(l)	Gearing ratio	n/a	50/560 × 100	50/620 × 100
			=8.9%	=8.1%

PROFITABILITY

Between 20X6 and 20X7 there was an increase in both gross profit margin and operating profit margin. However in 20X8, when revenue grew by 6%, both gross profit margin and operating profit margin decreased. However, the fall in the operating profit margin was relatively a great deal larger than that of the gross profit margin, indicating that expenses are increasing.

Return on capital employed did not follow the increases in profitability in 20X7 but instead fell due to a significant decrease in the asset turnover in that year. Asset turnover and non-current asset turnover both stabilised a little in 20X8 but ROCE still decreased due to the falling profit levels.

WORKING CAPITAL

One of the main problems with the business appears to be control of its working capital. Both the current ratio and the quick ratio are excessively high showing that there are large amounts of capital being tied up in receivables, inventory and cash balances which could perhaps be used more profitably in other areas of the business.

The main problem areas appear to be receivables and payables. The receivables' collection period has increased from 38 to 52 days over the period whereas suppliers were being paid after just 25 days in 20X6 and still after only 30 days in 20X8. This means that cash is flowing out of the business much earlier than it is coming in.

Added to this the inventory holding period has also increased from 41 to 49 days over the three years meaning that even more cash is being tied up in these inventories.

6   (a)

	Flimwell	Hartfield	Groombridge
Gross profit margin	62.0%	56.8%	60.4%
Operating profit margin	12.0%	9.5%	13.5%
Return on capital employed	11.8%	8.5%	12.7%
Asset turnover	0.98	0.90	0.94
Inventory turnover	95 days	108 days	60 days
Payables' payment period	45 days	61 days	58 days
Sales per sq m	£225	£218	£240
Sales per employee	£19,286	£28,462	£18,462
Sales per hour worked	£17.70	£26.24	£16.96

Workings		Flimwell	Hartfield	Groombridge
	Cost of sales	$51 + 210 - 56$	$45 + 165 - 50$	$30 + 192 - 32$
		$= £205,000$	$= £160,000$	$= £190,000$
(i)	Gross profit margin	$\dfrac{335,000}{540,000} \times 100$	$\dfrac{210,000}{370,000} \times 100$	$\dfrac{290,000}{480,000} \times 100$
		62.0%	56.8%	60.4%
(ii)	Operating profit margin	$\dfrac{65,000}{540,000} \times 100$	$\dfrac{35,000}{370,000} \times 100$	$\dfrac{65,000}{480,000} \times 100$
		12.0%	9.5%	13.5%
(iii)	Return on capital employed	$\dfrac{65,000}{550,000} \times 100$	$\dfrac{35,000}{410,000} \times 100$	$\dfrac{65,000}{510,000} \times 100$
		11.8%	8.5%	12.7%
(iv)	Asset turnover	$\dfrac{540,000}{550,000}$	$\dfrac{370,000}{410,000}$	$\dfrac{480,000}{510,000}$
		0.98	0.90	0.94
(v)	Average inventory	$\dfrac{51 + 56}{2}$	$\dfrac{45 + 50}{2}$	$\dfrac{30 + 32}{2}$
		£53,500	£47,500	£31,000
	Inventory days	$\dfrac{53,500}{205,000} \times 365$	$\dfrac{47,500}{160,000} \times 365$	$\dfrac{31,000}{190,000} \times 365$
		95 days	108 days	60 days
(vi)	Payables' payment period	$\dfrac{25,800}{210,000} \times 365$	$\dfrac{27,500}{165,000} \times 365$	$\dfrac{30,500}{192,000} \times 365$
		45 days	61 days	58 days
(vii)	Sales per sq. m.	$\dfrac{540,000}{2,400}$	$\dfrac{370,000}{1,700}$	$\dfrac{480,000}{2,000}$
		£225	£218	£240

(viii)	Sales per employee	$\dfrac{540,000}{28}$	$\dfrac{370,000}{13}$	$\dfrac{480,000}{26}$
		£19,286	£28,462	£18,462
(ix)	Sales per hour worked	$\dfrac{540,000}{30,500}$	$\dfrac{370,000}{14,100}$	$\dfrac{480,000}{28,300}$
		£17.70	£26.24	£16.96

(b) REPORT

To:	Sales Director
From:	Accounts assistant
Date:	xx.xx.xx
Subject:	Performance of stores

I have considered the performance figures for our three stores in Flimwell, Hartfield and Groombridge for the first six months of the year and have calculated a number of performance indicators (see part a). The key factors that have appeared from these figures are addressed below.

Flimwell has the highest gross profit margin but the highest operating profit margin and return on capital employed are generated by Groombridge. Clearly therefore Groombridge has better control of its expenses than the other two stores and if the Groombridge practices can be emulated in the other two stores this could improve their profitability.

The Hartfield store has problems with profitability, having significantly lower gross profit margin, operating profit margin, return on capital employed and asset turnover figures than the other two stores. Possibly one of the reasons for the lack of profitability is in the high inventory levels at Hartfield. The inventory turnover in days is almost twice as high as that for Groombridge with inventories being held for about three and half months.

Hartfield, however, does have the highest productivity levels in terms of sales per employee and sales per hour worked as these are all very much higher than the other two stores. This might imply that the Hartfield store is understaffed which may also be part of the problem with profitability. As the gross profit margin of Hartfield is much lower than the other two stores it may be that Hartfield has to charge lower prices for the goods due to the understaffing in order to attract customers.

Groombridge appears to have the best control over its working capital with inventory only held for two months and suppliers paid after a similar period. If the inventory control and payables' control of Groombridge can be introduced into the other two stores this will help in their performance. Groombridge also has the highest sales per square metre therefore their store layout may be of interest to the other two stores.

If Filmwell's payables' payment period of 45 days was lengthened to that of Hartfield of 61 days the cash balance of Filmwell would increase by £9,205 (£210,000/(365 × 16)).

7 (a) Gross profit margin $= \dfrac{\text{Gross profit}}{\text{Revenue}}$

44% $= \dfrac{\text{Gross profit}}{£106,500}$

44% × £106,500 $=$ Gross profit

Gross profit $=$ £46,860

(b) Gross profit margin $= \dfrac{\text{Gross profit}}{\text{Revenue}}$

37.5% $= \dfrac{£105,000}{\text{Revenue}}$

Revenue $= \dfrac{£105,000}{0.375}$

Revenue $=$ £280,000

(c) Gross profit $=$ £256,000 × 41%

$=$ £104,960

Operating profit $=$ £256,000 × 13.5%

$=$ £34,560

Expenses $=$ £104,960 – 34,560

$=$ £70,400

(d) ROCE $= \dfrac{\text{Operating profit}}{\text{Capital employed}}$

12.8% $= \dfrac{£50,000}{\text{Capital employed}}$

Capital employed $= \dfrac{£50,000}{0.128}$

$=$ £390,625

(e) ROCE $=$ Operating profit margin × Asset turnover

15% $=$ 10% × Asset turnover

$\dfrac{15\%}{10\%}$ $=$ Asset turnover

Asset turnover $=$ 1.5

(f) Average inventory $=$ $\dfrac{118{,}000+104{,}000}{2}$

$=$ £111,000

Inventory turnover $=$ $\dfrac{\text{Cost of sales}}{\text{Average inventory}}$

$=$ $\dfrac{£118{,}000+465{,}000-104{,}000}{£111{,}000}$

$=$ 4.3 times

(g) Receivables' collection period $=$ $\dfrac{\text{Receivables}}{\text{Revenue}}\times 365$

64 days $=$ $\dfrac{64{,}000}{\text{Revenue}}\times 365$

Revenue $=$ $\dfrac{64{,}000}{64\ \text{days}}\times 365$

$=$ £365,000

8

		Balanced scorecard perspective
Operating profit margin	19.9%	Financial or internal
Return on capital employed	24.7%	Financial
Inventory turnover	91 days	Customer
Asset turnover	1.24	Internal
Research costs as % of production costs	31.25%	Innovation and learning
Training costs as a % of labour cost	22.5%	Internal

Workings

(a) Operating profit margin $\quad = \quad \dfrac{\text{Operating profit}}{\text{Revenue}} \times 100$

$$= \quad \dfrac{68+6}{372}$$

$$= \quad 19.9\%$$

– financial perspective or possibly internal perspective as this is a measure of the control over the resources of the business

Note that operating profit is profit before interest therefore the interest deducted in the income statement must be added back – however if the profit after interest had been used this would be the net profit margin.

(b) Return on capital employed $\quad = \quad \dfrac{\text{Operating profit}}{\text{Capital employed}} \times 100$

$$= \quad \dfrac{68+6}{200+100} \times 100$$

$$= \quad 24.7\%$$

– financial perspective

(c) Inventory days $\quad = \quad \dfrac{\text{Average inventory}}{\text{Cost of sales}} \times 365$

Average inventory $\quad = \quad \dfrac{19+21}{2}$

$$= \quad 20$$

Inventory days $\quad = \quad \dfrac{20}{80} \times 365$

$$= \quad 91 \text{ days}$$

– customer perspective – the more inventory that is held the less likely it is that customer demand cannot be satisfied

(d) Asset turnover $\quad = \quad \dfrac{\text{Revenue}}{\text{Capital employed}}$

$$= \quad \dfrac{372}{300}$$

$$= \quad 1.24$$

– internal – intensity of asset use

(e)   Research costs/production $=$ $\dfrac{\text{Research costs}}{\text{Production costs}} \times 100$

$$= \dfrac{25}{80} \times 100$$

$$= 31.25\%$$

– innovation and learning perspective

Note: In this calculation we have used cost of sales of £80,000 as production costs however it would also have been acceptable to use production cost of £82,000 (28 + 40 + 14)

(f)   Training costs/labour cost $=$ $\dfrac{\text{Training costs}}{\text{Labour costs}} \times 100$

$$= \dfrac{9}{40} \times 100$$

$$= 22.5\%$$

– internal perspective

CHAPTER 8 Cost management

1

		Type of cost of quality
(a)	products scrapped due to faulty raw materials	Internal failure
(b)	training for quality control staff	Prevention
(c)	costs of customer after sales service department	External failure
(d)	lost contribution on defective products sold as seconds	Internal failure
(e)	costs of inspection of raw materials	Appraisal
(f)	maintenance of quality control equipment	Prevention
(g)	cost of replacing faulty products returned by customers	External failure
(h)	costs of production delays due to re-working defective products discovered in quality inspection	Internal failure
(i)	claims from customers relating to defective products	External failure
(j)	performance testing of finished goods	Appraisal

2

Cost of quality	Amount £	Category of cost
Repair of returned goods	£20,000	External failure
Advertising costs	£40,000	External failure
Lost customers	Unknown	External failure

Working

Repair of returned goods

$5,000,000/3,000 \times 60\% \times £20 = £20,000$

3

Cost of quality	Amount £	Category of cost	Explicit or implicit
Quality inspection	£60,000	Appraisal	Explicit
Lost contribution from defective units	£70,000	Internal failure	Implicit
Replacement of units	£37,500	External failure	Explicit
Lost customers	Unknown	External failure	Explicit

Workings

Lost contribution

$2,000 \times (£80 - £45)$ £70,000

Replacement of defective units

$1,000,000/1,000 \times 75\% \times £50$ £37,500

4

Cost per after sales service customer	£4.67
Sales returns as a % of sales	8%
Repair cost per returned units	£10.00
Complaints as a % of unit sales	6%

Workings

Cost per after sales service customer	=	$\dfrac{£280,000}{60,000}$	= £4.67
Sales returns as a % of sales value	=	$\dfrac{£120,000}{£1,500,000}$	= 8%
Repair cost per returned unit	=	$\dfrac{£40,000}{4,000}$	= £10.00
Complaints as a % of unit sales	=	$\dfrac{3,000}{50,000}$	= 6%

5   Total Quality Management (TQM) is a quality management system in an organisation that involves all areas of the organisation not just the production element. The philosophy behind quality management must be applied in all the activities of the business – design, production, marketing, administration, purchasing, sales and even the finance function.

TQM can be defined as a continuous improvement in quality, productivity and effectiveness.

Continuous improvement is the basic principle behind TQM. This can be described as the concept of "getting it right first time" and "getting it even more right next time". By getting it right first time the costs of internal failure and external failure will be reduced to the point where they should not occur at all. Costs of prevention are less than the costs of correction.

TQM seeks to ensure that the goods produced or the services supplied are of the highest quality.

In order for TQM to work in all areas of an organisation, training and motivation of staff is vital in order for each individual to have the attitude of constantly seeking improvement in what they do. All staff within the organisation must be taught that they have customers. These may be external customers of the business or internal customers in the form of colleagues in the business that use an individual's work. Each individual should endeavour to ensure that they get it right first time and therefore that their excellent work is passed on in the chain.

Another important concept behind TQM is that every employee is involved and anyone with an idea should be allowed to put this forward. This is often done by groups of employees being formed within the organisation known as quality circles.

These quality circles normally consist of about ten employees with a range of skills, roles and seniority who meet regularly to discuss problems of quality and quality control and to perhaps suggest ways of improving processes and quality. This means that there is input from all levels within the organisation and from different disciplines such as marketing, design, engineering, information technology and office administration as well as production.

6   **Development and launch stages**

During this period of the product's life there are large outgoings in terms of development expenditure, non-current (fixed) assets necessary for production, the building up of inventory (stock) levels and advertising and promotion expenses. It is likely that even after the launch sales will be quite low and the product will be making a loss at this stage.

Growth stage

If the launch of the product is successful then during the growth stage there will be a fairly rapid increase in sales and a move to profitability as the costs of the earlier stages are recovered. This sales increase, however, is not likely to continue indefinitely.

Maturity stage

In the maturity stage of the product demand for the product will probably start to slow down and become more constant. In many cases this is the stage where the product is modified or improved in order to sustain demand and this may then see a small surge in sales.

Decline stage

At some point in a product's life, unless it is a consumable items such as chocolate bars, the product will reach the end of its sale life. The market will have bought enough of the product and sales will decline. This is the point where the business should consider no longer producing the product.

INDEX

Notes

REVIEW FORM

How have you used this Text?
(Tick one box only)

☐ Home study

☐ On a course_____

☐ Other _____

Why did you decide to purchase this Text? *(Tick one box only)*

☐ Have used BPP Texts in the past

☐ Recommendation by friend/colleague

☐ Recommendation by a college lecturer

☐ Saw advertising

☐ Other _____

During the past six months do you recall seeing/receiving either of the following?
(Tick as many boxes as are relevant)

☐ Our advertisement in Accounting Technician

☐ Our Publishing Catalogue

Which (if any) aspects of our advertising do you think are useful?
(Tick as many boxes as are relevant)

☐ Prices and publication dates of new editions

☐ Information on Text content

☐ Details of our free online offering

☐ None of the above

Your ratings, comments and suggestions would be appreciated on the following areas of this Text.

	Very useful	Useful	Not useful
Introductory section	☐	☐	☐
Quality of explanations	☐	☐	☐
How it works	☐	☐	☐
Chapter tasks	☐	☐	☐
Chapter Overviews	☐	☐	☐
Test your learning	☐	☐	☐
Index	☐	☐	☐

	Excellent	Good	Adequate	Poor
Overall opinion of this Text	☐	☐	☐	☐

Do you intend to continue using BPP Products?   Yes ☐   No ☐

Please note any further comments and suggestions/errors on the reverse of this page. The author of this edition can be e-mailed at: suedexter@bpp.com

Please return to: Sue Dexter, Publishing Director, BPP Learning Media Ltd, FREEPOST, London, W12 8BR.

REVIEW FORM (continued)

TELL US WHAT YOU THINK

Please note any further comments and suggestions/errors below.

왓칭

왓칭
WATCHING

신이 부리는 요술

김상운 지음

정신세계사

왓칭

ⓒ 김상운, 2011

김상운 지은 것을 정신세계사 정주득이 2011년 4월 25일 처음 펴내다. 편집주간 이균형,
김우종이 다듬고, 김윤선이 꾸미고, 김진혜가 그리고, 경운출력에서 출력을, 한서지업사
에서 종이를, 영신사에서 인쇄와 제본을, 기획 및 영업부장 김영수, 하지혜가 책의 관리
를 맡다. 정신세계사의 등록일자는 1978년 4월 25일(제1-100호), 주소는 03040 서울시
종로구 자하문로 21 4층, 전화는 02-733-3134, 팩스는 02-733-3144, 홈페이지는
www.mindbook.co.kr, 인터넷 카페는 cafe.naver.com/mindbooky이다.

2017년 11월 10일 펴낸 책(초판 제105쇄)

ISBN 978-89-357-0346-3 03320

사람은 위기를 마주한 순간에 마음의 눈을 뜨게 된다고 한다. 나에게
도 위기의 순간이 있었다.

할머니가 세상을 떠난 뒤 몇 년 사이로 할머니를 그리던 아버지마저
뒤를 따랐다. 정직하게 농사일에만 파묻혀 지낸 인생들이었다. 나는 신이
정의롭다면 그들에게 말년이나마 편안함을 선사할 줄 알았지만, 그게 아
니었다. 낙상 후 3년 동안 누워 있던 할머니의 피부는 얇은 비닐처럼 변
해버렸고, 등에는 피부가 짓물러 심한 욕창이 났다. 아버지도 말년에 시
도 때도 없이 콧물과 침을 질질 흘렸고, 대소변도 맘대로 못 보는 고통을
맞았다. 고통을 지켜보는 것 자체도 고통이었다. 떠나보내는 것 또한 고
통이었다. 신은 왜 그런 고통들을 만들어냈을까? 머릿속이 온통 고통으
로 가득 차오르니 내 몸에도 마침내 이상이 찾아왔다. 체중이 갑자기 크
게 줄고, 머리털도 한 움큼씩 쑥쑥 빠져나갔다. 시도 때도 없이 가슴이 방
망이질을 해댔다. 지하철 역 바닥에 앉아 구걸하는 사람들을 보면 나도
모르게 눈물이 고였다. 만나는 사람들마다 "어디 아픈데 있어요?" 하고
물었다. TV 프로를 녹화할 땐 바짝 마른 얼굴을 숨기기 위해 "카메라 좀

당겨주세요"라고 부탁하곤 했다. 그러던 어느 날 밤 문득, 나는 화장실 거울에 비친 내 모습을 깊은 눈으로 바라보았다.

'고통으로 일그러진 저 얼굴…. 저 고통은 왜 생겼을까?'

비로소 나를 객관적인 관찰자의 눈으로 바라보는 순간이었다. 내게 늘 기쁨과 희망을 주는 아이들의 얼굴도 떠올랐다. 시골의 텅 빈 집에 덩그러니 홀로 남은 어머니의 모습도 아리게 스쳐왔다. '이러다간 정말 큰일 나겠구나' 하는 생각이 퍼뜩 들었다. 벗어나야겠다고 마음먹자 이런 의문이 고개를 들었다.

'신이 고통을 만들어놓았다면 그걸 꺼버리는 장치는 안 만들어놓았을까?'

조물주가 고통만 만들어놓고 그걸 꺼버리는 장치는 깜빡했을 리 만무하지 않은가? 그 장치가 뭘까? 다행히 나는 기자다. 감정에 파묻히지 않고 매사를 객관적으로 바라보는 게 직업상의 철칙이다. 모르는 게 있으면 취재해서 알아내면 그만이라는 생각으로 살아온 세월이 20여 년이었다.

우선 심리치료에 관한 해외 명저들을 집중적으로 주문해 읽기 시작했다. 뉴욕타임스 베스트셀러에 올라 있는 권위 있는 책들은 모조리 읽었다. 그러면서 놀라운 사실을 깨달았다. 내 마음의 병은 스스로의 생각에 지나치게 함몰돼 생긴 것이었다. 함몰된 시각에서 몇 발짝 벗어나 객관적인 눈으로 내면을 바라보는 순간 마음의 병은 거짓말처럼 사라졌다.

그러자 마음이 맑아지기 전에는 보지 못했던 것들이 보이기 시작했다. 파고들수록 새로운 사실이 드러나는 정신세계가 너무나 신기했다. 특히 책을 통해 양자물리학의 세계적인 권위자들을 만날 때 느끼는 감정은 경외감 그 자체였다. 밤마다 명상을 하며 조용히 산책하는 혼자만의 시간도 더없이 즐거웠다. 그렇게 1년이 지나고, 2년이 지나고, 3년이 지나면서 마침내 나는 왓칭watching(관찰)만으로 인간의 모든 고통이 해결된다는 우주 원리에 완전히 눈을 떴다. 그건 고통을 만들어준 신이 고통 해결의 열쇠로 인간의 손에 쥐여준 선물이었다.

그러던 차에 한국외국어대학교에서 강의를 맡게 되었다. 4학년 졸업반 학생들을 대상으로 한 국제 커뮤니케이션 강의였다. 학생들은 오로지 목전에 둔 취업 걱정으로 불안에 떨고 있었다. 그 불안한 마음을 위로하고 싶었던 나는 자연스럽게 강의주제를 왓칭이 일으키는 '관찰자 효과'로 정하였다. 강의를 해나가면서 학생들이 강의 내용을 어떻게 받아들이는지, 또 어떻게 변화해나가는지를 주의 깊게 관찰할 수 있었던 것은 나에게 의미 있는 경험이었다. 학생들도 왓칭으로 기대 이상의 변화를 겪었다. 이 책에 기록한 사례들은 모두 사실에 바탕을 둔 것들이다.

내가 좋아하는 말이 있다.

"난 모든 걸 할 수는 없다. 하지만 할 수 있는 게 분명히 몇 가지는 있다. 할 수 없는 것 때문에 할 수 있는 것까지 포기하지는 않겠다."

3년 전, 나는 아주 작은 가능성의 문을 열어놓고 호기심 가득한 기자의 눈으로 왓칭이 부리는 요술을 엿보기 시작했다. 그러자 그 문은 점점 크게 열리기 시작했고 지금은 더없이 활짝 열려 있다. 왓칭은 신이 누구에게나 똑같이 내려준 선물이다. 나는 기자이기 이전에 평범한 직장인이다. 나와 학생들이 변화를 체험했다면 누구든 왓칭을 통해 신기한 변화를 경험할 수 있다. 우주의 원리는 누구에게나 쉽고 공평하게 똑같이 적용되기 때문이다.

차 례

왓칭, 신이 부리는 요술

1 왓칭은
모든 것을 바꿔놓는다

마 음 을 바 꿔 놓 는 다

막무가내로 생떼를 쓰는 아이. 순식간에 뚝 그치게 할 수 있을까?

그 비밀에 눈뜨는 순간, 당신은 그 누구의 마음도 쉽게 바꿔놓을 수 있다.

"엄마가 그건 안 된다고 했지?"

엄마들은 대개 이렇게 을러댄다. 그러면서 함께 감정의 불길에 뛰어든다. 언젠가 마트에 갔을 때도 그랬다. 장난감 코너 앞에서 한 남자아이가 닌텐도 게임기를 사달라며 얼굴이 뻘게지도록 악을 쓰며 울어대고 있었다.

"요게 정말!"

쩔쩔매던 엄마는 아이의 볼기짝을 때렸다. 아이는 뚝 그치기는커녕 자지러질 듯한 울음으로 응수했다. 엄마도 뿔이 날 대로 났다. 거세게 팔을 잡아끌었지만 아이는 막무가내로 내팽개쳤다. 그 엄마는 아이가 품고 있는 불만 덩어리를 억누르려 하고 있었다. 억누르려 드니 고무공처럼 자꾸만 튀어 올랐다. 심리학에서 말하는 '아이러니 효과(irony effect)'이다.

14

"애, 너 저 게임기 갖고 싶지?"

내가 자신의 불만을 끄집어내 객관적으로 바라보도록 하는 순간, 아이는 울음을 뚝 그치고 나를 올려다보았다.

"아저씨도 엄청나게 갖고 싶단다. 그런데 돈이 없어서 못 사고 있어. 그런데 저게 얼만지 알아?"

아이가 호기심 어린 표정을 지으며 머리를 내저었다.

"굉장히 비싼 거야. 그럼 어떻게 해야 할까?"

아이는 또 고개를 좌우로 흔들었다.

"저걸 갖는 방법은 두 가지야. 첫째, 돈을 꼬박꼬박 모아서 사는 거야. 동전을 모아도 좋아. 둘째, 누가 선물로 줄 때까지 기다리는 거야. 넌 어떤 방법이 좋다고 생각하니? 방법은 너 스스로 정하는 거야."

아이가 잠시 생각하더니 대답했다.

"나중에 돈 벌어서 살 거예요."

자존심이 무척 강한 아이였다. 아이는 엄마 손을 잡고 언제 난리를 떨었느냐는 듯 깡총깡총 사라졌다. 아이는 왜 울음을 뚝 그쳤을까? 낯선 내가 무서웠거나 내 설득력에 감동해서였을까? 나는 그저 자신의 불만에 함몰돼 있던 그 아이가 그 불만을 끄집어내 객관적인 눈으로 바라볼 수 있도록 유도해줬을 뿐이었다. 그 불만은 바라보는 순간 저절로 물러갔다.

내 안에서 치솟은 화도 남의 일인 양 객관적으로 바라보면 쉽게 사라진다. 일요일 당직을 서던 날이었다. 느지막하게 초밥집을 찾아갔다. 식사가 중간쯤 돼가는데 웨이트리스가 샐러드 접시를 테이블에 땡그랑 떨어뜨렸다.

"어머!"

샐러드 소스와 유리조각들이 내 바지로 마구 쏟아져 내렸다. 얼굴이 찡그려졌다. 바지 오른쪽이 온통 샐러드 소스에 뒤덮였다. 엉망이 된 바지를 입고 사무실에 드나들 생각을 하니 화가 치솟았다. 예전 같으면 반사적으로 화를 냈을 것이었다. 순간적으로 화에 휩싸여 괴로워했다. 심장이 뛰고, 눈이 충혈되고, 독기가 온몸에 퍼져 나갔다. 화는 내 머릿속에서 나오는 것이니 당연히 나와 한 몸뚱이라고 생각했다.

하지만 지금은 다르다. 무조건 화를 내게서 분리시켜놓고 바라본다. 화를 낼 것인가, 참을 것인가? 화를 내고 나면 늘 후회한다. 그래서 나는 피어오르는 화 덩어리에 "화"라는 딱지를 붙여 바라본다. 바로 그 순간 화는 생명을 잃어가기 시작한다. 마치 맑은 하늘의 구름 한 조각처럼 살포시 물러간다.

"정말 죄송해요, 손님!"

웨이트리스는 새로 세팅을 하며 연신 사과했다. 나의 화는 이미 온데간데없었다.

눈에 안 보이는 화 덩어리도 저마다 독자적인 생명력과 지능을 갖고 있다. 에너지장 촬영장치인 키를리안 사진기(Kirlian camera)로 찍어보면 화 덩어리가 머리에서 빠져나와 가슴으로 되돌아가는 게 선명하게 목격된다. 그래서 그걸 그대로 구겨 넣고 살면 마침내 병이 되지 않는가? 아인슈타인이 "화도 어린아이처럼 달래줘야 하는 에너지 덩어리"라고 누누이 강조했던 것도 그래서다. 따라서 화 덩어리는 가슴에 품어두지 말고 따로 떼어내 남처럼 객관화시켜 바라보아야 한다. 그 간단한 행위만으로 쉽게 누그러진다.

키를리안 사진기로 찍은
인간의 에너지장

"감정과
건강 상태에 따라
에너지장의 형태와
색깔이 변화한다."

　화가 사라지면 연민의 감정이 밀려온다. 문득 딸아이의 얼굴이 떠올랐다. 내 아이도 나중에 크면 이런 일을 아르바이트로 할지 모르지 않는가? 만일 이런 실수를 저지른다면? 설사 손님이 화를 내지 않더라도 그날 온종일 기분이 가라앉을 것이다. 지금 그 웨이트리스도 신경이 곤두서 있을 것이다.

　내가 "접시 떨어뜨려서 깜짝 놀랐죠?" 하며 미소 지었더니 그녀도 방긋 따라 웃었다. 그 한 마디로 그녀도 자신의 '깜짝 놀란 마음'을 바라보게 되었고, 바라보는 순간 불안은 날아갔다. 아마도 그녀는 그 작은 실수를 잊고 그날 오후를 홀가분한 마음으로 보낼 수 있었을 것이었다.

관찰자 효과는 내 머리도 순식간에 바꿔놓았다. 전에는 짧은 기사 하나를 쓰다가도 생각이 막히면 얼굴에 화기가 오르고 골치가 지끈지끈 아팠다. 배도 더부룩해져 소화도 안 됐다. 그렇게 앉아 있다고 멋진 기사가 써지는 것도 아니었다. 게다가 나이가 들면서 기억력도 점점 떨어져 가는 것 같았다. 자주 만나는 사람들의 이름을 까먹어 어색해진 경우가 한두 번이 아니었다. 언젠가는 매일 걸던 고향집 전화번호가 돌연 떠오르지 않아 무척이나 당황했다.

'벌써 치매가 찾아온 건가?'

그런데 관찰자 효과를 이해하면서 뜻밖의 변화가 찾아왔다. 우선 기사를 쓰는 속도나 독서 속도가 놀랍도록 빨라졌다. 아이디어도 불쑥불쑥 잘 떠오르고 선명해졌다. 특히 내게 전혀 생소했던 양자물리학 책들이 머리에 쏙쏙 들어온다. 어느 땐 저자들이 책에 써놓은 것보다 저자들의 의도를 더 깊이 파악하기도 한다. 하도 신기해서 이런 생각도 들었다.

'그럼 내 영어 실력도 좋아졌을까?'

호기심에서 미국의 대학원 입학 자격시험 격인 GRE를 다시 응시해보았다. GRE는 20년 전 경제부 기자 시절 미국 대학원에 연수를 가기 직전 딱 한 번 쳐본 게 전부였다. 나는 시험성적을 받아보고는 깜짝 놀랐다. 영어부문에서 전체의 최상위 1퍼센트에 든 것이다. 물론 미국학생들을 포함해서 말이다. 신기한 일 아닌가? 무려 20년간이나 영어공부를 따로 하지도, 영어학원에 다니지도 않았다. 그렇다고 중학교에 들어가기 전까지는 알파벳도 몰랐으니 영어 조기교육의 효과가 남아 있는 것도 아니었다.

도대체 관찰자 효과가 내 머리에 어떤 요술을 부린 걸까? 머리를 확 터놓은 걸까? 시각을 전환하는 것만으로 지능에 정말 신기한 변화가 저절로 일어나는 걸까?

한 초등학교 교사는 성적이 형편없는 빈민지역 1학년 아이들을 '학자'라고 불러주기 시작했다. 아이들이 자기 자신을 학자로 바라보도록 한 것이다. 그는 교실에 누가 찾아오면 아이들을 학자라고 소개했다. 또 아이들로 하여금 학자가 무슨 뜻인지 방문객에게 직접 설명해주도록 유도했다.

"어린이 여러분, 학자가 뭐하는 사람이라고 했죠?"

"학자는 새로운 걸 배우고, 배움을 즐거워하는 사람입니다."

아이들은 일제히 목청 높여 이렇게 대답하곤 했다. 교사는 이런 말도 해주었다.

"여러분은 학자예요. 그날 배운 걸 집에 가서 가족들에게 가르쳐주세요. 학자는 남에게 가르쳐주는 것도 좋아하거든요."

공부라면 얼굴부터 돌리던 아이들이 정말 배움을 즐거움으로 여기게 됐다. 그리고 몇 달 후 시험을 쳐보니, 아이들의 성적은 놀랍게도 벌써 2학년 수준에 도달해 있었다.

"여러분은 이제 2학년생입니다."

교사는 실제로 봄방학이 되기 전에 1학년 수료식을 열어주었다. 1년 과정을 불과 몇 달 만에 마친 아이들은 스스로를 "2학년생"이라고 부르며 즐거워했다. 그리고 1학년이 끝나갈 때쯤 되자 아이들의 90퍼센트 이상이 3학년 수준을 뛰어넘는 읽기 능력을 갖게 됐다. 불과 아홉 달 전까지만 해도 그 지역에서 가장 공부 못했던 말썽꾸러기들이 가장 공부 잘하는 우등생들로 탈바꿈한 것이다. 미국 조지아 주의 초등학교 교사였던 존스(Crystal Jones)의 이야기다.

성적은 그렇다 치자. 그럼 예술적 재능은 어떨까? 예술적 재능도 자신을 어떻게 바라보느냐에 따라 껑충 뛰어오를까?

연아와 선아는 피아노를 배운 적이 없다. 타고난 재능도 똑같다. 부모의 교육 수준도 똑같다. 부모나 조부모, 가까운 친척들 가운데 피아노에 재능을 발휘한 사람도 없다. 유전적 환경이 비슷한 이 두 아이에게 똑같은 조건에서, 똑같은 방법으로, 똑같은 양의 연습을 시키면 나중에 그 실력도 똑같을까?

심리학자 맥퍼슨(Gary McPherson)은 악기를 연습중인 어린이 157명을 장기간 추적해보았다. 그런데 9개월쯤 후부터 아이들의 실력이 크게 벌어지기 시작했다.

"거참 이상하네. 연습량도 똑같고 다른 조건도 다 비슷한데 도대체 왜 이렇게 차이가 벌어지는 거지?"

그는 문득 연습을 시작하기 전 아이들에게 던졌던 질문을 떠올렸다.

"넌 음악을 얼마나 오래 할 거지?"

아이들의 대답은 크게 세 가지였다.

"전 1년만 하다가 그만둘 거예요."

"전 고등학교 졸업할 때까지만 할 거예요."

"전 평생 하며 살 거예요."

그는 아이들의 실력을 비교해보고 깜짝 놀랐다. 평생 연주할 거라는 아이들의 수준이 1년 만 하고 그만둘 거라는 아이들보다 무려 네 배나 더 높았기 때문이다! 똑같은 기간 동안 똑같은 시간 연습했는데도 말이다.

"그럼 평생 하겠다는 아이들의 연습량을 확 줄여보면 어떨까?"

더욱 놀라운 결과가 나왔다. 평생 하겠다는 아이들은 설사 일주일에 불과 20분씩만 연습하더라도 한 시간 반씩이나 연습하는 다른 아이들보다 실력이 훨씬 더 좋았기 때문이다.

결론은 자명했다. "전 1년만 하고 그만둘 거예요"라고 말한 아이들은 자신들을 음악가라고 생각하지 않는다. 반면 "전 평생 하며 살 거예요"라고 말한 아이들은 '난 음악가'라고 생각한다. 자신을 마음속에서 음악가로 바라보는 아이들은 남들보다 훨씬 적게 연습해도 마치 이미 훌륭한 음악가가 된 것처럼 특출한 재능을 발휘하게 되는 것이다.

단지 자신을 누구로 바라보느냐 하는 단순한 시각의 차이가 재능의 차이를 이토록 어마어마하게 벌려놓다니, 도대체 왜 이런 일이 일어날까?

자신을 음악가로 바라보는 아이는 음악을 완전히 받아들일 자세가 돼 있다. 즉, 음악에 관한 한 마음을 활짝 열어놓는 것이다. 반면, 1년만 연주하다가 그만둘 것이라는 아이는 마음의 일부만 열어놓는다. 마음을 활짝 열어놓고 "난 음악가"라고 바라보는 것만으로 음악적 재능이 무려 네 배도 넘게 껑충 뛰어오르는 것이다. 관찰자 효과를 알게 된 뒤 내 머리가 돌연 확 트인 느낌을 갖게 된 것도 바로 이런 이유 때문 아닐까? (관찰자 효과로 지능을 높이는 방법은 제2부에 자세히 설명돼 있다).

몸을 바꿔놓는다

바라보는 것만으로 몸도 깜짝 변신할 수 있을까? 예를 들어 만병의 근원인 뱃살도 바라보면 저절로 쉽게 빠져나갈까?

나는 전에는 호리호리한 체형이었는데도 허리 사이즈가 33인치 이상 되는 바지를 입었었다. 똥배가 볼록 튀어나왔기 때문이었다. 샤워하고 나서 거울에 옆모습을 비춰보면 참 꼴불견이었다. 책상 앞에 오래 앉아 있을 땐 남몰래 혁대 버클을 풀어놨다가 일어설 땐 슬쩍 다시 매곤 했다. 줄넘기 등 운동을 해도 똥배는 영 빠지지 않았다.

돌이켜보면 이유는 간단했다. 똥배는 보통 무의식적으로 서서히 찌는 살이다. 일단 무의식에 저장된 정보는 의지만으로는 지워지지 않는다. 의지보다 무의식이 불가항력적으로 더 강하기 때문이다. 하지만 관찰자 효과는 무의식에 저장된 정보까지도 쉽게 바꿔놓는다.

나는 밤 11시쯤 동네 운동장을 걷는 습관이 있다. 그래서 관찰자 효과를 알고 나서는 배가 출렁이는 느낌이 들도록 일부러 빨리 걸었다. 그리고 걸을 때마다 이렇게 생각했다.

'내 배가 출렁거리면서 지방질이 다 빠져나가고 있어.'

그렇게 30분쯤 걷다 보면 실제로 배가 텅 비어가는 느낌이 오기 시작한다. 그런 느낌을 갖고 걸으면 기분도 좋고 기운도 더욱 솟아오른다. 몸속을 바라본다는 건 어려운 게 아니다. 그냥 몸속의 움직임을 느껴본다는 뜻이다. 움직임을 생생히 느낄수록 그만큼 제대로 바라보는 것이다.

이런 식으로 했더니 불과 몇 주 만에 똥배가 쑥 들어갔다. 덕분에 지금은 허리 사이즈가 31인치 이하로 줄었다. 그렇다고 걱정이 완전히 사라진 것은 아니다. 이틀 정도만 건너뛰어도 그놈의 똥배가 또다시 슬금슬금 튀어나온다. 걷기 운동을 안 할 땐 똥배를 바라보지 않게 되기 때문이다.

그런데 꼭 이렇게 시간을 내서 운동을 해야만 하는 것일까? 그렇지 않다. 왓칭은 내면의 작업이므로 언제 어디서든 실천할 수 있다.

하버드 대학의 심리학자 랭거(Ellen Langer) 교수는 호텔 청소부들을 유심히 지켜보았다. 그들은 하루 평균 호텔방 열다섯 개를 부지런히 치워야 했다. 침대 시트를 갈고, 방바닥을 쓸고 닦고, 화장실을 반짝반짝하게 치우고… 눈코 뜰 새 없이 바쁘게 몸을 움직여야 했다. 그런데도 그들은 운동부족으로 인한 온갖 증세를 보이고 있었다.

"혈압이 너무 높아 걱정이에요."

"배도 불룩해서 움직이기 어려워요."

"도무지 운동할 짬을 내기 힘드네요."

랭거 교수는 여러 호텔의 청소부 84명의 건강 상태를 조사해보았다. 그들은 대부분이 과체중인데다가 배가 볼록 나오고 혈압도 높았다. 그 후 교수는 84명 중 절반을 비밀리에 따로 불러 청소 활동의 운동 효과에 대해 설명해주었다.

"여러분의 운동량은 충분하고도 남아요. 생각해보세요. 15분간 시트를 가는 데만 40칼로리가 소모됩니다. 진공청소기를 들고 15분간 청소하면 50칼로리가 더 빠져나가요. 방 하나를 청소하는 데도 땀을 뻘뻘 흘리며 10분간 운동하는 것과 똑같은 효과가 있답니다. 하루에 열다섯 개의 방을 치우는 것은 두 시간 반 동안 운동을 하는 것과 똑같아요."

랭거 교수는 차트까지 그려가며 자세히 설명해주었다.

청소 종류	청소 시간	칼로리 소비량
시트 갈기	15분	40칼로리
진공청소기	15분	50칼로리
욕조 닦기	15분	60칼로리

한 달 후 이 설명을 들은 청소부들의 건강을 검진해보았더니 신기한 변화가 나타났다. 불룩 나왔던 배가 쑥 들어가고 삼중턱도 사라졌다. 혈압도 떨어졌다. 그들이 따로 운동을 한 건 절대 아니었다. 다만 교수의 설명을 들은 것뿐이었다. 반면, 설명을 듣지 못한 청소부들의 몸에는 아무런 변화가 없었다.

* 몸의 변화를 바라보며 청소했다 → 체중, 허리둘레, 지방, 혈압 감소
* 무심코 청소했다 → 아무 변화 없음
* 고역이라고 여기며 청소했다 → 피로독소 증가

왜 이런 차이가 나타났을까? 랭거 교수는 이렇게 설명한다.

"청소하며 몸을 움직일 때마다 칼로리가 빠져나간다고 생각하니 실제로 지방이 빠져나간 겁니다. 그런 생각을 안 하며 청소할 땐 오히려 피로독소만 쌓이는 거죠."

랭거 교수

"청소할 때마다 살이 빠져나간다고
생각하는 것만으로 실제로 살이 빠진다."

다시 말해 청소라는 행위를 바라보는 눈이 달라지니 몸도 변화한 것
이다. '청소는 지겹고 힘든 것'이라고 바라보았을 땐 청소가 건강에 오히
려 해가 됐다. 하지만 청소할 때마다 이렇게 생각해본다면 어떨까?

"난 지금 시트를 가는 중이야. 또 40칼로리가 빠져나가겠군."

"지금처럼 진공청소기로 바닥을 청소할 때마다 50칼로리가 빠진다고
했지."

청소할 때마다 무의식적으로 살이 빠져나간다고 바라보니 실제로 살
이 빠져나갔던 것이다. 이것이 굳이 시간과 돈을 들여 따로 운동하지 않
고도 날씬하고 건강해지는 비결이다.

물질을   바꿔놓는다

그럼 사람의 몸과 마음이 아니라 음식이나 쇠붙이 같은 물질은 어떨
까? 그런 것들도 왓칭만으로 원하는 대로 변화시킬 수 있을까?

우선 우리가 매일 마시는 물부터 짚어보자.

"당신은 물을 마시며 어떤 생각을 하는가?"

이렇게 물으면 당신은 아마 "그냥 무심코 마신다"고 대답할 것이다. 그런데 입장을 바꿔서 물에게 당신을 어떻게 생각하는지를 묻는다면 어떨까?

"뭐, 생각? 두뇌도 없는 물이 무슨 생각을 한다고 그래?"

당신은 내 말에 이렇게 눈을 부라릴 것이다. 하지만 놀랍게도 실제로 물은 당신의 생각을 정확하게 읽고 있다. 당신이 무시하면 물도 당신을 무시한다. 거꾸로 당신이 물에 감사하면 물도 더 많은 영양분을 만들어낸다. 뚱딴지같은 소리만 한다고 펄쩍 뛸지 모른다. 하지만 이는 분명한 사실이다. 당신이 물을 마시기 위해 물병을 잡는 순간, 그 물은 이미 당신의 마음을 읽고 변화해 있다.

"물이 정말 그런 지능을 가지고 있을까?"

캐나다 맥길 대학의 생물학자인 그래드(Bernard Grad) 교수는 여러 개의 화분에 보리 씨앗을 20개씩 심어두었다. 그리고 물에 대한 호감도가 다른 세 사람에게 각기 물병을 하나씩 나눠주고 30분간 두 손으로 잡고 있도록 해보았다.

⟨보리 씨앗에 뿌려줄 물병⟩

물병 1. 물을 좋아하는 자연주의자가 잡고 있었다.
물병 2. 정신이 혼란한 정신병 환자가 잡고 있었다.
물병 3. 정신병 환자지만 물을 좋아하는 사람이 잡고 있었다.
물병 4. 아무도 잡고 있지 않았다.

그리고 이들 세 사람이 잡고 있던 물병을 수거해 여러 개의 화분에 각기 뿌려주었다. 그로부터 몇 주 후, 파릇파릇한 보리 싹들이 꽤 크게 자랐다. 하지만 자란 높이는 각각 달랐다. 과연 누가 만졌던 물이 보리를 가장 많이 자라게 했을까?

〈보리가 자란 속도〉

물병 1을 뿌려준 화분 → 가장 많이 자랐다.

물병 2를 뿌려준 화분 → 가장 적게 자랐다.

물병 3을 뿌려준 화분 → 두 번째로 많이 자랐다.

물병 4를 뿌려준 화분 → 두 번째로 적게 자랐다.

교수는 눈이 휘둥그레졌다.

"물이 귀신처럼 사람의 마음을 읽어내고 있어!"

정말 그랬다. 물에 대한 호감도와 보리의 키가 거짓말처럼 정비례했다. 물은 자신을 긍정적으로 바라볼수록 그만큼 더 많은 영양분을 만들어내는 게 틀림없었다.

생각해보라. 인체의 70퍼센트는 물이다. 따라서 어떤 마음으로 물을 바라보느냐에 따라 반드시 우리의 몸도 달라지게 된다.

그럼 물병을 손으로 잡지 않고 물병에 글자만 써서 붙여놓으면 어떨까? 물이 글자에 담긴 마음까지도 읽고 변화할까?

"뭐? 물이 글자를 읽는다고?"

당신은 이제 펄쩍 뛸 것이다. 하지만 널리 알려진 에모토 마사루(江本 勝)

masaru-emoto.net

사랑, 감사 딱지를 붙였던 물의 결정체(왼쪽)와 증오, 악마 딱지를 붙였던 물의 결정체(오른쪽)

박사의 실험을 좀더 깊이 살펴보자. 일본 IHM 종합연구소의 소장인 그는 한쪽 유리병에 물을 담아놓고 '사랑', '감사' 등의 단어를, 다른 병에는 '증오', '악마' 등의 단어를 써서 붙여놓았다.

한 달 후 물 입자를 분석해봤더니 물의 결정체가 위와 같이 판이하게 달라졌다. '사랑', '감사' 딱지를 붙인 왼쪽 물은 곧고 반짝이는 아름다운 결정체로 변해 있었다. 반면 '증오', '악마' 등 부정적인 딱지가 붙어 있던 물의 결정체는 형태가 흐리고 기형적으로 일그러져 있었다. 단어에 담긴 사람의 마음을 두뇌도 없고, 글자도 안 배운 물이 어떻게 읽었을까?

우리가 매일 먹는 밥도 마찬가지다. 한 개의 유리병엔 '감사', '사랑'이란 딱지를 붙여놓고, 다른 한 개엔 '증오', '망할 놈' 등의 딱지를 붙여놓았다. 한 달 후 살펴보니 '감사' 딱지를 붙여놓은 밥은 잘 발효된 누룩 냄새를 풍기고 있었다. 반면 '증오' 딱지가 붙은 밥은 곰팡이가 슬었고 검게 썩어 악취가 진동했다.

'감사', '사랑' 딱지가 붙은 밥은
누런 누룩으로 변했고(왼쪽)
'증오', '망할 놈' 딱지가 붙은 밥은
검게 썩어 악취를 풍겼다(오른쪽).

정말 이상하지 않은가? 밥이 어떻게 글자에 담긴 마음까지 읽었단 말인가? 의문을 품은 세계 각지의 아마추어들이 너도나도 여러 나라 말로 직접 실험해봤지만 어김없이 똑같은 결과가 나왔다. 영어로 하든, 프랑스어로 하든, 한국어로 하든, 그 결과는 똑같다.

이쯤 되면 당신은 아마 이런 뜨악한 생각도 들 것이다.

"그럼 반찬 없다고 툴툴거리며 밥을 먹으면 밥도 나를 못마땅하게 여길까?"

모든 관계가 그렇지 않은가? 예를 들어 직장 상사가 썩 내키지 않은 표정으로 당신에게 일을 시키면서 "이 친구한테 이런 중요한 일 맡겨도 될지 모르겠네. 하지만 당장 맡길 사람이 없으니 어쩔 수 없지…"하고 투덜댄다면? 그럼 당신은 최선을 다해 일해주고 싶은 생각이 들까?

마찬가지 이치로, 밥도 불만을 품은 채 당신의 뱃속에 들어가면 소화가 잘 되도록 순순히 협조를 해줄까? 호기심이 동한 과학자들이 스웨덴 여성들과 태국 여성들에게 같은 음식을 주는 실험을 해보았다. 스웨덴 여성들은 고춧가루가 뻘겋게 올라앉은 태국음식을 보고는 눈살부터 찌푸렸다.

"태국음식은 영 구미가 안 당겨."

반면 태국 여성들은 김이 모락모락 오르는 태국음식을 보고는 군침부터 돌았다.

"와, 맛있겠다! 공짜로 이런 음식 먹으니 감사한 일이야."

똑같은 음식이었지만 한쪽은 마지못해 꾸역꾸역 먹었고 다른 한쪽은 감사한 마음으로 맛있게 먹었다. 그리고 식사 후 여성들의 피를 분석해보니 태국 여성들은 음식에 들어 있는 철분을 스웨덴 여성들보다 50퍼센트나 더 많이 흡수했다.

이번에는 반대로 스웨덴 음식을 먹게 했더니 정반대의 결과가 나왔다. 태국 여성들의 철분 흡수량은 스웨덴 여성들보다 70퍼센트나 적었다. 음식을 먹긴 했지만, 굶은 거나 다름없었다.

초콜릿은 안 그럴까?

불교 승려들로 하여금 초콜릿 조각들을 사랑과 자비의 마음으로 각각 10초씩 바라보도록 해보았다.

'이 초콜릿을 먹고 몸과 마음이 건강해지도록 해주십시오.'

이렇게 바라본 초콜릿과 바라보지 않은 초콜릿을 사람들에게 제각기 하루 1온스씩 먹도록 했다. 5일 후 그들에게 물었다.

"심신이 어떻게 달라졌습니까?"

어떤 사람들은 전과 비교해 기운이 열 배나 더 넘쳐흐른다고 대답했다. 아무런 변화가 없는 사람들도 있었다. 기운이 넘쳐흐른다는 사람들을 살펴보니 신기하게도 모두가 사랑의 감정이 담긴 초콜릿을 먹은 사람들이었다. 그들은 닷새 만에 평균 67퍼센트나 활력이 더 넘치게 됐다고 응답했다. 반면 승려들이 바라보지 않은 초콜릿을 먹은 사람들은 아무 변화가 없었다. 프린스턴 대학의 라딘(Dean Radin) 박사가 실시한 실험이다.

라딘 박사

"감사와 사랑의 마음으로
음식을 먹으면 영양분
흡수율이 높아진다."

whatthebleep.com

왜 이런 일이 일어날까? 뇌세포도 없는 음식이 감사나 사랑의 마음으로 바라보면 어떻게 용케 그 마음을 알아차리고 영양분이 쑥쑥 흡수돼 에너지가 샘솟게 한단 말인가?

말랑말랑한 음식은 그렇다 치자. 그럼 딱딱하기 그지없는 기계마저도 어떤 마음으로 바라보느냐에 따라 변화할까? 물리학자인 슈미트(Helmut Schmidt) 박사는 사람들에게 헤드폰을 낀 채 기계에서 나오는 삐이 소리를 듣도록 했다. 삐이 소리는 왼쪽과 오른쪽 귀에 50:50으로 고르게 흘러나오도록 설정되어 있었다.

그는 이런 지시를 내렸다.

"삐이 소리가 왼쪽 귀에서 더 많이 흘러나오도록 생각해 보세요."

사람들은 시키는 대로 헤드폰을 낀 채 '왼쪽에서 삐이 소리가 더 많이 나오거라' 하고 반복해서 마음속으로 되뇌어보았다. 실험결과는 뜻밖이었다. 거의 모든 사람들이 왼쪽에서 더 많은 삐이 소리를 듣게 됐기 때문이다.

이번에는 '삐이 소리가 오른쪽 귀에서 더 많이 나오거라' 하고 생각해보았다. 그랬더니 예상대로 오른쪽 귀에서 더 많은 삐이 소리를 듣게 됐다. 다시 말해 사람들은 기계에 손가락 하나 안 대고도 마음만으로 기계의 성능을 변화시켰던 것이다.

박사는 이번에는 삐이 소리가 녹음된 테이프를 사람들에게 건네주며 말했다.

"이 테이프를 집에 가지고 가서 삐이 소리가 왼쪽 귀에 더 많이 들리도록 되뇌어보세요."

사람들은 지시대로 '왼쪽에서 삐이 소리가 더 많이 나오거라' 생각하며 테이프를 반복해서 들었다. 이튿날 그들의 테이프를 수거하여 오디오 확인 장치에 넣어 들어본 슈미트 박사는 어안이 벙벙했다.

"거참 기이한 일도 다 있군. 테이프들에서 나오는 삐이 소리가 정말 왼쪽 귀에 더 많이 들리도록 변하다니?"

테이프가 사람들의 생각만으로 변질된 것이었다. 그게 끝이 아니었다. 슈미트 박사가 따로 보관해두었던 테이프에서도 삐이 소리가 왼쪽 귀에 더 많이 들리는 것이었다. 그가 실험 직전에 확인한 바로는 분명히 양쪽 귀에 균등하게 삐이 소리가 녹음되어 있었는데 말이다.

"내가 가만히 내버려둔 테이프까지 변하다니… 대체 웬일일까?"

그는 잠시 후 무릎을 탁 쳤다. 그는 테이프들을 복사하면서 '왼쪽에서 삐이 소리가 더 많이 나게끔 되뇌도록 사람들에게 시켜야지' 하고 생각했었다. 바로 그 생각이 이미 테이프에 영향을 끼쳤던 것이다. 기이하지 않은가?

해스티드 교수

"생각의 힘은 거리에 상관없이
대상을 변화시킨다."

런던 대학의 해스티드(John Hasted) 교수는 어린이들을 대상으로 기발
한 실험을 고안해냈다.

그는 속임수가 통하지 못하도록 천장에 여러 개의 열쇠를 매달아놓
고, 어린이들에게 각기 90센티미터에서 3미터까지 떨어져 있도록 했다.
그리고 각각의 열쇠에는 끌어당기는 힘 등을 측정할 수 있는 작은 신장계
(strain gauge)를 부착해놓았다.

"어린이 여러분, 생각만으로 천장에 매달려 있는 열쇠를 구부려보세
요."

어린이들은 각기 앞에 매달린 열쇠를 구부리기 위해 열심히 생각을
집중했다. 그러나 열쇠가 엿가락처럼 구부러지는 경우는 없었다. 역시 생
각의 힘이란 공허한 것이었을까?

"어, 저 열쇠는 마구 흔들거리네?"

"금이 간 열쇠도 있어요!"

어린이들이 생각을 얼마나 집중하느냐에 따라 좌우로 흔들리는 열쇠

도 있었고, 가늘게 금이 가는 열쇠도 있었다. 해스티드 교수는 신장계에 기록된 수치들을 살펴보고는 입이 딱 벌어졌다. 신장계에 기록된 전압 펄스 그래프가 최고 한계를 뛰어넘어 10볼트까지 치솟는 경우도 있었기 때문이다. 더구나 생각의 힘은 90센티미터가 떨어져 있든, 3미터가 떨어져 있든 그 거리와는 상관이 없었다. 오로지 얼마나 강한 의도를 품고 바라보느냐에 따라 쇠붙이에 미치는 변화도 컸던 것이다.

'저 열쇠를 구부려야지.'

이렇게 마음먹고 바라보면 제아무리 단단한 쇠붙이라도 그 마음을 읽고 형태가 변형되기 시작한다.

2 왜 바라보는 대로 변할까?

이처럼 이 세상에 존재하는 모든 것들은 당신의 속마음을 귀신처럼 속속들이 읽어낸다. 그리고 그 속마음이 바라보는 대로 변화한다. 몸이건 물이건 밥이건 쇠붙이건 가릴 것 없이 말이다. 그렇다면 이런 현상은 도 대체 왜 일어나는 걸까?

이런 원초적인 질문을 던져보자.

"만물은 뭐로 만들어져 있는가?"

몸을 쪼개고 쪼개서 더 이상 쪼갤 수 없을 때까지 쪼개면? 미립자가 나온다.

밥을 쪼개고 쪼개서 더 이상 쪼갤 수 없을 때까지 쪼개면? 역시 미립 자가 나온다.

그럼 생각을 실은 뇌파를 더 이상 쪼갤 수 없을 때까지 쪼개면? 그것 도 역시 미립자다.

눈에 보이는 것이든 안 보이는 것이든, 만물은 죄다 미립자가 최소 구 성 물질이다. 다시 말해 우주가 몽땅 흙으로 만들어져 있다면 미립자는 가장 작은 흙먼지인 셈이다. 그럼 이 흙먼지, 즉 미립자의 정체는 뭘까? 정체가 뭐기에 사람의 마음을 그처럼 척척 읽어내는 걸까?

비 밀 은   미 립 자 에   있 다

미립자의 정체를 알기 위해 이런 상상을 해보자.

먼저 미립자들을 어마어마하게 부풀려 야구공만 하게 확대시킨다. 그런 다음 자동발사기에 장전시킨 뒤 하나씩 발사한다.

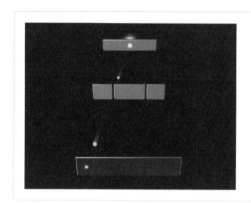

이중슬릿 실험 1

누군가가 바라보면, 미립자가 슬릿을 직선으로 통과해 뒷면에 알갱이 자국이 남는다.

위 그림을 보면, 중간의 벽에는 두 군데의 슬릿slit(가늘고 긴 틈)이 뚫려 있다. 당신은 거기를 향해 미립자들을 발사한다. 그럼 미립자들은 하나씩 직선으로 날아가 두 슬릿 중 한 곳을 통과하고 그 뒤의 벽면에 부딪혀 알갱이 자국을 남긴다. 그걸 바라보는 당신은 이렇게 말할 것이다.

"뭐 이래? 하나도 신기하지 않아. 뻥 뚫린 구멍을 통해 야구공을 던지는 것과 뭐가 달라?"

하지만 기절초풍할 일은 당신이 자리를 비운 사이에 나타난다. 잠시밖에 나갔다가 돌아온 당신은 소스라치게 놀란다.

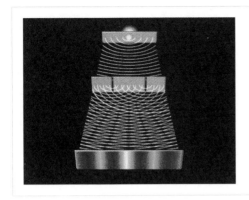

이중슬릿 실험 2

누군가가 바라보지 않으면, 미립자는 물결처럼 통과하며 벽면에 물결 자국을 남긴다.

"아니, 이런 귀신이 곡할 노릇이 다 있나? 벽면에 알갱이가 아니라 물결 자국들이 나 있네?"

당신이 바라보지 않는 사이에 자동으로 발사된 미립자들은 알갱이가 아니라 물결로 돌변해 두 슬릿을 통과한 것이다. 따라서 슬릿 뒤의 벽면에는 알갱이 자국들이 아니라 여러 개의 물결들이 서로 간섭하면서 만들어낸 자국이 남았다. 토끼 눈을 한 당신은 기가 막힐 뿐이다.

"미립자들이 귀신에 홀렸나? 내가 바라보고 있으면 미립자가 직선으로 날아가 알갱이 자국을 남기고, 바라보지 않으면 물결처럼 퍼져 나가 물결 자국을 남기다니?"

당신은 부랴부랴 친구를 불러 다시 한 번 실험을 해보라고 한다. 하지만 결과는 마찬가지다.

"내가 쳐다봐도 그래. 쳐다보면 무조건 알갱이처럼 행동하는 거야. 안 쳐다보면 물결처럼 행동하고."

미립자들은 왜 이런 요술을 부리는 걸까?

"왜 내가 바라볼 때만 고체 알갱이로 행동하는 거지?"

당신은 곰곰이 생각하다가 무릎을 탁 친다.

"오호라! 난 미립자를 바라볼 때마다 '미립자는 고체 알갱이야'라고 생각하고 있어. 그래서 미립자가 내 생각을 읽고 고체 알갱이처럼 행동하는 거야."

이처럼 미립자는 당신의 속마음을 귀신처럼 읽어낸다. 거짓은 통하지 않는다. (이상은 쉽게 풀어쓴 설명으로, 실제 실험 절차에서는 미립자의 궤적을 좇는 입자검출기의 설치 유무에 따라 미립자가 벽면에 남기는 패턴이 달라졌다.)

"만물이 내 마음을 척척 읽어내는 미립자들로 만들어져 있으니 내가 바라볼 때마다 변화할 수밖에 없는 거로군!"

정말 기막힌 요술 아닌가? 온 세상이 당신이 바라보는 대로 춤을 추다니! 당신 인생은 정말 당신 스스로가 창조하는 것이다.

이게 바로 양자물리학 분야에서 최고 권위를 자랑하는 이스라엘의 와이즈만 과학원이 1998년에 실시한 이중슬릿 실험(double-slit experiment)이다. (실험과정은 'google' 동영상 사이트에 들어가 'observer effect'를 클릭하면 자세히 볼 수 있다.) 세계적인 물리학 전문지 〈물리학 세계(Physics World)〉는 이 실험을 "과학사에서 가장 아름다웠던 실험"으로 선정하기도 했다.

아인슈타인 이후 최고의 물리학자로 꼽히는 노벨 물리학상 수상자 파인만(Richard Feynman) 박사도 한목소리를 냈다.

"그 실험을 보면 우리의 마음이 어떤 원리로 만물을 변화시키고 새 운명을 창조해내는지 한눈에 알 수 있어요."

사실 이중슬릿 실험을 처음 실시한 건 이스라엘 과학원이 아니었다.

양자물리학자 울프 박사

"내가 바라볼 때마다 만물이
변화하는 건 '신이 부리는
요술'이다."

whatthebleep.com

한 세기가 넘도록 세계 최고의 물리학자들이 비슷한 실험을 끊임없이 실
시해왔지만 결과는 늘 똑같았다. 즉, 미립자들은 사람들이 어떤 마음으로
자기를 바라보는지 언제나 컴퓨터처럼 정확하게 읽고 거기에 맞춰 변화
한다.

이처럼 실험자가 미립자를 입자라고 생각하고 바라보면 입자의 모습
이 나타나고 물결로 생각하고 바라보면 물결의 모습이 나타나는 현상을,
양자 물리학자들은 '관찰자 효과(observer effect)'라고 부른다. 이것이 만물
을 창조하는 우주의 가장 핵심적인 원리다. 다시 말해 미립자는 눈에 안
보이는 물결로 우주에 존재하다가 내가 어떤 의도를 품고 바라보는 바로
그 순간, 돌연 눈에 보이는 현실로 모습을 드러내는 것이다. 그래서 양자
물리학자 울프 박사는 관찰자 효과를 '신이 부리는 요술(God's trick)'이라
고 부르고, 미립자들이 가득한 우주공간을 '신의 마음(Mind of God)'이라
고 일컫는다.

신이 부리는 요술은 내가 얼마나 깊이 있게 바라보느냐에 따라 변화
의 폭이 다르다. 생각에도 층이 있기 때문이다. 깊은 마음으로 바라보면
깊이 변화하고, 얕은 마음으로 바라보면 티끌밖에 움직이지 못한다.

이 요술이 얼마나 경이롭던지 덴마크의 노벨물리학상 수상자인 보어 (Niels Bohr)는 "이 요술에 충격을 받지 않는 사람은 이해하지 못한 것이 다"라고까지 말했다. 독일의 노벨물리학상 수상자인 하이젠베르크 (Werner Heisenberg)도 미립자들을 "무한한 가능성의 알갱이들"이라고 불렀 다. 인간이 원하는 모든 정보와 모든 걸 창조할 수 있는 모든 가능성이 담 겨 있기 때문이다.

"미립자들은 우주의 모든 정보와 지혜, 힘을 갖고 있고 모든 걸 알고 있다. 그래서 동물이나 식물, 물과 바위 등 어떤 것으로든 현실화될 수 있 는 모든 가능성을 가진 마법의 알갱이들이다."

미립자들은 불가사의하게도 거리에도 전혀 영향을 받지 않는다. 특히 단 한 번이라도 인연을 맺었던 미립자들은 바로 곁에 있든, 우주 정 반대 편에 떨어져 있든, 아무 상관 없이 빛보다 빠른 속도로 영원히 서로 정보 를 주고받는다.

"그게 무슨 소리지?"

이를테면 이런 거다. 당신의 입천장에서 세포 몇 개를 떼어내 시험관에 넣는다. 그리고 당신 몸과 시험관에 각각 피부반응 감지기를 부착한다. 그런 다음 당신은 가만히 있고, 당신의 입천장 세포들이 든 시험관만 옆 건물에 갖다놓는다. 심심해진 당신은 비디오를 틀어본다.

"맑은 날 구름이 뭉게뭉게 떠 있는 비디오군. 내 마음도 평화로워지는걸."

당신의 몸에 붙여놓은 피부반응 감지기엔 '평온'의 반응이 나타난다.

"그럼 옆 건물에 갖다놓은 내 입천장 세포들은?"

과학자들이 당신의 입천장 세포들과 연결된 피부반응 감지기를 살펴보니 놀랍게도 당신이 '평온'을 느끼는 바로 그 순간, 세포들도 '평온'을 기록한 것으로 나타난다.

"이번엔 공포 비디오를 틀어볼까?"

마찬가지다. 당신이 비디오를 보면서 공포를 느끼는 순간, 옆 건물에 있는 당신의 세포들도 역시 '공포' 반응을 보인다.

"그럼 옆 건물이 아닌 20킬로미터 떨어진 곳에 세포들을 갖다놓으면 어떨까?"

그래도 결과는 역시 마찬가지다. 당신이 '평온'을 느끼면 세포들도 '평온'을, 당신이 '공포'를 느끼면 세포들도 '공포'를 느낀다. 정확하게 똑같은 찰나에 말이다.

"거참 이상하군. 두뇌도 없는 세포들이 어떻게 분리된 세포 주인과 똑같은 감정을 느끼는 거지?"

과학자들은 좀더 극단적인 방법을 써보기로 한다. 세포들을 떼어낸 지 무려 닷새나 지나고 나서 자그마치 80킬로미터나 떨어진 다른 도시에 세포들을 옮겨다 놓고 똑같은 실험을 하는 것이다.

"닷새나 지났고, 아주 멀리 떨어져 있으니 이젠 주인과 인연이 끊어졌겠지?"

하지만 웬걸? 당신의 입천장 세포들은 여전히 당신의 마음을 컴퓨터처럼 정확히 읽고 똑같이 반응하는 것 아닌가! 아무리 거리가 떨어져 있어도 아무 상관 없다. 세포 속에 들어 있는 미립자들은 인간의 두뇌로는 도저히 이해할 수 없는 불가사의한 능력을 갖고 있는 것이다. 1998년, 미국 국방부가 실시한 실험이다. 피붙이가 아무리 멀리 떨어져 있어도 영원히 끈끈한 사랑을 느끼는 것도 바로 이래서다.

러시아 과학자들은 잔인하지만 이런 실험도 해보았다. 어미 토끼를 새끼들과 떼어놓고 두뇌에 전극(electrode)을 삽입했다. 그리고 새끼들을 잠수함에 태워 수천 킬로미터 떨어진 북대서양 심해로 데려가서 한 마리씩 처형했다. 그런데 놀랍게도 새끼들이 처형되는 바로 그 순간마다 어미 토끼의 뇌파는 크게 치솟았다. 볼 수도, 들을 수도, 냄새를 맡을 수도 없는 수천 킬로미터 밖의 일인데도 말이다. 사람도 그렇다. 이역만리 떨어진 자식에게 어디 아픈 데라도 생기면 부모도 뭔가 편치 않은 구석이 생기지 않는가? 따라서 만일 한국의 부모가 미국에 가 있는 자식을 위해 기도해도 그 기도가 담긴 미립자 에너지는 즉시 목적지에 도달한다. 자식이 설사 달나라에 가 있더라도 빛보다 더 빠른 속도로 에너지가 전달된다. 비록 자식이 의식적으로는 느끼지 못하더라도 말이다.

뚱뚱한 사람을 친구로 둔 사람은 자신도 점점 뚱뚱해진다는 얘기를 들어본 적 있는가?

하버드 대학의 크리스타키스(Nicholas Christakis) 교수가 32년간 12,000명을 추적해봤더니, 친한 친구가 뚱뚱하면 나도 뚱뚱해질 가능성이 무려

크리스타키스 교수

"우리는 자주 바라보는
이미지대로 변화해간다."

christakis.med.harvard.edu

세 배나 높아졌다. 뚱뚱한 친구가 나와 얼마나 멀리 떨어져 사느냐는 아무 상관이 없었다. 지구 정반대 편인 브라질에 살든, 태양계의 저 끝 토성에 올라가 살든, 내가 그 친구 모습을 좋아하는 마음으로 자주 떠올려 바라볼수록 나도 모르게 점점 몸이 뚱뚱해진다. 내가 끌어당겨 자주 바라보는 이미지가 내 몸도 변화시키는 것이다. 미립자들이 이처럼 공간의 영향을 받지 않고 서로 영향을 미치는 현상을 양자물리학에서는 '비국지성(non-locality)'이라고 부른다. 아인슈타인은 이런 현상을 '멀리서 일어나는 으스스한 행동(spooky action at a distance)'이라고 부르기도 했다.

이처럼 불가사의한 미립자들로 만들어진 이 세상의 모든 만물은 저마다 특유의 지능을 갖고 있다. 단지 얼마나 많은 미립자들이 어떤 방식으로 모여 어떤 물질을 이루느냐에 따라 지능의 특성만 각기 다를 뿐이다. 우리는 인간만이 만물 가운데 독보적인 지능을 가진 것으로 알고 있지만, 그건 지능을 누구의 어떤 잣대로 정의하느냐의 문제다. 예를 들어 어떤 철새들은 해마다 수천 킬로미터를 날아 정확히 목적지에 도착한다. 깊은 바다 속에서 길을 잃지 않고 역시 수천 킬로미터씩 오가는 물고기나 거북

이들도 있다. 어떤 코끼리들은 수백 킬로미터 떨어진 가족을 찾아가기도 한다. 우리처럼 지도도 보지 않고 말이다. 만일 그들에게 인간의 지능을 어떻게 평가하느냐고 물으면 어떤 대답이 나올까?

"지도 없이는 십 리 밖도 못 가는 저능아들!"

그들은 자기네끼리 이렇게 낄낄거릴지 모른다.

대지에서 꼭 필요한 만큼의 자양분만 흡수하고 탄생하는 밥 등의 음식들도 그렇다. 비록 아무 말도 못하고 혼자서는 어디를 나돌아다니지도 못하지만, 필요도 없는 음식을 배가 터지도록 계속 먹어대는 우리를 보고, "이 인간, 자기 배가 얼마나 부른지도 모르고 먹어대네?" 하고 혀를 끌끌 찰 수도 있다.

우리가 감지할 수 있는 건 고작 오감을 통해 보고, 듣고, 만지는 것 등에 국한된다. 우리는 모르는 건 "존재하지 않는 것"으로 치부하고 무시해버린다. 심지어 우리 몸뚱이가 두뇌보다 더 똑똑한 지능을 갖고 있다는 사실조차 모른다. 이런 예를 들어보자.

큰 강당에 천 명이 모여 있다. 그들에게 각기 밀봉된 봉투 하나씩 나눠준다. 봉투 500개엔 인공감미료가, 나머지 500개엔 천연비타민C가 들어있다. 물론 참석자들은 뭐가 들어 있는지를 모른다.

"여러분, 이제 봉투를 각자의 가슴에 대보세요."

그런 다음 간단한 방법으로 참석자 전원의 근력을 시험해본다. 이를테면 두 명씩 짝을 지어 팔의 힘을 시험하도록 하는 식이다. 그런데 시험 결과 신기하게도 정확하게 500명은 전보다 힘이 세졌고, 나머지 500명은 힘이 약해졌다. 웬일일까?

"여러분, 각자 봉투를 뜯어보세요."

호킨스 박사

"몸은 두뇌보다 더 똑똑하다."

힘이 강해진 사람들의 봉투를 뜯어보니 한결같이 천연비타민C가 들어 있다. 반면, 약해진 사람들의 봉투 속에는 예외 없이 인공감미료가 들어 있다. 두뇌는 밀봉된 봉투 속에 뭐가 들어 있는지 깜깜하다. 하지만 뇌세포도, 눈도 없는 몸뚱이는 어떤 봉투 속에 몸에 이로운 비타민C가 들어 있는지 용케도 알아맞힌다. 정신의학자인 호킨스(David Hawkins) 박사는 지금도 많은 사람들 앞에서 강연할 때 종종 이런 시연을 한다.

"내 몸이 두뇌보다 더 똑똑하다니!"

참석자들은 늘 이렇게 놀라워한다. 하지만 조금만 더 깊이 생각해보면 그리 놀라운 일도 아니다. 잠시 책을 덮고 심장에게 말해보라.

"심장아, 10초간만 멈춰볼래?"

심장은 당신의 생각대로 멈추지 않는다. 만일 심장이 당신의 생각대로 멈춰버린다면 당신은 죽는다. 이처럼 심장은 두뇌보다 더 똑똑한 지능을 갖고 움직인다. 고도의 지능을 가진 미립자들로 만들어져 있으니 그럴 수밖에 없다. 단지 우리가 그런 사실을 모를 뿐이다. 우리는 인간의 오감보다 더 섬세한 차원에서는 어떤 대화가 오가는지 깜깜하다.

만물이 모두 지능을 갖고 있다는 사실은 영적 깨달음을 얻은 많은 사

노벨물리학상 수상자 플랑크

"고도의 지능을 가진 배후의 마음이
 모든 걸 창조한다"

람들을 통해 이미 수천 년 전부터 꽤 알려져 온 사실이다. 단지 과학이 그
걸 입증할 수준에 미치지 못했을 따름이었다. 뒤늦게나마 양자물리학자
들은 모든 피조물이 고도의 지능을 가진 미립자들로 만들어졌으며, 사람
의 속마음을 척척 읽어낸다는 사실을 밝혀냈다. 이에 따라 "두뇌가 없으
면 지능도 없다"는 생각도 두뇌를 가진 인간이 빚어낸 어이없는 착각임
이 여지없이 드러났다.

그럼 이렇게 요술 같은 지능을 가진 미립자는 대체 누가 창조해낸 걸
까? 독일의 노벨물리학상 수상자인 플랑크(Max Planck)는 "이 요술의 배후
에는 의식적이며 고도로 지능적인 마음이 존재한다. 이 마음이 모든 걸
창조한다"고 말했다. 아인슈타인도 "우주에는 인간의 상상을 초월하는
거대한 마음이 있다"고 밝혔다.

그렇다면 미립자들로 구성된 이 세상은 내가 원하는 대로, 생각하는
대로 수시로 바뀔 수 있다는 얘긴가? 그런 일이 흔하게 일어나지는 않는
다. 왜냐하면 우리는 대부분 그 무한한 가능성을 제대로 이해하거나 바라
보지 못하기 때문이다. 정신적 깨달음도 마찬가지다. 누구에게나 가능성

46

은 열려 있지만, 그 가능성을 진심으로 바라보지 못한다. 그래서 예수는 천국이 모든 곳에 있지만 사람들이 그걸 보지 못한다고 한탄했다. 그러면서 "누구든지 하느님의 말씀을 받는 자는 신神"이라고 했다. 제대로 바라보기만 하면 신처럼 모든 능력을 갖게 된다는 뜻이다. 또 석가모니도 "생명이 있는 모든 중생에게는 깨달을 수 있는 불성이 있다(一切衆生 皆有佛性)"고 했다. 누구나 제대로 바라보기만 하면 그처럼 깨달음을 얻을 수 있다는 것이다. 하지만 이런 말을 듣고 선뜻 "그래, 나도 노력하면 정말 신이 될 수 있을 거야"라든가, "맞아. 나도 마음만 먹으면 깨달음을 얻을 수 있어"라고 받아들이는 사람들은 지극히 드물다. "내가 감히 어떻게…", "노력해서 되는 일이 따로 있지…" 하고 가능성부터 쾅 닫아버린다. 가능성을 닫고 바라보니 가능성이 보이지 않는 것이다.

미립자는 사람의 속마음을 읽는다

내가 텅 빈 커피잔을 들고 진심으로 기도한다고 가정해보자.

"이 잔으로 커피를 마실 때마다 마시는 사람이 건강해지도록 해주십시오."

기도를 마친 뒤 잔을 알루미늄포일로 정성스럽게 감싸 미국에 사는 친구에게 보낸다. 미국에 유학중인 친구는 돈이 없다. 그래서 싸구려 커피를 마신다. 싸구려 커피는 노화방지물질의 농도가 높지 않다. 하지만 그 싸구려 커피를 내가 보내준 잔에 부어 마셨더니 신기하게도 맛이 확 달라지는 것 아닌가?

"어, 싸구려 커피가 고급 커피 맛을 내다니! 이 잔에 마법이 들어 있나?"

그래서 이번엔 평소 자신이 쓰던 잔에 부어 마셔봤더니 맛이 도로 확 떨어진다.

"친구가 보내준 잔이 마법을 부리는 게 틀림없어!"

도저히 믿기지 않아 실험실에 분석을 의뢰했더니 실제로 내가 보내준 잔에 커피를 붓기만 하면 노화방지물질의 농도가 훌쩍 높아지는 것 아닌가! 나는 그 소식을 전해 듣고 다른 커피잔에도 똑같은 기도를 해본다. 이번엔 여러 번 한다. 기도가 반복될수록 커피잔의 마법은 더욱 강력해진다. 기도를 하면 할수록 효과는 더욱 빨리 나타난다. 내 기도가 싸구려 커피를 고급 커피로 둔갑시키는 요술을 만들어내는 것이다.

1년쯤 후부터 더욱 놀라운 현상이 나타난다. 내가 기도하던 그 방에서는 기도를 한 잔이든 아니든, 그 어떤 잔에 커피를 마셔도 똑같은 기도 효과가 나타나는 것이다. 방 안 전체에 기도의 기운이 서려 있기 때문이다. 거짓말 같은 얘기라고 생각할 것이다. 하지만 이는 스탠퍼드 대학의 양자물리학자 틸러(William Tiller) 박사가 수도 없이 실험해서 얻은 결과다.

그는 원래 수소이온 농도 측정기로 이런 실험을 했었다. 먼저 그 기계에 대고 "이 기계로 측정하면 수소이온농도가 높아지도록 해주십시오" 하고 기도했다. 그런 다음 3,200킬로미터나 떨어진 실험실로 보내 그곳의 물을 측정해보도록 했다. 그랬더니 평소보다 수소이온 농도가 1도 이상 높아지는 것이었다. 그리고 한 장소에서 기도를 반복할수록 그 장소 전체에 기도의 기운이 스며들어 나중엔 기도를 안 해도 똑같은 효과가 나타났다.

틸러 박사

"기도가 반복될수록
그 효과는 점점 더 강해진다."

whatthebleep.com

이처럼 커피잔이건 기계건, 내 주변의 모든 것들을 구성하는 미립자들은 내 마음을 읽을 뿐 아니라 그 정보를 고스란히 저장해두는 지능까지 갖고 있다. 평소 공부하던 교실에서 시험을 보면 점수가 더 잘 나오고, 평소 연습하던 경기장에서 경기하면 실력이 더 잘 발휘된다는 널리 알려진 실험결과들은 이런 사실들을 과학적으로 뒷받침해준다. 따라서 기도의 효과가 당장 눈앞의 현실로 나타나지 않는다고 실망할 필요는 없다. 한 삽, 두 삽의 흙을 파냈다고 금방 우물물이 솟아오르지는 않는다. 수천 번, 수만 번 삽질을 해내려 가다 보면 갈수록 깊어지다 어느 순간 갑자기 물이 콸콸 솟아오른다.

기도에 담긴 뜻은 일일이 우주에 기억되고 저장된다. 어디로 가는 게 아니다. 내가 남에게 입히는 마음의 상처도 마찬가지다. 내 잘못을 뉘우치지 않는 한 가차없이 언젠가 내게 돌아온다. 만일 내 생전에 현실로 나타나지 않는다면 내세에, 혹은 후손들에게 나타날 수도 있다. 이것이 인과응보의 법칙이다.

많은 사람들의 염원이 합쳐지면 변화의 폭은 더욱 커진다.

날씨도 그렇다. 이런 의문을 품어본 적 있는가? 고등학생들이 수능시험을 보는 날엔 왜 어김없이 '수능추위'가 찾아올까? 또 졸업식 날엔 왜 어김없이 날씨가 좋을까?

프린스턴 대학의 넬슨(Roger Nelson) 박사는 졸업식 날만 되면 궂던 날씨도 돌연 좋아지는 게 이상하다고 생각했다.

"수천 명의 학부모와 학생들이 좋은 날씨를 바라보며 모여드니 그런 걸까?"

그는 30년간의 졸업식 당일과 전후의 날씨들을 면밀히 분석해보았다. 놀라운 결과가 나왔다. 30년간 졸업식 당일에 대학과 인접지역에 비가 내릴 확률은 33퍼센트였다. 그런데 신기하게도 그 지역 한복판에 있는 대학 교정에 비가 내릴 확률은 28퍼센트에 불과했다. 같은 지역인데도 경축 인파가 우글거리는 대학 교정은 쏙 빼놓고 주변지역에만 비가 내리는 경우가 많았던 것이다.

더 기이한 건 졸업식 전후로 며칠간 비가 오더라도 졸업식 당일엔 돌연 비가 뚝 그친 경우가 너무나도 많았다는 것이다. 예를 들어 1962년의 졸업식 날엔 예외적으로 어마어마한 폭우가 쏟아졌는데, 신통하게도 졸업식이 끝나는 바로 그 순간이 돼서야 봇물이 터진 듯 갑자기 쏟아지기 시작했다는 식이다. 마치 졸업식이 끝나길 참고 기다렸다는 듯 말이다.

이처럼 많은 사람들이 따뜻한 눈으로 어느 특정한 날의 날씨를 바라보면 실제로 화창한 햇볕이 찾아온다. 반면 차가운 눈으로 날씨를 바라보면 매서운 바람이 찾아온다. 이렇게 보면 수능추위도 우연의 일치로만 치부하긴 어렵다. 긴장과 걱정으로 꽁꽁 얼어붙은 수험생들과 부모들의 마음이 분명 일조를 하고 있는 것이다.

더욱 신기한 일도 있다. 우주가 마치 족집게 점술가처럼 미래를 척척 예측해낸다는 것이다.

2001년에는 110층짜리 뉴욕 무역센터 건물이 폭파되는 9/11 테러 사건이 벌어졌다. 그런데 우주는 사건발생 네 시간 전부터 쌍둥이 고층건물이 무너져 내리고 수천 명이 죽게 될 것임을 손바닥 들여다보듯 훤히 내다보고 있었다.

그걸 어떻게 증명하느냐고? 프린스턴 대학의 넬슨 교수 등 전 세계 41개국의 내로라하는 물리학자 75명은 이미 1997년부터 세계적인 재앙과 천재지변을 추적해오고 있었다.

"세계적인 충격을 주는 뉴스거리들을 우주는 얼마나 빨리 알아차릴까?"

그들은 전 세계 곳곳에 무작위사건발생장치(REG, random event generator)들을 설치해놓고 있었다. 요컨대 동전을 1,000번 던지면 앞면과 뒷면이 나올 확률은 500:500이다. 그게 자연의 법칙이다. 하지만 세계적으로 충격적 사건이 일어날 때면 이 확률이 요동친다. 500:500이 아니라 700:300, 800:200 등으로 완전히 균형을 잃는다. 영국 다이애나 왕세자비의 교통사고 사망, 클린턴 미국 대통령 탄핵 등 큰일들이 터졌을 때도 그랬다. 그 가운데 9/11 테러는 가장 큰 충격을 준 사건이었다. 벌써 네 시간 전부터 REG 기계의 바늘은 뾰족하게 치솟기 시작했다. 그걸 보고 과학자들은 숨을 죽였다.

"또 어마어마한 사건이 터지려는가 보군. 설마 미국 대통령이 저격당하는 건 아니겠지?"

아니나 다를까. 네 시간 후 테러범들은 피랍 여객기를 몰아 쌍둥이 건

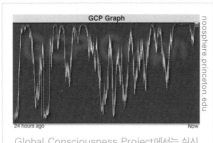

GCP Graph

noosphere.princeton.edu

24 hours ago   Now

Global Consciousness Project에서는 실시간으로 전 세계의 REG를 모니터링하고 있다.

물을 들이박았다. 우주는 테러범들의 무시무시한 살의를 미리 읽고 있었던 것이다. 그 후에도 REG 바늘은 무려 나흘간이나 800:200, 900:100 언저리를 맴돌며 날카롭게 치솟아 있었다.

기계의 바늘을 지켜본 네덜란드 암스테르담 대학의 물리학자 비에르만(Dick Bierman) 교수는 이렇게 말했다.

"기계가 수십억 지구인들이 받은 마음의 충격만 읽은 건 아닐 겁니다. 우주 삼라만상이 모두 사람의 마음을 읽으니까요."

우주는 사람들의 마음 구석구석을 속속들이 들여다본다. 따라서 우주에서는 그 어느 누구의 거짓도 통하지 않는다. 누군가 범행의도를 품고 있다면 범행이 채 일어나기도 전에 이미 우주에 그 범행의도가 고스란히 기록되기 때문이다. 우주만물이 사람의 마음을 읽는 미립자들로 구성돼 있으니 그럴 수밖에 없다.

그렇다면 살아 있는 식물은 어떨까? 커피잔이나 기계보다 내 마음을 더 훤히 읽어낼까? 심지어 미묘한 감정의 변화까지도?

1966년 어느 날 아침, 미국 중앙정보국(CIA) 최고의 거짓말 탐지 권위자였던 백스터(Cleve Backster)는 사무실에서 화분을 바라보다 문득 생각했다.

'저 드라세나 식물의 뿌리에서 가장 꼭대기의 잎사귀까지 물이 올라가는 데 시간이 얼마나 걸릴까?'

그는 거짓말 탐지장치의 하나인 피부반응 감지기를 잎사귀에 붙여놓았다. 그리고는 깜짝 놀랐다. 물을 주자 감지기 모니터에 즉각 '기쁨'의 반응이 나타났기 때문이다.

'드라세나 잎사귀가 사람의 감정과 같은 반응을 보이다니 이상한 걸?'

피부반응 감지기는 지극히 민감한 장치다. 혈압, 땀, 맥박의 섬세한 움직임을 감지해 감정의 변화를 읽어낸다. 누가 거짓말을 한다면 감지기 그래프도 튀어 오른다. 스트레스를 받아도 그렇다.

백스터는 드라세나 잎사귀에 정신적 충격을 줘보기로 했다.

'잎사귀 하나를 떼어내 태워보면 어떨까? 사람처럼 공포감을 느낄까?'

그는 옆 사무실에 가서 성냥을 가져오려고 걸음을 떼다가 혹시 하는 생각으로 감지기 그래프를 바라보았다. 입이 딱 벌어졌다. 감지기 그래프가 마구 요동치고 있었기 때문이다.

'엇? 이건 공포 반응 아닌가?'

화초는 '공포'의 반응을 그래프에 그려내고 있었다. 그래프가 차트의 꼭대기로 치솟았다. 성냥개비를 긋기는커녕 그저 생각만 했을 뿐인데도 말이다.

화초가 자신의 머릿속에 든 생각을 읽어내다니? 그는 얼른 옆 사무실로 달려가 성냥을 가져왔다. 성냥개비를 그어 잎사귀 밑으로 불을 가까이 해보았다. 감지기 그래프는 차트 맨 꼭대기 한계까지 치솟아 올랐다. 그가 옆 사무실에 성냥을 도로 갖다놓고 오니 그제야 그래프는 정상으로 떨어졌다.

'식물이 내 생각을 읽는 게 틀림없어.'

어느 날 한 과학자가 그의 실험실에 들렀다. 드라세나 실험을 직접 확인해보고 싶어서였다. 그래서 그도 '드라세나 잎사귀를 태워버려야지' 하고 생각해보았다. 예상대로 잎사귀에 붙여놓은 감지기 그래프가 공포 반응을 기록했다.

또 한 번 해보았다. 또 공포반응을 보였다. 하지만, 그가 네 번째 위협적 생각을 떠올리자 잎사귀는 공포 반응을 멈췄다. 과학자가 물었다.

"왜 공포 반응을 멈췄죠?"

백스터가 어깨를 으쓱하며 되물었다.

"박사님은 어떻게 생각하세요?"

과학자는 고개를 갸웃거리며 말했다.

"혹시 드라세나가 제 의도까지 알아챈 건 아니겠죠? 진짜로 태워버리려는 의도는 아니라는…"

백스터는 미소를 지었다.

"맞아요, 박사님. 식물이 속마음을 다 읽고 있어요."

양자물리학이 정신세계를 본격적으로 파고들기 전까지 백스터는 오랫동안 과학계의 조롱거리였다. 하지만 프린스턴 대학 교수를 지낸 독일의 생물 물리학자 포프(Fritz-Albert Popp) 박사, 상트 페테르부르크 기술대학 물리학 교수인 코로트코프(Konstantin Korotkov) 박사 등이 개발해낸 최첨단 빛 촬영장치(GDV)를 통해 그의 실험결과는 모두 사실로 확인됐다.

코로트코프 박사는 화분 식물들을 GDV와 연결시킨 후에 연구원들에게 분노, 저주, 슬픔, 사랑, 기쁨 등의 감정을 품어보도록 했다. 식물들은 그 감정들을 정확히 읽어냈다. 코로트코프 박사는 이렇게 선언했다.

"사람의 뇌파도, 식물도, 모두 똑같은 미립자로 만들어져 있다. 식물이 사람의 생각을 읽어내고 정보를 주고받는 건 지극히 당연한 일이다."

3 깊이 바라보려면?

마음속의 수다를 잠재워라

점심식사 후 사무실로 돌아오는 길이다. 그런데 저 앞에서 한 직장동료가 걸어오는 게 보인다. 꽤 친하게 지내는 입사 동기다. 당신은 가벼운 미소를 건넨다.

'어, 날 못 봤나?'

당신은 이번엔 크게 손을 흔들어본다. 하지만 그 친구는 이번에도 무반응이다.

'왜 못 본 척하는 거지?'

당신은 당황한다. 아무리 생각해도 그가 당신을 못 봤을 리는 없다.

'짜식! 승진했다고 날 무시하는 거야?'

가만히 생각해보니 그가 저번에 마주쳤을 때 시큰둥해보였던 것도 결코 우연이 아닌 것 같다는 의심이 든다. 좀더 깊이 생각해보니 그는 아예 처음 만났을 때부터 믿을 만한 친구가 아니었다는 생각도 퍼뜩 떠오른다.

'얼굴도 못생긴 주제에!'

당신은 전엔 그가 못생겼다는 생각을 한 번도 해본 적 없다. 하지만 곰곰이 생각한 결과 그는 원래 정말 못생긴 게 틀림없다는 결론에 도달한다.

'윗사람들에게만 굽실거리는 간신배 같은 녀석!'

그가 간신배 같다는 것도 역시 오늘 새삼 깨닫게 된 생각이다. 씩씩거리던 당신은 문득 자신을 돌아보게 된다.

'근데 난 왜 이 모양 이 꼴이지? 난 왜 승진도 못하고 인정도 못 받는 거지?'

당신은 갑자기 초라해진다. 그리고 회사와 관련된 모든 게 다 싫어진다. 승진인사를 그처럼 개판으로 하다니! 회사 사람들은 죄다 정의감이라곤 티끌만큼도 없는 파렴치한 인간들 같고, 출세를 위해서는 간이고 쓸개고 서슴없이 몽땅 빼내줄 듯 행세하는 간신배들 같다.

'차라리 직장을 때려치운다?'

때려치운다면 뭘 할 수 있을까? 당신의 머릿속에서는 온종일 온갖 목소리들이 속삭여댄다. 잠자리에 누워도 그 목소리들은 끊이지 않고 당신을 괴롭힌다.

가만히 생각해보자. 당신 친구가 당신을 일부러 무시했다는 증거가 있는가? 그가 혹시 평소 끼고 다니던 콘택트 렌즈를 깜빡 잊고 출근했던 것은 아닐까? 하지만 당신의 머릿속에서는 끝없는 수다가 이어진다. '어, 날 못 봤나?' 하는 단 하나의 생각이 갈수록 많은 가지를 치며 뭉게뭉게 피어오른다. 친구를 전면 부정하는 생각으로 부풀어 올랐다가 곧 그 생각은 사라지고, 대신 당신 자신을 불신하는 생각이 피어오른다. 잠시 후, 이번엔 그 생각이 사라지고 직장을 때려치울까 하는 생각이 몽실몽실

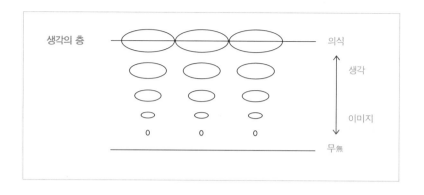

숫아오른다. 이렇게 수다가 많아질수록 당신의 머릿속은 그만큼 혼란해진다. 당신의 의지와는 상관없이 피어오르는 수다이다. 잠들고 싶어도 멈추지 않는다. 이렇게 피어오르는 생각들을 킨슬로우(Frank Kinslow) 박사는 위와 같은 그림으로 설명한다.

우리 의식의 표면은 이처럼 늘 생각으로 뒤덮여 있다. 가만히 생각해 보라. 이제까지 살면서 단 한 번이라도 생각이 멈춘 적 있는가? 아마 없을 것이다. 한 가지 생각이 사라지면 곧바로 다른 생각들이 꼬리를 물고 이어진다. 심지어 꿈속에서도 끊임없이 생각한다. 이처럼 생각의 바다에 빠져 살아가다 보니 우리는 '생각은 곧 나'라고 착각한다. 그래서 누가 내 생각을 비난하면 대뜸 "너 왜 날 공격하는 거야?" 하고 눈을 치켜뜬다. 자신의 생각을 지키기 위해 목숨까지 내걸기도 한다. 하지만 생각은 정말 '나'인가? 위 그림을 다시 보라.

생각은 무無에서 티끌만 하게 싹이 튼다. 점점 뭉게뭉게 버섯구름처럼 피어올라 의식의 표면을 완전히 덮어버린다. 주로 언어로 하는 얕은 생각이다. 심리학자 워런(Neil Warren)에 따르면, 보통 사람들은 1분에 평균 최고 1,300단어로 혼자서 수다를 떤다고 한다. 이런 생각은 피상적이며 선명한 이미지를 남기지 못한다. 반면, 생각이 깊어질수록 마음속의 잔 목소리들은 잦아들고 마음은 맑아진다. 그러면서 선명한 이미지가 형성된다.

예를 들어 당신이 너무나 재미난 소설을 읽는다고 가정해보자. 당신의 눈은 깨알 같은 글자들을 훑고 있지만, 머릿속은 글자들이 묘사해내는 생생한 이미지들로 가득 채워진다. 이미지는 한계가 없다. 상상대로 퍼져나간다. 그 이미지들은 10년이 지나도, 20년이 지나도 좀처럼 잊히지 않는다. 반면, 당신이 시험공부를 위해 지루한 교과서를 달달 외우고 있다면? 생생한 이미지들이 선명하게 그려지기는커녕 온통 깨알 같은 글자들만 두뇌 속에서 맴돌 따름이다. 그 글자들은 시험만 끝나면 기억에서 금방 사라진다.

이처럼 생각이 깊고 선명해야 형성되는 이미지도 선명하다. 거꾸로 이미지가 선명해지면 생각도 선명해진다. 세계적인 천재들이 한결같이 "난 말이 아니라 그림으로 생각한다"고 말하는 것도 그런 이유다. 심지어 물리학자인 파인만조차도 "난 복잡한 문제를 풀 때 큰 그림부터 그린다. 수학적 계산은 나중에 한다"라고 말했다.

만물을 구성하는 미립자들도 의식의 표면에서 겉도는 얇은 생각이 아니라, 의식 저 밑바닥에 그려지는 깊고 선명한 이미지를 읽고 변화한다. 우리가 깊이 생각해 바라볼수록, 선명한 이미지를 그려 바라볼수록, 그만큼 깊은 변화가 일어나는 게 당연하다. 반면, 얇은 생각은 티끌밖에 움직이지 못한다.

그럼 이렇게 우리 머릿속을 점령한 얕은 생각들은 어떻게 잠재울 수 있을까?

방법은 뜻밖에도 너무나 간단하다. 뭉게뭉게 피어오르는 생각 덩어리들을 상상 속의 스크린이나 백지에 투사시켜 가만히 바라보는 것이다. 바라보면 바라보는 의도를 읽어내고 저절로 물러간다. 하지만, 곧 또 다른 생각이 피어오른다. 그럼 또 바라보라. 또 사라진다. 이렇게 몇 번 되풀이하다가 이번엔 이런 질문을 속으로 되뇌어보라.

"다음 생각은 어디서 나올까?"

고요한 마음으로 다음 생각이 피어오르는 걸 기다려보라.

1초, 2초, 3초…

이렇게 몇 초가 흘러가도 아무 생각도 피어오르지 않는다. 텅 빈 공간만 보일 뿐이다. 신기한 일 아닌가? 억누르려 들면 기승을 부리며 더욱 피어오르던 생각이 어서 나오길 기다리며 지켜보면 청개구리처럼 오히려 냉큼 나오지 않는다. 이게 생각의 속성이다. 어린아이도 울지 말라며 억누르려 들면 되레 더욱 발악을 해대지 않는가? 생각 덩어리도 지능을 갖고 있다는 사실을 상기하라. 잡념이 걷잡을 수 없이 솟아올라 골치 아플 땐 마치 어린아이를 다루듯 따뜻한 눈으로 가만히 바라보라. 그럼 저절로 사그라진다. 만일 이 방법이 잘 안 된다면?

더 손쉬운 방법도 있다. 뭉게뭉게 피어오르는 생각 덩어리를 바라보며 조용히 이런 질문을 던져보라.

"지금 피어오르는 생각의 뿌리는 어디지?"

생각 덩어리의 뿌리를 찾아 점점 아래로 내려가며 바라보는 것이다. 그럼 결국 아무것도 없는 텅 빈 무無에 이르게 된다. 그리고 나서 다음 생각이 피어오르는 걸 기다리면 텅 빈 공간은 더욱 길게 지속된다.

"그런데 그 텅 빈 공간은 대체 뭐지?"

이런 호기심이 들 것이다. 아무 생각도 없는 텅 빈 공간, 그건 바로 '나'다. 원래의 '나'는 생각에 가득 차 있는 게 아니라 텅 비어 있다. 원래부터 수다쟁이가 아니다. '생각은 곧 나'라는 생각도 착각이다. 생각은 아무것도 없는 무無(nothing)에서 피어오른다. 사실은 우주에 존재하는 모든 것이 몽땅 무에서 생긴다. 그래서 세계적인 양자물리학자인 봄(David Bohm)은 "눈에 보이는 것이든, 안 보이는 것이든, 모든 것은 무에서 창조된다"라고 말했다.(생각을 잠재우는 방법은 〈왓칭 요술 #5〉에 자세히 언급돼 있다.)

고 요 한 마 음 으 로 바 라 보 라

둘째 아이가 유치원에 다니던 시절 우유를 잘 마시지 않았다. 체질적으로 유지방을 제대로 소화시키지 못하는 것 같았다. 그래서 나는 아침에 출근준비를 하면서 종종 계란반숙을 준비해주곤 했다. 냄비에 물과 계란을 넣고 5분쯤 지나 보글보글 소리가 나면 흰자는 거의 다 익고 노른자는 살짝 익는다. 그런데 이상한 현상을 발견했다. 보글보글 소리가 나기를 기다리며 계속 지켜보면 더디 끓는다는 것이다. 거꾸로 냄비를 지켜보지 않고 신문을 보고 있으면 어느새 보글보글 소리가 난다.

"그건 심리적 느낌이겠지. 설마 지켜본다고 계란이 더디 익을까?"

당신은 아마 이렇게 일축할 것이다. 나도 그렇게 생각했다. 하지만 과학자들은 느낌으로 말하지 않고 정밀한 실험 증거로 말한다. 결론부터 말하면 냄비가 빨리 끓기를 조바심치며 지켜보고 있으면 실제로 더디 끓는다.

하버드 대학 출신의 물리학자인 이타노(Wayne Itano) 박사는 전자파를 발사하여 베릴륨 원자 5,000개를 가열해보았다. 이 상황을 쉽게 설명하면 원자들은 냄비 속의 계란이고, 전자파는 냄비에 가해지는 열과 같다. 가열시간은 250밀리세컨드(ms), 즉 1/4초였다.(레이저 광선을 이용하면 지극히 짧은 순간마다 원자들의 가열상태를 들여다볼 수 있다.)

1. 250ms 중 한 번도 바라보지 않음
   → 원자들이 100퍼센트 익었다(계란이 완전히 익었다).
2. 250ms 중 62.5ms, 125ms, 187.5ms, 250ms 등 일정한 간격으로 모두 네 번 바라보았다.
   → 원자들의 3분의 1만 익었다.(계란이 3분의 1만 익었다.)
3. 250ms 중 일정한 간격으로 16번, 32번, 64번 바라보았다
   → 바라보는 횟수가 늘어날수록 익는 정도도 줄어들었다. 64번 바라보았더니 원자들이 전혀 익지 않고, 원래의 냉동상태에 머물렀다.(자주 바라볼수록 계란은 그만큼 더디 익었다.)

"지켜보는 냄비는 끓지 않는다(A watched pot never boils)"는 서양속담이 양자물리학적으로 생생하게 입증된 것이다. 왜 이런 결과가 나왔을까? 냄비를 가스레인지에 올려놓자마자 바라보면 아직 끓고 있지 않는 상태다. 끓고 있지 않은 냄비를 자꾸만 바라보는 심리상태는 뻔하다. 마음 한 구석에 "이 물은 도대체 왜 이렇게 안 끓는 거지?" 하고 조바심치는 생각

이 섞여 있다. 이 생각은 보글보글 끓고 있는 냄비가 아니라, 끓지 않는 냄비의 이미지를 그려낸다. 따라서 냄비 속의 물은 자연이 끓지 않는 냄비 이미지를 읽고 현실로 나타낸다. 조바심치는 얕은 생각보다 이미지가 훨씬 더 강한 것이다. 그러다 보니 끓는 속도가 더뎌질 수밖에….

그럼 냄비가 빨리 끓도록 하려면 어떻게 해야 할까? 머릿속에서 조바심치는 잔 목소리들부터 완전히 잠재워야 한다.

'도대체 왜 이렇게 안 끓는 거지?'

'빨리 안 끓으면 지각할 텐데.'

이런 조급한 목소리들을 꺼버리고 고요한 마음으로 끓는 냄비의 이미지를 떠올려야 한다.

"시간이 되면 끓게 되겠지."

이렇게 의도(intent)만을 던져놓은 채 고요히 바라보는 행위가 원하는 현실을 창조해낸다. "선명한 이미지만 그릴 수 있다면 얼음 위에 올려놓아도 냄비는 끓는다"는 것이 이타노 박사의 설명이다. 이게 무슨 소리냐고? 이런 상상을 해보자. 영하 수십 도를 오르내리는 혹한의 날씨에 당신은 얇은 옷만 걸친 채 바깥에서 달달 떨며 앉아 있다. 그때 누군가 나타나 양동이에 가득 담긴 얼음물을 당신 몸에 확 끼얹었다. 당신은 이렇게 소리 지를 것이다.

"으악! 나 얼어 죽어!"

설사 얼어 죽진 않더라도 최소한 당신은 기절하고 말 것이다. 이유는 간단하다. 혹한의 날씨에 얼음물을 끼얹으면 죽는다는 이미지가 자동적으로 그려지기 때문이다.

"난 정말 얼어 죽긴 싫어!"

이렇게 아무리 죽기 싫다는 생각을 하며 발버둥쳐봐야 소용없다. 말로 하는 생각은 이미지를 당해내지 못하기 때문이다. 티베트의 승려들은 이런 이치를 훤히 꿰고 있다. 그래서 그런 상황에서도 편안히 잠을 잘 수 있다. 하버드 의대의 벤슨(Herbert Benson) 교수가 똑같은 상황에서 그들의 몸에 얼음물을 끼얹은 담요를 덮어뒀더니 금세 증발돼 말라버렸다. 이것이 널리 알려진 '툼모'(티베트 승려들에게 전승되는 수행법) 현상이다.

그들은 어떤 욕망이나 투지로써 그렇게 할 수 있는 걸까? 아니다. 욕망이나 투지가 개입된다면 그들 역시 얼어 죽게 된다. 그들은 먼저 머릿속의 모든 속삭임을 완전히 잠재운다. 그러고는 명상을 통해 점점 뜨겁게 달아오르는 몸을 선명하게 그린다. 그럼 그 이미지대로 몸이 불덩이처럼 달아올라 얼음물도 순식간에 증발시켜버린다. 공부나 일도 마찬가지다. 마음이 집중되지 않고 머릿속에서 온갖 잡념이 피어오르는데 억지로 투지를 불태우는 것은 지극히 비생산적이다. 말로 하는 생각(투지)으로 말로 하는 생각(잡념)을 물리치기 어렵기 때문이다. 따라서, 그럴 땐 조용히 잡념이 피어오르는 걸 바라보아야 한다. 바라보면 저절로 사라진다.

의지보다 강한 이미지를 이용하라

학생들에게 고속 롤러코스터를 타본 적 있느냐고 물었더니 손을 든 사람은 뜻밖에도 20여 명 중 다섯 명 남짓이었다.

"너무 무서워서요."

"속이 울렁거리는 느낌이 너무 싫어요."

모두 같은 대답이었다. 사실은 나도 그랬다. 딸아이가 여섯 살쯤 됐을 때 함께 탔는데 짜릿한 스릴은커녕 속만 울렁거렸다. 괜히 돈 내고 생고 생만 했다는 생각뿐이었다. 이렇게 짓눌린 마음으로 억지로 타면 정말 위험한 일이 생길 수도 있다. 실제로 세계에서 가장 빠른 일본 후지큐 놀이 공원의 롤러코스터를 타다가 뇌혈관이 파열된 사례들이 몇 건 있었다. 미국에서도 마찬가지였다. 미국 두뇌부상협회가 롤러코스터의 위험성을 조사한 적이 있었는데, 평소 심장질환을 앓던 사람이 롤러코스터를 타면 뇌혈관의 피가 뭉쳐져 두뇌손상을 초래할 수 있다는 결론이 나왔다.

한 여학생은 "고속으로 가파르게 내려갈 때 꼭 추락할 것 같아요"라고 말했다. 수십 미터 상공에서 땅바닥으로 패대기쳐진다고 상상해보라. 온몸이 자라목처럼 바짝 오그라든다. '떨어지면 안 돼! 떨어지면 난 산산조각나고 말 거야!'라고 이를 악물고 젖 먹던 힘을 다해 손잡이를 움켜잡는다. 하지만 이렇게 의지를 불태울수록 내 몸이 까마득한 저 아래로 추락하는 이미지는 더욱 무섭게 소용돌이친다. 이미지는 말로 하는 생각(의지)보다 강하기 때문이다. 결국 이미지가 의지를 완전히 압도하게 된다. 이를 어찌나 악물었는지 눈물까지 찔끔거리며 롤러코스터에서 초주검 상태로 내려서는 어른들을 종종 목격할 수 있다. 하지만 롤러코스터를 즐기는 사람들은 완전 딴판이다. 딸아이도 그중 하나다.

"넌 무섭지 않니?"

"왜 무섭죠? 안전장치가 튼튼해서 전혀 떨어질 염려가 없는데?"

딸애는 롤러코스터를 '땅에 추락할 수 있는 괴물'로 상상하는 게 아니라 '하늘을 자유롭게 나는 새'로 상상하고 있었다. 의지로 이미지와 싸워 이기려 드는 게 아니라, 무서운 이미지 대신 즐거운 이미지를 그리는 것이었다. 그러니 롤러코스터 타는 게 즐거울 수밖에 없다.

이미지를 이용해 먹고 싶은 충동도 쉽게 잠재울 수 있다. 이런 상상을 해보자. 당신이 식사를 마친 후 앉아 있는데 웨이터가 아이스크림을 후식으로 갖다놓는다.

"아, 내가 가장 좋아하는 아이스크림!"

아이스크림이 입안에서 스르르 녹는 이미지가 그려진다. 하지만 당신은 다이어트중이다.

'저건 먹으면 안 돼.'

이렇게 의지의 힘만으로 이미지를 짓누르자니 힘들다. 더 강한 다른 이미지를 그려야 한다.

'저 아이스크림 속에서 구더기 세 마리가 꿈틀거리고 있어. 꿈틀꿈틀 아이스크림을 파먹으며 누런 배설물도 배출하며 말이야.'

이런 이미지가 생생하게 그려지면 그려질수록 먹고 싶은 충동도 그만큼 쉽게 가라앉는다.

의지는 말로 하는 생각이기 때문에 두뇌 속에서 맴돈다. 반면, 이미지는 어떤가? 아마존 강 유역의 깊은 밀림을 상상해보라. 빽빽한 열대식물들과 활을 든 토착민들의 이미지가 금방 떠오른다. 이처럼 이미지는 두뇌의 한계를 멀찌감치 벗어난다. 그러니, 의지보다 수만 배, 수백만 배 더 강할 수밖에 ―.

"난 TV 인터뷰는 절대 안 해요."

인터뷰 섭외를 할 때 상대가 이렇게 나오면 보통 요지부동이다. 따라서 이런 말이 나오기 전에 상대의 기분을 좋게 만들어야 한다. 이럴 때도 말보다 강한 이미지를 이용하면 쉬워진다. 그래서 상대방에게 전화를 걸기 전 그의 웃는 얼굴을 그려본다. '좋다, 싫다, 될 거다, 안 될 거다' 등의 어떤 가치판단도 없이 상대의 웃는 얼굴을 짧은 순간 몇 차례 떠올린다. 길게 떠올리면 내 의지나 의심이 스며든다. 그런 다음 편안한 목소리로 전화를 건다.

"안녕하세요. 저는 MBC 아무개라고 합니다. 거기 누구누구 맞으시죠?"

상대편에서는 십중팔구 호의적인 목소리가 흘러나온다.

나는 낯선 사람을 만날 때도 같은 방법을 쓴다. 문을 열고 들어가기 전 몇 차례 그의 웃는 얼굴을 그린다. 그럼 영락없이 그는 기분 좋은 표정이다. 설사 웃고 있지 않더라도 호의적이다. 이런 일들은 그저 우연의 일치일까?

"무뚝뚝한 사람을 원격으로 웃게 만든다? 설마!"

당신은 아마 이렇게 생각할 것이다. 하지만 이미지는 거리와 상관없다. 눈을 감고 미국에 건너간 친구의 얼굴 이미지를 그려보라. 그가 한국에 있을 때 그려보던 그의 얼굴 이미지와 차이가 있는가?

배스터 대학과 워싱턴 대학의 과학자들이 실제로 실험을 해보았다.

그들은 평소 마음이 잘 통한다는 커플들을 모집했다. 그리고 커플을 서로 분리시켜 10미터 떨어진 다른 방에 각자 들어가 있도록 하고는 한쪽 사람들에게 말했다.

"다른 방에 있는 짝에게 미소를 보내보세요."

10미터 떨어져 있는 상대가 미소 짓는 이미지를 그려보라는 것이었다. 그런다고 과연 상대가 미소를 짓게 될까? 과학자들은 fMRI로 상대의 두뇌를 촬영해보았다. 놀랍게도 한쪽에서 미소를 그릴 때마다 다른 쪽 사람의 시각피질(visual cortex) 내 혈중 산소치(blood oxygenation)가 급증했다. 미소를 그리지 않을 땐 아무 변화가 없었다.

과학자들은 이런 결론을 내렸다.

"이미지를 받는 사람은 이미지를 보낸 사람과 똑같은 이미지를 본다."

내가 마음속으로 미소를 보내면 상대방도 자신도 모르게 미소를 짓게 된다. 상대가 아무리 멀리 떨어져 있어도 마찬가지다. 따라서, 만일 말다툼을 벌인 누군가와 화해하고 싶다면 먼저 그가 미소 짓는 얼굴을 생생하게 그려보라. 그가 설사 이역만리 먼 곳으로 떠나갔더라도 다음에 그와 만나는 순간, 그는 언제 싸웠냐는 듯 당신에게 미소를 머금고 있을 테니까!

나를 바꿔놓는
요술 일곱 가지

내가 원하는 몸 만들기

체중이 날로 불어나 걱정이다. 하지만 그놈의 식탐은 통제 불능이다. 어떻게 하면 음식욕구를 쉽게 줄일 수 있을까?

함께 일하던 한 후배 여직원은 키가 160센티미터 정도였다. 하지만 체중은 65킬로그램을 넘었다.

"먹지 말아야지 하고 마음먹어도 음식만 보면 저절로 손이 가요."

유심히 살펴보니 정말 잘도 먹었다. 점심도 많이 먹었고, 누가 간식을 시켜도 마다치 않고 먹었다. 저녁 회식 때도 마찬가지였다. 뭔가 채워지지 않는 내면의 욕구가 있었을까?

"혹시 어머니는 집에 안 계신가?"

"엄마는 바빠요. 어릴 때부터 늘 바빴어요."

"그럼 식사는 누가 차려주고?"

"각자 알아서 먹어요."

그녀의 어머니는 종교에 빠져 있었다. 모든 건 종교가 해결해준다고 믿었고, 어릴 적부터 가정보다 종교 활동이 우선이었다. 알고 보니 그녀는 어머니로부터 못 받는 애정을 무의식적으로 음식으로 채우려 드는 것이었다.

"음식 충동을 외면하지 말고 어린아이처럼 달래봐."

'식탐'이라는 욕구도 엄연히 독자적인 생명과 지능을 가진 존재이다.

"달래다니요? 어떻게요?"

"'식탐'은 마음속에 존재하는 괴물이지? 그러니까 마음속에서 먹이를 실컷 먹여봐. 그럼 잠잠해질 테니까."

그녀는 농담이려니 생각했는지 픽 웃었다. 그래서 내가 다시 말했다.

"뭔가 먹고 싶을 때 마음속에서 실컷 먹어봐. 실제로는 먹지 말고─."

얼마 후 그녀는 다른 부서로 발령이 났다. 나도 다른 층으로 사무실을 옮겼다. 6개월쯤 지나 회사 앞에서 그녀와 마주친 나는 깜짝 놀랐다. 그 사이 뚱뚱하던 몸집이 반쪽이 됐기 때문이다.

"그동안 다이어트를 열심히 했나 봐?"

"상상 속에서 실컷 먹었더니 식욕이 정말 떨어졌어요."

그녀는 실제로는 먹지 않았다. 단지 실컷 먹는 이미지만 그려 바라본 것뿐이었다. 그러자 그녀의 머릿속에 도사리고 있던 충동이 누그러졌고, 실제로 실컷 먹은 것처럼 식욕도 떨어졌다.

카네기멜론 대학 연구진은 이런 효과를 실험을 통해서 확인했다. 남녀 4백 명을 두 그룹으로 나누고, 절반에게는 초콜릿을 한 알씩 옮기는 이미지를 그려보도록 했다. 그리고 다른 절반에게는 한 알씩 먹는 이미지를 상상하도록 했다. 그런 다음 모두에게 진짜 초콜릿을 주고 말했다.

"여러분이 원하는 만큼 자유롭게 드세요."

어느 쪽이 더 많이 먹었을까? 초콜릿을 먹는 이미지를 상상했던 사람들은 다른 그룹에 비해 절반밖에 먹지 않았다. 먹고 싶은 충동을 억누르지 않고 끄집어내 객관적인 눈으로 따뜻하게 바라보니 충동이 누그러져 실제로 이미 먹은 효과가 나타났던 것이다.

실험을 주도한 모어웨지(Carey Morewedge) 교수는 이렇게 조언한다.

"햄버거를 먹고 싶은 충동이 들면 햄버거를 잔뜩 먹는 이미지를 그려 바라보세요. 고기를 먹고 싶다면 고기를 잔뜩 먹는 이미지를 그려 바라보세요. 그럼 먹고 싶은 충동이 가라앉으니까요."

우리가 자신도 모르게 많이 먹게 되는 건 먹고 싶은 충동을 억누르기 때문이다. '식탐' 괴물도 나름대로 지능과 자존심을 갖고 있다. 만일 당신이 '식탐'이라면 화나지 않겠는가?

"왜 억눌러 대는 거야? 왜 날 무시해?"

당신은 오기가 생겨 더욱 이를 갈며 먹어댈 것이다. '식탐'도 마찬가지다. 따라서 당신이 '식탐'의 감정을 이해해주고 따뜻한 마음으로 바라보면 '식탐'도 조용해진다. 어차피 그가 원하는 건 실제 음식이 아니라 마음속의 가짜 음식 아닌가?

'서 있는 것도 운동'이라고 생각하라

사람들은 대개 자신의 몸이 딱딱한 뼈와 탄탄한 근육, 탄력 있는 피부로 둘러싸인 고정된 물질이라고 믿는다. 하지만, 몸도 역시 다른 만물처럼 사람의 생각을 읽어내는 지능을 갖고 있다. 간단한 실험을 해보자.

손바닥 아래 가로선을 기준으로 양손을 맞댄다. 그런 다음 양쪽 가운뎃손가락 길이를 서로 비교해보라.

양손을 편 뒤 두 가운뎃손가락 길이를 서로 비교해보라. 비슷하게 보이지만 사실은 길이가 다르다. 손바닥 아래 가로선을 기준선으로 양손을 서로 맞대보라. 대개 왼쪽 가운뎃손가락이 더 짧다. 사실 어느 쪽이 짧든 상관없다. 다시 양손을 떨어뜨린 뒤 짧은 쪽 가운뎃손가락을 가만히 바라보며 되뇌어보라.

'가운뎃손가락아, 점점 길어져라.'

이렇게 생각하며 바라보노라면 손가락이 간질간질해지는 걸 느끼게 된다. 손가락이 당신의 생각을 읽고 변화하는 것이다. 1분 후 다시 양손을 맞대어 비교해보라. 놀랍게도 짧았던 쪽이 더 길어져 있다. 이처럼 몸은 고정된 게 아니다. 내가 어떻게 바라보느냐에 따라 수시로 변화한다. 뱃살도 마찬가지다.

당신이 뱃살이 자꾸 불어나 고민이라고 가정해보자.

"운동할 시간은 없고, 굶기는 싫고, 뱃살은 늘어나고… 뭐 좋은 방법 없나?"

당신의 머릿속에 그려지는 이미지는 불어나는 뱃살이다. 그러니 뱃살이 불어나는 게 당연하다. 이제부터는 거꾸로, 길을 걸을 때마다 이렇게 상상해보라.

"한 걸음 걸을 때마다 지방이 몇 방울씩 빠져나가겠군."

서 있을 때도 마찬가지다.

"서 있는 시간만큼 뱃살도 빠져나가겠지."

계단을 오를 때도, 청소할 때도, 설거지를 할 때도 그런 이미지를 바라보라. 한 달쯤 지나 안 입던 바지를 꺼내 입다가 당신은 깜짝 놀랄 것이다.

"어? 한 달 전에 입었던 바지가 왜 이렇게 헐렁해졌지?"

건강검진을 받아보니 복부지방 수치도 떨어졌다. 당신은 따로 운동을 한 적이 없다. 단지 뱃살이 빠져나간다고 바라보았을 뿐이다.

팔을 운동할 때도 마찬가지다. 운동을 하면서 '아, 지금 내 팔의 근육이 강해지고 있어'라고 생각해보라. 팔 근육이 그 생각을 읽고 실제로 강해진다. 영국 헐 대학의 마찬트(David Marchant) 교수는 사람들에게 팔 운동을 시키면서 세 가지 생각을 해보도록 했다.

방법 1. 근육만을 생각한다. '아, 내 근육이 지금 열심히 움직이고 있어.'
방법 2. 운동기구만을 생각한다. '이 운동기구는 참 편리하게 만들어졌단 말이야.'
방법 3. 아무거나 생각한다. '지금 친구는 어디쯤 가고 있을까.'

그러고는 이두박근(biceps)의 전기적 활동량을 측정해보았다. 측정 결과, 근육의 움직임을 생각하는 첫 번째 방법으로 운동할 때 근육의 전기적 활동량이 가장 많은 것으로 나타났다. 즉, 근육운동량이 가장 많았다는 얘기다. 마찬트 교수는 운동선수들이나 일반인들이 근력강화 운동을 할 때 근육을 상상하면 근육이 더 빨리 형성된다고 조언한다.

따라서 당신이 헬스클럽에서 러닝머신 위를 걸으며 신문을 읽거나 TV를 시청하는 건 좋은 방법이 아니다. 왜냐하면 다리가 당신의 생각을 훤히 읽고 있기 때문이다.

"뭐야? 나한텐 걸게 시켜놓고 TV만 보다니!"

입장을 바꿔놓고 생각해보라. 무시당한 다리 근육은 최선을 다해 운동효과를 내주지 않는다. 생각과 다리 근육이 서로 따로 놀게 된다. 이 때문에 운동하고 나서도 영 개운치 않다. 따라서 운동할 땐 자신의 몸이 어떻게 움직이는지 조용히 귀를 기울여 바라보아야 한다. 그러면 운동 효과도 몇 배로 늘어나고 마음도 샘물처럼 맑아진다.

그럼 걷기나 서 있기 등 일상의 평범하고 습관적인 행위들은 어떨까? 운동이라고 생각하면 몸이 그 생각을 읽고 실제로 운동효과가 생기도록 해줄까?

예를 들어 연아는 출퇴근길에 걸으면서 이렇게 생각한다.

"걷는 것도 운동이야."

버스를 기다리거나 버스 안에 서 있을 때도 마찬가지다.

"서 있는 것도 훌륭한 운동이야."

과연 연아는 실제로 땀을 뻘뻘 흘리며 운동하는 것처럼 살이 빠지고, 몸도 튼튼해질까?

우선 "난 운동하고 있어" 혹은 "난 운동 못 해"라는 식의 간단한 생각이 몸에 어떤 영향을 끼치는지부터 알아보자.

스웨덴의 생리학자인 살틴(Bengt Saltin)은 젊은이들에게 이렇게 말해보았다.

"앞으로 3주간 아무 운동도 하지 말고 침대에 누워 푹 쉬세요."

이들은 자연히 '난 운동 못해'라는 생각을 갖고 멀뚱멀뚱 천장만 바라

살틴 교수

"몸은 우리의 생각을 읽고
변화한다."

보며 누워 지냈다. 드디어 3주가 지났다. 건강상태를 확인해본 살틴은 자신의 눈을 의심했다.

"맙소사! 겨우 3주 사이에 20년이나 폭삭 늙어버리다니!"

그들은 벌써 40~50대처럼 주름이 생기기 시작했고 근육도 크게 줄어들었다. '난 운동 못 해'라는 생각을 갖고 누워 지내니, 실제로 몸이 그 생각을 읽고 운동을 못하는 모드로 전환됐던 것이다. 기억력도 역시 큰 폭으로 떨어졌다.

"그럼 누워 있지 않고 서 있도록 하면 어떨까?"

이번에는 그들에게 하루에 5분씩 침대에서 내려와 서 있도록 해보았다. 돌아다니거나 팔다리 운동을 하도록 한 게 아니었다. 그런데도 놀랍게도 불과 며칠 만에 노화됐던 몸이 정상으로 되돌아왔다. '난 운동 못 해'라는 생각을 털어버리고, '난 서 있을 수 있어'라는 생각만을 갖도록 한 것이었는데도 뜻밖의 엄청난 변화가 일어난 것이다. 다시 말해 특별한 운동을 하지 않고 그냥 서 있더라도 '서 있는 것도 운동이야'라고 생각하면 실제로 운동이 되는 것이다.

그럼 노화로 인해 운동능력을 상실한 노인들은 어떨까? '난 늙어서

76

운동 못 해'라는 생각에서 벗어나 '난 운동할 수 있어'라는 생각으로 전환시키면 몸도 크게 변화할까?

터프츠 대학의 과학자들은 먼저 60세 이상의 노인들에게 석 달 동안 일주일에 세 번씩 규칙적인 역기운동을 시켜보았다. 그것도 최고능력의 80퍼센트를 발휘하도록 강도 높게 훈련시켰다.

처음에 노인들은 이렇게 반응했다.

"나 같은 노인에게 무슨 운동을 하라고 그래요?"

"운동 안 한 지 벌써 30년이 넘은 걸요."

하지만 조금씩 '늙으면 운동 못 해'라는 고정관념이 깨져가면서 온몸에 놀라운 변화가 일어나기 시작했다. 다시는 늘어나지 않을 것 같았던 근육은 두 배, 세 배 이상 커졌고 무거운 물건도 번쩍번쩍 들어올렸다. 무기력증, 우울증 등의 증세도 사라졌다. 과학자들은 더 큰 호기심이 들었다.

"95세 이상 노인들도 이렇게 변화할까?"

처음에 95세가 넘은 백발노인들은 손가락 하나 까딱 안 하려 들었다.

"내가 저걸 들었다간 그 자리서 기절할지 몰라요."

하지만 실험결과 그들 역시 운동량이 늘어가면서 마치 20대 젊은이들처럼 혈기왕성하게 돌변했다. 신기한 건 팔 운동을 시키면 다리까지 튼튼해지고, 다리 운동을 시키면 팔까지 튼튼해진다는 사실이었다. 의아한 생각이 든 과학자들은 젊은 여자 육상선수들의 골밀도를 검사해보았다. 달리기만 하는 육상선수들인데도 다리뼈가 단단한 건 물론이고 운동을 전혀 하지 않은 팔뼈까지 단단한 것으로 나타났다.

"아하, 선수들이 다리 운동을 시작하는 순간 온몸이 '난 운동해'라고 받아들이는 거로군!"

즉, '난 운동을 한다'고 생각하며 뛰기 시작하는 순간, 몸이 그 생각을 읽고 몸 전체에 운동 효과가 나타나도록 해주는 것이다.

그럼 거꾸로 '난 운동 안 한다'라고 생각한다면 어떨까?

스탠퍼드 대학의 외과의사인 보츠(Walter Bortz)는 사람이 육체 활동을 하지 않기로 마음먹으면 생리현상 전체가 위축된다는 사실을 발견했다. 심장, 관상동맥 등 심혈관계가 약화되고, 비만이 심해지며, 조기노화 증세가 나타나기 시작하는 것이다.

양자물리학자들은 이렇게 설명한다.

"몸과 마음은 한 덩어리의 전기 에너지다. 마음을 간질이면 몸이 웃는다."

쉽게 말해 내가 손가락 하나를 까딱이며 '손가락을 까딱이는 것도 운동이야'라고 생각하면 몸 전체에 운동 효과가 나타난다는 것이다. 따라서 '걷는 것도 운동이야', '서 있는 것도 운동이야'라고 바라보면 실제로 운동 효과가 온몸에 고스란히 나타난다. 관찰자 효과가 부리는 요술이다.

시 간 여 행 으 로 돌 연 젊 어 진 노 인 들

2009년 8월, 경기도 한 한적한 마을에 버스 석 대가 스르르 미끄러져 들어왔다. 마을 사람들은 학처럼 목을 쑥 뺀 채 수군거렸다.

"이런 오지 마을에 웬 관광버스 행렬이람?"

버스에서 내리는 사람들을 보고는 더욱 의아해했다.

"다들 꼬부랑 할머니, 할아버지들이네. 대체 뭘 하려는 거지?"

지팡이에 의지해 간신히 발걸음을 떼는 할아버지들, 눈이 침침한지 연신 눈을 껌뻑거리는 할머니들…. 노인들은 꾸역꾸역 마을회관처럼 생긴 큰 집에 들어갔다. 그들이 짐을 푸는 걸 훔쳐본 동네 아이들이 소곤거렸다.

"정말 이상해. 먼지가 잔뜩 쌓인 케케묵은 옛날 물건들만 가져왔어."

정말 그랬다. 짐들은 하나같이 20년 전인 1989년 8월 이전의 것들이었다. 의아해하기는 집에 들어선 노인들도 마찬가지였다.

"이게 꿈이여, 생시여? 눈에 띄는 게 죄다 20년 전 것들이니—."

독서대의 신문도, 잡지도, 서가의 책도, 음반도, 집안의 가구도, 부엌의 냉장고도 모조리 20년 전 것들이었다. TV를 틀어보고는 눈이 더욱 휘둥그레졌다.

"노태우 대통령은 오늘…"

노태우 대통령이 동유럽을 방문하는 뉴스가 흘러나오고 있었다.

"기막힌 일도 다 있군. 내가 정녕 꿈을 꾸고 있는 건가!"

그들은 서로 볼때기를 꼬집어보기도 하고, 옆구리를 찔러보기도 했다.

"아얏!" 분명히 꿈은 아니었다. 그때 이상야릇하게 생긴 집주인이 스르르 나타나 더욱 괴상망측한 주문을 하는 것이었다.

"여러분은 앞으로 일주일간 이곳에 머물면서 1989년 이전에 일어난 일에 대해서만 말하고 생각해야 합니다. 보는 것도 20년 전 것들만 보고, 행동도 20년 전처럼 해야 해요. 20년 전 사진을 붙인 신분증도 늘 목에 걸고 다녀야 합니다."

노인들의 입에서는 탄식이 터져 나왔다.

"어허! 꼬부랑 노인들에게 시간여행 배우 노릇을 시키는구먼!"

그렇게 하루 이틀 지나면서 조금씩 이상한 현상이 나타나기 시작했다. 20년 전 것들만 바라보고, 20년 전처럼 행동하고 말하고 생각하니 몸도 점점 20년 전을 향해 거꾸로 돌아가는 것 아닌가? 꼬부랑 허리는 날이 갈수록 꼿꼿해지고, 관절통도 사라지며, 얼굴 주름살도 펴지는 것이었다. 돋보기를 쓰던 노인들은 돋보기를 벗어버렸고, 지팡이를 들었던 노인들은 지팡이를 내던졌다.

일주일이 지나자 의사들은 정밀 검진을 해보았다.

"아니, 세상에 이럴 수가!"

의사들은 딱 벌어진 입을 다물지 못했다. 손의 악력, 팔다리의 근력, 시력, 청력, 혈압, 콜레스테롤 등 모든 면에서 노인들의 몸이 놀랍도록 젊어졌기 때문이다. 심지어 지능까지 높아졌다.

이런 꿈같은 일이 가능할까? 이는 실제로 일어난 일이다. 하버드 대학의 랭거 교수가 75세 이상 노인들을 대상으로 1979년 미국 뉴햄프셔 주의 한 한적한 마을에서 실시한 실험과 똑같은 상황이다. 그녀는 모든 걸 20년 전인 1959년처럼 꾸며놓고 노인들의 몸이 어떻게 변하는지 살펴봤다. 당시 일주일간의 실험을 마친 뒤 노인들의 몸을 검진했던 의사들은 정말 기이한 현상을 발견하고는 혀를 내둘렀다. 특히 손가락 길이가 확연하게 길어진 것에 놀랐다.

"사람은 30대 후반부터 조금씩 척추 디스크가 닳아버리면서 키도 줄어들어요. 손가락 마디에 관절염이 생기면 손가락 길이도 짧아지고요. 그

BBC에서 방영된
〈The Young Ones〉

런데 불과 일주일 사이 손가락 길이가 이렇게 늘어나다니 정말 불가사의한 일이네요."

그로부터 30여 년의 세월이 흐른 2010년 9월, 영국의 BBC-TV가 랭거 교수의 자문을 받아 비슷한 실험을 해보았다. 이제는 꼬부랑 노인들이 된 20~30년 전의 인기 스타들을 한곳에 모아놓고 옛날처럼 행동하고 생각하고 말하도록 했던 것이다. 그들이 사용하는 모든 소품도 몽땅 옛날 것들이었다. 그들의 몸도 역시 변했을까?

일주일간의 실험기간이 끝난 뒤 시청자들의 눈은 토끼 눈처럼 동그라졌다. 뇌졸중으로 쓰러져 휠체어를 타고 실험을 시작했던 팔순의 여배우는 휠체어를 버리고 혼자서 걸어서 나왔다. 거동이 힘들었던 왕년의 인기 남자연예인은 무대에 나와 탭댄스를 추었다. 지팡이에 의지해야 했던 옛 뉴스앵커는 지팡이 없이 뚜벅뚜벅 무대계단을 걸어서 올라갔다.

의사들이 출연자들의 몸을 검진해보니 실제로 젊어진 것으로 나타났다. 머릿속이 온통 젊은 시절의 이미지들로 꽉 차버리면 몸도 저절로 젊어지는 것이다. BBC는 이 실험을 〈The Young Ones〉라는 제목으로 방영했다.

그럼 거꾸로, 세월을 한꺼번에 확 앞당겨 은퇴 시절을 상상하도록 하면 어떨까? 몸도 그만큼 더 빨리 늙을까?

심리학자 바그(John Bargh)는 대학생들에게 '늙은', '은퇴한', '힘없는', '회색의', '휴양지' 등과 같은 단어들을 넣어 짧은 글을 짓도록 해보았다. 학생들은 다음과 같은 문장을 만들었다.

"나는 은퇴하면 따뜻한 휴양지에 가서 여생을 보내고 싶다."

"늙은 노숙자들을 보면 마음이 아프다."

"도시가 온통 회색빛으로 보인다."

바그는 강의실을 나서는 대학생들을 따라나섰다. 그리고 학생들이 걷는 속도를 쟀다. 학생들의 걸음걸이가 글짓기 전보다 눈에 띄게 느려졌다. 노화와 관련된 단어들을 사용했다는 사실만으로도 걸음속도가 떨어진 것이다. 비록 짧은 순간이나마 약 40여 년 후의 은퇴 시절을 바라보도록 하니 몸도 마치 빨리감기를 시킨 테이프처럼 벌써 빨리 늙어갈 기미를 보이기 시작했던 것이다.

"그럼 도대체 젊어지려면 어떻게 하란 말이야? 집안을 온통 20년 전으로 꾸며놓을 수도 없는 노릇이고."

당신은 아마 이렇게 항변할 것이다. 랭거 교수의 대답은 간단하다.

"나이가 들면 몸도 불가항력적으로 늙어갈 수밖에 없다는 바로 그 생각이 몸을 늙게 만드는 겁니다. 시각만 바꾸면 몸도 얼마든지 변할 수 있다는 사실을 깨닫는 것 자체만으로 노화속도도 변하기 시작하죠."

다시 말해 '나도 나이에 상관없이 젊어질 수 있다'는 가능성을 열어놓는 것 자체만으로 젊음이 스며든다는 것이다. 반면 '노화는 불가항력적으로 일어나는 현상'이라고 바라보면 노화는 가차없이 진행된다. 이처럼 우리의 몸은 바라보는 대로 현실화된다.

일란성 쌍둥이인데 왜 수명이 다를까?

아래 사진을 보라. 올해 97세인 두 할머니는 똑같은 유전자를 갖고 태어난 일란성 쌍둥이다. 하지만 겉모습부터 달라 보인다. 왼쪽의 테소로 할머니는 젊은이처럼 등이 곧고 이도 튼튼하다. 교회나 시장에 갈 때 직접 운전도 한다. 하지만 몇 초 뒤에 태어난 오른쪽의 동생은 이미 엉덩이뼈가 부러져 인공뼈를 이식받았고, 시력도 거의 완전히 상실한 상태다. 대소변도 마음대로 못 가리는데다 몇 년 전부터 치매까지 찾아왔다.

일란성 쌍둥이인 테소로 할머니(왼쪽)와 동생(오른쪽)

이들만 그런 게 아니다. 모든 일란성 쌍둥이의 건강상태나 수명은 서로 다르다. 둘 다 똑같은 유전자를 물려받고, 똑같은 부모 밑에서 어린 시절을 보냈고, 같은 지역에서 젊은 시절을 보냈는데 왜 이렇게 다를까?

예일 대학의 레비(Becca Levy) 박사팀이 노년기에 접어든 노인들에게 물었다.

"여러분은 나이가 들어가는 걸 어떻게 생각하시나요?"

어떤 노인들은 이렇게 대답했다.

"나이 들면 건강은 나빠지게 돼 있어요. 내 건강도 당연히 나빠질 겁니다."

또 다른 사람들은 나이 듦을 달리 바라보았다.

"나이가 무슨 상관인가요? 나이 들어도 얼마든지 건강할 수 있는데."

연구팀은 20년 후 노인들을 추적해보고 깜짝 놀랐다. "나이 들면 건강은 당연히 나빠지게 돼 있다"고 대답했던 노인들은 하나같이 건강이 나빴거나 사망했다. 반면 "나이가 들어도 얼마든지 건강할 수 있다"고 응답했던 사람들은 하나같이 건강했다. 후자들은 전자들보다 무려 평균 7년 반이나 더 오래 살았다. 바라보는 대로 현실로 나타난 것이다.

심장병을 막는 가장 큰 비결은 잦은 병원치료가 아니라 바로 마음이라고 한다.

핀란드 의학자들이 심장병 위험이 있는 중년 남성들에게 1년에 몇 차례에 걸쳐 이런 조언을 해줬다.

"붉은 고기 대신 채소와 과일을 많이 드세요. 동물지방은 많이 섭취되면 혈관을 막아버리거든요. 매일 규칙적으로 걸으세요. 걸을수록 지방이 발산되고 혈액순환이 잘 돼 혈관이 깨끗해지니까요. 그리고 담배를 끊으셔야 합니다. 니코틴은 혈관을 딱딱해지게 하거든요."

자신의 몸을 스스로 돌아보도록 하는 조언이었다.

또 다른 중년 남성들에겐 전혀 다른 방법으로 접근했다. 정기적으로 꼬박꼬박 자주 병원 치료를 받도록 하고, 혈압과 콜레스테롤 수치를 낮추는 약도 먹도록 했다. 몇 년 후 두 그룹 중년 남성들 간의 건강상태를 비

초프라 박사

"어떤 정보를 입력하느냐에 따라
몸은 늙기도 하고 젊어지기도 한다."

© Mitchell Aidelbaum

교해보았다. 어떤 그룹이 더 건강해졌을까? 놀랍게도 엄격한 병원치료를 받았던 중년남성들보다 건강관리에 대한 자세한 설명을 들은 중년남성들의 사망률이 더 낮았다.

심장병 예방연구 사례로 유명한 '헬싱키 연구(Helsinki Study)'이다. 왜 이런 결과가 나왔을까? 〈타임〉이 '20세기 100대 인물'로 선정한 세계적인 의학자인 초프라(Deepak Chopra)는 이렇게 말한다.

"건강관리에 관한 설명을 들으면 자신의 몸을 제대로 바라볼 수 있게 된다. 바라보면 몸도 변화한다. 병원이나 약에 의존하는 것보다 머릿속에 얼마나 긍정적인 정보를 입력해놓느냐가 더 중요하다."

그는 "젊음과 노화도 선택하는 것이다. 젊음에 관한 정보를 많이 입력하면 젊어지고, 노화에 관한 정보를 많이 입력하면 늙어간다"라고 설명한다.

머릿속을 어떤 이미지로 채울 것인가?

수업시간에 한 학생을 앞으로 불러 간단한 실험을 해보았다.

"진표 군, 한 팔을 옆으로 쭉 뻗어보세요. 그리고 조용히 눈을 감고 가장 수치스러웠던 장면을 떠올려보세요."

그가 눈을 감고 나서 조금 지나 내가 팔을 슬쩍 내리눌렀다. 팔이 힘없이 툭 떨어졌다.

"이번에는 가장 평화로운 장면을 떠올려보세요."

내가 또 팔을 슬쩍 내리눌렀다. 이번에는 팔이 끄떡없었다. 내가 더 힘을 줘서 눌렀는데도 그의 팔은 내려가지 않았다. 왜 이런 현상이 나타날까?

머릿속에
수치스런 장면을 입력시키면
기운이 빠진다.

머릿속에
평화로운 장면을 입력시키면
힘이 생긴다.

수치스러운 장면을 떠올리면 얼른 도망치거나 숨고 싶다. 몸이 바짝 오그라들면서 자기 방어를 위한 벽을 세우게 된다. 반면 평화로운 장면을 떠올리면 긴장이 풀린다. 방어의 벽이 허물어지고 몸이 열린다. 마음의 벽을 세우면 우주의 기운이 스며들지 못하고, 벽을 허물면 스며들어오는 것이다. 눈에 보이지 않는 벽도 눈에 보이는 벽과 똑같은 위력을 발휘한다는 사실을 상기하라.

당신이 끔찍한 실연을 겪었다고 상상해보자. 머릿속이 돌연 텅 빈 느낌이다. 하루 24시간 머릿속을 채웠던 연인이 떠났다고 생각하니 실제로 머릿속이 텅 비는 것이다. 정신이 멍해지니 밥도 먹기 싫고, 누구를 만나거나 책을 보는 것도 싫다. 그러면서 온몸의 힘도 빠져나가 초주검 상태로 누워 있기만 한다. 그러던 차에 웬일로 옛 연인이 전화를 걸어와 울먹이며 용서를 구한다.

"헤어지고 나니 온몸이 아파서 꼼짝도 못하겠어요. 용서해주세요. 다시 만나주세요."

당신은 침대에서 벌떡 일어난다. 텅 비었던 머릿속이 다시 연인에 대한 사랑으로 가득 차오르면서 초주검 상태에서 초능력 상태로 깜짝 변신한다. 정신의학자 호킨스(David Hawkins)는 평화, 기쁨, 사랑 등을 느낄 때 가장 많은 에너지가 흐르고 수치심, 죄책감, 무관심 등을 느낄 때 가장 적은 에너지가 흐른다고 분석한 바 있다.

캘리포니아 대학의 사회학자인 필립스(David Phillips)가 미국 군인 1,251명의 사망률을 조사해보니, 생일을 두세 달 앞두었을 때가 가장 낮았고 생일이 지난 뒤 3개월 이내가 가장 높았다. 생일 때 가족들로부터 축하연락을 받는다는 기대가 커지면 에너지가 넘쳐흘렀다가 기대가 사라지면 에너지가 빠져나갔기 때문이다.

그럼 노인들은 어떨까? 필립스는 중추절(중국의 추석)을 전후한 중국 노인들의 사망기록도 조사해보았다. 아니나 다를까. 중추절 전주의 사망률은 35퍼센트나 뚝 떨어졌고, 중추절 다음 주의 사망률은 거꾸로 37퍼센트나 쑥 치솟았다. 중추절 전주엔 멀리 떨어졌던 사랑하는 가족들의 얼굴들이 머릿속을 가득 채우니 온몸에 힘이 넘쳐흘렀고, 중추절 다음 주엔 가족들이 한꺼번에 떠나버린 텅 빈 집안만 보이니 힘도 쑥 빠져나갔기 때문이다.

이처럼 내 머릿속을 어떤 이미지로 채우느냐에 따라 내 몸도 달라진다. 젊은 이미지로 채우면 몸도 젊어지고, 평화롭고 사랑스런 이미지로 채우면 몸도 활기차고 건강해진다. 당신은 오늘 하루 어떤 이미지로 머릿속을 채우고 살아갈 것인가?

나를 남으로 바라보면 효과 백 배

어느 날 이메일을 열어보니 한 여학생이 면담을 요청해왔다. 그런데 평소 얌전하고 공부 잘하는 그 학생의 입에서 뜻밖의 말이 튀어나왔다.

"선생님, 제가 골초예요. 술도 많이 마시고요. 어떻게 해야 끊을 수 있을까요?"

담배는 중학교 때부터, 술은 고등학교 때부터 시작했다는 거였다. 유별난 행동을 들춰보면 유별난 뿌리가 숨겨져 있는 법. 그녀의 가슴에도 어릴 적 상처가 도사리고 있었다.

"엄마는 어릴 적부터 늘 제게 예쁘고 매력적으로 행동하고 말하라고 했어요. 제가 엄마에게 애정과 인정을 받으려면 시키는 대로 해야만 했죠. 엄마는 저를 예쁘게 꾸며 쇼핑이나 파티에도 데리고 다니곤 했어요. 하지만 파티가 파하고 나면 저는 안중에도 없었죠."

한번은 파티에서 이런 일도 있었다. 모든 사람이 멋진 옷을 차려입고 음식과 대화를 즐기고 있었다. 어린 그녀도 예쁜 옷차림으로 엄마의 무릎 위에 앉아 있었다.

"저도 그렇게 앉아 있으니 특별한 기분이었어요."

그때 엄마가 이렇게 말했다.

"혜정아. 저쪽에 앉아 있는 여자아이 예쁘지? 네가 가서 볼에 살짝 뽀뽀해주고 오렴."

그녀는 난처한 얼굴로 대답했다.

"하지만 엄마. 난 저 애 몰라. 마음에 들지도 않고."

"그게 무슨 당치 않은 소리니? 네가 좋아할 만한 애야. 냉큼 가서 뽀뽀해주고 와."

엄마가 시키는 대로 꼭두각시처럼 행동하라는 거였다. 아무리 어린아이지만 자신의 존재를 완전히 무시당한 것이었다. 엄마의 사랑은 허울뿐인 사랑이었다. 파티가 끝나면 우아하던 엄마의 미소도 함께 사라졌다. 그리고 엄마는 다시 예전의 무심한 마음으로 돌아갔다.

물론 남들이 보면 참 행복해 보였다. 물질적으로는 엄마가 모든 욕구를 채워주었다. 하지만 정작 정신적 도움이 필요할 땐 기댈 수 없었다. 엄마는 딸을 자신의 만족을 채우기 위한 분신으로 보았을 뿐이다. 엄마는 자신이 예전에 못했던 것들을 딸을 통해 대리만족을 얻으려 했다. 심지어 졸업 후 결혼할 남자까지 이미 점찍어놓았다. 물론 엄마 입맛에 맞는 돈 많은 남자였다.

어릴 적부터 그런 식으로 억눌린 그녀의 감정은 출구를 찾고 있었다. 그 출구가 바로 술과 담배였다. 하지만 어쨌든 술과 담배는 끊어야 했다. 그래서 담배 대용으로 최근에 나온 수증기를 뿜어내는 전자담배도 피워보고, 피부 패치도 붙여 보는 등 온갖 방법을 다 써보았다. 하지만 아무리 결심을 단단히 해도 술자리에만 가면 모래성처럼 허물어지곤 했다. 끼리끼리 모인다고 했던가. 친구들도 대부분 술과 담배를 즐겼다. 그런 자리에서 술기운이 돌면 자연이 긴장이 풀리고 결심도 풀렸다.

"이번만 딱 한 번 피우고 정말 끊지 뭐."

그런 패턴이 반복되면서 자신감도 사라졌다. 결심과 후회가 상습화돼버렸다. 그녀의 잠재의식에 각인된 건 금연하는 자신의 모습이 아니라 담배를 피워 물고 낙담하는 자신의 얼굴이었다. 잠재의식에 새겨진 이미지는 의지만으로 지우기 힘들다. 이미지가 의지보다 훨씬 더 강하기 때문이다. 따라서 이미지는 더 강한 다른 이미지로 밀어내야 한다. 그럼 어떤 이미지를 어떻게 그려 바라보아야 골초 습관을 끊을 수 있을까?

나를 타인처럼 바라보면 완전히 바뀐다

나는 오하이오 주립대학의 리비(Lisa Libby) 교수가 실시한 실험이 떠올랐다. 그는 2004년 대선을 하루 앞두고 대학생 146명을 두 그룹으로 나눴다. 그리고 A그룹 대학생들에게 주문했다. "내일 투표장에서 여러분이 투표하는 모습을 각기 1인칭으로 떠올려보세요." 즉 '나는 투표용지에 후보를 찍고 있어'와 같은 식으로 1인칭인 '나'의 시각으로 내 모습을 상상하라는 것이었다. 학생들은 시키는 대로 눈을 감고 자신들이 투표장에 걸어 들어가 투표용지에 후보를 선택하는 장면을 각기 자유롭게 상상해보았다. 몇 초씩 반복해서 상상하든, 몇 분간 지속적으로 상상하든, 그건 자유였다.

B그룹 학생들에게도 그런 방식으로 자유롭게 상상하도록 했다. 단지 3인칭(저 사람)의 시각으로 상상하도록 한 것만 달랐다. "여러분이 투표하는 모습을 '저 사람은 투표용지에 후보를 찍고 있어'라는 식으로 떠올

려 바라보세요. 자신을 남으로 보는 겁니다."

이튿날 두 그룹 사이에는 어떤 차이가 나타났을까? 자신이 투표하는 모습을 1인칭의 시각으로 상상한 학생들은 72퍼센트가 투표했지만, 3인칭의 시각으로 상상한 학생들은 무려 90퍼센트나 투표장에 갔다. 조사대상이 아니었던 다른 학생들의 투표율은 20퍼센트를 밑돌았다.

〈대학생들의 투표율〉
* 상상하지 않는다 → 20퍼센트 미만
* 1인칭으로 상상 : "나는 투표하고 있어." → 72퍼센트
* 3인칭으로 상상 : "그는 투표하고 있어." → 90퍼센트

단 한 차례의 상상만으로도 이런 놀라운 차이가 나타났다. 반복할수록 투표율은 더욱 높아진다.

이 실험은 중요한 메시지를 던진다. 나의 행동을 변화시키고 싶다면 내가 원하는 새로운 행동을 머릿속에서 미리 이미지로 그려 바라보라는 것이다. 그럼 관찰자 효과에 따라 그 이미지가 현실로 나타난다. 그런데 이미지를 어떤 방식으로 그리느냐에 따라 또 차이가 난다. 나를 나라고 상상하는 것보다 나를 남이라고 상상하는 게 훨씬 성공률이 높다(예를 들어 자신을 'A'라는 이름의 낯선 사람으로 보아도 좋다).

왜 이런 차이가 날까? 나의 눈으로 나를 바라보면 나의 감정에 휘말려 들어 나를 객관적으로 바라보지 못한다. 그럼 선명한 이미지 형성에 방해가 된다. 하지만 나를 남이라고 상상하면 나를 객관적으로 바라볼 수 있어 이미지가 더 선명해진다. 이미지가 선명할수록 제대로 바라보게 되고,

현실로 나타날 가능성은 그만큼 더 높아진다.

리비 교수는 이렇게 설명한다.

"잠재의식에 새겨진 뿌리 깊은 습관은 잠재의식이 바뀌지 않는 한 고쳐지지 않아요. 의지력에는 한계가 있죠."

머릿속에 그린 이미지를 제3자의 눈으로 객관화하면 우리 잠재의식은 이를 당연히 받아들여 믿게 되고, 이렇게 믿음의 강도가 높아지면 분명한 현실로 나타나는 것이다.

술 과 담 배 를 단 박 에 끊 다

나는 권혜정 학생이 쉽게 금연할 수 있을 거라고 판단했다. 왜냐하면 그녀는 분명한 의도를 갖고 있었기 때문이다. 못 말리는 골초이면서도 끊고자 하는 의도조차 없는 사람들이 세상에는 얼마나 많은가? 나는 리비 교수와 똑같은 방법을 시도해보기로 했다.

"흡연 유혹을 가장 강하게 받을 때가 언제죠?"

"그야 다른 사람들이 담배를 피울 때죠."

"그럼 일단 눈을 감고 다른 사람들이 흡연하는 장면을 그려보세요."

그녀가 눈을 감고 상상에 잠기자 내가 다시 말했다.

"흡연하고 싶어 근질근질할 겁니다. 그 흡연 충동에도 끄떡없이 금연하는 혜정 양의 모습을 그려보세요." 상상에 잠긴 그녀를 보고 내가 물었다.

"어때요? 남들이 흡연해도 안 흔들리나요?"

그녀는 고개를 끄덕였다. 자신을 남의 눈으로 바라보니 흔들리지 않았다.

"흡연 유혹을 이겨내는 혜정 양 모습을 가장 보고 싶어하는 사람이 누굴까요? 엄마, 아빠, 아니면 약혼자?"

"약혼자와 아빠요."

"그럼 아빠와 약혼자가 혜정 양의 꿋꿋한 금연 자세를 지켜보고 흐뭇해하는 모습들을 그려보세요. 다시 말해 혜정 양이 금연하는 모습을 가족들과 함께 관객처럼 지켜보는 겁니다."

그녀는 시키는 대로 했다. 나는 담배를 피우고 싶은 충동이 고개를 들 때마다 그렇게 해보라고 했다.

다음주 강의가 끝난 뒤 핸드폰 문자메시지가 왔다. 잘 버티고 있다는 거였다. 한 달쯤 지나면서부터 그녀의 얼굴에 화색이 완연했다.

"이젠 니코틴의 유혹에서 완전히 벗어난 얼굴이네요?"

나도 관찰자 효과가 실제로 성과를 거두고 있다는 사실이 기뻤다.

"이젠 담배뿐 아니라 알코올 중독에서도 완전히 해방된 걸요."

그녀가 자랑스러운 표정으로 털어놓은 성공담은 이랬다. 담배를 끊은 지 이틀쯤 지나 친구들과 저녁식사를 했다. 식사가 끝나자 예상대로 술이 돌았고, 몇몇 친구들이 담배를 피워 물었다. 담배냄새가 살살 코를 자극했다.

'충동이 드는 순간 금연하는 이미지를 떠올려라.'

친구들 앞에서 돌연 눈을 감고 상상에 잠길 수는 없는 노릇이었다. 그래서 그녀는 그 자리에서 눈을 뜬 채 이미지를 그렸다. 흡연을 즐기는 친구들 옆에서 담배 연기를 맡고도 초연한 표정으로 앉아 있는 자신의 모습

자신이 변한 모습을
여러 명이 함께 바라보는
이미지를 그리면
현실화가 가속화된다.

을 상상했다. 자신을 남이라고 객관화시켜 바라보았다.

"저 사람은 역시 금연 약속을 깨지 않는군. 새로운 모습이야. 대단해."

그 이미지 속에 아빠와 약혼자도 관객으로 등장시켰다. 금연 유혹을 꿋꿋하게 떨쳐내는 그녀를 보고 아빠가 중얼거렸다.

"우리 혜정이가 이제 정말 담배를 끊었나 봐."

그 모습을 상상한 그녀는 으쓱해졌다. 오랜만에 아빠를 기쁘게 해드렸다는 뿌듯한 자부심도 밀려왔다. 상상으로 이렇게 고비를 넘기자 그다음부터는 점점 더 쉬워졌다. 우선 상상 자체가 쉬워졌다. 흡연 욕구가 고개를 들 때마다 불과 몇 초씩 금연하는 자신의 이미지를 떠올리면 그만이었다. 그녀는 이런 호기심도 들었다.

'금연하는 나의 모습을 종이에 그리면 어떨까? 마찬가지 효과가 있을까?'

금연 욕구가 들 때마다 종이쪽지에 얼른 금연 이미지를 그려놓고 가만히 바라보았다. 신기한 일이었다. 그 자체만으로도 충동이 사라지는 것이었다. 이 역시 자신을 객관화시켜 바라보는 방식이기 때문이다.

그녀는 폭음 습관도 마찬가지 방법으로 이겨냈다. 사실상 단 한 차례의 상상만으로 10년 가까이 계속돼온 흡연, 음주 습관을 끊어버렸다.

상상 속에 청중을 등장시켜라

한 남학생은 발표할 때만 되면 좌불안석이었다. 연신 헛기침을 해대고 손을 비비적거렸다. 연단에 나가서도 벌건 얼굴로 더듬거리기 일쑤였다. 그러니 의사전달이 제대로 될 리 없었다. 그 모습을 보니 불현듯 내가 무대공포증에 떨던 순간이 떠올랐다. 방송국에 들어가 10여 년쯤 됐던 때였다. 어느 날 보도국장이 찾았다.

"바쁘지? 다음주부터 저녁뉴스 프로를 강화할 계획이네. 자네가 앵커 좀 맡아줘."

당시 나는 정치부 기자로 총리실 취재를 담당하고 있었다. 사실 그 일만으로도 바빴다. 하지만 새로운 경험을 해보는 것도 기회라 생각했다. 하지만 막상 방송할 날이 바짝 다가오자 나도 모르게 떨리기 시작했다. 바로 전날 밤에는 잠을 못 이루고 뒤척거렸다.

'생방송 하다가 말을 더듬기라도 하면 무슨 망신이지? 방송사고가 나면 어떡하지?'

총리실에 나갔다가 돌아와 초긴장 상태로 10분 정도 일찍 스튜디오에 들어가 앉았다. 마이크와 이어폰, 큐시트 등을 확인하고 나니 마음이 좀 놓였다. 드디어 생방송의 시작을 알리는 큐 신호가 들어왔다.

"여러분, 안녕하십니까?"라는 인사말과 함께 헤드라인 몇 개를 읽었다. 그리고 첫 앵커 멘트를 끝내고 해당 기자의 리포트가 나갈 때 한숨을 돌렸다. 그러고 나니 긴장도가 확 떨어졌다. 그다음부터는 쉬웠다. 그때 느낀 건 "역시 한 번 해보고 나면 안 떨린다"는 사실이었다. 방송 시작 전 내가 그토록 떨렸던 건 어떤 상황에서 어떤 말을 해야 할지 한 번도 해보지 않았기 때문이었다.

한 번 해보고 나면 왜 안 떨릴까? 그건 내가 어떤 상황에서 어떤 말을 해야 할지 분명하고 선명한 이미지가 그려지기 때문이다. 즉, 미래의 행동이 선명한 이미지로 그려질수록 떨리지 않게 되고, 자신감을 갖게 되는 것이다. 선명한 이미지는 완벽한 리허설이 만들어낸다.

세계적인 명연설가였던 미국의 존 F. 케네디 대통령은 대중연설이 계획된 전날은 잠자리에 들기 전 반드시 상상 속에서 연설을 하곤 했다. 머릿속으로 연단에 올라선 자신의 모습을 떠올리면서 약 10분 동안 연설 내용을 쭉 훑어보는 것이었다. 연설 내용뿐 아니라 연설 속의 상황도 세세하게 그렸다. 청중들이 환호하는 모습, 자신이 취해야 할 제스처, 미소, 목소리 톤까지 구체적으로 그렸다. 이것을 지겹다는 생각이 들 정도로 연습하고 나면 떨리는 마음은 멀찌감치 달아나고 어서 빨리 연단에 서고 싶어 안달이 나기 마련이었다. 여기서 특이한 점은 그는 상상 속에 반드시 청중을 등장시켰다는 점이다.

캐나다 요크 대학의 배스케스(Noelia Vasquez) 교수는 상상 속의 청중이 어떤 차이를 만들어내는지 실험해보았다. 그는 대학생들에게 이렇게 말했다.

"오늘은 3분씩 자유 연설할 시간을 주겠습니다. 각자 마음속으로 연설 리허설을 해보세요."그는 학생들을 두 그룹으로 나눴다. A 그룹에게는 이렇게 말했다.

"자신의 모습을 1인칭으로 바라보며 리허설 하세요. 즉 자신을 '나'의 시각으로 보는 겁니다."

반면, B 그룹에게는 자신을 3인칭으로 바라보라고 했다.

"자신을 청중과 함께 남으로 바라보는 장면을 상상해보세요. 여러분 스스로도 청중이 되는 겁니다."

연설 리허설이 끝난 뒤 학생들에게 물었다.

"자, 리허설이 끝났죠? 여러분은 이제 얼마나 성공적으로 연설을 할수 있을까요? 성공에 대한 자신감을 1~10점까지의 점수로 매겨보세요."

1인칭의 눈으로 자신의 리허설을 바라본 A그룹은 평균 5점 정도의 자신감을 보였다. 반면, 청중과 함께 자신의 리허설을 남의 눈으로 객관화시켜 바라본 B그룹은 평균 9점이 넘었다. 다수의 청중들로 하여금 자신의 리허설을 바라보도록 하면 왜 이처럼 자신감이 껑충 뛰어오를까? 배스케스 교수의 분석은 이렇다.

"한 사람이 한 가지를 바라볼 때 변화가 일어난다면 여러 사람들이 한꺼번에 바라볼 땐 더 큰 변화가 일어나는 건 당연하죠. 지켜보는 사람들이 많아질수록 자신을 더욱더 객관적으로 바라볼 수 있기도 하고."

이 실험결과는 2008년 베이징 올림픽에 참가했던 미국 올림픽 선수들의 심상화 훈련에 그대로 활용됐다.

부 정 적   기 억 들   지 워 내 기

그럼 과거의 기억은 어떨까? 나를 괴롭히는 과거의 불행한 추억도 자신의 눈으로 회상하는 것보다 다수의 제3자들과 함께 돌이켜보면 긍정적으로 회상될까?

코넬 대학의 길로비치(Thomas Gilovich) 교수는 예일 대학, 오하이오 주립대학 교수들과 공동으로 그 답변을 찾아보았다. 그들은 내성적인 성격 때문에 고등학교 시절을 우울하게 보냈다는 대학생들에게 이렇게 주문했다.

"고교시절 가장 창피했던 순간을 회상해보세요."

A그룹에게는 1인칭 시각으로, B그룹에게는 다수의 제3자, 즉 급우들의 시각으로 회상해보도록 했다. 결과는 예상대로였다. 1인칭 시각으로 회상한 학생들은 과거의 창피했던 순간을 그대로 떠올리고는 금방 우울해졌다. 고교시절과 비교해 지금도 사교성이 나아지지 않았다고 보았다.

반면 여러 급우들의 시각으로 회상한 학생들은 창피했던 순간을 보다 객관적으로 보게 됐다. 그러면서 "난 대학생이 된 뒤 사교성이 좋아졌어요"라고 대답했다. 불행했던 과거를 다수의 제3자 시각으로 바라보면 '그게 별게 아니었구나' 하며 긍정적인 면을 더욱 부풀려보게 된다. 이런 자세는 곧바로 행동에도 반영된다.

제3자의 시각으로 과거를 회상한 학생들은 설문조사가 끝난 뒤 낯선 사람을 만나자 먼저 말을 거는 등 실제로 더욱 사교적으로 행동했다. 생각이 변하니 행동도 변했던 것이다. 길로비치 교수는 이렇게 분석한다.

"난 이제 변했어. 내 성격은 이미 좋아졌어. ─ 이렇게 믿게 되면 실제로 그렇게 행동하게 되죠. 그래서 더욱 많이 변화할 수 있는 동기가 생기게 됩니다. 반면, 변화를 원하는 당사자가 자신만의 시각으로 과거를 바라보면 큰 진전을 이룬 게 별로 없어 보이죠. 과거의 감정에 휩싸여 더욱 우울해질 뿐이거든요."

이런 결과는 우울증 치료에서도 그대로 나타난다.

한 실험에서 우울증 치료를 받는 대학생들에게 첫 치료시간을 회상토록 해보았다. 절반에게는 "당시 상황을 자신의 눈으로 바라보세요"라고 주문했다. 나머지 다른 절반에게는 "제3자의 눈으로 당시 상황을 바라보세요"라고 지시했다. 그런 다음 첫 치료에 대한 평가를 0~10점의 눈금으로 표시해보도록 했다. 자신의 눈으로 회상한 학생들은 치료의 효과를 평균 5.6점, 제3자의 눈으로 회상한 학생들은 7.8점으로 평가했다.

오하이오 주립대학의 리비(Lisa Libby) 교수는 이렇게 조언한다.

"자신을 남으로 객관화시켜 바라보는 건 인생의 긍정적 변화를 유도하는 데 매우 훌륭한 기술이죠. 노력에 대한 만족도가 높아지고, 그러다 보면 목표 달성을 위한 노력도 더 많이 하게 되지요."

말기 암을 완치한 할머니의 기도

내가 담당하는 해외정보 TV 프로인 〈지구촌 리포트〉에는 보통 사람들의 기적 같은 실제 사례들이 많이 소개된다. 얼마 전에는 관찰자 효과로 온몸에 퍼졌던 암세포를 일주일 만에 말끔히 털어버린 말기 암 환자의 이야기를 방송했다. 71세인 하이벨(Ellen Heibel) 씨가 그 주인공이다.

그녀는 6년 전 의사로부터 청천벽력 같은 선고를 받았다.

"식도암이 간, 폐, 척추, 흉골 등 온몸에 이미 다 퍼져버렸네요. 어떤 치료를 받더라도 소용없어요. 집에 가서 그냥 편히 쉬세요."

죽을 날만 기다리라는 얘기였다. 의사는 그러면서 방사선과 화학 치료를 받으면 암의 진행속도가 늦춰져서 잘하면 6개월 정도 살 수 있을 거라고 말해주었다. 하지만 그녀는 나을 수 있다는 믿음을 버리지 않았다.

때마침 한 친구가 실로스^(Francis Seelos) 신부 이야기를 해주면서 그를 떠올리며 함께 기도해보자고 했다. 실로스는 19세기 미국 메릴랜드 주에서 활동했던 신부로, 성자의 전 단계인 복자로 추대됐을 만큼 추앙받는 인물이었다. 지푸라기라도 잡고 싶었던 그녀는 곧장 9일 기도에 들어갔다. 신부의 뼛조각이 담긴 목걸이도 줄곧 몸에 지니고 다녔다. 그리고 불과 일주일 후, 기적이 일어났다.

"병원에 갔더니 의사들이 암이 다 사라졌다며 깜짝 놀랐어요. 기도를 시작한 날과 검사받던 날 사이에 모두 사라진 겁니다."

어떻게 그토록 순식간에 암이 완치될 수 있는지 의사들도 설명하지 못했다. 단지 화학 치료만으로는 그런 일이 불가능하다는 말만 반복할 뿐이었다. 하지만 그녀는 알고 있었다.

"신부님이 제 암을 씻어내는 장면을 생생하게 그리고 또 그렸어요. 신부님과 함께."

다시 말해 믿음이 강한 신부와 그녀 자신이 함께 제3의 관찰자가 됐던 것이다. 그러다 보니 혼자서 암이 사라지는 걸 그리는 것보다 효과가 몇 배나 강해졌다는 얘기다.

교회는 실로스 신부를 성자로 시성해달라고 교황청에 조사를 의뢰했다. 성자가 되려면 보통 사후에 두 건 이상의 기적을 일으켜야 한다. 실로스 신부의 경우에는 지난 1966년에도 말기 간암 환자를 완쾌시킨 기적을 일으킨 바 있다. 그 환자 역시 온몸에 암세포가 퍼져 수술 불가 판정을 받았지만 실로스 신부에게 기도한 끝에 완쾌됐었다.

방송이 나간 뒤 한 시청자가 이런 전화를 걸어왔다.

"저도 사실은 환자예요. 방송에 나온 하이벨 할머니처럼 기댈 만한 사

실로스 신부와
하이벨 할머니

람이 없는 경우엔 어떻게 기도해야 하나요?"

하이벨 할머니 사례의 실로스 신부처럼 의지할 만한 제3자를 떠올리기 어려운 사람들은 어떻게 기도해야 하느냐는 의문이었다.

기도하는 방식에 따라 기도 효과는 어떻게 달라질까? 미국의 생물학자 레인(Glen Rein)은 어떤 식의 기도가 암세포의 성장을 가장 억제하는지 실험해보았다. 우선 다섯 개의 세균배양 접시(petri dish)에 각기 똑같은 수의 암세포들을 집어넣었다. 그런 다음 한 심리치료사에게 다섯 가지 방식으로 기도해보도록 했다.

〈다섯 가지 기도방법〉

1. "암세포들이 자연의 질서를 회복해 다시 정상적으로 자라도록 해주세요."
2. "암세포가 세 개만 남도록 해주세요."
3. "신의 사랑과 연민이 암세포에 미치도록 해주세요."
4. "암세포들에게 무조건적인 사랑과 연민을 보내주세요."
5. "암세포들을 파괴시켜주세요."

결과는 이랬다.

1. "암세포들이 자연의 질서를 회복해 다시 정상적으로 자라도록 해
   주세요."
   → 암세포들의 성장 속도가 39퍼센트 떨어졌다.
2. "암세포가 세 개만 남도록 해주세요."
   → 암세포들의 성장 속도가 21퍼센트 떨어졌다.
3. "신의 사랑과 연민이 암세포에 미치도록 해주세요."
   → 2번처럼 21퍼센트 떨어졌다.
4. "암세포들에게 무조건적인 사랑과 연민을 보내주세요."
   → 아무 효과가 없었다.
5. "암세포들을 파괴시켜주세요."
   → 아무 효과가 없었다.

"자연의 질서를 회복해달라"는 1번 기도가 왜 가장 효과가 컸을까?
아인슈타인이 지적했듯, 사람의 몸은 전기 에너지 덩어리다. 온몸의 구석
구석마다 에너지 물결이 흐르고 있다. 건강한 사람의 몸은 에너지 물결이
고르고 균형을 이룬다. 이게 자연의 질서다. 반면 암이 생긴 부위의 에너
지 물결은 고르지 못하다. 키를리안 사진기로 촬영해보면 물결이 들쭉날
쭉하고 색깔도 다르다. 자연의 질서가 깨진 것이다. 따라서, "자연의 질
서를 회복해달라"는 기도가 가장 효율적일 수밖에 없다.
레인의 실험결과가 말해주는 또 다른 사실은 암세포들도 사람처럼 부
정적인 메시지보다는 긍정적인 메시지에 훨씬 더 적극적으로 반응한다

는 것이다. 파괴시키겠다는 의도를 품고 기도하면 고집스럽게 버티려 들지만, 따뜻한 마음으로 정상적으로 자라게 해달라고 기도하면 순순히 말을 듣는다. 또한 똑같이 사랑과 연민을 보내달라고 기도하더라도 '신'을 명시하는 것과 않는 것 간엔 큰 차이가 벌어졌다. 막연한 기도보다는 자신이 갈망하는 바를 구체적으로 요구하는 기도가 훨씬 더 잘 통한다는 사실도 확인됐다.

키가 8센티미터나 커진 대학생

몇 년 전의 일이었던가. 방송국 사무실에서 기사를 쓰고 있는데 전화가 걸려왔다. 회사 선배였다.

"김 부장, 혹시 인턴 필요하지 않아?"

"인턴요? 글쎄요."

사실 인턴사원이 붙어 있어봐야 거추장스럽게 느껴지기만 한다. 기사를 쓸 수 있는 것도 아니고 심부름을 알아서 척척 해줄 수 있는 것도 아니다. 일거리를 만들어줘야 하고, 점심때가 되면 점심도 사줘야 한다. 하지만 친한 선배의 부탁이니 안 들어줄 수도 없는 노릇이었다.

"어느 학교 다니는 학생인데요?"

"응, 프린스턴 대학교 2학년이야. 여름방학 때 방송국에 한 달만 다니고 싶대."

한 달만이라니? 한 달이 얼마나 긴 시간인데….

그 학생의 이름은 김인수. 키는 168센티미터 정도로 호리호리한 편이었다. 말씨도 사근사근하고 예의가 발라 호감이 갔다. 졸업 후 희망이 뭐냐고 했더니 로스쿨에 들어가는 거라고 했다.

"로스쿨이라⋯. 그럼 방송국 일은 배워봐야 말짱 헛거구만. 괜히 시간 낭비하지 말고 여기 앉아서 공부나 열심히 해. 인턴 수료증서는 원하는 대로 써줄 테니."

인수는 사무실에 나와서 시키는 대로 공부만 하다 갔다. 인턴을 수료했다는 증서는 약속대로 잘 써주었다.

그 이듬해 여름방학 때 인수한테서 전화가 걸려 왔다. 찾아와서 인사를 하겠다는 거였다. 젊은 친구가 참 인사성 바르다는 생각이 들었다. 그런데 그를 보는 순간 깜짝 놀랐다.

"어? 인수야, 웬 키가 이렇게 커졌지? 키 커진 거 맞지?"

그는 씩 웃었다.

"네, 1년 사이 8센티미터나 커졌어요. 고등학교 때도 안 크던 키가 대학 2학년 때 갑자기 커졌어요."

세상에 희한한 일도 다 있다고 생각했다. 그는 벌써 23살이었다. 20살만 넘으면 척추 마디의 성장판이 닫혀버려 더 이상 키가 안 큰다는 게 의학계의 정설이다. 실제로 X-레이 사진을 찍어보면 성장판이 닫혀 있는 게 목격된다. 의학적으로는 불가능한 일이다. 하지만 이 학생은 하느님에게 부탁하면 모든 게 이뤄진다고 굳게 믿고 있었다. 그래서 매일 마음속으로 기도를 드렸다.

"하느님. 키가 10센티미터만 더 커지게 해주세요. 이 정도는 해주실 수 있으시죠?"

그는 친구에게 말하듯 틈만 나면 졸랐다. 그 결과 1년 만에 키가 훌쩍 커졌던 것이다. 중학교 다닐 때까지만 해도 맨 앞줄에 앉아 있었고, 대학교 3학년 때도 작은 축이었던 그가 이제는 평균 키를 웃돌게 됐다. 기도를 어떻게 했느냐고 내가 물었다.

"제 기도는 꼭 이뤄진다고 믿었을 뿐이에요. 하느님은 저를 사랑하시니까요."

내가 재차 물었다.

"그런 말은 딴 데서도 많이 들어봤어. 구체적인 방법을 말해봐. 기도할 때 어떤 식으로 했는지."

그제야 그는 털어놓았다.

"매일 밤 자기 전에 누워서 제 척추 마디마디가 조금씩 늘어나는 이미지를 그렸어요. 그걸 보고 기뻐하시는 부모님과 동생도 이미지에 함께 그렸죠. 가족들도 제 키가 커지는 걸 너무나 원하고 있었거든요."

나는 나중에 궁금증이 들어 그에게 일부러 국제전화를 걸었다.

"그런데 그때 관찰자 효과를 어떻게 알고 있었지?"

"사실은 우리 학교에 유명한 양자물리학 교수님들이 많거든요. 그래서 한 과목 청강했어요."

과연 아인슈타인이 교수로 재직했던 프린스턴 대학은 다른 점이 있구나 하는 생각이 들었다.

과정을 바라보면 쉽게 달성된다

관찰자 효과 수업 중 한 남학생이 좀 느닷없는 질문을 던졌다.

"마음의 눈으로 열심히 취직에 성공한 장면을 그려 바라보면 정말 취직도 되나요?"

낄낄거리는 소리가 흘러나왔다. 많은 자기개발 전문가들이 목표만 간절히 상상하면 어느 순간 거짓말처럼 현실로 나타난다고 외쳐대고 있지 않은가? 정말 그런 식으로 목표를 이룰 수 있을까?

펜실베이니아 대학의 외팅겐(Gabriel Oettingen) 교수는 졸업반 학생들에게 얼마나 자주 취직한 장면을 상상하느냐고 물어보았다. 그리고 2년 후 열심히 상상한 만큼 결실을 맺었는지 추적해보았다. 결과는 뜻밖에도 거꾸로였다. 취업에 성공한 상상에 빠진 학생들일수록 취직률도 떨어졌고, 보수도 적게 받았다. 살빼기의 심상화도 마찬가지였다. 살찐 여성들이 살이 쪽 빠진 자신의 미래 모습을 열심히 상상했는데도 살이 빠지기는커녕 오히려 체중이 더 불었던 것이다.

캘리포니아 대학의 팸(Lien Pham) 교수도 학생들에게 며칠 뒤 치를 중간고사에서 높은 점수를 얻는 장면을 매일 몇 분씩 상상해보도록 했다.

"간절한 마음으로 좋은 성적을 얻고 기뻐하는 장면을 생생히 떠올려

외팅겐 교수

"심상화를 열심히 한 사람들은 왜 오히려 나쁜 결과를 얻었을까?"

보세요."

이들의 심상화 노력은 과연 좋은 결실을 맺었을까? 그들의 점수를 다른 학생들과 비교해보았다. 그런데 심상화에 매달린 학생일수록 점수가 오른 게 아니라 오히려 떨어졌다. 도대체 성공하는 장면을 상상하면 상상할수록 결과는 왜 거꾸로 나오는 걸까? 꿈은 도대체 어떻게 이뤄지는 걸까?

한 17세 소년은 고급 자가용을 손에 넣는 게 꿈이었다. 그런데 꿈을 꾸기 시작한 지 2년 만에 정말 거짓말처럼 그 꿈이 현실로 나타났다. 돈 한 푼 안 들이고 포르셰 승용차를 손에 넣게 된 것이다. 어찌된 일일까? 목표만 간절히 상상한 결과였을까? 목표는 어떻게 이뤄진 걸까?

2년 전 친구로부터 중고 휴대전화를 얻은 게 시작이었다. 소년은 그걸 벼룩시장에 올려 조금 더 나은 휴대전화와 맞바꾸었고, 그걸 다시 고급 mp3 아이팟으로 바꾸었다. 그 후 그걸 산악용 오토바이로 바꾸었고, 다시 오토바이를 애플사의 맥 노트북과 바꾸는 데 성공했다. 그런데 놀랍게도 노트북과 도요타 자동차를 맞바꾸자는 사람이 나타났다.

"그분은 자동차가 이미 세 대나 있는데, 맥 노트북의 녹음 성능이 좋아 갖고 싶어했어요"

하지만 그 자동차를 운전하고 다니기에는 그가 너무 어렸다. 그래서 그걸 전동 골프차와 맞바꿨다. 그리고 전동 골프차를 다시 산악용 오토바이로 바꿨다가 일반 오토바이와 교환했다. 그러다가 그걸 수집가들이 탐내는 1975년산 포드 브론코로 바꿨고, 그걸 다시 은색 포르셰로 바꾸는 데 성공했다. 뉴스가 됐던 미국의 오티즈(Steven Ortiz) 군 실화이다.

그가 부지런히 이런 무수한 과정들을 거치지 않았더라면 과연 포르셰를 손에 넣을 수 있었을까? 자나깨나 목적지만 상상하고 있으면 설사 가는 길을 몰라도 저절로 도착할 수 있을까?

언제, 어디서, 어떻게… 실행 과정은 구체적으로

상습적으로 리포트를 늦게 내는 학생이 있었다. 그 버릇을 어떻게 고쳐줄 수 있을까? 나는 마지막 리포트 과제를 내주고 나서 그를 따로 불러 실험 삼아 이렇게 물어보았다.

"이번 리포트는 무슨 요일에 쓸 거죠?"

그가 머리를 긁적거리더니 대답했다.

"아마, 금요일쯤엔 쓸 수 있을 거 같아요."

"금요일 몇 시쯤?"

"글쎄요, 아마 저녁 먹고 9시쯤 시작할 수 있을 것 같아요."

"밤 9시라. 그럼 어디서 쓸 건가요?"

"그거야 물론 제 방에서 써야죠. 컴퓨터가 제 방에 있거든요."

그러고 나서 일주일 후 깜짝 놀랄 일이 벌어졌다. 강의 시작 전 그가 빙긋거리며 나오더니 리포트를 제일 먼저 제출하는 것 아닌가!

우리가 목표를 정해놓고 실행하지 못하는 건 실행 과정을 구체적으로 머릿속에 미리 그려 넣지 않기 때문이다. 과정 없는 결과는 없다. 언제, 어디서, 어떻게 실행할 것인지를 구체적으로 그려 바라보면 그대로 일어난다. 과정이 구체적일수록 이미지도 그만큼 더욱 선명하게 그려진다. 초일류 스포츠 선수들이 이미지 훈련을 할 때도 경기 과정을 최대한 생생하게 그린다. 그러다 보면 우승컵을 거머쥔 장면도 자연히 쉽게 그려질 수밖에 없다. 과정을 생략한 채 억지로 성공 이미지만 그리려 들면 무의식적으로 의심이 스며들어 이미지가 흐려진다. 이미지는 의지로 그려지는 게 아니라 고요한 마음으로 그려지기 때문이다.

이는 이 분야 세계 최고 권위자인 뉴욕 대학의 골비처(Peter Gollwitzer)와 독일의 심리학자 브란트스타터(Veronika Brandstatter) 교수가 실험으로 확인한 바 있다. 그들은 이틀간의 크리스마스 연휴가 시작되기 전 독일 대학생들에게 이런 주문을 했다.

"여러분은 크리스마스 이브를 어떻게 보낼 거죠? 어떻게 보냈는지에 대한 에세이를 써서 12월 26일까지 제출하세요."

그런 다음 학생들을 A, B 두 그룹으로 나눠 B그룹 학생들만 따로 불러 물어보았다.

"여러분은 언제, 어디서, 어떻게 에세이를 쓸 생각인가요? 구체적으로 말해보세요."

학생들은 제각기 대답했다.

"저는 크리스마스 날 아침 일찍 일어나 쓸 작정이에요. 다른 식구들이 일어나기 전 아빠 책상에서 조용히 말입니다. 아빠의 볼펜으로요."

"저는 식구들과 아침 식사를 마치자마자 후딱 해치울 거예요."

교수들은 에세이가 완성되면 우편으로 보내달라고 요청했다.

드디어 크리스마스 연휴가 끝나고 다시 몇 주일이 더 흘렀다. 두 그룹 중 어느 쪽이 목표를 더 많이 달성했을까?

*A그룹 : 12월 26일까지 쓰겠다는 목표만 정해놓은 학생들
  → 평균 7.7일 걸려 에세이 완성
*B그룹 : 언제, 어디서, 어떻게 쓰겠다는 구체적인 실행 과정까지
  그려본 학생들
  → 평균 2.3일 만에 에세이 완성

에세이를 완성하는 데만 차이가 벌어진 게 아니었다. A그룹은 완성한 에세이를 제출하는 데도 또 다시 시간을 질질 끌었다.

*A그룹 : 평균 12.6일 만에 에세이 제출
*B그룹 : 평균 4.9일 만에 에세이 제출

더 중요한 문제가 있다. 두 그룹 중 어느 쪽이 에세이 제출이라는 최종 목표를 더 많이 달성했을까?

* A그룹 : 32퍼센트만 에세이 제출
* B그룹 : 75퍼센트가 에세이 제출

왜 이런 차이가 날까? 교수들은 이렇게 입을 모은다.

"크리스마스 날 아침 일찍, 아빠 방에서, 아빠의 펜으로 에세이를 쓰겠다는 식으로 실행과정을 구체적으로 그릴수록 이미지도 그만큼 생생해집니다. 반면 과정이 막연하면 목표를 달성하는 이미지가 생생하게 그려지지 않아요."

이미지가 생생할수록 현실로 나타날 가능성도 높아지는 것이다.

교수들은 몇 년 후 비슷한 실험을 또 해보았다. 크리스마스 연휴 중 학생들에게 뭘 할 건지 물어본 것이다.

학생들은 "리포트 원고를 끝내야 해요", "아파트를 새로 구해야 해요", "부모님을 찾아뵙고 화해해야 해요" 등으로 제각기 대답했다. 그들은 일부 학생들에게 그 목표를 언제, 어디서, 어떻게 실행할 것이냐고 추가로 물었다. 그리고 연휴가 일주일쯤 지난 뒤 학생들의 몇 퍼센트가 목표를 달성했는지 확인해보았다.

* 그냥 목표를 세운 학생들 —→ 23퍼센트만 달성
* 구체적 과정까지 상상한 학생들 —→ 82퍼센트가 달성

규칙적인 운동을 목표로 세울 때도 마찬가지다. 그냥 목표만 세우는 것과 목표를 세워놓고 세부적인 실행과정을 떠올리는 것 사이에는 큰 차

이가 난다. 심리학자들이 학생들에게 두 가지 방법으로 목표를 정해 실행하도록 해보았다.

* A그룹 : "나는 앞으로 매주 조깅을 하겠다"라는 문장을 완성토록 했다.
* B그룹 : "나는 앞으로 매주 조깅을 하겠다"라는 문장을 완성토록 한 다음, 다음과 같은 문장을 추가로 완성토록 했다. "나는 ( )부터 매주 ( )요일마다 ( )에서 최소한 ( )분간 조깅을 하기로 했다."

한 달 후 두 그룹이 목표를 달성한 비율은 각각 얼마나 됐을까?

* A그룹 학생들 중 29퍼센트가 목표 실행
* B그룹 학생들 중 91퍼센트가 목표 실행

공 부 안 하 는 아 이 공 부 하 게 만 들 기

만일 당신의 아이가 공부는 안 하고 매일 TV나 보며 빈둥거린다면? 속이 터질 것이다. 그렇다고 "빨리 네 방에 가서 공부해!" 하고 버럭 소리 지른다면? 그것도 별 효과가 없다. 강요받은 마음은 공부를 잘 받아들이지 못하기 때문이다.

셰필드 대학의 쉬랜(Paschal Sheeran)과 웨브(Thomas Webb) 교수는 학생들에게 "다음 주에는 몇 시간이나 공부할 거죠?" 하고 물었다.

"35시간요."

"40시간은 해야죠."

교수들이 다시 말했다.

"그럼 목표로 정한 공부시간을 종이에 적어볼래요?"

학생들이 지시대로 목표 시간을 적은 뒤, 교수들이 일부 학생들을 따로 불러 딱 한 가지 질문을 보태보았다.

"언제, 어디서, 몇 시간씩 공부할 건가요? 그것도 종이에 적어볼래요?"

학생들이 또 시키는 대로 종이에 적었다. 일주일이 지났다. 이들은 몇 시간이나 공부했을까?

* 총 공부 시간만 목표로 적은 학생들 : 평균 10시간 공부
* 언제, 어디서 공부할 건지도 함께 적은 학생들 : 평균 35시간 공부

아이가 영 공부를 안 해 속이 상하는가? 아이에게 스스로 목표를 정하도록 유도한 뒤 구체적인 실행과정을 종이에 적어보도록 하라. 백 번 잔소리 하는 것보다 백 배 낫다.

걸림돌을 미리 바라보면 넘어지지 않는다

고등학교 시절 시험지만 받아들면 너무 긴장해 얼굴이 벌게지고 손이 달달 떨리는 친구가 있었다. 그런 상태로는 머리가 제대로 돌아가지 않는

다. 그래서 그런지 그는 시험만 끝나면 늘 "오늘 시험도 또 망쳤어!"라고 버릇처럼 중얼거리곤 했다. 이른바 '시험 불안증(test anxiety)'이다. 이처럼 목표를 실행하는 과정에는 대개 장애물이 생기기 마련이다.

골비처 교수는 이를 간단히 해결하는 방법을 발견했다. 그는 어느 날 수학시험지를 들고 들어가 학생들에게 엄포를 놓았다.

"오늘 치는 시험은 아주 어려운 수학시험입니다. 고도의 집중력과 사고력을 요하는 시험이죠."

그 말을 듣고 학생들은 더욱 불안해졌다. 설상가상으로 교수는 학생들의 책상 위에 놓여 있는 컴퓨터 스크린에서 재밌는 동영상 광고까지 흘러나오도록 했다. 마음을 어수선하게 만드는 소음공해까지 겹치니 학생들의 불안은 극에 달했다.

그런 다음 교수는 학생들을 강의실 오른편과 왼편 두 편으로 갈라놓더니 오른편 학생들에게 이렇게 말했다.

"시험문제를 풀면서 동영상 광고가 거슬리면 '수학문제에만 집중해야지' 하고 생각해보세요."

동영상 광고로 인한 불안한 마음을 억지로 외면하고 목표에만 집중하라는 얘기였다. 그러나 왼편 학생들에게는 다른 주문을 했다.

"시험문제를 풀면서 동영상 광고가 거슬리면 '그냥 무시하면 되지'라고 생각해보세요."

불안한 마음이라는 장애물을 외면하지 말고, 오히려 정면으로 바라보고 그 해결책까지 미리 생각해보라는 얘기였다.

불안한 마음을 억누르고 목표에만 집중하려 든 오른편 학생들과, 목표 실행 과정에서 나타날 장애물에 대한 해결책까지 미리 생각해둔 왼편 학생들… 과연 어느 편 학생들이 문제를 더 많이 풀었을까? 결과는 이랬다.

* 오른편 학생들 : '수학에만 집중해야지'
  → 54문제를 풀었다
* 왼편 학생들 : '광고가 나오면 그냥 무시하면 되지'
  → 78문제를 풀었다

　불안한 마음이 들 때 투지나 의지로 억지로 덮어버리거나 저항하려 들면 오히려 역효과가 난다. 억누를수록 더욱 거세게 일어나는 생각의 속성 때문이다. 덮어버리려거나 저항하지 말고, 있는 그대로 바라보고 그냥 흘러가도록 내버려두는 게 훨씬 낫다. 앞으로 시험을 앞두고 마음이 불안하다면 조용히 이렇게 되뇌보라.

　"만일 시험 칠 때 불안한 마음이 생기면, 그럼 무시하고 흘려보내면 되지 뭐!"

　이렇게 해결책까지 미리 상상해두면 불안한 마음이 닥치더라도 금방 사라진다. 이게 바로 골비처 교수가 개발해낸 걸림돌 자동 제거 장치 'if-then'(만일 ~하면, 그럼 ~하면 되지 뭐) 공식이다.

　알코올 중독자들은 "난 앞으로 절대 술 안 마시겠어!" 하고 아무리 단단히 결심해도 막상 술을 보는 순간 그 결심은 온데간데없이 증발해버린다. 음주 욕구가 잠재의식에 깊이 각인돼 있으니 의지만으로 눌러버리기 어려운 게 당연하다. 따라서 마음속으로 잠재의식에 신호를 보내야 한다. 음주 욕구가 솟아오르는 순간, 즉각 'if-then' 공식을 떠올려라.

"만일 음주 충동이 들면, 그럼 껌을 씹으면 되지 뭐.(혹은 그럼 물을 마시면 되지 뭐.)"

이렇게 해결책까지 미리 상상해두면 설사 술자리에 앉아 있더라도 유혹에 넘어가지 않는다.

외팅겐과 골비처 교수는 독일 고등학교 3학년 여학생들을 두 그룹으로 나누어 수학시험을 치도록 해보았다. 객관식 14문제였다. 시험을 치기 전 A, B 두 그룹에게 똑같이 다음과 같은 지시사항을 읽고 암기하도록 했다.

"나는 최대한 많은 문제를 침착하게 풀 것이다!"

목표의식을 갖도록 하는 글이었다. 그런 다음 B그룹에게만 따로 다음과 같은 내용을 추가로 암기하도록 했다.

"만일 어려운 문제와 마주치면, 그럼 '난 풀 수 있어' 하고 다짐해야지!"

목표를 실행해가는 과정에서 풀기 어려운 장애물이 나타나더라도 그 장애물에 대한 마음가짐까지 상상해두라는 말이었다. 어떤 그룹이 더 많은 문제를 풀었을까? 난제를 미리 상상한 B그룹이 두 배나 더 많은 문제를 풀었다.

우산을 깜빡하지 않는 법

한 남학생이 비를 흠뻑 맞은 채 헐레벌떡 강의실에 뛰어들어왔다. 보기에 민망할 정도로 머리며 옷이 젖었다. 웬일이냐고 물으니 지하철 선반에 우산을 깜빡 놓고 내렸다는 거였다.

"관찰자 효과를 이용하지 그랬어요?"

지하철로 통학하거나 통근하는 사람치고 우산을 잃어버리지 않은 사람은 드물 것이다. 나도 꽤나 많은 우산을 잃어버렸다. 나는 빈 좌석이 생기더라도 그냥 서 있는 버릇이 있다. 그래서 우산은 대개 문 옆에 기대어 세워둔다. 그러고 나서 신문이나 책을 꺼낸 뒤 가방을 선반에다 올려놓는다. 하지만 내릴 때 가방을 깜빡한 적은 없다. 왜냐하면 읽던 신문이나 책을 가방에 도로 집어넣어야 하므로 자동적으로 가방을 찾기 때문이다. 하지만 문 옆에 기대어 둔 우산은 까맣게 잊는 경우가 많았다.

이젠 그런 일이 사라졌다. 'if-then' 공식대로 우산을 기대어 놓으면서, '만일 내가 선반의 가방을 집어들면, 그럼 우산도 함께 집어들면 되지' 하고 미리 잠깐 상상해두기 때문이다. 가방을 집어들면 자동적으로 우산을 집어들도록 상상 속에서 연결고리를 맺어두는 것이다.

잘게 쪼개면 가벼워진다

토익 성적 올리는 방법은 없느냐고 물었던 한 여학생이 하소연했다.

"남들은 900점 이상 척척 받는데 저는 아무리 해도 어림도 없어요.

500쪽짜리 토익 책을 여는 순간, 아휴, 이걸 언제 떼나 싶어 골치가 지끈 지끈 아파와요."

몇 달째 씨름을 해오고 있었지만 겨우 100쪽 언저리에서 제자리걸음 이었다.

"500쪽짜리 영어책을 바윗덩어리처럼 무겁게 바라보고 있군요? 그러니 머리가 짓눌리는 거죠."

짓눌린 머리는 새 정보를 받아들이지 못한다. 억지로 책상 앞에 붙어 있어봐야 말짱 헛거다. 잡념만 무성하게 피어오른다. 잡념은 심신을 더욱 지치게 한다. 악순환이다. 그럼 시각을 돌려 500쪽짜리 책을 잘게 쪼개 바라보면 정말 머리에 쏙쏙 들어올까?

이스라엘 헤브루 대학의 심리학자 브레츠니츠(Shlomo Breznitz)가 그 해답을 찾아보았다. 그는 몇 그룹의 군인들에게 똑같이 40킬로미터 행군을 시켰다. 하지만 각 그룹에게 다른 말을 들려주었다.

한 그룹에게는 이렇게 말했다. "오늘 행군거리는 30킬로미터입니다." 그리고 30킬로미터 행군이 끝난 뒤 다시 10킬로미터를 더 행군하도록 했다.

다른 그룹에게는 이렇게 말했다. "오늘 행군거리는 60킬로미터입니다." 하지만 그 그룹이 실제로 행군한 거리도 역시 40킬로미터였다.

브레츠니츠는 행군이 끝난 뒤 각 그룹의 혈액을 채취해 스트레스 호르몬 수치를 측정해보았다. 측정 결과, 스트레스 호르몬 수치는 실제 행군거리와는 상관없이 앞으로 얼마나 더 걸어야 하느냐 하는 생각에 따라 요동쳤던 것으로 나타났다.

브레츠니츠 교수

"아무리 힘든 목표라도
작게 쪼개서 생각하면 쉬워진다."

즉 군인들의 몸은 현실에 반응하는 게 아니라 그들이 현실로 바라보는 이미지에 반응하는 것이었다. 쉽게 말해 모든 군인이 똑같이 40킬로미터를 행군했지만, 30킬로미터짜리 행군이라고 상상하며 걸었던 군인들은 30킬로그램의 짐을 짊어지고 걸었던 것과 비슷한 신체적 반응을 보였고, 60킬로미터짜리 행군이라고 상상하며 걸었던 군인들은 60킬로그램의 짐을 짊어지고 걷는 것처럼 탈진상태의 신체적 반응을 보였던 것이다.

생각해보라. "60킬로미터 행군"이라는 말을 듣는 순간 어떤 이미지가 떠오르는가? 60킬로미터나 되는 먼 거리가 이역만리처럼 까마득한 이미지로 떠오른다. 출발 전부터 피곤해진다. 하지만 60킬로미터를 1킬로미터씩 쪼개서 행군한다고 생각하면 어떨까? 1킬로미터 행군은 그리 힘겨운 일이 아니다. 다음 1킬로미터도 역시 힘겹지 않다. 그다음 1킬로미터도 역시 마찬가지다. 이렇게 생각하며 걸으면 60킬로그램의 바윗덩어리를 짊어진 게 아니라 1킬로그램의 가벼운 짐을 짊어진 기분으로 바뀐다.

이 원리는 무슨 일을 하든 똑같이 적용된다. 내가 지금 책을 쓰는 것도 그렇다. 300쪽에 가까운 책을 끝내야 된다고 생각하면 한숨부터 나온다.

머리가 짓눌려 지끈지끈 아파온다. 하지만 300쪽을 쪼개 오늘 하루 사이 오직 두 쪽만 쓴다고 생각을 돌리면 마음이 거뜬해진다.

내가 매일 한 시간씩 걷기로 결심했다고 하자. 결심하자마자 '어휴, 한 시간을 지루해서 어떻게 걷지?' 하고 생각하면 걷기가 무거운 짐으로 둔갑한다. 걷고 나서도 몸이 가뿐해지는 게 아니라 중노동을 한 것처럼 피로독소만 쌓인다.

마라톤 선수들도 42.195킬로미터를 그냥 뛰는 게 아니다. 한 번에 그 긴 거리를 뛰어야 한다고 생각하면 힘이 쭉 빠진다. 대신 이를 여러 구간으로 쪼개놓고 각 구간별로 목표 시간을 정해놓는다. '이번 5킬로미터는 15분 내에 달려야 해.' 그리고 5킬로미터 구간만 생각하며 달린다. 그럼 몸도 가볍다.

운동생리학자들은 이렇게 잘게 쪼갠 목표들을 '서브 골(sub goal)'이라 부른다. 널리 알려진 것처럼 1마일(1,609m) 경주에서 세계 최초로 4분 벽이 깨진 건 1954년이었다. 1852년 4분 28초의 기록이 세워진 이후 102년간 내로라하는 세계 최고의 선수들이 4분 안에 돌파해보겠다며 도전했지만, 모두 실패하고 말았다. 언론들은 불가능한 일이라고 입을 모았다. 무리하게 4분 내에 달리면 폐와 심장이 파열돼 죽음을 초래할 것이라고 경고하는 의사들도 있었다. 당시 영국 옥스퍼드대학 의대생이었던 배니스터(Roger Bannister)는 마의 4분 벽이 심리적 장벽이라고 생각했다. 이를 어떻게 깨야 할까? 그는 연습할 때마다 3분 59초라고 적은 작은 종이쪽지를 운동화에 집어넣고 달렸다. 그는 뛸 때마다 이렇게 되뇌었다.

"난 이미 4분 1초의 기록을 세워놓았어. 1초만 더 빨리 달리면 4분, 거기서 1초만 더 빨리 달리면 3분 59초야. 바로 그거야. 내 기록보다 2

최초로 마의 4분 벽을 깬 배니스터

초만 더 빨리 달리면 되는 거야."

다른 선수들의 마음속엔 도저히 넘어설 수 없는 4분 장벽이 버티고 있었다. 하지만 그는 2초만 단축시키면 그만이라고 생각했다. 2초를 둘로 쪼개면 1초, 우선 1초를 뛰어넘으면 되는 거였다. 드디어 1초를 뛰어넘었다. 그러자 더욱 자신감이 생겼다. 1954년 26세의 그는 1마일 경주의 출발선에 섰다.

'오늘 또다시 1초만 더 단축시키면 성공이야.'

그는 죽기를 각오하고 달렸다. 마침내 1마일을 3분 59초 4의 기록으로 주파해내는 데 성공했다. 목표의 실행 과정을 1초 단위로 잘게 쪼개 바라본 결실이었다.

잘 게   쪼 개 면   행 복 해 진 다

내가 방송국에 입사한 지 2년쯤 됐을 때의 일이다. 어느 날 아침 보도국장이 불렀다.

"사장이 한 달 뒤에 유럽 출장을 간대. 자네가 함께 가줘야겠어."

사장 비서실에 한 달간 파견근무 명령을 받았다. 알고 보니 사장이 국

내 언론사 사장단과 함께 20여 일간 유럽에 가는데 통역 겸 비서로 따라 가라는 것이었다. 아마 내가 대학원에서 통역을 전공했으니 통역으로는 적격이라고 판단했던 것 같았다.

출장 일정은 환상적이었다. 국제 언론협회 회의는 오스트리아의 빈에서 열리는데 그 전후로 영국, 프랑스, 독일, 스페인, 이탈리아 등의 주요 방송국을 방문하는 것이었다. 그 일정 사이사이로 세계적인 관광명소들도 들르게 되어 있었다. 그전까지 내가 외국을 가본 건 입사한 지 얼마 안 돼 파리를 가본 게 전부였다. 그 이전엔 비행기 한 번 타보지 못한 왕 촌놈이었다. 하지만 나는 출발 전부터 마음이 편치 않았다.

'내가 사장 비서나 하려고 방송국 들어온 줄 알아? 기자 시험을 쳐서 들어왔어. 근데 왜 나한테 이런 일을 시키는 거지?'

이런 마음을 갖고 있으니 모든 게 힘겹게 느껴졌다. 출장 일정을 확인하고 외국 방송사 사장들과의 면담자료를 준비하는 일들이 번거롭기 짝이 없었다. 한 술 더 떠 사장이 여행중 불시에 던질지 모를 잡다한 질문에 대한 답변까지 외워두라고 하니 더욱 짜증이 났다. 이를테면 이런 거였다. 만일 사장이 여객기를 탔을 때 "이 비행기 길이는 몇 미터나 되지?" 하고 묻거나, "BBC 방송국의 직원은 총 몇 명인가?" 하고 물을 때 주저 없이 척척 대답할 수 있어야 한다는 게 비서실장의 주문이었다.

공항에서 보니 함께 출국하는 언론사 사장단 부부는 10여 쌍이 넘었다. 그 큰 무리를 보니 더욱 기가 질렸다. '타 언론사 사장 부부들까지 내가 안내해야 할 판인가?'

사실 안내하는 일이 그리 큰 문제는 아니었다. 정해진 일정대로 움직이면 그만이었다. 또 유럽의 최고급 호텔에 머물며 책에서나 봤던 최고의 역사적 명소들을 돌고 유럽 최고의 방송사 사장들과 면담하는 일들은 호기심을 자극하기에 충분했다. 하지만 내 생각이 문제였다. 시시콜콜한 잡일까지 해야 한다는 게 갈수록 짜증스럽게 느껴졌다.

"미스터 김, 사진 좀 찍어주세요."

"우리도요!"

관광지에 가면 여기저기서 사진 찍어달라는 말이 쏟아져 나왔다. 물건을 사오라면 가게에 뛰어가 사다 줘야 했다. 사장단 부인들이 쇼핑할 땐 지루하기 짝이 없었다. 사장이 일어나기 전에 먼저 일어나 그날 일정은 물론 심부름할 일이 없는지도 확인해야 했다. 사장이 외국 방송사 사장과 면담하기 전에는 면담내용을 준비하고, 통역하고, 면담이 끝나면 보고서도 써야 했다. 내 머릿속에서는 볼멘소리가 끊임없이 흘러나오고 있었다.

'난 비서가 아니고 기자야. 내가 왜 이런 일을 해야지?'

'내가 자기네들 몸종인가?'

'난 이 사람들과 다니는 게 싫어.'

나는 최고의 호텔에서 최고의 대우를 받으며 최고의 구경을 하고 있었다. 하지만 생각은 늘 다른 곳에 떠다니고 있었다. 난 점점 지쳐가고 있었다. 급기야 독일 방송국에서 회의 도중 코피까지 터뜨리고 말았다.

내가 그토록 지쳐갔던 이유는 내게 주어진 일을 지겹고 성가신 일로 바라보았기 때문이다. 그러다 보니 내 머릿속은 잡념으로 꽉 들어차 있었다. 예를 들어 내 몸뚱이는 대영박물관에 와 있는데도 머릿속은 '난 비서처럼 따라다니는 게 정말 싫어'라는 불만이 가득했다. 사장 부인들의 쇼핑을 지켜보면서는 '남들 쇼핑하는데 난 괜히 이게 뭐하는 짓이야?'라고 투덜대고 있었다. 몸은 현재에 와 있는데 생각은 과거나 미래에 매달려 현재의 순간들을 비웃거나 심판하고 있었다. 몸과 생각이 완전히 따로 놀았다. 만일 내가 그때 나에게 주어진 일들을 잘게 쪼개 바라보았더라면 어땠을까?

'오늘 하루는 어떤 일을 해야지?'

'앞으로 한 시간 동안 뭘 해야지?'

'지금 당장 내가 할 일은 뭐지?'

이렇게 쪼개서 바라보았더라면 몸과 마음이 일치를 이뤄 일도 가볍고 잡념도 비집고 들어서지 못했을 것이다. 나는 일도 하고 관광도 하면서 여행을 즐겼을 것이고, 덕분에 나와 함께 했던 사장단 일행도 더욱 편안했을 것이다. 하지만 어쭙잖은 자존심이 피워낸 불필요한 잡념으로 인생의 귀중한 순간들을 허공에 날려버리고 말았다.

지능을 껑충 높이려면?

"지극히 평범한 아이를 천재로 만들 수 있을까?"

호기심을 못 이긴 한 심리학자가 마침내 신문에 이색 광고를 냈다.

"저와 결혼해주실 지극히 평범한 여자분 급구. 천재 만들기 실험용 아기 낳아주실 여자분."

광고를 보고 사람들이 수군거렸다.

"망측해라. 실험 목적으로 구혼광고를 내다니."

"머리가 헷가닥 돌아간 사람인가 보군."

하지만 신통하게도 그 광고를 보고 결혼하겠다는 여자가 나타났다. 크게 똑똑하거나 크게 멍청하지도 않은 어중간한 지능의 여자였다. 얼마 후 계획된 대로 첫 아이도 낳았다. 딸이었다. 딸아이는 예상대로 네 살이 될 때까지 아무런 특별한 재능도 보이지 않았다.

"이 아이를 어떤 분야의 천재로 만들까? 과학? 수학? 음악? 철학? 문학?"

고민 끝에 그는 첫 아이를 체스 천재로 만들기로 결정했다. 이유가 있었다. 당시만 해도 여자는 선천적으로 체스를 못한다는 고정관념이 팽배해 있었다. 실제로 전 세계적으로 체스 명인 가운데 여성은 단 한 명도 없었다. 그는 그게 고정관념 때문이라는 걸 입증하고 싶었다.

또한 그가 깨고 싶었던 것은 지능이 유전된다는 고정관념이었다. 그는 사실 체스엔 문외한이었다. 부인은 더더욱 체스엔 젬병이었다. 또, 양가 선조들 가운데 체스 말을 만져본 사람조차 없었다. 따라서 만일 딸아이가 체스 천재가 된다면 그건 성별로 보나, 유전적으로 보나, 타고난 재능과는 전혀 무관한 일이었다.

그는 천재성을 이끌어내는 가장 큰 힘은 동기유발이라고 보았다. 그래서 아이가 볼 때마다 너무나 재미있는 표정을 지어 보이며 혼자서 체스를 두었다. 호기심이 동한 아이가 다가와 체스 말을 만지면 이렇게 말했다.

"좀 참아. 이렇게 재밌는 건 좀더 커야만 할 수 있단다."

아이는 체스를 하고 싶어 도저히 못 견디고 마구 울곤 했다. 그는 그제야 조금씩 알려주었다. 체스에 관한 그림책들도 많이 사다 놓았다. 아이의 체스 실력은 쑥쑥 늘었다. 그 자신도 아이를 가르치기 위해 직장을 그만두고 체스 공부에 전념했다. 체스에 관한 모든 책을 사다 아이와 함께 읽었다. 체스 명인들의 대국 비디오도 많이 사다 보았다. 서가에는 어느새 만 권이나 되는 체스 책들이 빽빽하게 꽂혀 있었다.

그는 아이를 학교에 보내지 않고 부인과 함께 집에서 가르쳤다. 학교에 보내면 지능에 대한 유전적, 성별적 고정관념에 물들어버릴 게 불을 보듯 뻔해서였다. 대신 집에서 국어, 수학, 과학, 외국어 등 다른 과목들을 틈틈이 가르쳤다. 주입식이 아니라 스스로 재미를 느껴 깨우치도록 자극만 주는 방식을 택했다. 5년 후 둘째 딸이 태어났고, 또다시 2년 뒤엔 셋째 딸도 태어났다. 그들에게도 똑같은 방법으로 체스를 가르쳤다. 온

최연소 체스 챔피언이 된
막내 주디트(좌)와 언니 소피아(우)

식구가 체스에 파묻혀 살았다. 세 딸들은 정말 체스 천재가 됐을까?

첫째 딸은 17세 때 여성으로는 세계에서 처음으로 세계 체스 명인전 예선을 통과했다. 하지만 당시 여성은 본선에 진출할 자격이 없었다. 그런 전례가 없었기 때문이다. 2년 후엔 세 자매가 한 팀으로 세계 대회에서 우승했다. 다시 1년 후, 첫 딸은 역시 여성으로는 사상 처음으로 세계 최고 명인이 됐다. 한동안 세계 정상에 섰다가 최근 은퇴를 선언했다. 둘째와 셋째 딸도 역시 최고 명인 자리에 올랐다. 셋째 딸의 경우 15세에 세계 체스 사상 최연소 명인이 됐다. 그녀는 지금도 세계 1위의 여성 체스 명인인데다, 지난 수년간 남녀를 통틀어 꼬박꼬박 세계 10위 안에 꼽힌다.

"어느 아이든 천재가 될 수 있다고 바라보면 천재가 된다"는 아버지의 신념이 정확히 현실로 나타났다. 헝가리의 교육 심리학자 폴가(Laszlo Polgar)의 이야기다.

지능에 대한 두 가지 착각

양자물리학자들은 지능에 대한 두 가지 고정관념을 지적한다. 첫째는 "지능은 타고나는 것"이라는 고정관념이다. 둘째는 "지능은 내 머릿속에서 나오는 것"이란 고정관념이다. 이런 고정관념들이 지능을 고정시킨다.

1. "지능은 타고나는 것, 즉 고정된 것"으로 바라본다.
   → 관찰자 효과에 따라 지능은 더 이상 높아지지 않는다.
2. "지능은 내 머릿속에서 나오는 것"으로 바라본다.
   → 관찰자 효과에 따라 내 머릿속에 든 생각만 돌고 돈다.
   → 새 아이디어는 떠오르지 않는다.

이 두 가지 착각을 떨쳐버리면 닫혀 있던 지능은 저절로 열리게 된다. 즉, "지능은 내가 바라보는 대로 변화하는 것", "지능은 내 머리 밖에서 나오는 것"이라고 생각하면 사고의 폭이 획기적으로 넓어지고 지능도 저절로 껑충 올라간다.

"설마, 지능이 그렇게 쉽게 변할까? 그럼 머리 나빠 출세 못 하는 사람이 세상에 왜 그리도 많단 말인가?"

아마 당신은 즉각 이렇게 반문할 것이다. 그건 당신이 착각의 감옥에 갇혀 있기 때문이다.

첫 번째 착각을 살펴보자. 지능은 정말 고정된 것일까?

빈에서 회의를 마치고 한 음식점에 들렀을 때의 일이다. 우리 일행은 현지 교민들까지 합쳐 30명이 넘었다. 그런데 웨이터가 그 많은 손님의 식사주문을 종이에 적지도 않고 받는 게 아닌가?

"저러다가 다 까먹고 엉뚱한 식사 내놓는 거 아냐?"

사람들마다 한 마디씩 했다. 하지만 그건 기우였다. 30여 명분의 식사는 주문대로 아무 실수 없이 척척 나왔다. 더구나 웨이터는 누가 어떤 주문을 했는지까지 빠삭하게 기억하고 있었다.

"거 참! 여기 웨이터들은 천재들인가?"

나는 나중에 러시아의 심리학자 차이가르닉(Bluma Zeigarnik)이 쓴 책을 보고서야 빈의 웨이터들의 전설적인 기억력이 왜 가능한지 알게 됐다. 그녀도 어느 날 빈의 커피숍에서 커피를 홀짝거리다가 한 웨이터가 무려 20명이나 되는 손님들의 주문을 외우는 걸 목격했다.

그들은 머리가 좋아서 그 많은 주문을 한 번 듣고 척척 외우는 걸까? 그녀는 여러 차례 실험을 해보았다. 대답은 놀랍도록 간단했다. 그건 단지 상황을 바라보는 시각에 달려 있었다.

'주문을 받아야지' 하고 마음먹으면 두뇌도 활짝 열린다. 다른 건 모두 잊고 온 신경이 오로지 주문 내용에만 쏠린다. 그럼 손님들의 주문 내용은 물론 얼굴 표정까지 생생하게 입력된다. 차이가르닉은 이를 '심리적 긴장(psychic tension)' 상태라고 불렀다. 하지만 신기하게도 주문이 끝나는 순간 언제 그 많은 주문을 외웠었느냐는 듯 한꺼번에 깡그리 잊어버린다.

'주문은 다 끝났어. 머리를 비워야지.'

이렇게 생각하고 두뇌를 바라보면 실제로 두뇌가 깡그리 비워지는 것이다. 즉, '내 머리는 활짝 열렸다'고 생각하고 어떤 정보를 받아들이면 실제로 두뇌가 활짝 열려 천재적인 암기력이 생기고, '내 머리를 몽땅 비웠어'라고 생각하면 정말 두뇌에 들어 있던 내용들이 마치 먼지를 털어내듯 일시에 털려나가 깜깜해지는 것이다.

독일의 심리학자 지그프리트(Siegfried Lehrl) 교수는 '머리를 비운다'는 생각이 정말 IQ를 떨어뜨리는지 조사해보았다. 신기하게도 '난 머리를 비웠어'라는 마음가짐으로 2주간 해변에 휴가를 간 사람들의 IQ는 실제로 무려 20포인트나 떨어졌다. 더 신기한 건 휴가가 끝난 뒤 '일하려면 머리를 다시 채워야지' 하는 마음가짐으로 직장에 나가면 불과 나흘 만에 떨어졌던 IQ 20포인트가 다시 제자리로 되돌아간다는 것이었다. 내가 내 머리를 어떻게 바라보느냐에 따라 실제로 내 지능도 오르락내리락하는 게 틀림없지 않은가?

그럼 우리나라 여학생들이 수학에 약한 것도 바로 그런 시각 때문일까? 한 설문조사 결과, 수학교사들의 66퍼센트가 "여학생들이 남학생들보다 수학에 약하다"고 응답한 바 있다. 우리 문화는 성차별도 심하다. 반면 성차별이 존재하지 않는 스칸디나비아 국가들에서는 신기하게도 남녀 간의 수학 성적 차이가 아예 존재하지 않는다.

여학생들을 바라보는 시각이 정말 수학 성적을 춤추게 하는 걸까? 한 교수가 시험 직전 남녀학생들에게 딱 한 마디씩 던져보았다.

한 그룹에게는 이렇게 말했다.

"과거 시험의 결과, 남녀 간의 차이가 꽤 크게 나타났던 시험입니다."

여학생들에게 '여학생은 수학에 약해'라는 편견을 떠오르게 하는 한 마디였다. 그리고 다른 그룹에게는 이런 편견이 들지 않도록 말해보았다.

"과거 시험의 결과, 남녀 간의 차이가 나타나지 않았던 시험입니다."

결과는 짐작대로다. '여학생은 수학에 약해'라는 편견을 퍼뜩 떠올린 채 시험을 치른 여학생들의 성적은 남학생들보다 떨어졌다. 반면 이런 편견을 잊은 채 시험을 본 여학생들은 남학생들과 같은 수준의 성적을 거뒀다. 스탠퍼드 대학의 스틸(Claude Steele) 교수가 실시한 실험이다.

그럼 만일 여교사가 학생들 앞에서 무심코 이런 말을 중얼거린다면 어떨까?

"어휴, 난 왜 계산이 서툴지? 여자라 그런가 봐."

1년 후 수학시험을 쳤더니 그 반 여학생들의 수학성적이 형편없이 떨어졌다. 기이하게도 남학생들의 성적이나 다른 반 여학생들의 성적엔 별 변화가 없었다. 이는 실제로 시카고 대학의 베일록(Sian Beilock) 교수가 초등학교 1~2학년생들을 대상으로 실험해 얻은 결과다. 여교사가 무심코 흘리는 편견의 말 한 마디가 어린 여학생들의 평생 수학 능력에 돌이킬 수 없는 상처를 냈던 것이다.

그럼 거꾸로 여학생들의 수학점수를 끌어올리는 편견은 없을까? 미국에서는 한국, 중국, 인도 등 아시아계 학생들은 남녀를 불문하고 수학을 잘한다는 고정관념이 널리 퍼져 있다. 신기하게도 수학시험을 칠 때이 고정관념을 퍼뜩 떠올리도록 유도하면 아시아계 여학생들의 수학점수도 쑥 올라가는 기현상이 일어난다.

"이런 고정관념이 수학점수에 얼마나 강력하게 나타날까?"

하버드 대학의 쉬(Margaret Shih) 교수는 아시아계 여성들을 세 그룹으로 나눠 수학시험을 쳐보도록 했다. 먼저 시험을 치기 직전 각기 간단한 설문조사에 응하도록 했다.

* A그룹 : 인종에 관한 설문조사
  → '수학 잘하는 아시아계'라는 고정관념을 상기시킴.
* B그룹 : 성에 관한 설문조사 → 고정관념과는 상관없음.
* C그룹 : 전화서비스에 관한 설문조사 → 고정관념과는 상관없음.

예상은 적중했다. 자신을 '수학 잘하는 아시아계'로 바라보며 시험을 친 A그룹의 수학점수가 B나 C그룹보다 삐죽하게 솟아올랐다.

"정말 신기한 일이야. 자신을 어떻게 바라보느냐가 이런 차이를 만들어내다니. 그럼 고정관념이 존재하지 않는 곳에서는 점수 차이도 안 날까?"

교수는 이번에는 캐나다의 밴쿠버를 실험장소로 택했다. 미국과는 달리 그곳은 중국, 홍콩, 대만, 한국, 인도의 일반 이민자들이 워낙 많이 뒤

섞여 사는 곳이다. 수학 잘하는 유학생들이 몰려 있는 미국과는 다르다. 따라서 "아시아인은 수학 잘 한다"라는 고정관념도 사실상 존재하지 않는다. 교수는 그곳에 사는 아시아계 여성들도 앞서와 똑같이 A, B, C 세 그룹으로 나눠 똑같은 실험을 해보았다. 이번에도 A그룹의 수학점수가 높았을까? 결과는 그렇지 않았다.

"정말 신기하군. 고정관념이 없는 곳에서 시험 치니 점수 차이도 생기지 않는걸."

자신이 특별한 수학적 재능을 가졌다고 바라보는 사람들이 없으니 특별한 수학점수가 나올 리 없었던 것이다.

미국에서는 "흑인들은 백인들보다 머리가 나빠"라는 고정관념도 팽배하다. 아무리 똑똑한 흑인들이라도 자신도 모르게 이런 편견에 빠져든다. 그래서 백인들과 지능이 비교된다는 생각이 드는 순간 지능은 저절로 떨어진다.

스탠퍼드 대학의 스틸 교수는 SAT 시험을 치르기 직전 흑인학생들에게 인종을 명시하도록 해보았다. 인종을 명시하는 난에 '흑인'이라는 단어를 기입하는 순간, 흑인학생들의 머릿속에서는 '머리 나쁜 흑인'이라는 편견이 번쩍 떠올랐다. 그러면서 '나도 머리 나쁜 흑인이라는 말을 듣게 되면 어쩌지' 하는 불안이 머리를 꽉 채워버렸다. 풀어야 할 문제는 머리에 들어오지 않았다. 결국 그들의 점수는 형편없이 떨어졌다.

이번에는 대학원 수능시험 격인 GRE의 고난도 문제들만 골라 흑인과 백인 대학생들에게 동시에 풀게 했다. 먼저 한 그룹에게 이렇게 말했다.

"이 시험은 중요한 거 아니니까 마음 푹 놓고 편하게 풀어보세요."

스틸 교수

"'난 머리 나쁜 사람'이라는 편견을 상기하는 것 자체만으로 성적이 크게 떨어진다."

또 다른 그룹에게는 몹시 중요한 시험이라고 강조했다.

"이 시험은 여러분의 지능을 정확하게 알아 보려는 거니까 최선을 다하세요."

점수를 채점해본 스틸 교수는 깜짝 놀랐다. 가벼운 마음으로 시험을 친 첫 그룹의 흑인 대학생들 점수는 백인들과 비슷했다. 하지만 지적 능력을 시험한다는 말을 들었던 둘째 그룹 흑인들의 점수는 크게 떨어졌다. 왜일까? 그들은 자신들을 바라보는 고정관념에 휩싸였다. 그래서 스스로를 '난 머리 나쁜 흑인'이라는 시각으로 바라보았고, 그런 시각이 실제로 점수를 떨어뜨렸던 것이다. 이와는 반대로 백인들은 자신감에 가득 찼다. 그래서 '흑인들은 공부 못하는 사람들'이라는 시각으로 시험 친 흑인들은 평소보다 점수가 나빴고, '백인들은 공부 잘하는 사람들'이라는 마음으로 시험 친 백인들은 오히려 점수가 더 올라갔던 것이다.

흥미로운 사실은 백인 학생들에게 시험 직전 "지금 우리가 치려는 시험의 과거 성적을 보면 동양인이 백인들보다 점수가 좋았다"고 말하면, 백인들의 성적이 평소보다 정말 떨어진다는 것이다.

한 교수가 평소 공부를 잘하는 백인 남학생들에게 시험지를 나눠주며 말해보았다.

"아시아계 학생들은 수학을 잘한다고 하죠. 이 시험은 바로 그 비결을 캐내려는 실험의 일부입니다."

그 말을 듣는 백인 남학생들의 표정이 순간적으로 바짝 얼어붙었다. '백인들은 아시아계보다 수학에 약해'라는 고정관념이 불쑥 떠올랐기 때문이다. 아니나 다를까. 그들의 점수는 어이없이 툭 떨어졌다. 고정관념을 암시받지 않은 남학생들보다 열여덟 문제 중 무려 평균 세 문제나 더 틀렸다. 실험을 주도한 뉴욕 대학의 아론슨(Joshua Aronson) 교수는 혀를 끌끌 찼다.

"그 학생들은 모두 SAT 점수가 800점 만점에 750점 이상인 우수한 학생들인데. 말 한 마디에 그처럼 큰 폭으로 점수가 떨어지다니…."

그 남학생들은 교수의 말 한 마디를 듣고 자신들을 '아시아계들보다 수학에 약한 백인들'이라고 바라보았고, 바라본 대로 고스란히 현실로 나타났던 것이다.

정말 거짓말처럼 간단한 일 아닌가? 나의 지능을 높이고 싶다면 나의 지능을 높게 바라보면 그만이다. 전적으로 내 두뇌를 어떻게 바라보느냐에 달린 문제다. 그래서 컬럼비아 대학의 심리학자 드웩(Carol Dweck) 교수는 "내 지능은 내가 어떻게 바라보느냐에 따라 고무줄처럼 줄기도 하고 늘어나기도 한다"고 말한다.

정말 신기한 일 아닌가? 고정된 건 줄로만 알았던 지능이 고무줄처럼 늘었다 줄었다 하다니? 지능은 전혀 고정된 게 아닌 것이다.

드웩 교수

"지능은 어떻게 바라보느냐에 따라
고무줄처럼 줄기도 하고 늘어나기도 한다."

stanford.edu

그럼 두 번째 착각은 어떤가? 과연 "지능은 내 머릿속에서 나오는
것"일까?

미국 펜실베이니아 주에 사는 샌트하우스(Christina Santhouse) 양은 여덟
살 때 두뇌가 바이러스에 감염돼 두뇌의 좌반구를 완전히 들어냈다. 수술
한 지 2년이 지나 기자들이 방문해보니 그녀는 마당에서 친구들과 자유
롭게 깡충깡충 뛰어놀고 있었다. 근처 호수에서 보트도 탔다. 수영도 했
고, 다이빙도 즐겼다. 교회 성가대의 일원으로도 활약했다. 기자들이 물
었다.

"학교에선 무슨 과목이 가장 재미있니?"

"물론 수학이죠."

그녀는 반쪽 두뇌로 학교에서도 우등생이었다. 전 과목에 걸쳐 최고
점수를 받아 대학에도 진학했다. 영국의 버사(Bursa)라는 소녀도 역시 똑
같은 수술을 받았지만 몇 년 후 네덜란드어와 터키어를 유창하게 구사하
게 되었을 만큼 머리가 좋다. 두뇌의 반쪽을 잃었다고 해서 반드시 반쪽
짜리 지능이 되는 건 아니다. 이런 일이 어떻게 가능할까? 특정기억은 두

샌트하우스
반쪽밖에 없는 두뇌지만 반쪽짜리 인간은 아
니다. 그녀는 최우등으로 졸업했다.

뇌의 특정 부위에 저장된다는
의학계의 오랜 정설이 왜 들어
맞지 않는 걸까?

미국의 신경생리학자 래실
리(Karl Lashley) 박사는 쥐들에게
미로를 달리는 훈련을 시켰다.
그런 다음, 쥐들의 뇌를 외과적
으로 제거한 뒤 다시 미로를 달
리도록 해보았다. 쥐들은 종종 비틀거리기는 했지만 뇌의 상당 부분이 제
거됐는데도 기억력을 유지한 채 미로를 제대로 찾아갔다.

이번에는 인디애나 대학의 생물학자인 피취(Paul Pietsch) 교수가 도마
뱀을 대상으로 실험해보았다. 먼저 도마뱀들에게 먹이를 찾아 먹는 방법
을 완전히 기억할 때까지 가르쳐주었다. 그런 다음 두개골을 열고 두뇌의
거의 대부분을 끄집어내 고기 저미는 기계에 넣고 잘게 갈았다. 도마뱀들
의 기억을 완전히 지워버린 것이다. 그러고는 두개골에 도로 집어넣었다.

"이젠 도마뱀들이 먹이 찾아 먹는 방법을 기억해내지 못하겠지?"

하지만 웬걸? 도마뱀들은 두뇌가 산산조각나기 전에 배웠던 것들을
그대로 기억해냈다.

더 단적인 예는 아메바이다. 아메바는 두뇌도, 신경조직도 없는 단세
포 원생동물이다. 하지만 위족僞足(가짜다리)으로 세균이나 다른 원생동물
을 끌어들여 잡아먹는다. 두뇌도 없는 아메바가 뭘 잡아먹고, 어떻게 싸
우거나 도망칠 것인지를 척척 궁리해낸다. 두뇌는 없지만 분명히 생존을
위한 지능을 갖고 있다. 이 지능 덕분에 수백만 년간 생존해올 수 있었다.

지능이 두뇌에만 국한된 것이라면 대체 이게 가능한 일인가?

스탠퍼드 대학의 세계적인 신경생리학자 프리브램(Karl Pribram) 교수도 수많은 환자들을 치료하면서 의문이 들었다.

"환자들은 뇌의 상당 부분을 제거했는데도 왜 기억의 일부가 상실되지 않는 거지?"

심지어 치매환자들도 그랬다. 한 환자는 치매가 워낙 심해 마지막 10년간을 식물인간 상태로 지냈다. 아들들을 봐도 누가 누군지 알아보지 못하고 말도 못했다. 그러다가 어느 날 돌연 얼굴빛이 회색으로 변하더니 의자에서 앞으로 고꾸라졌다. 아들이 의사를 부르려 하자 뜻밖에도 정신이 깜깜하던 아버지가 말을 하는 것 아닌가?

"아들아, 의사 부를 필요 없단다. 어머니에게 사랑한다는 말을 전해주렴. 나는 괜찮다는 말도 함께."

아버지가 숨을 거둔 직후 부검을 해보니 뇌세포 대부분이 치매로 파손돼 있었다. 사실상 두뇌가 없는 거나 마찬가지였다. 그런데도 마지막 순간 어떻게 돌연 정신이 말짱해져 그런 말을 할 수 있었을까?

또한 영국의 뇌과학자 로버(John Lorber) 박사가 뇌세포의 90퍼센트가 파손된 뇌수종 환자들을 조사해보니 지능지수(IQ)는 놀랍게도 발병 이전과 변함이 없는 것으로 나타났다. 어떻게 이런 일이 가능할까? 두뇌는 지능이 생기는 곳이 아니라, 어디선가 지능을 받아들이는 기능만 하는 걸까?

두뇌과학자들은 오랫동안 아인슈타인의 지능이 그의 두뇌에 들어 있는 것으로 착각했다. 그래서 그가 죽은 뒤 두뇌를 방부제인 포름알데히드가 든 유리병에 넣어 보관해뒀다. 결국 나중에는 여러 과학자들이 연구를 한다며 서로 여러 조각으로 나눠 가졌다. 그럼 그의 지능도 여러 조각들로 쪼개졌을까? 그의 지능은 그중 어느 조각에 들어 있을까?

창밖을 내다보면 왜 성적이 오를까?

이처럼 지능이 두뇌에서 나오는 게 아니라면 도대체 어디서 나올까?

한 초등학교 이야기다. 그 학교는 창문이 거의 없는 낡은 건물이었다. 낮에도 형광등을 켜야 할 만큼 어두컴컴했다. 설상가상으로 선생님들은 학생들의 집중력을 높인다며 수업할 때 커튼까지 쳐놓곤 했다. 학생들의 성적은 전국에서 꼴찌를 맴돌았다.

선생님들은 한탄했다.

"이 아이들은 머리가 너무 나빠. 아무리 가르쳐도 따라가지 못해."

얼마 후 창문이 널찍한 새 학교 건물로 이사를 갔다. 밖이 훤히 내다보였다. 학생들은 공부하다가도 문득문득 무한히 펼쳐진 창공과 확 트인 들판을 바라보며 마음까지 확 트임을 느꼈다.

그러자 놀랍게도 1년 만에 학생들의 평균 성적이 20퍼센트 이상 수직 상승했다. 꼴찌였던 학교가 일등으로 올라섰다. 미국 캘리포니아 주 포오우크스Four Oaks 초등학교에서 일어난 일이다.

이 소식을 전해 들은 캐나다 앨버타 교육청도 다섯 개 초등학교에 일제히 널찍한 창문을 달도록 해보았다. 놀랍게도 똑같은 결과가 나왔다. 성적만 좋아진 게 아니었다. 불과 2년 만에 학생들의 평균 키도 2센티미터 넘게 쑥 커졌다. 충치 발생률은 9분의 1로 뚝 떨어졌다. 이 소식이 전해지자 북미의 초등학교들이 일제히 창문을 넓히기 시작했다.

고등학생들은 안 그럴까? 미시간 대학의 마쯔오카(Rodney Matsuoka) 교수는 101개 고등학교들을 대상으로 조사해보았다. 결과는 마찬가지였다. 창밖의 자연을 얼마나 많이 내다보느냐에 따라 성적도 들쭉날쭉했다. 조사결과를 요약하면 이렇다.

"창밖으로 내다보이는 식물들이 많으면 많을수록, 자주 내다볼수록, 창문이 크면 클수록 학생들의 성적도 좋고, 대학진학률도 높았다."

왜 창밖의 자연을 내다보면 성적이 오를까? 굳이 창밖이 아니라도 그렇다. 방 안에서 자연을 연상하기만 해도 지능이 오른다. 일본의 심리학자 시바타 세이지와 스즈키 나오토는 어떤 사무실에는 화분을 놓아둔 반면, 다른 사무실에는 전혀 놓지 않았다. 식물 대신 잡지걸이를 놓아둔 사무실도 있었다. 그런 다음 직원들에게 다양한 창조적 활동을 해보도록 했다. 실험 결과, 식물을 바라본 직원들의 창조성이 단연 압도적으로 높았다.

텍사스 A&M 대학의 울리치(Robert Ulrich) 교수는 식물을 사무실에 놓아두면 아이디어 제안 건수가 15퍼센트나 증가한다는 사실을 발견했다. 어린이들도 마찬가지였다. 황량한 야외 공간보다는 식물이 가득한 뜰에서 놀게 했을 때 훨씬 더 창조적인 놀이를 하는 것으로 나타났다.

세계적인 철학자들이나 예술가들, 과학자들은 어떤가? 그들이 하나같이 자연을 바라보며 산책했던 것도 지능의 마력에 홀려서였을까?

독일의 철학자 이마누엘 칸트는 평생 자신이 살던 도시 쾨니히스베르크를 벗어나 본 적이 없었다. "난 여행을 하지 않는다. 자연 속에서 모든 해답을 얻을 수 있는데 왜 굳이 돈과 시간을 들여 여행을 하는가?" 그는 매일 정확하게 오후 3시 30분에 늘 똑같은 거리를 산책했다. 걷는 속도도 변함이 없었다. 동네 사람들이 그가 집 앞을 지나가는 시간을 보고 시계를 맞추었다는 유명한 일화도 여기서 나왔다.

우울증에 시달렸던 베토벤은 심지어 비가 억수같이 쏟아지는 날에도 우산이나 모자도 쓰지 않은 채 성곽의 큰 공원을 산책했다. 산책하지 않으면 새로운 아이디어가 떠오르지 않는다고 생각했기 때문이다. 루소와 에머슨, 키르케고르는 산책할 때 반드시 작은 노트를 챙겼다고 한다. 걷다가 생각이 떠오르면 기록하기 위해서였다. 《리바이어던》을 쓴 영국의 철학자 홉스는 지팡이 끝에 아예 작은 잉크병을 집어넣고 다녔다고 전해진다. 궁금하기 짝이 없다. 창밖을 내다보거나 밖에 나가 자연을 바라보며 산책하면 왜 머리가 더 잘 돌아가거나 생각이 더 잘 떠오를까?

한 신기한 자연현상에서 힌트를 얻어보자.

일본인들이 많이 기르는 관상어 중에 '고이'라는 잉어가 있다. 고이는 작은 어항에 넣어두면 5센티미터 정도밖에 자라지 않지만 연못에 풀어주면 25센티미터까지 자라게 된다고 한다. 또, 강물에 방류하면 무려 1미터 안팎까지 자란다. 그런데 알고 보면 고이만 그런 게 아니다. 우리가 흔히 보는 금붕어도 큰 연못에 넣어두면 40센티미터가 넘게 자란다. 네덜란드의 한 남성이 길렀던 금붕어는 47.4센티미터나 자랐던 것으로 기네스북은 기록하고 있다. 강물에 방류하면 1미터도 넘게 자란다. 그뿐인가? 큰 곳에 살면 수명도 늘어난다. 영국의 '티시(Tish)'라는 이름의 금붕어는 무려 43년간이나 살아 역시 기네스북에 올랐다. 얼마나 넓고 멀리 바라보며 자라느냐에 따라 물고기의 크기가 스무 배나 넘게 차이 나고, 수명도 부쩍부쩍 늘어난다.

그럼 지능은 어떨까? 지능도 넓고 멀리 바라보면 부쩍부쩍 늘어날까?

사람도 자연의 섭리를 벗어나지 못한다. 방 안에 갇혀 지내면 지능이 떨어지고 확 트인 자연을 바라보면 지능이 높아지는 게 당연하다. 그럼 아예 자연이 아닌 우주를 바라보면 어떨까? 관찰자 효과에 따라 우주만큼 사고의 폭도 넓어지는 걸까?

기발한 아이디어는 우주에서 떨어진다

특이한 방법으로 대박을 터뜨린 사람이 있다.

그녀는 1년 동안 백수였다. 자신이 방송작가로 일하던 TV 프로가 졸지에 폐지됐던 것이다.

"시청률이 너무 떨어져 어쩔 수 없네요. 광고가 안 들어와요."

눈앞이 캄캄했다. 이제 겨우 유치원에 다니는 딸아이 얼굴이 퍼뜩 떠올랐다. 불행은 한꺼번에 찾아온다더니, 바로 1년 전부턴 해외 연수를 간다고 미국에 갔던 남편마저 연락을 끊은 상황이었다.

그녀는 무슨 영문인지도 몰랐다. 조금 지나니 차라리 잘 됐다는 생각도 들었다. 늘 밖으로만 나돌던 남편, 어차피 바늘방석처럼 불안했던 결혼생활이었기 때문이다. 하지만 잘리고 나서 어디를 둘러봐도 비집고 들어갈 직장이 없었다. 평범한 외모, 30대 중반의 나이, 싱글 맘, 실무경험 전무… 스스로 생각해봐도 자신 있게 내놓을 만한 장점이 아무것도 없었다. 그렇다고 남을 탓할 수도 없었다. 남을 탓하는 건 자신의 운명을 스스로 남의 손에 넘겨주는 짓이라는 걸 잘 알고 있었다. 딸아이는 어떻게든 먹여 살려야 했다. 그러다가 눈에 띈 게 TV 단막극 공모 광고였다.

"가장 자신 있는 것 딱 한 가지, 거기에 혼신의 힘을 쏟아라. 그럼 반드시 길이 뚫린다."

어느 책에선가 읽었던 말이 떠올랐다. 그녀는 방송작가 시절 끼적거리다 처박아두었던 극본 원고를 다시 끄집어냈다. 그리고 거기에 정말 미친 듯이 매달렸다. 쓰고 고치고 쓰고 고치고… 딸아이가 잠들거나 혼자 노는 틈만 나면 오로지 그 생각뿐이었다. 석 달 동안 그 짓만 했다. 어느덧 마감 시한이 일주일 앞으로 다가왔다. 그런데도 원고가 영 제대로 풀리지 않았다.

"내 머리로는 도저히 안 되는 건가 봐."

어느 날 새벽, 그녀는 쪽방 책상 앞에서 앉아 이렇게 중얼거렸다. 몸으로 때우는 거라면 몸이 부서져라 수백 번이고 수천 번이고 해보겠는데, 머리가 안 돌아간다 생각하니 정말 어쩔 수 없다는 절망감이 들었다. 한겨울의 냉기가 뼛속까지 파고들었다. 춥고 외로웠다. 하지만 포기할 수도 없는 일이었다. 자신과 딸아이의 실낱같은 희망은 오로지 거기에 걸려 있었다. 머리가 쪼개질 듯 아파왔다. 벌떡 일어서서 벽에 걸린 긴 거울에 비친 자신의 모습을 바라보았다. 며칠째 감지 않아 기름이 조르르 흐르는 생머리, 핏기 하나 없는 피부, 앙상해진 몰골, 퀭한 눈….

"세상살이 참 힘들지? 네 힘으로 안 되면 하늘의 힘을 빌려보렴."

거울 속에서 스며 나오는 나지막하고 따스한 음성. 그녀는 소스라치게 놀랐다. 3년 전 돌아가신 아버지의 음성이었다. 환청이었을까? 그녀는 그 자리에 스르르 구겨져 내렸다. 울음이 터져 나왔다. 엉엉 울었다. 잠시 후 정신을 차린 뒤 원고를 다시 움켜잡았다.

"하느님, 제발 완벽한 원고를 보내주세요."

자신도 모르게 굴러 나온 말이었다. 그러고는 기절하듯 잠이 들었다. 다음날 눈을 뜨는 순간 부리나케 볼펜부터 찾았다. 뭔가에 홀린 듯 정신 없이 메모해나가기 시작했다.

"그건 분명히 내 머리에서 나온 건 아니었어요. 완벽한 원고가 고스란히 보였으니까요. 제목까지도—."

예감대로 그녀는 응모에 당선됐고, 대박을 터뜨렸다. 신기하지 않은가? 자신의 머릿속만 바라보고 머리를 쥐어짤 땐 기발한 아이디어가 튀어나오지 않았다. 하지만 너무나 절박한 나머지 자신도 모르게 하늘을 향해 애원하는 순간 고대하던 아이디어는 저절로 굴러떨어졌다. 이런 비결을 터득한 사람들은 의도적으로 매번 그렇게 한다.

공포소설의 천재 스티븐 킹은 《미저리》의 아이디어를 어떻게 얻었느냐는 질문을 받고 이렇게 대답했다.

"비행기를 타고 영국에 가던 중이었죠. 졸음이 쏟아지기 직전 우주에 이렇게 부탁했어요. '멋진 공포소설 줄거리가 떠오르게 해주세요.' 그러고 나니 꿈속에서 여성 테러범이 나타났어요. 그 여성은 한 작가를 인질로 잡더니 금방 죽여버리고는 탑승객들이 보는 앞에서 칼을 꺼내 죽인 작가의 피부를 모두 벗겨내는 것이었어요. 그리고 시체는 돼지한테 집어던져 아귀아귀 씹어먹게 하고, 벗겨낸 피부는 책을 장정하는 데 썼죠. 잠에서 깬 후 그 장면을 얼른 메모해뒀다가 《미저리》로 완성했답니다."

146

《보물섬》을 쓴 로버트 스티븐슨도 자서전에서 비슷한 방법을 썼다고 털어놓았다. 그는 잠들기 전 손가락으로 머리를 가리키며 이렇게 주문했다.

"머리야, 똑똑히 들어라, 우주에서 어떤 이야깃거리들이 쏟아지는지 잘 기억해다오. 많은 사람들이 읽고 싶어 안달할 이야기 말이야."

뉴턴은 아침에 일어나자마자 침대에 쪼그리고 앉아 밤사이 우주에서 떨어진 생각들을 반추하곤 했다. 그럴 땐 식사하라는 소리도 듣지 못했다. 이처럼 우주에 존재하는 가능성을 믿고 바라보는 사람에겐 바라보는 대로 나타나는 것이다.

두뇌가 잠들어 있을 때 문제가 저절로 풀리는 신기한 현상은 실험으로도 입증된다. 독일 루에벡Luebeck 대학의 보른(Jan Born) 교수는 사람들에게 골치 아픈 수학문제들을 내주고 풀어보라고 했다. 아무도 풀지 못했다. 그래서 한 그룹에게는 밤을 새워 문제를 계속 풀어보라고 했다. 다른 한 그룹에게는 잠을 잔 뒤 다음날 아침에 일어나 다시 풀어보도록 했다. 어느 그룹이 문제를 풀었을까? 밤새워 끙끙거린 피험자들은 여전히 문제들을 풀지 못했지만, 잠을 푹 자고 난 피험자들은 일어나자마자 세 배나 더 많은 문제들을 풀어냈다. 두뇌가 잠들어 있는 사이 문제를 술술 풀어낸 건 누구인가?

가능성을 닫으면 두뇌도 닫혀버린다

그럼 우주엔 얼마나 많은 가능성이 들어 있을까?
이런 상상을 해보자.

* 당신이 차를 타고 가다가 아슬아슬한 사고를 당했다.
  다행히 사고는 모면했다.
* 다른 우주에 사는 또 다른 당신은 똑같은 사고를 당해
  불행히도 숨지고 말았다.
* 또 다른 우주에 사는 당신은 간신히 목숨을 건져
  병원에서 치료를 받고 퇴원했다.
* 또 다른 우주에 사는 당신은 치료를 받고 퇴원하다가
  돌부리에 걸려 넘어졌다.

당신은 아마 "말도 안 되는 허튼소리" 혹은 "공상과학 같은 소리"라고 생각할 것이다. 하지만 이 모든 가능성이 사실이라면? 사실이 아니라는 걸 당신은 어떻게 입증할 수 있는가? 이 세상 아무도 입증할 수 없다.
옥스퍼드 대학의 도이치(David Deutsch) 교수 등 저명한 과학자들은 2007년에 위와 같은 상상이 수학적으로 완벽한 사실이라는 걸 입증했다. 프린스턴 대학과 UCLA 대학 등의 많은 과학자들도 이른바 평행우주 (parallel universes)들의 존재가 수학적으로 딱 들어맞는 사실이라고 입을 모은다. 천체물리학의 천재 스티븐 호킹 박사도 동의한다. MIT의 물리학자 구스(Alan Guth) 교수는 "엘비스 프레슬리가 아직 살아 있는 우주는 존재

카쿠 교수

"평행우주는 반드시 존재한다."

한다"고 단언한다. 이 우주에 살고 있는 당신은 지금 안락한 의자에 앉아 책을 읽고 있지만, 다른 우주에선 똑같은 얼굴을 가진 또 다른 당신은 돌도끼를 쳐들고 새끼 공룡과 사투를 벌이고 있을 수도 있다. 노벨물리학상 수상자인 와인버그(Steven Weinberg)는 이런 가능성들을 라디오 채널에 비유한다.

"당신이 살고 있는 공간은 여러 나라의 수십 개 방송국에서 송출한 수백 가지 전파로 가득하다. 그러나 당신은 그 가운데 단 한 가지만 청취할 수 있다. 나머지 전파들은 그저 가능성으로만 존재하다가 채널을 돌리는 순간 현실로 나타난다."

당신이 상상할 수 있는 모든 상황이 무수한 평행우주에서 실제로 펼쳐진다는 얘기다. 뉴욕 시립대학의 물리학자 카쿠(Michio Kaku) 교수는 앞으로 수조 년 후 우리가 사는 우주가 완벽하게 얼어붙기 전, 인간은 다른 평행우주로 대이동할 기발한 방법을 고안해낼지 모른다고 예측하기도 한다.

그럼에도 불구하고 대부분의 사람들이 이를 "허튼소리"로 치부하는 이유는 단 하나다. 모르기 때문이다. 우리는 머릿속에 든 지식을 잣대로 우리 현실과 너무 동떨어진 일은 무조건 "허튼소리"라고 일축하고 가능성의 문을 완전히 닫아버린다. 하지만 가만히 생각해보자. 우리 머릿속에 들어 있는 게 뭔가? 어릴 적부터 가정에서, 학교에서, 사회에서 배우고 체험한 것들이 전부다. 그걸 찧고 까불러 굴려내는 생각들이 고작이다. 그런데도 그게 틀림없는 사실이라고 믿고, 그 믿음의 틀 속에 틀어박혀 꿈쩍도 하지 않는다.

다시 한 번 생각해보라. 우리가 틀림없다고 믿었던 지식들이 늘 들어맞았는가? 우리는 오랫동안 태양계가 속한 은하수가 우주의 전부라고 믿었었다. 그러다가 관측기술이 좋아지면서 은하수와 같은 은하가 수십억 개도 넘게 존재한다는 사실에 눈을 떴다. 우리 우주엔 지구의 모래알보다 더 많은 별들이 존재한다는 것이었다. 하지만 놀랍게도 그게 다가 아니었다. 최첨단 인공위성과 우주왕복선이 전송한 데이터들을 분석해보니, 우리 우주와 비슷한 또 다른 우주들이 무수히 존재할 가능성이 어마어마하게 컸다. 우리는 사막의 모래알보다 작은 사고의 틀 속에 꼭꼭 틀어박혀 있었던 것이다. 당신은 여전히 이렇게 생각할지 모른다.

"설사 무수한 평행우주가 실제로 존재한다 한들 그게 나와 무슨 상관인가? 내가 벌어먹고 사는 데 무슨 쓸모가 있는가?"

평행우주는 무한한 가능성을 뜻한다. 이 우주에 사는 당신은 봉급쟁이에 불과할 수 있지만, 다른 우주에 사는 똑같은 당신은 수천억 원대의 재산가일 수도 있다. "난 머리가 나빠"라고 한탄하는 당신이 다른 우주에선 천재 과학자일 수도 있다. 이 우주에 사는 당신은 다리뼈가 부러졌을 수 있지만, 다른 우주에 사는 당신의 다리는 멀쩡할 수도 있다. 이 우주에 사는 당신은 한숨을 푹푹 내쉬며 신세한탄만 할 수 있지만, 다른 평행우주에선 재산가일 수도, 천재 과학자일 수도, 다리뼈가 멀쩡할 수도 있는 것이다. 당신과 외모도, 머리도, 유전자도 똑같은 사람들이다. 단지 생각만 다를 뿐이다. 다시 말해 생각만 돌려 바라보면 당신이 바로 그렇게 변신하는 것이다.

"나는 무수한 평행 우주에 존재하는 무수한 나 가운데 어떤 나를 선택할 것인가?"

진심으로 이렇게 마음을 먹고 선택하면 그 선택이 바로 현실이 된다. 당신은 여전히 의심을 품고 있을지 모른다. 하지만 가능성만큼은 열어놓아야 한다. 가능성을 열어놓아야 머리도 열린다. 반면 가능성을 닫아버리면 관찰자 효과에 따라 머리도 닫혀버린다. 우주의 무한한 가능성이 접근 금지 상태가 된다.

평행우주의 가능성을 받아들여 온갖 심신의 병을 치료하는 사람들도 있다. 킨슬로우(Frank Kinslow) 박사도 그 중 하나다.

예를 들어 내가 교통사고로 허리를 다쳤다고 가정해보자. 병원에 가서 촬영해보니 네 번째 척추 마디가 삐끗 어긋났다. 앞서 언급했듯 우주엔 무수한 가능성이 존재한다. 네 번째 척추 마디가 삐끗한 척추가 있는가 하면, 다섯 번째가 어긋난 척추도 있다. 멀쩡한 척추도 있다. 몽땅 망가진 척추도 있다. 눈을 감고 우주 속에서 멀쩡한 척추를 고른다. 우주엔 시공간 개념이 없다. 그 척추를 내 몸속에 옮겨놓는 모습을 고요한 마음으로 그린다. 건강한 척추와 다친 척추가 교체되는 순간 눈을 떠보면 거짓말처럼 척추가 완치된다. 킨슬로우 박사는 이것이 사람의 지능으로 되는 일이 아니라고 설명한다.

킨슬로우 박사

"우주엔 무한한 가능성이 존재한다. 그 가능성을
진심으로 받아들이면 심신의 온갖 질병도 즉각
적으로 치유할 수 있다."

"나는 몸만 빌려준다. 우주의 지능을 빌리면 즉각적인 치유 효과가 나
타난다."

그는 전 세계의 많은 환자들을 그런 식의 상상으로 치료한다. 인터넷
동영상으로 치료법을 강의하기도 한다(www.quantumentrainment.com, 그의 저
서는 참고문헌에 수록돼 있음).

여전히 황당무계한 소리로만 들릴지 모른다. 하지만 이런 가정을 해
보자.

당신은 시간여행을 통해 원시인들을 만난다. 그들에게 당신이 쓰는
핸드폰의 존재에 대해 열심히 설명한다.

"말도 안 되는 허튼소리로군!"

"어디서 튀어나온 미친놈이야!"

당장 이런 반응이 나올 것이다. 원시인들은 자신들이 갖고 있는 지식
을 잣대로 당신을 "미친놈"으로 치부하는 것이다. 그들의 고정된 두뇌는
도저히 휴대폰을 상상할 수 없다. "휴대폰은 미친놈이 만들어낸 엉뚱한
쇠붙이" 정도의 상상만 가능하다. 새로운 가능성을 진실로서 받아들일

수 없는 것이다.

만일 어떤 원시인이 "휴대폰은 존재할 수도 있어"라고 모든 가능성을 열어놓고 귀를 기울인다면? 그는 진실을 보게 될 것이다. "지구가 태양을 돈다"는 사실을 발견했던 코페르니쿠스나 "지구는 둥글다"는 사실을 수학적으로 증명했던 갈릴레오는 온갖 조롱과 핍박, 박해를 받았다. 진실이 아닌 허튼소리를 퍼뜨린다는 이유였다. 모든 사람들이 "지구는 평평하다"고 믿던 시대에 그들은 미치광이들이었다. 수백만 년, 수억 년 후의 후손들이 어떤 진실을 밝혀낼지는 아무도 모른다. 그들은 우리를 "무식한 21세기 원시인들"로 여길 수도 있다. 우주에 대한 진실을 "허튼소리"라고 일축하던 원시인들 말이다.

물리학자 에버렛 3세(Hugh Everett III)는 "조금이라도 가능성이 있으면 그 사건이 발생하는 우주가 반드시 존재한다. 각 우주에 살고 있는 사람들은 자신의 우주만이 유일한 현실이며 다른 우주는 허구라고 믿는다"라고 꼬집었다. 무한한 가능성은 무한한 문제에 대한 모든 해답을 갖고 있다. 옥스퍼드 대학의 도이치 교수는 "우주에 모든 물음에 대한 해답이 들어 있다"고 말한다. 아인슈타인도 "우주에 완벽한 두뇌가 존재한다"고 누누이 말했었다.

두뇌를 활짝 열어젖히고 우주의 모든 가능성을 바라보는 것, 이게 바로 지능을 획기적으로 높이는 비결이다. 실제로 새롭고 기발한 아이디어로 성공한 사람들에게 물으면 대답은 한결같다. 우주에서 떨어졌다는 것이다.

두뇌를 활짝 열어 놓아라

해리포터 시리즈로 단숨에 세계적인 거부가 된 영국의 작가 롤링(J.K. Rowling)은 기자들이 어디서 영감을 얻었느냐고 묻자 이렇게 대답했다.

"마치 누군가가 내 머리에 아이디어를 확 집어넣는 것 같았어요. 그 아이디어가 전개되는 걸 선명하게 볼 수 있었죠. 나는 보았던 걸 적어놓은 것뿐이에요."

미국의 시인인 롱펠로도 자신의 뛰어난 작품이 투지가 아니라 대부분 갑작스런 영감에 의해 탄생했다고 털어놓았다.

"지난밤, 나는 12시가 넘도록 난롯가에 앉아 담배를 피우고 있는데 문득 〈헤스페러스 호의 발라드(Ballad of the Hesperus)〉 구상이 떠올랐다. 그 구상은 그림으로 생생하게 보였다. 그래서 얼른 써놓고 잠자리에 들었는데 잠은 안 오고 다른 생각들이 역시 그림으로 계속 떠올랐다. 그래서 또 그 생각들을 추가했다. 전혀 어떤 노력도 필요하지 않았다. 몇 줄씩 떠오른 게 아니라 작품 전체가 통째로 떠올랐다."

러시아의 작곡가 차이콥스키도 비슷한 말을 했다.

J.K. 롤링

"기차를 타고 가는데 누군가가 내 머리에
아이디어를 확 집어넣는 것 같았어요."

"작품에 대한 아이디어는 갑작스럽고 돌발적으로 떠오른다. 그 아이디어는 놀라운 힘으로 땅을 가르고 솟아올라 가지와 잎을 내밀며 꽃을 활짝 피운다."

그것들을 생생하게 보았다는 말이다.

아버지를 따라 유럽 연주 여행을 다니던 열네 살의 모차르트는 이탈리아의 시스티나 성당에서 알레그리의 유명한 성가곡 〈미제레레〉를 단한 번 듣고는 숙소에 돌아가 그대로 옮겨 적었다. 당시 교황은 이 아름다운 악보가 외부에 흘러나가는 걸 엄격히 금지시키고 있었다. 만일 옮겨적었다가 들키면 파문하겠다는 포고령까지 내렸다. 1년에 딱 한 주간만연주하고는 악보를 금고에 넣고 잠가두었다. 그런데 모차르트는 기억만으로 교황청의 금기를 깨버렸다.

물리학자 라즐로 박사는 이렇게 설명한다.

"모차르트와 같은 천재 음악가들에게 그건 대단한 일이 아니다. 그들은 기발한 영감과 아이디어로 가득한 곳을 알고 있다. 그곳에서 그런 악보들을 끊임없이 본다. 그러니 쉽게 기억할 수밖에 없다."

UCLA 연구진이 천재들의 두뇌를 촬영해보니 그들은 뭔가를 깊이 생각하는 순간 두뇌 에너지가 뚝 떨어졌다. 반면 보통 사람들은 애써 생각할 때마다 두뇌에너지가 급증했다. 천재들은 두뇌를 열어놓고 우주에서아이디어를 얻으니 많은 에너지를 소모할 필요가 없는 것이다.

이처럼 지능은 내 머릿속에 고정돼 있는 것도 아니요, 내 머릿속에서나오는 것도 아니다. 두뇌의 문을 활짝 열어놓고 우주의 모든 가능성을바라볼 때 저절로 흘러들어온다. "난 그런 거 안 믿어" 하고 가능성을 닫아버리면 관찰자 효과에 따라 지능도 닫혀버린다. 지능은 시야를 넓혀 바라보기만 하면 저절로 높아지는 요술방망이 같은 것이다.

세상을 깜짝 놀라게 하는 아이디어를 얻는 비결도 바로 이거다. "아이디어는 내 머릿속에서 나온다"고 생각하면 기존의 생각들을 벗어나기 힘들다. 아무리 머리를 쥐어짜도 그 생각이 그 생각이다. 비슷한 생각이 돌고 도는 것이다. 그러다 보면 골치만 지끈지끈 아파와 쥐가 날 지경이다. 반면 생각을 돌려 '아이디어는 우주에서 떨어진다'라고 본다면? 우주에 무수하게 떠다니는 온갖 새롭고 기발한 아이디어들이 모두 내 선택의 대상이다. 나는 그저 머리를 활짝 열어놓고 사냥하다가 그중의 하나를 덥석 낚아채면 그만이다. 아무리 오랫동안 생각에 잠겨 있어도 골치가 지끈지끈하거나 머리에 쥐가 나는 경우는 없다. 비좁은 두뇌 속이 아닌 무한한 우주를 사냥하기 때문이다. 오히려 마치 최면에 걸린 듯 생각에 점점 깊이 빠져든다. 식사도 잊고 잠도 잊은 채 생각에 잠긴다. 천재들이 한 가지 문제에 몇 달, 혹은 몇 년씩 몰입할 수 있는 것도 바로 이 때문이다.

"난 머리가 좋은 게 아니다. 그저 문제를 오래 생각할 따름이다."

아인슈타인의 말은 그냥 나온 말이 아니었다.

지 능 에   대 한   착 각 의   위 험 성

그럼 만일 '내 지능은 타고난 것, 내 머릿속에 들어 있는 것'이라는 생각을 갖고 살아가면 어떻게 될까? 관찰자 효과에 따라 내 지능은 정말 꼼짝없이 감옥에 갇혀버릴까?

컬럼비아 대학의 드웩(Carol S. Dweck) 교수는 초등학교 5학년생 400여

명에게 간단한 문제들을 풀어보도록 한 뒤 다음과 같은 두 가지 문장으로
칭찬해보았다.

　＊ "넌 참 똑똑하구나!" ⟶ '지능'을 칭찬해주었다.
　＊ "넌 참 열심히 공부했구나!" ⟶ '노력'을 칭찬해주었다.

　'지능'을 칭찬받은 아이들과 '노력'을 칭찬받은 아이들 간엔 어떤 차
이가 생겼을까? 드웩 교수는 얼마 후 이들을 다시 한 번 시험해보았다.

　"여기 쉬운 문제와 어려운 문제, 두 가지 문제가 있어. 어떤 문제를 풀
어보겠니?"

　어떤 칭찬을 들었느냐에 따라 아이들의 반응은 정반대였다. '노력'을
칭찬받았던 아이들의 90퍼센트는 어려운 문제를 선택했다. 반면, '지능'
을 칭찬받았던 아이들은 대부분 쉬운 문제를 골랐다.

　칭찬 한 마디가 왜 이런 차이를 만들어낼까?

　'지능'을 칭찬받은 아이들은 '지능은 타고나는 거야'라고 생각하게
된다. '지능은 고정돼 있는 것'이라고 생각하니 어려운 문제를 기피하게
된다. 노력해도 문제가 풀리지 않을 수도 있기 때문이다. 반면, '노력'을
칭찬받은 아이들은 '지능은 노력에 따라 변하는 것'이라고 생각한다. 그
러니 어려운 문제가 두렵지 않다. 설사 지금 안 풀리더라도, 노력하면 곧
풀릴 것이기 때문이다.

　이런 자세는 나중에 성적에도 영향을 미쳤다. '노력'을 칭찬받았던 아
이들은 처음보다 성적이 30퍼센트나 뛰어올랐다. 그러나 '지능'을 칭찬
받았던 아이들은 거꾸로 20퍼센트나 떨어졌다. 드웩 교수 스스로도 이런

결과에 크게 놀라워했다. 아이들에게 노력을 칭찬해주면 '난 뭐든지 노력하면 할 수 있어'라고 믿게 되지만, 타고난 지능을 칭찬해주면 '내가 잘할 수 있는 건 타고날 때부터 정해진 것'이라고 생각하게 되는 것이다.

드웩 교수는 지능을 칭찬받으며 자라난 아이들이 중학교에 들어가서는 어떤지 더 오래 추적해보았다. 그랬더니 점입가경이었다. 지능의 힘만 믿고 중학생이 된 아이들은 일단 성적이 떨어지면 회복불능 상태에 빠져버렸다. 성적을 올리기 위해서는 노력을 해야 하지만, 이들은 노력의 힘을 믿지 않았던 것이다.

드웩 교수는 나중에 이런 진리를 교육현장에서 생생히 확인할 수 있었다. 그녀는 어느 날 뉴욕 할렘가의 한 중학교로부터 전화를 받았다.

"교수님, 학생들의 수학성적이 해마다 떨어져요. 방법이 없을까요?"

드웩 교수는 학교로 달려갔다. 가장 큰 문제는 학생들의 지능에 대한 착각을 뜯어고치는 거였다.

"이 지역의 가난한 아이들은 원래 공부를 못해요."

"저희 부모님도 공부를 못했대요."

그는 학생들 700명을 두 반으로 나눠 A반에겐 효율적인 공부법만을 가르쳐주었다. 그리고 B반에게는 공부법과 함께 "지능은 타고나는 게 아니야"라고 자세히 설명해주었다. 적절한 자극을 받으면 지능도 높아진다는 내용의 글을 읽어주기도 하고, 과학 비디오도 보여주었다.

"사람의 뇌는 고정돼 있는 게 아니야. 근육처럼 많이 쓸수록 좋아지는 거란다."

6개월 후 학생들에게 수학시험을 치게 했다. 놀라운 변화가 일어났다. 공부법만 배운 A반 학생들의 수학성적은 별 변화가 없었지만, "지능은 변화하는 것이다"라는 사실을 깨닫게 된 학생들의 수학성적은 극적으로 상승했던 것이다.

　제아무리 IQ가 높은 사람도 '나는 IQ 천재'라고 바라보면 마치 마법에 걸린 듯 지능의 감옥에 갇혀 버린다. 세계에서 가장 IQ가 높은 미국의 사반트(Marilyn vos Savant)라는 여성을 보자. 그녀는 영국 기네스북에 세계 최고의 IQ 기록 보유자로 기록된 사람이다. 10세 때 치른 IQ 시험성적이 228이었다. 그때부터 '난 IQ 천재'라는 딱지를 붙이고 살아왔다. 얼핏 생각하면 굉장한 칭찬으로 들린다. 하지만 사실은 지능을 두뇌라는 비좁은 감옥에 집어넣는 말이다. 그러면 'IQ 천재'라는 한계를 벗어날 수 없다. 실제로 그녀는 벌써 중년이 됐지만 아직 이렇다 할 천재적 재능은 보이지 않는다. 한 잡지의 일요판 칼럼니스트로 일하면서 이따금 책을 쓰고 강연하는 게 고작이다. IQ 천재들이 대개 그녀와 같은 운명을 맞는다. 어릴 땐 천재로 반짝 유명세를 날리다가 나중엔 지능의 감옥에 갇혀 버린다.

　이렇게 보면 "난 머리가 나빠", "내 머리로는 도저히 안 돼", "난 IQ 150이야", "난 하버드 대학을 나온 사람이야" 하는 식의 말들이 얼마나 무의미하고 위험한 것인지 알 수 있다. 자신의 지능을 무한한 우주를 향해 열어놓지 못하고 비좁은 두뇌에 가둬놓는 말들이다. "우주에 존재하는 완벽한 우주의 지능과 비교하면 인간의 모든 생각과 행동은 너무도 무의미하다"라는 아인슈타인의 말이야말로 불변의 진리인 것이다. 그렇다면 우주에 있는 이 "완벽한 지능"의 정체는? 이 궁금증은 〈제3부 : 나 이상의 나 바라보기〉에서 스르르 풀리게 된다.

골칫덩어리 소녀가 있었다. 나이는 이제 겨우 여덟 살. 숙제를 내주면 늦게 내거나 아예 안 해 가기 일쑤였다. 글씨체도 도저히 알아볼 수 없을 정도로 엉망이었다. 시험을 치면 반에서 늘 꼴찌였다.

"너만 보면 골치가 아파!"

선생님들은 노골적으로 그녀를 싫어했다. 아이들도 그랬다. 소녀는 수업중 자리에 채 1분도 진득하게 앉아 있지 못했다. 좀이 쑤시는 듯 몸을 이리저리 뒤틀다가 도저히 못 참겠다는 듯 책상 위에 있던 것들을 가방에 도로 집어넣거나, 가방에서 도로 털어내곤 했다. 벌떡 일어서서 소리를 지르는 경우도 있었다.

"조용히 못하겠어?"

선생님들이 버럭 소리를 질러도 그때뿐이었다. 못된 아이, 골칫덩어리, 조용히 해! 얼른 꺼져버려! … 그녀에겐 이런 말들이 아무렇지도 않았다. 귀가 따갑도록 들어봤기 때문이다. 채 한 학기가 끝나기도 전, 참다 못한 담임선생님이 부모에게 편지를 보냈다.

"주의력 결핍증세가 너무 심각합니다. 우리 학교에서는 도저히 다루지 못하겠어요. 약을 먹이거나 특수학교에 보내세요."

부모는 가슴이 철렁 내려앉았다. 드디어 올 게 온 것이었다. 다음날 엄마는 소녀에게 가장 멋진 옷을 갈아입히고 구두를 신겼다. 머리도 정성스럽게 빗긴 다음 함께 나가자고 했다. 소녀는 덜컥 겁이 났다.

"엄마, 어디 가요?"

엄마는 그냥 멋진 데 가보자고 했다. 지하철을 타고 가다가 다시 버스로 갈아탔다. 버스에서 내려 10분쯤 걷다 보니 큼지막한 건물이 나타났다. 엘리베이터를 타고 어느 방에 들어갔다.

"안녕하세요?"

검은 뿔테 안경을 쓴 키 큰 남자가 인사했다.

"넌 여기 조용히 앉아 있어."

엄마가 나지막하면서도 엄숙하게 명령했다. 소녀는 무서웠다. 소파에 앉아 있자니 또 손이 들썩거렸다. 무서운 마음에 두 손을 소파에 꽉 깔고 앉았다.

엄마는 그 남자와 오래 이야기를 나눴다. 학교에서도 문제가 많고, 집에서도 문제가 많다는 늘 듣던 얘기였다. 그 남자는 대화를 나누면서 간간이 소녀의 행동을 가만히 살펴보곤 했다. 소녀는 그런 눈길이 더욱 무서웠다.

'난 특수학교는 싫어. 절대로 안 가! 내가 왜 특수학교에 다녀야 해?'

그녀는 특수학교가 어떤 곳이라는 걸 잘 알고 있었다. 선생님들이 그런 말을 하는 걸 여러 번 들어봤기 때문이다. 모든 사람들이 그녀를 심한 문제아로 낙인찍어놓고 있었다. 선생님들도, 아빠도, 엄마도, 친구들도… 이 세상 사람 누구나 다 그렇게 생각한다면 자신이 정말 문제아인지도 모른다는 생각이 퍼뜩 들었다.

마침내 그 남자가 엄마와의 대화를 끝내고 벌떡 일어섰다. 뚜벅뚜벅 걸어와 소파에 앉았다.

"애야, 지루했지? 그런데도 용케 잘 참았다."

부드러운 말투였지만 소녀의 가슴은 사정없이 콩닥거렸다.

"애, 아저씨가 엄마랑 옆방에 가서 좀더 얘기할 게 있단다. 여기서 몇 분만 더 기다릴 수 있겠니? 금방 돌아올 거야."

소녀가 고개를 끄덕이자 남자가 책상 쪽으로 걸어가더니 은은한 음악을 틀어놓았다. 그러고는 엄마와 함께 밖으로 나갔다. 그가 복도에서 벽을 가리키며 말했다.

"이 벽에 작은 구멍이 뚫려 있죠? 이 구멍으로 따님이 뭘 하는지 가만히 들여다보세요."

잠시도 가만히 앉아 있지 못하는 소녀는 곧 일어서더니 몸을 움직이기 시작했다. 그들의 입이 딱 벌어졌다. 소녀는 음악에 따라 마치 물결처럼 우아하게 춤을 추는 것이었다! 어린아이가 그토록 자연스럽게 춤을 추다니!

그 남자가 조용히 속삭였다.

"따님은 문제아가 아닙니다. 저거 보세요. 타고난 댄서예요. 댄스 학교에 보내세요."

그는 유명한 심리학자였다. 엄마의 눈에 눈물이 핑 돌았다.

댄스학교에 들어간 소녀는 물을 만난 물고기였다. 그녀는 나중에 이렇게 술회했다.

"댄스 연습실에 처음 들어갔더니 모두가 나와 똑같은 사람들이었어요. 몸을 움직이지 않으면 좀이 쑤셔서 못 견디는 사람들요. 몸을 움직이지 않으면 아무 생각도 못하는 사람들 말입니다."

그녀는 신명이 났다. 학교에서도, 집에서도 매일 춤을 추었다. 아무도 시키지 않았는데도 새벽 일찍 일어나 연습하기도 했다.

마침내 그녀는 런던왕립 발레학교에 지원해 합격했다. 거기서 실력을 인정받아 왕립 발레단에 들어가 솔로이스트로 세계적인 명성을 날렸다.

20세기 최고의 발레리나이자
안무가인 질리언 린

은퇴 후엔 뮤지컬 극단을 창립해 런던과 뉴욕 등에서 대성공을 거두었다. 우리나라에서도 공연된 뮤지컬 〈캣츠Cats〉와 〈오페라의 유령(The Phantom of the Opera)〉이 역사상 가장 성공적인 명작으로 꼽히는 것도 그녀의 안무 없이는 불가능한 것이었다. 질리언 린Gillian Lynne의 이야기다.

그녀가 만일 "문제아"라는 착각의 감옥에서 풀려나지 못했더라면 그녀의 인생은 어떻게 달라졌을까?

지금도 얼마나 많은 사람들이 비좁은 착각의 감옥에 갇혀 자신의 재능을 사장시키고 있을까?

부정적 생각 꺼버리기

왜 자꾸만 휩싸이는 걸까?

한 여직원이 주말에 남자친구를 만나러 대전에 내려갔다. 그가 대전의 연구단지에서 일하기 때문이다. 그날은 두 사람이 만난 지 1주년이 되는 특별한 날이라 그녀는 콧노래를 부르며 차를 몰았다.

'오늘 하루는 영화도 함께 보면서 환상적으로 보내야지…'

두 시간 넘게 날아가듯 운전해 드디어 대전에 도착했다. 남자친구는 근사한 음식점에서 그녀가 좋아하는 스파게티를 사준 뒤, 평소 갖고 싶다던 음반도 선물로 주었다. 그녀는 정말 하늘을 날 것 같았다.

"우리 오후엔 영화 보러 갈까?"

그러자 남자친구 얼굴이 갑자기 어두워졌다.

"어? 어떡하지? 오후엔 다른 약속을 잡아놨는데. 친구들과 먼 데 가기로 했거든."

그녀의 얼굴이 하얗게 굳어졌다.

"엉? 이런 날 다른 약속을 잡아놨다고?"

그녀는 홱 토라졌다. 더 이상 변명을 듣고 싶지 않았다. 세상에 이럴

수가! 대전까지 일부러 차를 몰고 찾아왔는데 이런 냉대를 당하다니⋯. 그가 자신을 무시한다고 생각했다. 태도가 달라진 거 같다는 의심도 들었다. 그녀는 핸드백을 집어 들고는 벌떡 일어섰다. 당황한 남자친구는 멍한 눈으로 앉아 있었다. 그녀는 또각또각 걸어가 핸드백에 집어넣은 음반을 꺼내 쓰레기통에 탁 집어던졌다.

'저런 남자를 사귀어온 내가 바보지. 다시 만나주나 봐라.'

이튿날 남자친구가 전화를 걸어왔지만 받지 않았다. 그다음 날도 그가 메시지를 보내왔지만 답신하지 않았다. 관계는 그것으로 끝장나고 말았다. 하지만 지금 그녀는 그때 일을 후회한다.

"내가 홧김에 너무 충동적으로 행동했다는 생각이 들어요. 헤어진 건 인연이 그런가 보다 쳐도, 내가 어린애처럼 행동한 게 자존심이 상해요."

그녀는 평소 차분한 성격이고 지적인 능력도 갖추고 있다. 하지만 남자친구에게 무시당했다는 생각이 들자 앞뒤 안 가리고 폭발해버렸다.

지능이 높은 사람은 후회할 짓을 하지 않고 살아갈까?

미국 플로리다 주에서는 이런 사건이 일어났다. 고등학교 2학년 학생인 제이슨 군이 물리교사를 부엌칼로 찔렀다. 단순한 살인미수나 상해사건이 아니었다. 그는 전 과목 성적이 A로 늘 전교 1등을 놓치지 않던 수재였다. 미국 최고 명문인 하버드 의대 진학을 목표로 하던 공부벌레가 왜 그런 야만적인 짓을 저질렀을까? 이유는 단순했다. 얼마 전에 치른 물리시험에서 B를 받았다는 것이었다. 그는 점수를 보는 순간 분노가 폭발했다. 분노를 주체하지 못해 부엌칼을 가방에 숨긴 채 등교했다가 실험실에서 물리교사를 만났다.

"선생님, 점수를 A로 올려주실 수 없나요? 다른 과목은 모두 A인데 물리만 B거든요."

"그렇게는 안 돼. 공정하게 채점한 점수야."

"그럼 하버드 의대에 진학하려는 제 꿈은 물거품이 돼버려요."

"그건 네 사정이고. 점수를 그렇게 흥정해서 줄 수는 없어. 다른 학생들에게도 불공평하고."

대화 직후에 일어난 일에 대해서는 양측의 진술이 엇갈렸다. 분명한 건 잠시 후 제이슨 군이 부엌칼로 교사의 빗장뼈 부위를 찔렀다는 것이다. 그는 격투 끝에 교사에게 칼을 빼앗겼다.

판사는 제이슨 군에게 무죄를 선고했다. 정신과 의사 네 명이 법정에서 범행 당시 제이슨 군은 제정신이 아니었다고 진술했기 때문이다. 제이슨 군도 물리교사를 살해할 의도가 전혀 없었다고 주장했다.

"저는 선생님을 찌르기 위해 찾아간 건 아니었어요. 단지 설득해서 실패하면 선생님 앞에서 자살할 계획이었습니다. 하지만 선생님이 저의 간절한 생각을 무시한다고 느끼는 순간 완전히 정신착란 상태에 빠졌어요. 제가 선생님을 찔렀는지조차 기억나지 않는 걸요."

제이슨 군은 곧바로 다른 학교로 전학했다. 거기서도 그는 전교 1등을 하더니 수석으로 졸업했다. 사람들은 몹시 의아해했다. 그처럼 똑똑한 아이가 아무리 홧김이라지만 어떻게 그런 짐승 같은 끔찍한 짓을 저질렀을까? 왜 어떤 사람들은 부정적 감정에 휩싸여 인생을 망치기까지 하는 걸까?

자나깨나 생존에만 집착하는 요물 아미그달라

아래의 그림을 보라.

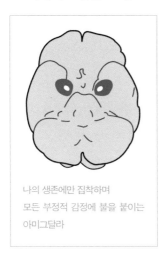

나의 생존에만 집착하며
모든 부정적 감정에 불을 붙이는
아미그달라

우리 두뇌 속의 모습이다. 양쪽 뇌의 빨간 부위가 바로 분노, 증오, 슬픔, 절망, 공포 등 모든 부정적 감정에 불을 댕기는 아미그달라(편도체)이다. 아미그달라는 생존을 책임진 만큼, 두뇌 한가운데의 변연계 가장 깊숙한 곳에 튼튼히 자리잡고 있다. 엄지손가락만 한 크기나 기능은 원시시대나 지금이나 변화가 없다. 그래서 생존에 위험이 닥치면 현대인도 원시인과 똑같이 폭발하고, 증오하고, 절망한다. 두뇌과학자들이 '원시적 두뇌(primitive brain)'라고 부르는 이유다.

원시시대를 생각해보자. 나는 가족과 함께 칠흑같이 어두운 동굴 속에서 잠을 자고 있다.

"부스럭! 부스럭!"

밖에서 부스럭 소리가 난다. 아미그달라가 순식간에 위험신호를 켠다. 호랑이? 소름 끼치는 뱀? 혹은 돌도끼를 든 낯선 원시인? 부스럭 소리는 점점 가까워진다. 벌떡 일어나 가시나무 몽둥이를 집어든다. 부스럭 소리가 동굴 입구에까지 이르렀다. 나는 방망이를 홱 내리친다.

"꽥! 꽥! 꽥!"

꽥꽥거리는 소리를 따라가며 몽둥이를 마구 내리치고 휘두른다. 나의 생존을 위해서는 어쩔 수 없다. 무조건 내 생존부터 챙기지 않으면 나와 내 가족이 당할 수 있다. 이처럼 내 생존에 위험이 닥치면 무조건 빨간불을 켜놓고 보는 위험경보장치가 아미그달라다. 시카고 대학의 클링(Arthur Kling) 박사가 아미그달라를 다친 원숭이 일곱 마리를 야생지대에 놓아주었더니 일곱 시간 만에 한 마리만 빼고 전부 맹수들에게 잡아 먹혔다. 생존을 위해서는 부정적 감정이 필수적인 것이다.

뇌신경과학자들에 따르면, 사람은 하루 평균 2만 가지 상황을 겪게 된다고 한다. 아미그달라는 이 모든 상황을 늘 '내 편'과 '네 편', '나'와 '적'의 두 가지로 분류해 두뇌 전체에 전달한다. 철저하게 나의 생존이라는 시각으로 모든 상황을 분류한다.

아 미 그 달 라 의   분 류 법

* 유쾌(pleasant) : 생존에 위험이 없다고 판단되면 '유쾌'로 분류한다. 어떤 사람이 나를 인정해주고 칭찬해주거나 높여주면 '유쾌'로 분류해 더 가까이 지내고 싶어한다.

* 불쾌(unpleasant) : 위험이 닥치거나 불안하게 느껴지면 '불쾌'로 분류한다. 나를 무시하는 행위, 남이 내 생각대로 움직이지 않는 상황 등도 불쾌다. 불쾌로 분류되면 위험신호를 켜서 분노, 공포 등의 부정적 감정을 일어나도록 한다. 불쾌로 분류된 사람은 잠재적 적으로 인식돼 기피하게 된다. 첫눈에 불쾌한 인상을 준 사람이 이유 없이 점점 싫어지는 것도 이 때문이다.

168

르두 박사

"아미그달라는 부정적 감정을 켜고 끄는 스위치이다."

* 중립(neutral) : 유쾌도 불쾌도 아닌 상황으로 별 의미가 없다면 분류하지 않는다.

아미그달라가 유쾌, 불쾌의 분류장치라는 사실은 우연히 발견됐다. 뉴욕 대학의 르두(Joseph LeDoux) 박사가 쥐들에게 여러 가지 실험을 하다가 두뇌에 탐침을 투입한 뒤 아미그달라를 마비시켜보았다. 그랬더니 쥐들이 화, 공포 등의 불쾌한 감정이라곤 티끌만큼도 느끼지 못하는 것이었다. 예를 들어 반복적으로 먹이를 줬다가 빼앗아도 화를 내지 않았다. 고양이가 앞에 나타나도 눈 하나 까딱하지 않았다.

"흠, 쥐가 고양이를 겁내지 않다니? 그럼 함께 놀도록 해볼까?"

쥐들은 끝내 고양이에게 잡아먹히면서도 신음소리 하나 내지 않았다. 르두 박사는 원숭이의 아미그달라도 마비시켜보았다. 역시 아무리 괴롭혀도 화를 내지 않았고, 전에는 낯선 음식을 보면 고개를 돌리더니 이제는 겁 없이 덥석덥석 받아먹는 것이었다. 심지어 독버섯까지 먹고 숨지는 사례도 있었다.

남가주 대학의 뇌신경과학자인 다마시오(Antonio Damasio) 박사는 아미그달라에 칼슘이 쌓여 기능을 못하는 환자에게 공포에 질려 비명을 지르는 여성의 비디오를 보여주었다. 그런 비디오를 보면 보통 사람들은 바짝 몸을 움츠리며 함께 공포를 느낀다. 그러나 그 환자는 전혀 딴판이었다.

"왜 저러는 거죠?"

환자는 공포에 질린 여성의 표정을 전혀 이해하지 못했다. 주삿바늘로 찌르거나 마취시키지 않고 이를 뽑아도 통증을 느끼지 못했다. 아무리 무시하거나 모욕적인 말을 던져도 화내는 일도 없었다. 아미그달라가 마비된 사람은 마치 불쾌한 감정의 스위치를 완전히 꺼버린 것처럼 행동했다.

내 정신연령은 5세 유아

상대의 얼굴을 모른 채 만나는 블라인드 데이트blind date를 해본 적 있는가? 이성과 첫눈이 마주치는 바로 그 순간 사실상 '저 여자는 마음에 안 들어' 혹은 '휴, 오늘 데이트는 꽝이야'라고 판결을 내려버린 적 없는가? 낯선 남자를 처음 만난 바로 그 순간 '이 남자는 왠지 가까이하기 싫어' 혹은 '이 남자는 좀 괜찮아 보이는군'과 같은 식으로 심판해버린 적 없는가? 아미그달라는 낯선 사람을 만나면 대번에 친구인지 적인지부터 가려내려 든다. 이렇게 첫눈에 호불호가 정해져 버리면 그대로 잠재의식 속에 저장된다.

신입생들이 대학 4년간 친하게 지낼 친구를 선택하는 것도, 학생들이 처음 대하는 교수들의 실력을 분간해내는 것도, 직장 친구를 정하는 것도 불과 몇 초 만에 결단난다. 프린스턴 대학의 토도로프(Alexander Todorov) 교수는 사람들에게 2000년, 2002년, 2004년 의회선거 출마자들의 흑백 사진들을 1초씩 보여주었다. 낯익은 출마자들의 사진은 제외했다.

"얼굴 사진만 보고 당선됐는지 낙선됐는지 알아 맞춰보세요."

출마자들에 대한 아무런 사전지식 없이 전적으로 얼굴만 살짝 보고 당락 여부를 맞춰보라는 것이었다. 사람들의 예측은 얼마나 들어맞았을까? 놀랍게도 적중률이 무려 70퍼센트에 달했다. 그들은 뭘 보고 당락을 점쳤을까?

"능력이 있어 보이는 인상이거든요."

"경험도 많고 성숙한 인상을 풍겨요."

아미그달라가 첫인상만으로 단숨에 내 편을 골라냈던 것이다.

수십 명이 모이면 대번에 친한 사람들과 그렇잖은 사람들로 양분되는 것도 아미그달라의 이분법적 본능 탓이다. 서로 말싸움 한 번 않고도 적이 생긴다. 심리학자 셰리프(Muzafer Sherif)가 흥미로운 실험을 해보았다. 미국 각지에서 모인 열두 살 안팎의 어린이 캠핑 참가자들을 두 반으로 나눠본 것이다. 지연이나 학연, 취미, 적성 등과는 전혀 관계없이 무작위로 말이다. 그런데 신기하게도 두 반으로 갈리자마자 그들 사이엔 미묘한 경쟁의식이 싹트기 시작했다. 두 반이 맞붙는 스포츠 경기를 시켰더니 경쟁의식은 순식간에 노골적인 적대감으로 발전했다. 경기에 진 팀은 이긴 팀이 부정행위를 저질렀다고 비난했고, 이긴 팀은 그런 비난을 비웃었다. 그러더니 야간에 서로 상대편의 숙소에 몰래 침입해 들어가 깃발을 훔쳐 불태우거나 침대를 뒤집어놓고 도망치기도 했다. 나중엔 캠프 관리자들에게 이렇게 호소하고 나섰다.

"우리 반은 야만적인 저런 친구들과는 같은 식당에서 식사할 수 없어요. 제발 식사를 따로 하게 해주세요!"

생면부지의 어린이들이 단지 두 반으로 나뉘었다는 사실 하나만으로 졸지에 원수지간이 됐던 것이다. 이렇게 철저하게 네 편과 내 편으로만 생각하려 드는 아미그달라의 정신연령은 그다지 높지 않다. 겨우 5세 유아 수준이다.

우리 두뇌는 5세 이전에는 아미그달라를 통해 분노, 증오, 절망 등 원시적 감정을 배우고, 5세부터는 대뇌피질을 통해 사회생활에 필요한 개념적인 걸 언어로 배운다. 우리가 5세 이전의 일들을 기억하지 못하는 것도 그래서다. 프로이트(Sigmund Freud)는 이처럼 5세 이전의 일들을 기억 못하는 현상을 '유아기 기억상실(childhood amnesia)'이라고 불렀다. 두 뇌과학자들은 기억력이 원시적 감정에서 개념적으로 바뀌는 5세를 '기억 전환 나이(Memory Transition Age)'라고 지칭하기도 한다.

원시적 감정은 5세를 넘으면 더 이상 발달하지 않는다. 이 때문에 5세 유아나 어른이나 원시적 감정은 똑같다. 제아무리 학식과 덕망을 갖춘 사람이라도 분노나 증오, 절망 등의 감정에서 완전히 해방될 순 없다. 만일 그런 감정을 못 느낀다면 그건 아미그달라가 고장 났다는 얘기다. 다시 요약하면 모든 부정적 감정은 생존에만 집착하는 머릿속의 5세 유아가 만들어내는 것이다. 이 유아는 생존에 위험이 닥쳤다고 판단되면 앞뒤 안 가리고 무조건 빨간불을 켜놓고 본다. 생존문제가 걸려 있는 만큼, 이 빨간불은 저절로 꺼지는 법이 없다. 반드시 위험이 사라졌다는 해제 신호를 보내줘야 꺼진다.

이영지 씨는 얼마 전 초등학교 동창으로부터 이런 전화를 받았다.

"영지야. 네 남편 오늘 늘씬한 여자와 호텔서 나오더라. 보통 사이가 아닌 거 같았어. 여자가 스스럼없이 팔짱까지 끼던걸."

너무나 충격적인 말이었다. 내 남편이 정말 맞느냐고 물었다.

"두 눈으로 똑똑히 봤어. 네 남편 오늘 빨간 넥타이 매고 나갔지? 양복은 짙은 감색이고?"

틀림없는 남편이었다. 동창은 "넌 너무 순진해서 탈이야. 잘 감시해. 앉아서 당하지 말고"라며 전화를 끊었다. 갑자기 숨이 턱 막혀오고 기절할 것만 같았다.

"이 이중인격자!"

남편이 말로만 듣던 겉 다르고 속 다른 이중인격자일 줄이야! 그녀의 머릿속 어린아이는 빨간불을 켰다. 남편의 배신은 곧 자신의 생존에 대한 위협이었다. 빨간불이 켜지니 눈앞이 캄캄하고 아무 일도 손에 잡히지 않았다. 학원에서 돌아온 딸아이가 외쳤다.

"엄마, 배고파. 밥 줘."

딸이고 밥이고 보이지 않았다. 그래서 소리를 뺙 질렀다.

"그놈의 밥, 한 번쯤 굶으면 병나니? 네가 차려 먹어!"

귀가한 남편의 얼굴을 쳐다보기조차 역겨웠다. 후다닥 화장실에 뛰어들어갔다가 남편이 옷을 갈아입는 사이 다시 밖으로 뛰쳐나갔다. 남편은 호텔에서 그 늘씬한 여자와 뭘 했을까? 그동안 얼마나 오랫동안 서로 놀아났으면 보란 듯이 팔짱까지 끼고 돌아다닐까?

"뻔뻔스러운 이중인격자! 더러운 철면피!"

그녀는 길가에 "퉤!" 하고 냅다 침을 뱉었다. 집에 돌아가서도 도저히 남편과 가까이할 수 없었다. 잠도 따로 잤다. 하지만 잠이 오지 않아 하얗게 샜다. 다음날 아침 남편이 출근하고 나서도 도무지 손가락 하나 까딱할 힘조차 없었다. 그동안 속고 살아왔다고 생각하니 오장이 뒤틀렸다. 그렇게 침대에 꼼짝 못한 채 누워 있는데 전화가 걸려왔다.

"언니, 형부가 어제 저녁 사줬어. 취직 축하한다고. 멋진 호텔에서."

"멋진 호텔?"

알고 보니 동창이 목격한 바로 그 호텔이었다. 동창은 그녀의 동생을 남편과 바람피우는 늘씬한 여자로 오해했던 것이다. 오해가 풀어지는 순간 그녀의 머릿속 어린아이가 켜놓았던 빨간불도 즉각 꺼졌다. 그녀는 하늘을 날 것 같았다. '그럼 그렇지. 그렇게 착실한 남편을 의심하다니.' 신바람이 절로 났다. 영문도 모른 채 아침을 굶고 나간 남편에게 미안한 생각이 가득 차올랐다. 장바구니를 낚아 들고 저녁을 준비하러 나가는 그녀의 발걸음은 나비처럼 가뿐했다.

머릿속 5세 유아는 이처럼 생존에 대한 위험을 감지하는 순간 반사적으로 빨간불을 켠다. 빨간불이 켜지면 머릿속에서는 부정적 생각이 꼬리를 물고 일어난다. 생존을 위해 상상가능한 온갖 최악의 상황을 가정해보는 것이다. 이런 상태가 계속되면 병이 된다. 하지만 위험이 사라졌다고 판단되는 순간 거짓말처럼 쉽게 꺼진다. 그러나 위험 해제 신호가 이처럼 명백하지 않을 수도 있다. 그럴 땐 5세 유아를 달래줘야 한다. 달래주는 최선의 방법은 바라보는 것이다. 바라보는 것만으로 5세 유아의 빨간불은 꺼진다.

한 여학생이 들려준 이야기다.

일요일 오전이었다. 그녀는 아침 늦게까지 방 안에서 나뒹굴고 있었다. 엄마가 먼지떨이로 톡톡 거리는 소리가 들렸다. 그녀가 부스스 일어나 화장실에 들어가려는 순간 엄마가 뒤에서 한 마디 쏘아붙였다.

"다 큰 여자애가 그게 뭐냐? 밤늦도록 쏘다니다 점심때나 겨우 일어나고. 네 동생은 벌써 도서관에 갔어."

또 그 잘난 남동생 타령이었다. 공부 잘하고 말 잘 듣는 아들. 이젠 정말 지긋지긋했다. 하지만 엄마는 멈추지 않았다.

"동생 하는 거 반만 따라 해봐. 누나가 돼가지고 동생 절반도 못 따라하니?"

그 말을 듣는 순간 머리가 홱 돌았다.

"엄마는 남하고 비교하는 버릇 좀 제발 고치세요!"

그렇게 말하고는 화장실 문을 쾅 닫아버렸다. 툭 하면 동생과 비교하는 엄마가 정말 지겨웠다. 어떻게 저런 엄마와 시집갈 때까지 견디고 산단 말인가? 끔찍했다. 과거의 분노와 증오, 절망감까지 꼬리를 물고 피어오르며 마구 소용돌이치기 시작했다.

그녀는 얼굴에 찬물을 끼얹었다가 거울을 보았다.

'분노로 일그러진 저 얼굴. 저 여자는 왜 저러고 있지?'

문득 화가 나면 머릿속의 어린아이를 바라보라는 말이 생각났다. 눈을 감았다. 머릿속에서 빨갛게 달아오른 어린아이를 떠올렸다.

'10, 9, 8, 7, 6, 5, 4, 3, 2, 1···'

속으로 숫자를 거꾸로 세면서 빨간 어린아이가 점점 파란색으로 식어가는 모습을 그려보았다. 그러자 화가 멈췄다. 신기하게도 평화가 찾아왔다.

이번에는 엄마의 머릿속을 상상해보았다. 어린아이가 만들어낸 온갖 부정적 생각들에 휩싸여 얼마나 고통스러울까? 돌연 고통에서 탈출하지 못하는 엄마가 불쌍하다는 생각이 들었다. 알고 보면 아빠 사업이 부도난 뒤 음식점에서 뼈 빠지도록 일하느라 병까지 얻은 엄마였다. 고교시절 시험 때면 아무리 피곤해도 잠든 딸의 잠자리를 토닥거린 후에야 눈을 붙였고, 꼭두새벽에 늘 먼저 일어나 딸을 깨워주곤 했었다. 그런 몸으로 온종일 음식점에 나가 일해야 했다. 대학 합격을 확인하는 순간 엄마는 아예 그 자리에 픽 주저앉아 엉엉 울기까지 했었다.

그녀는 화장실 문을 열었다.

"엄마, 죄송해요. 실망만 시켜 드려서 힘드시죠?"

빗자루를 들고 있던 엄마가 잠시 멍한 얼굴로 쳐다보았다. 그러더니 눈에 눈물이 가득 고이는 것이었다.

부정적 감정에 딱지를 붙여 바라보는 방법도 있다.

UCLA의 심리학자 리버만(Matthew Lieberman)은 부정적 감정이 일어날 때 사람들에게 "이건 분노야", "이건 불안이야", "이건 스트레스야" 등의 식으로 딱지를 붙여 제3자의 눈으로 객관적으로 바라보게 했다. 그랬더니 아미그달라는 거의 즉시 진정되는 것으로 나타났다.

"자신의 감정을 남의 눈으로 바라보는 순간 아미그달라는 식어버리기 시작합니다."

바라보는 단순한 행위가 머릿속 어린아이의 불쾌신호를 꺼주는 'off' 스위치라는 것이다.

부 정 적 감 정 의 자 연 수 명 은 9 0 초

정신의학자인 카바트 진(Jon Kabat-Zinn) 박사는 부정적인 감정이 소용돌이칠 때 조용히 주시하노라면 우리 두뇌가 만들어내는 그 소용돌이의 경이로움을 느낄 수 있다고 말한다.

"우리가 스스로 만들어내는 부정적인 소리에 귀를 기울여보세요. 인간이 부정적인 감정을 스스로 만들어낼 수 있다는 게 얼마나 경이로운 일인가요? 때로는 분노에 파묻혀 치를 떨기도 하고, 때로는 절망의 늪에 빠져 허덕이는 것도 다 우리 스스로 창조해내는 겁니다."

부정적인 감정이나 생각은 내 생존을 위해 생겨나는 것인 만큼, 그 존재를 인정하고 따뜻하게 받아들이라는 것이다.

"두뇌야, 고마워. 내 생존을 위해 이런 소용돌이 감정을 만들어내다니. 어차피 몇 분 만에 사라지겠지? 나에게 오늘은 어떤 깨달음을 주려고 이런 감정을 선사하는 거니?"

이렇게 반갑게 인사를 건네고 나면 어느새 평화가 온다.

하버드 대학의 테일러(Jill Taylor) 박사 역시 조용히 주시하는 것만으로 부정적인 감정이나 생각이 90초 내에 식어버린다고 말한다.

"부정적 생각이나 감정의 자연적 수명은 90초이다. 우리가 화를 내는

테일러 박사

"부정적 감정의 자연적
수명은 90초이다."

순간 스트레스 호르몬이 온몸의 혈관을 타고 퍼져 나가는데, 90초가 지
나면 저절로 완전히 사라진다."

그래서 화는 뿌리 없는 나무에서 활활 타오르는 불길과 같다고 한다.
시간이 흐르면 저절로 꺼지게 돼 있다. 그런데도 분노가 90초 이상 지속
되는 건 우리 스스로 화에 기름을 붓기 때문이다. 예를 들어 어떤 운전자
가 내 차 앞에 갑자기 끼어들어 화가 치밀어 오른다고 해보자.

"뭐, 저런 사람이 다 있어? 정말 이해 못할 놈이네."

이렇게 스스로 기름을 부으면 화는 90초가 넘어도 계속된다.

테일러 박사는 어느 날 음악에 도취돼 과속으로 차를 몰고 가다가 딱
지를 떼이게 됐다. 몹시 기분이 상했다.

"음악에 빠져 잠시 과속을 했기로서니 벌금을 100달러나 물리다니.
정말 못된 경찰관이야."

이렇게 생각하니 화가 더욱 불길처럼 치솟아 몹시 고통스러웠다. 그
러나 곧 자신이 화에 파묻혀 있음을 깨닫고는 머릿속의 어린아이를 남처
럼 조용히 바라보며 달래보았다.

"나를 생각해줘 고맙구나. 그런데 90초가 지났거든. 위험한 상황은

아니란다. 그런데도 여전히 화를 낼 필요가 있니? 조용히 물러가렴."

이렇게 달래자 화는 곧 가라앉았다.

억 누 르 면   병 이   된 다

전작인 《아버지도 천재는 아니었다》를 출간한 뒤 학부모들을 대상으로 강연할 기회가 있었다. 강연이 끝난 뒤 한 학부모가 이런 걱정을 털어놓았다.

"우리 애가 통 공부와 담쌓고 있으니 어떡하죠?"

얘기를 들어보니 정말 걱정할 만했다. 중2 때 상위권에 들던 현수는 웬일인지 성적이 떨어지기 시작해 고1 때 급기야 전교 255명 중 200등 언저리까지 떨어졌다.

"그래서 어머니께선 어떻게 하셨나요?"

"성적표를 받던 날 넋이 빠지도록 혼내줬죠."

초조해진 엄마는 갈수록 발악에 가까운 잔소리를 해댔다. "그 모양으로 공부해서 대학에나 들어가겠니?", "친구 아들은 또 전교 1등 했다더라", "다른 엄마들 만나기가 창피하다" 등등. 대부분 엄마들이 보통 안타까움과 초조함을 그런 식으로 표출시킨다. 하지만 부정적인 잔소리는 부정적인 감정만 부추긴다. 다행히 현수는 밖으로 나돌아다니지는 않았다. 그럴 푼수도 아니었다. 늘 책상 앞에 붙어 있는데도 성적은 날로 곤두박질하는 것이었다. 초조한 엄마는 속이 바싹바싹 타들어갔다.

"현수가 엄마의 잔소리를 좋아합니까?"

세상에 잔소리를 좋아할 사람은 아무도 없다.

"듣기 싫어 죽으려고 하죠. 요즘엔 손으로 귀를 틀어막기도 하고 문을 쾅 닫고 제 방으로 쑥 들어가 고슴도치처럼 처박혀 있기도 해요."

한번은 아무리 불러도 대답 않기에 문을 쾅쾅 두드려 열도록 했다. 현수는 양쪽 귀에 이어폰을 꽂은 채 음악을 듣고 있었다. 나는 물론 정신과 의사는 아니다. 하지만 뭐가 문제인지는 불을 보듯 뻔했다. 나는 충격을 주기 위해 일부러 이렇게 말했다.

"현수 성적이 떨어지는 건 어머님 때문이네요."

그녀는 뒤통수에 한 방을 된 탕 맞은 듯 두 눈을 동그랗게 떴다.

"쉴 틈 없이 싫은 소리를 퍼부어대면 현수의 머릿속은 오로지 싫은 소리로 가득 찰 수밖에 없지요. 생각해보세요. 싫다는 생각으로 가득 찬 머리가 뭘 받아들이겠습니까?"

싫다는 생각이 꽉 들어찬 머리는 모든 걸 거부한다. 아무리 책을 읽어도 비집고 들어갈 구석이 없다. 대부분의 사람들은 눈에 안 보이는 생각 덩어리쯤이야 무시하고 짓눌러도 아무 탈 없으려니 착각한다. 하지만 생각 덩어리도 엄연히 지능과 자존심을 갖고 있다. 무시하고 짓누르면 없어지는 게 아니라 머릿속에 똬리를 틀고 틀어박힌다. 쌓이고 쌓이면 병이 된다.

미 국립보건원의 정신과 의사인 헤이즈(Steve Hayes) 등 심리학자들은 100여 건이 넘는 연구보고서들을 분석한 결과, 대부분의 정신질환이 부정적 생각을 억누르기 때문에 일어난다는 사실을 확인했다.

"그럼 어떡하죠?"

"싫다는 생각부터 몽땅 털어내도록 해야죠. 그래야 뭔가 하고 싶다는 생각이 들어설 틈이 생길 거 아닙니까?"

그녀도 그럴싸하다고 생각했는지 고개를 끄덕이며 사라졌다.

몇 주 후 전화가 걸려왔다. 흥분한 목소리였다.

"선생님, 작전이 주효했어요!"

자초지종은 이랬다. 그녀는 그날 밤 현수와 마주 앉았다.

"현수야. 넌 엄마가 네 속마음을 전혀 모른다고 생각하지? 상위권이
던 성적이 어쩌다 딱 한 번 떨어졌는데 그렇게 막무가내로 야단만 쳤으
니."

그 순간 현수의 눈에 눈물이 핑 돌았다.

"엄마가 그렇게 혼내지만 않았더라도 나 스스로 잘 회복할 수 있었을
텐데, '성적이 갑자기 떨어져 나도 엄청 스트레스 받았는데…' 이런 생
각이 들지? 가뜩이나 힘 빠졌을 때 엄마가 힘이 돼주기는커녕 오히려 힘
만 빠지게 했구나. 그동안 무척 힘들었지?"

울먹거리던 현수가 갑자기 걷잡을 수 없는 울음을 터뜨렸다. 그녀의
눈에도 눈물이 고였다.

"그렇게 힘들었으면 왜 진작 말하지 그랬니?"

그러자 현수는 가까스로 울음을 억제하며 엄마의 눈을 노려보며 외
쳤다.

"엄마가 언제 제 아픔을 귀담아 들어보려고 한 적이나 있어요?"

그녀도 끝내 울음보가 터졌다.

"그래. 이 미련한 엄마는 자기 새끼 어려운 것도 모르고 몰인정하게
몰아붙이기만 했구나. 그동안 얼마나 힘들고 외로웠니?"

모자는 난생처음 서로 부둥켜안고 한참 울었다.

그녀가 내게 말했다.

"선생님, 전 그 후로 현수한테 공부하란 잔소리 절대 안 해요. 오히려 거꾸로 하죠. 좀 쉬면서 하라고. 그런데 어떤 일이 일어났는지 아세요? 현수가 완전 딴판이 됐어요!"

그날 이후로 현수는 표정이 점점 밝아져 갔다. 콕콕 찌르는 말 대신 온정어린 말이 들어가니 핏기없던 얼굴엔 화색이 돌기 시작했다. 공부도 머리에 쏙쏙 들어온다며 좋아했다. 머릿속에 잔뜩 구겨 넣었던 '공부는 싫다'는 생각 덩어리들을 끄집어내 따뜻하게 바라보게 되니 저절로 사라졌던 것이다.

거울처럼 비춰주면 저절로 꺼진다

한강 다리 5미터 높이의 트러스트 꼭대기.

한 남자가 아슬아슬하게 버티고 서 있다. 한강에 뛰어내리겠다며 벌써 30분 넘게 경찰과 대치중이다. 당장 생명을 집어삼킬 듯 아가리를 딱 벌리고 있는 무시무시한 부정적 감정이라는 괴물을 어떻게 잠재울 것인가? 경찰이 파악한 인적 사항은 대강 이렇다.

32세의 차영호. 2년 전 직장에서 쫓겨났다. 그 후 부인이 아이를 데리고 친정으로 도망쳤다. 곧 월세 집에서도 쫓겨나 친구들 집을 전전하다가 거기서도 쫓겨났다.

경찰이 확성기에 대고 계속 설득을 시도한다.

"차영호 씨, 사랑하는 가족들에게 슬픔을 안겨주지 마세요. 어서 마음을 풀고 내려오세요."

남자가 소리친다.

"개수작 떨지 말고 꺼져!"

몸을 수그리며 당장에라도 강에 뛰어들 태세다.

"영호 씨 생명은 소중합니다. 어서 가족의 품으로 돌아오세요."

"너도 주둥이만 살았구나! 이 세상 모든 놈들이 다 똑같아!"

그 사이 새로운 정보가 들어온다. 남자는 직장에서 상사와 말싸움 끝에 부당하게 해고됐으며, 고향의 부모는 직장을 구할 때까지 고향 근처에는 얼씬거리지도 말라고 했다는 것이다.

대치 상태가 한 시간을 넘어가면서 아침 러시아워가 다가온다. 운전자들의 볼멘소리가 여기저기서 터져 나오기 시작한다.

"뛰어내릴 거면 빨리 뛰어내리지, 저게 뭐야?"

"뛰어내릴 용기도 없으면서 왜 올라갔어?"

이런 험악한 말들이 귀에 들어가면 자살시도자들은 십중팔구 뛰어내리게 된다. 가느다란 희망의 끈마저 뚝 끊어버리는 차가운 말들이기 때문이다. 정말 일촉즉발의 상황이다.

그때 어디선가 한 중년 남자가 나타나 경찰로부터 확성기를 건네받는다. 설득전문가다.

"이봐요, 젊은이. 젊은이는 이 세상 아무도 젊은이 속마음을 모른다고 생각하죠? 가족들을 먹여 살리기 위해 발버둥쳤지만, 더 이상 손 쓸 수 있는 방법은 없다고 생각하죠?"

남자의 입에서 갑자기 뜻밖의 말이 나온다.

"당신이 그걸 어떻게 알아?"

설득전문가가 다시 말을 잇는다.

"맞아요. 이 세상 아무도 젊은이가 안고 있는 고통과 배신감을 모를 거라고 생각할 겁니다. 열심히 일했지만 직장에서 어이없이 쫓겨나고, 아내도 위로는 못해줄망정 아이를 데리고 도망치고. 게다가 친구들까지 등을 돌리고."

"맞아. 이 더러운 세상, 믿을 놈은 한 놈도 없어!"

남자의 목소리가 흔들리기 시작한다.

"그래요. 믿을 사람 아무도 없다는 생각이 들 수밖에 없을 거요. 모든 걸 끝장내고 영원히 쉬고 싶은 생각밖에 안 들 거요."

남자가 돌연 흐느끼기 시작한다. 그도 악한 사람은 아니었다. 단지 직장에서 못된 상사를 만났고, 차가운 아내와 결혼했고, 얄팍한 친구들을 사귄 게 죄였다.

"도대체 직장에선 어떤 일이 있었던 겁니까? 젊은이를 해고시킨 작자는 대체 어떻게 되먹은 인간이었나요?"

남자는 드디어 엉엉 울기 시작한다. 설득전문가가 슬그머니 사다리차에 오른다. 남자에게 다가가며 말을 계속한다.

"젊은이, 실컷 울어보세요. 나도 그런 억울한 일을 당해 울어본 적이 있다오."

사다리차가 트러스트에 닿는 순간, 설득전문가가 두 손을 뻗어 마치 어린아이를 얼싸안으려는 듯 남자의 두 손을 덥석 감싸 잡는다.

이 남자는 왜 뛰어내리지 않았을까? 설득전문가는 어떤 해답도 제시하지 않았다. 단지 그 남자의 감정을 거울처럼 비춰주어 그가 자신의 감

184

정을 객관적으로 바라보도록 했을 뿐이다. 바라보는 순간 자신을 집어삼킬 듯했던 거대한 감정 덩어리도 맥없이 사그라졌다.

반박하면 반발한다

평소 툭하면 아들 자랑인 50대 중반의 한 여선배가 어느 날 식사를 하다가 불쑥 이런 말을 꺼냈다.

"우리 아들 형철이가 말이야. 갑자기 자살하고 싶다는데 도대체 어떻게 해야지?"

그녀의 목소리에 공포가 배어 있었다. 형철이는 서울의 명문의대에 다닌다. 얼굴도 잘생기고 키도 훤칠한데다 공부까지 잘한다고 마냥 자랑스러워하던 아들이다. 그런데 그게 아니었다. 대학에 1년쯤 다니고 나서부터 아들이 이상증세를 보이기 시작했다. 공부하러 책상 앞에만 앉으면 가슴이 두근거리고 머리가 터질 듯 아파서 도저히 집중하지 못한다는 거였다.

"엄마, 의대 공부는 못할 것 같아요. 제 적성이 아니에요."

그녀는 속이 터질 것 같았다. 어떻게 고생고생 공부시켜 집어넣은 대학인데, 1년 만에 하차하도록 내버려둘 수는 없는 노릇이었다. 어떻게든 위기만 넘기면 된다고 생각했다. 엄마가 다그치자 아들도 꾹 참고 억지로 몇 개월 더 다녔다. 공부는 형편없이 뒤쳐졌다. 그러다가 난데없이 날벼락을 터뜨렸다.

"엄마, 인생은 살 만한 가치가 없는 것 같아요. 엄마만 없었다면 이미

자살하고 말았을 거예요."

그녀는 공황상태에 빠졌다. 아들이 그런 극단적인 생각까지 할 줄은
미처 몰랐다.

"아니야. 넌 똑똑하고 인물 좋고 탁월한 의사가 될 사람이야. 넌 참 행
복한 거야. 그런 생각은 꿈에도 하지 마."

그녀는 어떻게든 삶의 의욕을 북돋아 줄 양으로 이렇게 말했다. 하지
만 그녀가 그런 식으로 말하면 말할수록 아들은 오히려 더욱 큰 절망에
빠져들었다. 이제는 아예 학교도 가지 않으려 들었다. 나는 그녀의 설득
방법에 문제가 있다는 걸 금방 알아챘다.

"선배가 그렇게 말하면 형철이는 더 좌절감을 느낄 수밖에 없죠. 선배
의 말은 형철이의 아픔을 받아들이는 게 아니라 거꾸로 반박하는 거니까
요."

형철이는 책상 앞에만 앉으면 부정적 생각이 한꺼번에 마치 봇물 터
진 듯 밀려드는 '봇물 현상(flooding)'을 겪고 있었다. 공부에 넌더리가 난
머릿속의 어린아이가 책상만 보면 빨간 '불쾌' 신호를 켜놓는 것이었다.
그런데 엄마가 이 빨간불을 꺼줄 생각은 하지 않고 자신의 말을 반박하기
만 하니 아들은 더욱 막다른 골목에 들어섰다는 생각에 빠질 수밖에….
아들이 바라는 건 엄마가 자신의 정신적 고민과 고통을 공감하고 이해해
달라는 것뿐이었다.

며칠 후 선배로부터 전화가 걸려왔다. 우리가 대화를 나눈 그날 밤, 그
녀는 아들 방에 들어가 슬며시 손을 잡고 말했다.

"형철아, 네 마음을 아무도 몰라줘서 고통스러웠지? 자나깨나 로봇처
럼 책상 앞에만 달라붙어 있어야 하니, 이러려고 대학 들어왔나 하는 생

각도 들고 넌더리가 났지? 머리는 쪼개질 거 같은데 공부만 하라고 을러대는 엄마아빠가 야속하고 비정하게 느껴졌지? 네 말대로 인생은 힘겹고 고통스러운 순간도 참 많아. 나도 그럴 때가 있었단다. 너도 지금 그 힘겨운 순간을 맞은 것 같구나. 엄마한테 네 가슴속에 있는 고통을 털어놓아보렴. 내가 친구가 돼줄게."

그 말을 들으며 형철이는 눈물을 주르륵 쏟았다. 엄마가 자신의 마음을 거부하지 않고 받아들이자 아들의 빨간불도 꺼졌다. 그러고는 조금씩 입을 열기 시작했다. 다음날도 그녀는 아들의 고민을 부인하지 않고 받아들여 바라보도록 했다. 그러면서 자살 충동도 사라졌다. 형철이의 어린아이는 뾰족한 해결책을 원하는 게 아니라 자신의 고통을 털어내고 싶었던 것이다.

머릿속의 어린아이는 진짜 어린아이와 똑같다. 외면하지 않고 정면으로 받아들여 따뜻하게 바라보면 저절로 잠잠해진다.

우리 둘째 아이가 초등학교 1학년이었던 때의 일이다. 오후에 회사로 아들이 전화를 걸어왔다. 잔뜩 울먹이는 목소리였다.

"아빠, 아빠 때문에 학교에서 창피당했어!"

"아니, 왜?"

가슴이 철렁했다. 퇴근해 자초지종을 알아보니 좀 어이가 없었다. 학교 수업시간에 크리스마스 화환을 만든다고 해서 전날 밤 아이와 함께 문방구에서 몇 가지 장식물을 샀다. 금방울, 장식용 색깔 테이프, 장식용 별 등이었다. 그리고 집에서 철사로 화환 원형을 만들고 신문지를 돌돌 말아 철사를 휘감았다. 이튿날 아이는 준비물들을 챙겨 학교에 갔다. 하지만 학교에 가서 당황하고 말았다. 다른 아이들의 장식물들은 우리 아이와는 비교가 안 될 정도로 휘황찬란하고 요란했기 때문이다. 결국 화살은 준비물들을 초라하게 챙겨준 나에게 돌아왔다. 나는 아이를 이렇게 위로해주었다.

"괜찮아. 사람마다 크리스마스 화환 만드는 생각이 다 달라. 요란하게 만드는 아이도 있고, 좀 수수하게 만드는 아이도 있는 거지 뭐. 그게 그렇게 큰 문제는 아니지 않니?"

"아니야. 아빠는 몰라서 그래. 다른 아이들이 얼마나 많이 준비해왔는지 아빠는 몰라."

아이는 더욱 씩씩거렸다. 다시 생각해보니 나의 대처방법이 틀렸다는 걸 깨달았다. 아이의 아미그달라는 체면이 깎였다고 판단해 '불쾌' 신호를 켜놓았다. 그 신호를 꺼주는 게 급선무였다. 그 생각은 안 하고 아이의 분노를 부인하기만 했으니 아이가 더욱 화를 내는 건 당연했던 것이다.

"그래, 다른 아이들은 다 멋진 걸 많이 갖고 왔나 보구나. 너 혼자서만 조금밖에 챙겨가지 않았으니 당연히 속이 많이 상하지. 아빠라도 속이 많이 상했을 거야. 다음엔 좀더 많이 챙겨가자. 알았지?"

이렇게 말하자 아이는 고개를 끄떡였다. 금방 기분이 풀려 웃음을 터뜨리며 함께 놀았다. 아이가 원하는 건 큰 게 아니었다. 자신의 머릿속에 쌓인 불만을 따뜻하게 바라보고 이해해달라는 것뿐이었다. 바라보는 것만으로 기분이 저절로 풀리는 것이다.

가까이 지내는 지인 중 하나가 맏딸을 먼 지방대학에 입학시킨 뒤 갑자기 우울증에 걸렸다. 기운이 뚝 떨어지고 매사에 의욕을 잃었다. 새벽 늦게까지 뒤척이다 간신히 잠들곤 했다. 통통하던 얼굴도 쏙 빠져 홀쭉해졌다. 참 이상한 일이었다. 평소 활달하고 에너지가 넘치던 그녀였다.

"딸이 떨어져 나가 서운하긴 하지. 하지만 내게 뭔가 문제가 있는 게 분명해."

그녀가 맥없이 말했다.

"그러게요. 방학이 돌아오면 또 만날 텐데."

그녀는 돌연 어머니 얘기를 꺼냈다. 이미 40여 년 전에 세상을 떠난 어머니였다. 뭔가 문제가 있는 것 같았다.

"어머니는 참 좋은 분이셨지. 내가 열두 살 때였어. 초등학교 교사였던 어머니는 학교 운동장에서 학생들의 경주를 지켜보고 계셨어. 난 반드시 1등 해서 어머니를 기쁘게 해드리고 싶었거든."

그녀가 온 힘을 다해 달리던 중 어머니 쪽에서 돌연 소란이 이는 게 느껴졌다. 경주를 끝내고 가보니 어머니가 쓰러져 있었고, 사람들이 부산하게 움직이고 있었다. 그녀는 접근하려 했지만, 다른 사람들이 막았다. 이 대목을 말하면서 그녀의 눈이 그렁그렁해졌다.

"그때 난 들었어. 어머니가 사라져가는 목소리로 '누가 어서 신부님 좀 불러주세요'라고 말하는 것을. 어머니는 독실한 가톨릭 신자였거든. 그게 내가 들은 어머니의 마지막 목소리였어."

어머니는 급성 심장마비에 걸려 앰뷸런스가 채 도착하기도 전에 운동장에서 숨지고 말았다.

"내겐 한이 남아 있어. 어머니를 그렇게 비명에 잃고도 단 한 번도 제대로 울어본 적도 없으니까. 아버지가 워낙 엄하셨거든. '너희 어머니는 너희가 우는 걸 원치 않아. 강인하게 살아가야지'라고 말씀하시곤 하셨어. 그래서 우리는 장례식장에서조차 실컷 울어보지 못했어."

그녀가 솟아오르는 눈물을 억누르며 말했다.

"울음을 참지 마세요. 지금 맘껏 울어보세요."

말이 떨어지기 무섭게 그녀가 울먹이기 시작했다. 그러더니 돌연 '헉' 하는 소리와 함께 울음이 터져 나왔다. 얼마나 참았던 울음이었을까? 울음소리는 점점 커지더니 봇물이 터진 듯 걷잡을 수 없었다. 어찌나 슬프게 우는지 옆에서 지켜보는 나도 저절로 눈물이 나왔다. 그녀가 마침내 울음을 멈췄다.

"슬픔도 분노처럼 꽉 억눌러놓고 있으면 병이 된대요. 수십 년 전 장례식장에서 못 울었던 울음이 단 한 번으로 가라앉지는 않을 것 같네요. 실컷 울어보세요. 매일 밤 잠자리에 들기 전에도 울고, 어머니 묘지에 가서도 실컷 울어보세요."

그러고 나서 2주가 흘렀다. 그녀는 전혀 딴 사람으로 변해 있었다. 예전처럼 생기에 넘쳤고 얼굴엔 화색이 돌았다.

"그날 집에 돌아간 뒤 온종일 정말 목청이 터지도록 울었어. 어머니의 죽음에 대해 남편과 딸아이들에게도 다 털어놓고. 그날 밤엔 울면서 잠들었지."

이튿날 그녀는 개운한 마음으로 아침을 맞았다. 우울 증상은 거짓말처럼 싹 사라졌다.

"거참 신통한 일이야. 실컷 울었더니 몸과 마음이 새 사람처럼 달라지던걸. 의사가 이젠 우울증 약 안 먹어도 된대."

"정말 놀랍네요. 우울증이 하루 만에 싹 나아버리다니."

그녀가 맏딸과 떨어져 지내는 게 그토록 힘들었던 것도 바로 응어리진 슬픔 때문이었다. 그녀의 5세 유아는 어머니의 갑작스런 죽음에 충격을 받아 빨간불을 켜놓고 있었다. 하지만 그녀는 그걸 꺼줘야 한다는 생각은 아예 안 하고 40년간 억지로 짓눌러 놓고만 있었으니 응어리가 질 수밖에…. 응어리진 슬픔은 울음과 함께 털려나갔다.

위기를 기회로 뒤집는 설득 원리

머릿속의 5세 유아 아미그달라는 걸핏하면 "불쾌" 신호를 켜댄다. 이렇게 상대의 머릿속에 "불쾌" 신호가 켜져 있으면 내가 아무리 그럴싸한 말을 해도 먹히지 않는다. 따라서 상대를 설득할 땐 "불쾌" 신호를 꺼주는 게 최우선이다. 꺼주는 방법은 아주 간단하다. 불쾌한 감정을 바라보는 것, 즉 외면하지 않고 따뜻하게 인정해주는 것이다. 이것이 모든 설득의 핵심원리다. 이를 이용하면 구제불능의 위기 상황도 단숨에 값진 기회로 반전시킬 수 있다. 학생들에게 강의했던 내용 중 일부를 소개한다.

C 학 점 을   A+ 학 점 으 로   돌 려 놓 기

어느 날 한 여학생이 들어오자마자 스스럼없이 넋두리부터 늘어놓았다.

"선생님, 입사시험에서 또 떨어졌어요. 벌써 일곱 번째예요."

그녀만 떨어진 게 아니었다. 대부분 학생들이 벌써 몇 차례씩 고배를 마셨다. 그해 웬만한 대기업들의 취업경쟁률은 1,000 대 1이 넘는 곳이 많았다. 불과 열 명의 신입사원을 뽑는 방송사에도 시험을 쳤지만 지원자가 9,000명 넘게 몰려들었다.

여학생이 주저주저 물었다.

"선생님, 2학년 때 제 점수가 엉망이에요. 대부분 C 아니면 B거든요. 면접관이 왜 성적이 그리 나쁘냐고 물으면 뭐라고 해야죠?"

정말 큰일이 아닐 수 없었다. 면접시험 때마다 면접관들이 2학년 때 점수를 문제 삼으니 취직이 될 리 없었다. '학점이 뭐 그리 대수인가?' 하는 안이한 생각으로 동아리 활동에만 매달렸던 게 후회막급이었다. 학생들에게 어떻게 그런 위기에서 벗어나겠느냐고 되물었더니 대개 이런 식의 답변을 했다.

"아버님 병구완 때문에 성적이 나빴다고 하면 어떨까요?"

"학비를 벌려고 파트타임으로 일하느라 공부를 못했다고 하면 되지 않을까요?"

이런 핑계에 면접관이 넘어갈까? 면접관이 성적을 따지는 이유는 무엇인가? 면접관의 5세 유아는 '성적이 저렇게 나쁘다니? 불성실한 학생 아니야?' 하는 의구심으로 빨간불을 켜놓고 있다. 이 빨간불을 꺼놓지 않고 구구하게 설명해봐야 면접관의 귀에는 변명으로밖에 들리지 않는다.

"제 점수가 나빠서 우려되시죠? 사실 저 자신도 그런 걱정 많이 했습니다."

이렇게 먼저 아미그달라를 달래줘야 한다. 이 간단한 한 마디로 빨간불이 꺼진다. 그런 다음 성적보다 더 가치 있는 것을 언급하라.

"솔직히 분명한 인생목표를 세우지 못하고 한동안 방황했습니다. 대학 공부도 피상적으로 보였죠. 그래서 대신 많은 책을 읽으며 생각을 거

듭했습니다. 그 결과 인생 목표가 뚜렷해졌고 더욱 강한 내가 될 수 있었어요. 학교 점수는 나빴지만 내면은 가득 차올랐죠. 그 방황기가 없었다면 하루하루 최선을 다해 살아가는 현재의 나는 존재하지 않을 겁니다."

이런 말을 듣고 누군들 깊은 인상을 받지 않을 수 있겠는가? 치명적인 약점이 강점으로 둔갑하는 순간이다. 번번이 고배를 마시던 여학생은 정말 그 방법으로 다행히 다음 면접시험을 무사히 통과했다. 머릿속의 5세 유아는 이처럼 단순하다.

이번엔 당신이 한 작은 회사의 사장이라고 가정해보자. 출장을 보냈던 두 직원이 아주 흡사한 사고를 일으켰다. 첫째 직원은 돌아와 이렇게 인사를 한다.

"사장님, 걱정 많으셨죠? 다행히 잘 해결됐습니다."

둘째 직원은 첫 마디만 약간 다르다.

"사장님, 걱정 마세요. 다행히 잘 해결됐습니다."

그 말이 그 말처럼 들린다. 하지만 당신의 무의식 속에는 두 직원에 대한 평가가 판이하게 갈린다. 첫째 직원에 대한 신뢰가 급상승하게 된다. 왜 그럴까?

직원이 사고를 내면 당신의 아미그달라에는 '불쾌' 신호가 켜진다. "걱정 많으셨죠?"라는 한 마디는 그 불쾌한 감정을 바라보고 인정해주는 말이다. 불쾌감이 싹 지워지고 상대에 대한 호감이 솟아오른다. 반면 "걱정 마세요"라는 말은 불쾌감의 존재를 부정한다. 아미그달라의 '불쾌' 신호가 여전히 켜져 있다. 우리가 일상에서 별생각 없이 툭툭 내뱉는 간단한 말 한 마디의 작은 차이가 우리에 대한 평가나 인상을 결정짓고 나아가 인생까지 가를 수 있는 것이다.

아직 '설마' 하는 생각이 남아 있는가? 미국 유타 대학의 워너(Carol Warner) 교수는 학생들이 강의실 쓰레기통에 빈 깡통을 함부로 버리는 걸 보고 이런 실험을 해보았다. 먼저 강의실 쓰레기통에 스티커를 붙여보았다.

"빈 깡통은 버리지 마세요! 1층 입구의 재활용 쓰레기통에 버리세요!"

하지만 고분고분 응하는 학생은 고작 40퍼센트에 불과했다. 그래서 스티커에 딱 한 문장을 덧붙여보았다.

"빈 깡통은 버리지 마세요! 1층 입구의 재활용 쓰레기통에 버리세요! 귀찮겠지만, 중요한 일입니다!"

그랬더니 학생들의 재활용 참여율이 무려 80퍼센트로 껑충 뛰어올랐다. 왜 그랬을까? 학생들이 빈 깡통을 재활용하려면 일부러 1층 입구까지 가야 한다. 그들의 아미그달라는 1층에 버리라는 명령식 문장에 '불쾌' 신호를 켠다. 워너 교수는 이 불쾌감의 존재를 하나의 문장으로 인정해주고 어루만져주었다. 불쾌 신호가 꺼지니 마음이 열렸고, 그러다 보니 자연히 재활용 참여율이 높아질 수밖에!

못난 외모를 장점으로 바꿔놓은 한 마디

나도 언젠가 입사시험 면접관으로 들어갔던 적이 있다. 많은 지원자들 가운데 지금도 기억에 남는 사람이 있다. 그녀는 누가 봐도 외모가 많이 뒤진다는 평가를 받을 게 뻔했다. 면접관들의 아미그달라는 '저런 얼굴로 감히…'라는 '불쾌' 신호를 켜두었을 것이다. 하지만 그녀는 당당하게 자신을 이렇게 소개했다.

"제 첫인상을 보시고 실망하셨죠? 저런 얼굴로 어떻게 감히 방송국에 지원하나 하고요. 첫인상은 타고난 거라 저도 어쩔 수 없어요. 하지만 끝 인상만큼은 책임질 수 있습니다. 노력으로 할 수 있는 일, 뒷바라지가 필요한 일, 끝 인상을 책임질만한 일은 무조건 자신 있습니다."

나는 속으로 감동했다. 그녀는 그 몇 마디로 면접관들의 '불쾌' 신호를 일거에 꺼버렸다. 그런 다음 자신의 외적인 약점을 상쇄시키고도 남는 내적인 장점을 언급했다. 이것이 약점을 장점으로 뒤바꿔놓는 마술이다. 나중에 알고 보니 그녀는 당당히 합격했고, 지금도 그 부서에서 능력을 인정받고 있다는 얘기를 들었다.

약점은 숨기려 들면 오히려 더 커 보인다. 반면 스스로 드러내면 솔직해 보일 뿐 아니라 강점으로 둔갑할 수 있다. 그러기 위해서는 반드시 약점을 보완해주는 관련된 장점을 언급해줘야 한다. 약점과 무관한 장점은 언급해봐야 아무런 도움이 되지 못한다. 더 구체적인 사례를 보자. 어느 음식점의 다음 세 가지 광고 중 어느 게 가장 마음에 드는지 생각해보라.

1. "우리 음식점은 최고의 인테리어와 최신 냉난방 설비를 갖추고 있습니다. 분위기도 아늑합니다."
2. "우리 음식점은 최고의 인테리어와 최신 냉난방 설비를 갖추고 있습니다. 하지만 전용 주차장이 없어서 주차가 불편할 수는 있습니다."
3. "우리 음식점은 전용 주차장이 없을 만큼 공간은 작습니다. 하지만 작은 데서 오는 특유의 아늑함을 만끽할 수 있습니다."

첫 번째 광고는 자랑만 늘어놓아 신뢰가 가지 않는다. 반면 두 번째와 세 번째는 스스로 약점도 함께 언급해 솔직해 보인다. 두 번째 광고를 다시 보라. 장단점을 동시에 언급했지만, 장점과 단점 간에 아무런 관련성이 없다. 단점을 상쇄시키는 관련된 장점이 없다. 이번엔 세 번째 광고를 보라. 단점을 거론한 뒤 그 단점과 관련된 장점, 즉 단점을 상쇄시키는 특징을 함께 거론했다. 그래야만 단점이 장점이 된다.

실제로 사회과학자인 보너(Gerd Bohner) 박사가 조사해보니 사람들은 세 번째 광고가 가장 호소력 있다고 대답했다. 왜 그럴까? 음식점에 가고 싶어하는 고객의 관점에서 그 음식점의 단점을 보면 아미그달라에 '불쾌' 신호가 켜진다. 하지만 그 단점을 보완해주는 관련된 장점을 보면 불쾌 신호가 해제되면서 호감을 갖게 된다.

"흠, 음식점이 작긴 하지만 작아서 오히려 아늑하군."

그럼 같은 물건을 경쟁사보다 30퍼센트나 더 비싸게 팔아야 하는 상황이라면 어떻게 말하는 게 좋을까?

1. "사실 이 신제품은 기존제품보다 30퍼센트나 더 비쌉니다. 하지만 훨씬 빠르고 공간도 덜 차지하죠."

2. "사실 이 신제품은 기존제품보다 30퍼센트나 더 비쌉니다. 하지만 내구성과 전기사용량을 따지면 비싼 비용을 뽑고도 남죠."

정답은 당연히 2번이다. 비용에 관한 단점을 언급했으면 역시 비용에 관한 장점을 언급해야만 고객의 아미그달라에 켜진 불쾌 신호를 해제시킬 수 있다. 개인적인 실수도 마찬가지다. 실수를 어물어물 덮어버리려 들면 실수가 더 커져 보인다. 그보다는 실수를 솔직하게 인정하고 그 실수를 바로잡을 수 있는 능력이 있음을 보여주면 실수가 오히려 재산이 된다.

무경력을 최고 경력으로 둔갑시키기

자신을 30대 초반이라고 밝힌 한 가정주부가 이런 이메일을 보내왔다. "저는 선생님의 강의를 듣는 대학생의 언니예요. 동생이 요즘 '머릿속 5세 유아 바라보기' 강의를 듣고 있다고 자랑하더군요. 요점을 말씀드리면 저는 고등학교를 졸업하고 집안일을 도우며 지냈어요. 아버지 병구완 때문에 직장 다니기도 어려웠습니다. 아버지가 돌아가신 후 20대 초반에 결혼해서 아이 둘을 열심히 키워왔죠. 아이들은 이제 10세, 12세로 제가 직장을 다녀도 괜찮을 것 같다고 생각했어요. 남편 봉급만으로는 생활이 빠듯하기도 하고. 그래서 틈틈이 방송통신대학 강의도 들었습니다.

그런데 문제가 생겼어요. 입사 면접시험 때마다 실무경험이 없다는 게 어김없이 약점으로 지적되는 겁니다. 이 약점을 어떻게 해야죠?"

정말 그렇다. 아이들을 키운 뒤 뒤늦게 취직하고자 하는 주부들의 최대 약점은 실무경력이 없다는 거다. 면접관은 틀림없이 그 약점을 짚고 넘어가기 마련이다.

"이력서를 보니 일해본 경험이 전혀 없으시네요?"

경험 많은 경쟁자들도 많은데 하필 실무경험이 전혀 없는 주부를 써야 할 이유가 뭔가? 이 약점을 어떻게 강점으로 둔갑시킬 것인가? 열쇠는 역시 면접관의 머릿속에 든 아미그달라를 바라보고 달래주는 것이다.

"제가 직장생활 경험이 없어 우려하시는 점 잘 알고 있습니다. 직장경험이 없는 게 사실이죠."

이 단순한 한 마디로 면접관의 아미그달라에 켜졌던 빨간불은 꺼진다. 당신은 이 기회를 놓치지 말고 재빨리 약점을 강점으로 전환시켜야만 한다. 그러려면 직장경험보다 한 차원 높은 경험을 언급하라.

"아이 둘을 키우면서 틈틈이 공부해 방송통신대학도 졸업하고 취업준비도 해왔어요. 직장경험은 없지만, 아이들을 키우고 살림을 책임지면서 끈기와 열정, 사랑, 인내 등 더욱 값진 인간적 경험을 쌓았습니다."

직장 경험보다는 인간적 경험이 한 차원 더 높게 들린다. 논리가 아니라 가슴에 호소하는 것이다. 또한 정직하고 성실하며 신뢰감을 주는 답변이기도 하다.

상사와의 말다툼 끝에 직장을 때려치운 한 선배가 있었다. 그는 젊은 혈기에 바른말을 하고 뛰쳐나갔지만, 막상 새 직장을 잡으려니 여간 어려운 게 아니었다. 면접시험을 볼 때마다 그 문제가 꼬리표처럼 따라다녔다.

"그 좋은 직장을 뚜렷한 이유도 없이 왜 그만둔 거죠? 잘린 건가요?"

그 선배는 상사에 대한 반감이 아직 생생했던지라 이런 식으로 대답하곤 했다.

"그 상사는 부하직원들의 의견에 귀를 기울일 줄 몰랐습니다. 독단적이고 몹시 권위주의적이었죠. 다른 직원들도 불만이 많았습니다. 그래서 제가 참고 참다가 용기를 내서 이견을 제시했던 거였어요."

정의의 사도처럼 의로운 말로 들린다. 하지만 당신이라면 이런 사람을 채용할 것인가? 아마 고개를 내저을 것이다. 언제 당신의 권위에 도전하려 들지 모르기 때문이다. 그 선배는 번번이 취직에 실패하자 결국 어렵사리 유학길에 올랐다.

당신이 그 선배였다면 어떻게 대답하는 게 좋았을까?

면접관은 당신이 권위에 도전적인 성격인지 의구심을 품고 있다. 아미그달라에 빨간불이 켜져 있다. 이 불을 꺼주지 않고 구구한 말을 늘어놔 봐야 귀에 들어가지 않는다. 빨간불부터 꺼줘야 한다.

"제가 혹시 권위에 도전적인 성격이 아닌지 걱정되시죠?"

이 한 마디를 먼저 꺼내놓는 것만으로 빨간불은 꺼진다. 그런 다음 그 쓰라린 약점이 왜 장점이 됐는지 설득시켜야 한다. 가장 좋은 방법은 약점을 통해 과거의 '철없던 나'가 현재의 '더 나은 나'로 변신했음을 납득시키는 것이다.

"사실 저는 당시 경험도 없고 독선적이고 남의 의견을 경청할 줄도 잘 몰랐습니다. 설사 상사가 이치에 맞지 않는 말을 해도 이를 상사의 입장에서 다시 생각할 줄 아는 현명함도 없었습니다. 다행히 과거의 뼈아픈 실수는 저 자신을 돌아볼 수 있는 귀중한 계기가 됐습니다. 그런 일이 없었다면 모나지 않고 남의 시각에서 문제를 바라볼 수 있는 '더 나은 지금의 나'는 탄생하지 못했을 겁니다."

이렇게 말하면 직장에서 잘렸던 게 안 잘렸던 것보다 오히려 장점으로 비친다. 상대의 머릿속에 든 5세 어린아이는 마치 전기 스위치 같다. 불쾌하면 켜지고, 바라보면 꺼지니 말이다.

상대가 나를 좋아하도록 만드는 한 마디

당신이 아리따운 두 여성과 사귀고 있다고 가정해보자. 당신은 누구를 선택해야 할지 막판까지 갈팡질팡한다. 두 여성이 여러모로 너무나 닮은꼴이기 때문이다. 그러자 화가 치민 두 여성이 마침내 최후통첩을 선언한다.

"어서 마음을 정하세요. 삼각관계를 이대로 지속할 수 없어요."

먼저 여성 A가 당신에게 이런 말을 하며 떠난다.

"나를 좋아하는 이유 열 가지만 말해보세요."

여성 B는 좀 달리 말하며 자리를 뜬다.

"나를 좋아하는 이유 딱 한 가지만 말해보세요."

당신은 일주일간 고민한다. 과연 누구를 택해야 하나? 당신의 머릿속에는 두 여성의 마지막 이미지가 각기 다르게 떠오른다. 그들은 둘 다 "나를 좋아하는 이유를 말해보라"는 말을 남기고 헤어졌지만, 당신의 잠재의식 속에 한 여성은 약간 골치 아픈 인상으로 기억됐고, 다른 여성은 정다운 인상으로 새겨졌다. 정다운 인상을 남긴 건 누구일까?

뱅케(Michaela Wanke) 교수가 실시한 실험에 그 해답이 담겨 있다. 그는 A그룹의 대학생들에게 BMW 자동차 회사의 이런 광고를 보여주었다.

"BMW와 벤츠 중 어느 차를 타시겠습니까? BMW를 선택해야 하는 이유는 여러 가지가 있습니다. 열 가지를 대보시겠습니까?"

B그룹의 대학생들에게도 비슷한 문구의 광고를 보여주었다.

"BMW와 벤츠 중 어느 차를 타시겠습니까? BMW를 선택해야 하는 이유는 여러 가지가 있습니다. 딱 한 가지만 대보시겠습니까?"

어느 그룹이 BMW를 더 많이 타겠다고 대답했을까? B그룹에서 BMW를 타겠다는 대답이 압도적으로 많았다. 왜 그랬을까?

광고문구는 비슷하지만 풍기는 이미지가 다르다. "좋아하는 이유 열 가지를 대보라"고 하면 골치 아프다는 이미지가 형성된다. 아미그달라에 불쾌 신호가 들어온다. 반면 "딱 한 가지만 대보라"고 하면 정말 좋아하는 이미지가 선명하게 떠오른다. 아미그달라에 유쾌 신호가 켜진다. 사람들은 이처럼 단순하고 선명한 이미지를 좋아한다.

이미지는 오래 남는다. 만일 당신이 사귀던 여성과 어쩔 수 없이 오랜

이별을 해야 한다면 헤어질 때 "나에 대한 가장 좋은 추억을 딱 한 가지만 말해봐요"라고 말하라. 그럼 그녀는 가장 좋은 추억으로 당신을 기억하게 된다.

발음도 그렇다. 사람들은 발음하기 어려운 단어나 이름보다 발음하기 쉬운 단어나 이름을 더 좋아한다. 똑같은 편지라도 필체가 나쁠수록 설득력이 떨어진다. 나쁜 필체에 대한 거부감을 편지 내용이 어려운 탓이라고 착각한다. 또한 똑같은 말이라도 운율이 맞는 말이 내용도 맞는 것처럼 들린다. 아미그달라는 지극히 단순한 잣대로 '유쾌'와 '불쾌'를 결정짓는다는 사실을 기억하라.

내 요청을 꼼짝없이 받아들이도록 하는 법

특파원 시절 노근리 미군만행 사건과 관련해 미국 육군장관을 인터뷰하고 싶었다. 그가 그 사건에 관한 조사를 총 지휘하는 미국 국방부 내의 최고 책임자였기 때문이다. 하지만 녹록지 않은 일이었다. 왜냐하면 미국 기자들과 AP, 로이터 등 세계적인 통신사들도 나와 똑같은 생각을 갖고 이미 인터뷰를 신청해놓은 상황이었기 때문이다. 서면으로 신청해놓은 인터뷰 요청에 대한 답변은 백년하청이었다.

나는 이제나저제나 하다가 육군장관실 대변인에게 전화를 걸었다.

"한국의 MBC 특파원입니다. 인터뷰 요청한 거 어떻게 됐나요?"

"검토중이니까 기다리세요."

의례적인 답변이었다. 나는 일단 전화를 끊고 곰곰이 생각해보았다.

그리고 이튿날 다시 전화를 걸었다.

"오늘도 백악관, 국방부, 국무부 등 세 곳에 전화를 걸었는데 정확한 말을 할 수 있는 곳은 오로지 여기뿐이라고 합니다. 육군장관의 해명이 늦어지니 한국에서는 불필요한 의혹만 자꾸 증폭되고 있어요. 미국에 대한 불신도 커져가고 있구요. 굉장히 절박한 상황입니다."

그러자 대변인은 한 시간쯤 후 전화를 해주겠다고 했다. 마음 졸이며 한 시간을 기다리자 정말 전화가 왔다.

"다음주 월요일 오후 3시에 육군장관실로 오세요."

나는 날아갈 듯 기뻤다. 그는 수백 명의 다른 나라 특파원들을 제치고 왜 하필 내 부탁을 들어주었을까?

남에게 도움을 요청할 때는 그로 하여금 '내가 꼭 도와주지 않으면 안 되겠구나' 하는 불가피성을 느끼도록 하는 게 열쇠다. 예를 들어 목발을 짚은 사람이 책을 떨어뜨리면 옆에 있던 사람은 주저 없이 책을 주워준다. 아무런 보상을 기대하지 않고 선뜻 도와주는 건 '내가 도와주지 않으면 어쩔 수 없는 상황이구나' 하고 불가피성을 느끼기 때문이다. 도와주는 사람의 아미그달라는 이 순간 어떤 기분일까?

'저 사람은 내 도움 없이는 꼼짝할 수 없는 상황이군.'

하늘로 치솟는 존재 가치를 느낀다. 주저 없이 도와주고 싶은 충동을 느낀다.

"이것도 해보고 저것도 해보고 안 해본 게 없어요. 그런데도 안 돼요. 기댈 수 있는 건 당신밖에 없네요."

이런 말을 들으면 누구든 '난 특별한 능력을 가진 사람'이라는 착각에 빠진다.

반즈(Richard Barnes) 등 위스콘신 대학 심리학자들은 대학생들에게 이런 실험을 해봤다.

기말시험을 앞두고 한 동료 학생이 당신에게 전화를 걸어온다. 그리고 필기한 심리학 강의 노트를 좀 빌려줄 수 있느냐고 묻는다.

"안녕하세요. 저는 같은 수업을 듣는 학생인데요. 수업내용을 제대로 필기하지 못했어요. 필기하자면 할 수는 있는데, 왜 그런지 필기를 잘 못하겠어요."

"내 전화번호는 어떻게 알아냈죠?"

"출석부에서 봤어요."

당신은 수업시간에 그 학생을 본 것 같기도 하지만 가까이 지내는 사이는 아니다. 이럴 경우 필기 노트를 빌려주겠는가? 아마 주저할 것이다.

그럼 만일 그 학생이 이런 식으로 말했다면 어떨까?

"안녕하세요. 저는 같은 수업을 듣는 학생인데요. 온 힘을 다해 수업을 따라가려 해도 영 역부족이네요. 제가 난청이 심하거든요. 수업이 끝난 뒤 여러 학생들에게 필기한 내용을 물어봤지만 제대로 필기한 사람이 없어요. 그래서 필기를 가장 잘하는 분이라는 말을 듣고 감히 용기를 내서 이렇게 전화를 드렸어요."

이런 식의 말을 들으면 아마 선뜻 도와주고 싶은 생각이 들 것이다. 왜 그럴까? 그 학생이 겪고 있는 상황이 그의 통제밖에 있는 어쩔 수 없는 상황이라고 느껴지기 때문이다.

'저 학생이 스스로 할 수 있는 건 다 해봤는데 영 안 되는 모양이군. 도와줄 사람이 나밖에 없다니 어떻게 외면할 수 있겠어?'

심리학자들은 이처럼 어쩔 수 없는 상황이라는 느낌을 주면 선뜻 도움을 받게 된다는 사실을 여러 차례의 실험을 통해 거듭 확인했다. 하지만 '내가 부탁할 만한 사람들은 많이 있는데, 그래도 당신이 나를 도와주면 고맙겠어'라는 식으로 여러 선택이 가능한 것처럼 들리면 도움을 받기 어렵다. 왜냐하면 꼭 내가 도와주지 않아도 된다면 굳이 내 시간을 빼앗겨야 할 불가피성이 없기 때문이다.

이런 원리는 일상에서도 활용할 수 있다. 당신의 집에 있는 수도꼭지가 고장 났다고 가정해보자. 아무리 낑낑거려보아도 도저히 못 고칠 것 같다. 그래서 기술자인 이웃집 아저씨에게 도움을 청하기로 했다. 어떤 말로 도움을 청해야 할까?

* 부탁 1 : "저희 집 수도꼭지가 고장 났는데 좀 도와주시겠어요?"

이웃집 아저씨는 아마도 "그것 고치려면 시간 좀 걸릴 텐데요. 수선공을 불러보시지 그러세요?" 하고 말할 공산이 크다. 도와달라는 말은 곧 와서 해달라는 강요로 들리기 때문이다. 그의 아미그달라에 '불쾌' 신호가 켜진다.

* 부탁 2 : "저희 집 수도꼭지가 고장 났는데 저희 식구들 힘으로는 도저히 못 고쳐요. 혹시 어떻게 고칠 수 있는지 아세요?"

이 말을 들으면 이웃집 아저씨는 내심 우쭐해질 것이다. 그의 아미그달라에 '유쾌' 신호가 켜진다. 자신의 존재가치를 높이 띄워주기 때문이다. '내가 도와주지 않으면 꼼짝 못할 사람들이군. 불가피한 상황이야'라는 생각이 든다.

타이타닉호가 대서양에서 침몰했을 때 남성승객들은 겨우 20퍼센트밖에 구조되지 않았지만, 여성들은 70퍼센트나 구조됐다고 한다. 또한 3등실 승객들보다 1등실 승객들이 구조된 경우가 2.5배나 더 많았지만, 그럼에도 3등실 여성이 구조된 비율(47퍼센트)이 1등실 남성이 구조된 비율(31퍼센트)보다 높았다. 건장한 남성들보다는 나약한 여성들이 도움의 손길을 더 많이 필요할 거라는 인식이 낳은 차이였다. 심리학에서는 이를 '사회적 책임 규범(social-responsibility norm)'이라고 일컫는다.

상보성 원리로 인생이 갈린다

인생을 가르는 건 단순한 시각 차이

20여 년 전 앞집과 뒷집에 두 아기 엄마가 살고 있었다. 집 근처를 산책하다 보면 그들의 말소리가 흘러나오곤 했다. 그런데 앞집 사는 엄마의 말투는 늘 긍정적이었다. '할 수 있는 것'에 초점을 맞춰 말했다. 반면 뒷집 엄마는 늘 부정적이었다. "할 수 없는 것"에 초점을 맞춰 말했다.

어느 날 아이들이 동네 놀이터에 놀러가고 싶다고 했다. 뒷집 엄마는 이렇게 말했다.

아이 : "놀이터에 놀러가도 돼?"
엄마 : "안 돼. 아직 숙제도 안 했잖아."

똑같은 내용의 말을 앞집 엄마는 긍정적으로 돌려 표현했다.

아이 : "놀이터에 놀러가도 돼?"
엄마: "그럼. 숙제하고 가면 되지."

다음날 우연히 또 대화를 엿듣게 됐다. 이번에는 아이들이 친구 집에 놀러가고 싶다고 했다. 뒷집 엄마는 여느 때처럼 "안 돼"라는 말로 대답했다.

아이 : "엄마, 나 친구 집에 놀러가도 돼?"
엄마 : "안 돼. 5분쯤 있다가 점심 먹어야 해."

앞집 엄마는 어떻게 말하는지 귀를 바짝 기울여보았다.

아이 : "엄마, 나 친구 집에 놀러가도 돼?"
엄마 : "그럼, 물론이지. 5분 뒤 점심 먹고 실컷 놀아라."

20여 년이 지난 후 두 집 아이들은 어떻게 됐을까? 기막힌 우연의 일치인지 두 청년 모두 의대에 진학해 의사가 됐고, 각기 병원도 개업했다. 궁금증이 들어 슬그머니 병원에 들러 환자와의 대화를 엿들어보았다. 때마침 시한부 생명의 말기 암환자와 대화중이었다. 부정적인 말을 듣고 자란 뒷집 청년은 말투 역시 부정적이었다.

환자 : "저는 앞으로 얼마나 살 수 있을까요?"
의사 : "잘해야 6개월밖에 버티지 못하실 겁니다."

그 말을 듣고 몹시 낙담한 환자가 한숨을 푹 내뿜는 소리가 들렸다. 그래서 이번에는 긍정적인 말을 듣고 자란 앞집 청년의 병원에 달려가

보았다. 그도 역시 말기 암환자와 대화중이었다. 하지만 그의 말투는 영 달랐다.

환자 : "저는 앞으로 얼마나 살 수 있을까요?"

의사 : "잘하면 6개월간 가족과 행복한 순간들을 즐길 수 있으실 겁니다."

환자는 황금같이 귀중한 마지막 순간들을 잘 쓰겠노라며 의사에게 연신 허리를 굽혔다. 그로부터 얼마 후 뒷집 청년이 운영하던 병원이 문을 닫았다. 환자들이 모두 긍정적인 말을 해주는 앞집 청년의 병원으로 옮겨갔기 때문이다.

긍정적인 생각을 품고 자라면 긍정적인 사람이 되고. 부정적인 생각을 품고 자라면 부정적인 사람이 된다는 늘 듣는 얘기다. 진부하기 짝이 없는 이야기 같지만, 그 속에 인생을 결정짓는 신기한 원리가 숨겨져 있다.

아래 사진을 보라.

이 사진을 보는 순간 어떤 생각이 스쳐가는가?

"불쌍하다."

"부모의 마음이 얼마나 아플까?"

"양팔이 없으니 뭘 하며 살아갈까?"

아마 이런 연민을 느꼈을 것이다. 하지만 이 부모는 아이에게 자기연민을 심어주지 않았다. 대신 이렇게 가르쳤다.

"양팔이 없어도 할 수 있는 게 많단다. 매일 네가 새롭게 할 수 있는 게 뭔지 찾아보렴."

할 수 없는 건 철저히 무시하고, 오로지 할 수 있는 걸 찾는 데서 기쁨을 얻도록 유도했다. 아이는 할 수 있는 것만 바라보며 자라니 하루하루가 즐겁고 활기에 넘쳤다. 할 수 있는 게 점점 늘어갔다. 그러다 보니 남들이 하는 건 다하며 성장했다. 손 대신 발로 콘택트렌즈를 끼고, 휴대전화 문자도 보낸다. 피아노 연주도 문제없고, 태권도 검은 띠를 딴 유단자이기도 하다. 마침내 정식 비행기 조종사 자격증까지 땄을 때, 사람들의 입은 딱 벌어졌다. 요즘엔 스쿠버 다이빙과 서핑을 배우려는 꿈에 부풀어 있다.

"양팔 없이 그런 걸 할 수 있다는 걸 증명하려는 게 아니에요. 제가 진심으로 하고 싶어서 하는 것뿐이죠."

제시카 칵스_{Jessica Cox}의 이야기다. 양팔을 잃으면 대개 절망에 빠진다. 하지만 양팔이 있으면서도 절망 속에 살아가는 사람들도 부지기수다. 자포자기에 빠져 심지어 자살하는 사람들도 있다. 할 수 있는 걸 바라보지 않고 할 수 없는 것만 바라보기 때문이다.

"캐롤은 숙제를 해야 한다는 걸 기억해요."

헬싱키 대학의 심리학자 에로넨 (Sanna Eronen) 교수는 대학생들에게 다음과 같은 한 컷의 만화를 보여주었다.

캐롤이라는 이름의 한 평범한 여성이 TV를 시청하는 모습이 담긴 지극히 평범한 만화였다. 만화엔 "캐롤은 숙제를 해야 한다는 걸 기억해요"라는 캡션이 쓰여 있었다.

그런 다음 잠시 후 캐롤이 숙제를 해서 교수에게 제출하는 모습이 담긴 다른 만화 한 컷을 또 보여주었다. 교수로부터 숙제에 대한 평가도 받았다고 덧붙여 설명해주었다.

그러고 나서 교수가 학생들에게 물었다.

"여러분은 캐롤이 어떤 사람이라고 생각하나요?"

어떤 학생들은 캐롤이 숙제를 위해 즐겨보던 TV를 끌 줄 아는 부지런하고 똑똑한 여성일 거라고 대답했다. 아마 어려운 숙제도 꽤 잘해낼 것이라고 긍정적으로 평가했다.

"캐롤은 숙제를 해서 교수한테 평가를 받았어요."

하지만 캐롤을 부정적으로 평가하는 학생들도 있었다. 그들은 캐롤이 TV만 보는 게으른 여성이며, 숙제도 쉬운 것만 골라 할 것이라고 부정적으로 응답했다.

아무 감정도 담겨 있지 않은 지극히 중립적인 만화 두 컷을 보고, 어떤 학생들은 긍정적인 감정을 만들어냈고, 또 다른 어떤 학생들은 부정적인 감정을 만들어낸 것이었다. 여기까지는 놀라울 일이 없다. 시각은 사람마다 다르기 마련이니까. 놀라운 일은 훨씬 후에 일어났다.

에로넨 교수는 5년 후 실험에 참가했던 학생들을 추적해보았다. 그런데 캐롤을 부정적으로 평가했던 학생들은 대학을 졸업한 뒤 하나같이 불행한 삶을 살고 있었다. 취직을 못해 백수건달로 지내는 사람이 있는가 하면 직장에서 제대로 풀리지 못해 고민하는 사람들도 있었다. 돈벌이도, 이성관계도 시원치 않았다.

그럼 캐롤을 긍정적으로 평가했던 사람들은 어땠을까? 놀랍게도 하나같이 행복한 삶을 만끽하고 있었다. 좋은 직장에 취직해 좋은 대우를 받으며 승승장구하는 사람들이 많았다. 또, 맘에 드는 이성을 만나 결혼해 아이까지 낳고 보란 듯 살고 있는 사람들도 있었다.

아무 감정도 없는 똑같은 만화를 보고 부정적으로 평가했던 학생들은 불행한 삶을, 긍정적으로 평가했던 학생들은 행복한 삶을 살고 있었다. 신기하지 않은가? 바라보는 시각대로 인생이 펼쳐지는 것은 우연이 아니라 필연인 것이다. 왜 이런 현상이 일어날까?

긍정을 바라보면 부정은 보이지 않는다

다음 쪽의 그림은 흔히 볼 수 있는 것으로 아가씨로 보이기도 하고 노파로 보이기도 한다.

이 흔한 그림 속에도 우주의 진리가 숨겨져 있다.

다시 한 번 살펴보자.

그림을 아가씨로 보는 순간 노파는 의식에서 사라진다. 그렇다고 노파가 머릿속에서 완전히 지워지는 건 아니다. 잠재하고 있다가 노파로 바라보는 순간 표면으로 나타난다. 대신 이번엔 아가씨가 의식에서 사라진다. 하지만 한쪽만 보인다고 해서 그 한쪽이 전부는 아니다. 전체를 이루

아가씨의 옆얼굴로 보면 노파가 안 보이고, 노파의 얼굴로 보면 아가씨가 안 보인다.

는 두 쪽이 서로 보완적 관계에 있다. 그래서 양자물리학에서는 이를 '상보성의 원리(principle of complementarity)'라고 부른다.

뇌파도 TV 전파처럼 전자기파이기 때문에 일어나는 현상이다. 한 가지 것을 두 가지로 동시에 바라보지 못한다. TV가 두 가지 채널을 동시에 내보내지 못하는 원리와 똑같다. KBS를 틀면 MBC가 안 나오고, MBC를 틀면 KBS가 안 나온다.

내가 입사시험에 열 번 떨어졌다 치자.

"제길, 또 실패야. 난 왜 늘 이 모양이지?"

나는 즉각 이런 부정적 감정에 빠져든다. 나는 그게 시험 실패 때문이라고 생각한다. 하지만 정말 그런가? 상황은 아무런 감정이 없다. 철저한 중립이다.

"이번 실패에선 어떤 교훈을 얻을 수 있지?"

이렇게 돌려 생각하면 부정적 감정도 사라진다. 우리는 어떤 상황을 나름대로 해석하고, 거기에 파묻혀 버리는 습성이 있다.

실패는 더 배우라는 우주의 신호다. 모든 실패에는 어김없이 교훈이 들어 있다. 교훈을 잘 배우면 실패 수업은 곧 끝나지만, 교훈을 못 배우면 실패 수업은 자꾸만 되풀이된다.

캘리포니아 대학의 심리학자 루보미르스키(Sonia Lyubomirsky)는 고등학교 졸업반 학생들이 원하는 대학에 지원했다가 떨어졌을 때 어떻게 반응하는지 궁금했다. 그래서 그녀는 "제 인생은 너무나 행복해요"라거나, 정반대로 "제 인생은 너무나 불행해요"라고 시각이 분명한 학생들만 골라 조사해보았다.

예를 들어 어떤 학생이 미국의 최고 명문 프린스턴 대학과 일종의 안전판으로 무명의 한 지방 대학에 동시에 지원서를 냈다고 치자. 결과를 보니 프린스턴 대학에는 떨어지고 지방 대학에는 붙었다. 이럴 경우 평소 불행하다는 학생들은 이렇게 반응했다.

"난 역시 프린스턴 대학 수준은 안 돼. 수준 낮은 무명 대학에나 가는 수밖에 없어."

쉽게 말해 불행한 학생들은 가장 어두운 면에만 초점을 맞췄다. 자신의 실력과 자신이 다니게 될 학교를 전보다 오히려 더 낮게 평가했다.

그럼 평소 행복하다는 학생들은 어땠을까? 그들은 이런 반응을 보였다.

"프린스턴 대학에 못 들어가면 어때? 지방 대학도 알고 보니 재미난 점이 너무 많은걸. 집에서 다니기도 가깝고. 오히려 잘 됐어."

그들은 불행한 학생들과는 정반대로 가장 밝은 면에만 초점을 맞추는 것이었다.

행복한 사람들은 늘 그렇게 살아갈까? 루보미르스키 교수는 한 번 더 실험해보았다.

사람들에게 자신이 가장 좋아하는 후식을 고르도록 했다. 행복한 사람과 불행한 사람이 각기 치즈케이크, 아이스크림, 바나나 파이 순으로

좋아하는 후식을 골랐다고 가정해보자. 교수는 두 사람이 가장 선호하는
치즈케이크 대신 일부러 선호도가 가장 낮은 바나나 파이를 줘봤다.

반응은 판이하게 달랐다. 불행한 사람은 바나나 파이를 받자마자 강
한 거부감을 보였다.

"어휴! 맛이 형편없군! 오늘 후식들은 다 이 모양이겠지?"

그는 바나나 파이뿐 아니라 자신이 선호했던 치즈 케이크를 포함한
후식 전체를 전보다 형편없다고 평가했다. 하지만 행복한 사람의 반응은
완전 딴판이었다.

"바나나 파이도 뜻밖에 맛있네! 오히려 잘 됐어!"

자신이 가장 낮게 평가했던 후식이었지만 일단 그걸 먹게 되자 거기
에 숨겨진 긍정적인 면을 찾아내 즐겼던 것이다. 교수는 행복과 불행은
이처럼 환경이나 운, 혹은 머리가 만들어내는 게 아니라 스스로 창조해내
는 것이라는 사실을 확인했다.

위인으로 추앙받는 사람들은 알고 보면 밝은 면에만 초점을 맞춰놓았

216

던 사람들이다. 잘 알려진 대로 링컨은 40대 후반까지 무려 여덟 번이나 선거에 낙선했고, 사업이나 해볼까 시도했지만 두 번 모두 실패했다. 발명왕 에디슨은 평생 1,093가지나 되는 발명품을 만들어냈지만, 그걸 위해 수십만 차례나 실패했다. 특히 축전지를 발명하기 위해서는 무려 5만 번의 실패를 극복해야 했다. 농구 황제 마이클 조던은 자서전에서 고등학교 농구팀에 지원했다가 거절당하자 집에 돌아가 방문을 걸어 잠그고 온종일 울었다고 술회하고 있다.

"저는 선수생활 중 9,000번이나 넘는 슛에 실패했고, 300차례의 경기에서 졌습니다. 제 손에 동점골을 깨라는 기회가 주어진 게 26차례나 됐지만, 모두 실패했습니다. 평생 수없이 실패했습니다. 그리고 그 때문에 슛을 잘 날릴 수 있게 됐습니다."

톨스토이가 죽은 뒤 그의 방을 정리하던 사람들이 방 안에 빼곡하게 쌓여 있는 실패작들을 보고 놀랐다는 유명한 일화도 있다. 셰익스피어도 평생 154편의 시를 썼는데 성공한 몇 편만 빼고는 형편없는 졸작이었다. 또 다윈은 〈진화론〉 말고 평생 119편의 논문을 발표했고, 프로이트는 650편이나 되는 논문을 발표했다. 음악 신동의 대명사인 모차르트도 평생 무려 600편이나 되는 곡들을 발표했지만, 대부분이 작품성이 형편없어 빛을 보지 못하고 있다는 사실을 사람들은 모르고 있다. 이렇게 심혈을 쏟아 만들어낸 작품들의 99퍼센트 이상이 졸작으로 사장되고, 겨우 나머지 1퍼센트 정도만이 인정받아 위대한 인물로 기억되는 것이다.

크게 성공한 사람들은 하나같이 어둠 속에 숨겨진 밝은 면에 초점을 맞춰놓고 몰입했다. 그러다 보면 밝은 면이 점점 커져서 어두운 면을 완전히 덮어버리게 된다.

장점에 초점을 맞추면 단점이 사라진다

그는 수업시간에 늘 뒷줄에만 앉아 있곤 하던 남학생이었다. 키도 크고 인물도 좋았다. 군대에 다녀와 복학을 해서 다른 학생보다 나이가 두세 살 많았다. 허우대도 멀쩡했다. 그런데도 항상 의욕이 없어 보였다. 졸업 후 진로를 모색하는 일에도 관심이 없어 보일 정도였다.

수업이 끝난 뒤 이런저런 이야기를 나누면서 보니 그는 전형적인 '마마보이'였다. 그래서 혼자서는 아무 일도 못했다. 왜일까? 그와 대화를 나누면서 단서를 잡게 되었다.

"어렸을 때예요. 엄마랑 실내 수영장에 갔었는데 저는 물이 겁났어요. 실내 수영장의 그 울림도 싫었고요. 엄마는 계속 들어가서 다른 아이들처럼 재미있게 놀라고 했는데 잘 안 되더라고요. 제가 주저하니까 엄마는 계속 저를 재촉했지요. 그러다 엄마가 갑자기 뒤에서 절 밀었어요. 저는 너무 놀랐고요. 다행히 튜브가 있어 몸은 붕 떴어요. 그걸 보더니 엄마가 '그것 봐. 괜찮잖아!'라고 하는 거예요. 괜찮기는 했지만 충격이었어요. 이후 저는 '난 누가 떠밀어 줘야지만 할 수 있어'라고 생각하게 되었어요. 엄마도 그런 거 같아요. '우리 아들은 내가 떠밀지 않으면 혼자서는 어떤 일도 할 수 없어'라고요. 좋지는 않지만 엄마와 저 모두 동의한 한계였죠. 누가 떠밀어줘야 하는 태도는 고칠 수 있다고 생각하지만, 그조차도 누가 떠밀어줘야 할 수 있을 거 같아요."

어엿한 청년의 입에서 '누가 떠밀어주면 하겠다'는 소리가 나오다니 안타까운 일이었다. 그는 매사에 자신감이 없고, 자신이 경험하는 모든 일을 부정적 시각으로 해석했다. 하루에도 수십 가지의 일을 경험하면서 자신이 스스로 못한 일에만 생각을 모았다.

'난 역시 스스로는 어떤 일도 못해. 오늘도 스스로 한 일이 하나도 없거든.'

하지만 그건 사실이 아니었다. 하루에 스무 가지의 크고 작은 일을 했다고 치면, 그 가운데 적어도 열다섯 가지 이상은 스스로 한 일이었다. 그러나 남이 시켜서 한 일 다섯 가지에만 초점을 맞추다 보니 '난 역시 스스로 못하는 게 맞아'라는 생각을 자꾸만 강화시킬 따름이었다.

그런 습관을 고치는 방법은 뜻밖에도 간단하다. 부정적인 면만 바라본 탓에 부정적 성격이 됐으니 거꾸로 긍정적인 면만 바라보면 긍정적 성격으로 변하게 되는 것이다. 문제는 무기력증에 빠진 그로 하여금 어떻게 자발적으로 실천토록 하느냐였다. 강요하려 들면 더욱 무기력증에 빠진다.

"앞으로 한 달간 형민 군 자신을 남이라고 가정해보면 어떨까요? 자신을 남이라고 생각하고 그가 어떻게 변화하는지 우리 둘이 함께 관찰해보는 겁니다."

자기 자신을 객관적인 관찰자의 눈으로 바라보면 놀라운 변화가 너무도 쉽게 일어난다는 사실을 자세히 설명해주었다. 성과가 좋으면 성적에 반영해주겠다는 말도 덧붙였다.

의논 끝에 그는 스스로 실험계획을 세웠다. 지극히 단순한 실험이었다. 호주머니에 메모지와 볼펜을 넣고 다니며 남이 시킨 게 아니라 스스로 한 일이나 행동이 있을 때마다 메모지에 동그라미를 그려 넣는다는 것이었다. 그는 하루 일과가 끝나면 동그라미가 몇 개나 있는지 기록했다. 그러고 나서 일주일마다 만날 때 그 기록을 내게 보여주겠다는 거였다.

그는 자신의 의지에 따라 하는 온갖 자질구레한 일들, 이를테면 아침에 잠자리에서 일어나는 것, 옷을 입는 것, 가게에 가는 것, 전화를 거는 것 등을 모조리 적어나갔다. 그러면서 놀랐다.

'우와, 내가 생각한 것보다 나는 자발적인 일을 많이 하네. 오늘도 스스로 한 일이 이렇게 많다니!'

그는 점점 재미가 붙고 자신감도 생겼다. 하루하루 동그라미가 늘어났다. 결국 한 달 만에 마마보이 성격은 완전히 바뀌어버렸다. '난 스스로 할 수 있다'는 생각에 초점을 맞추다 보니 어느새 긍정적 성격이 돼버렸던 것이다. 이처럼 자신의 어느 면에 초점을 맞춰 바라보느냐에 따라 우리는 완전히 새로운 성격으로 탈바꿈할 수 있다.

마찬가지 원리로 집 나간 남편을 제 발로 되돌아오게 한 아내도 있다.

어느 날 평소 꼬박꼬박 일찍 귀가하던 남편이 회식이 있다며 전화를 걸었다.

"오늘 좀 늦을 거야. 기다리지 말고 먼저 자."

처음 있는 일이라 그녀는 잠 안 자고 기다려보기로 했다. 하지만 그게 화근이 됐다. 1시가 넘고, 2시가 넘고… 그녀는 남편 휴대폰에 전화를 걸었다. 꺼져 있었다. 조금씩 짜증이 나기 시작했다. 남편이 지금쯤 무슨 일을 하고 있을까 온갖 추측이 몽실몽실 피어올랐다. 한 친구가 귀띔해준 얘기가 귓가에 생생했다.

'새벽 3~4시 넘어도 귀가 안 하면 잘 살펴봐. 밖에서 의심할 만한 행동을 한 거라고 보면 맞아.' 남편은 새벽 5시가 넘어서야 술 냄새를 풍풍 풍기며 귀가했다. 그녀는 가슴을 두근거리며 밤을 꼬박 새웠으니 초주검

이 다 되어 있었다. 그 얼굴을 본 남편은 대뜸 화부터 냈다.

"아니, 아직도 안 자고 기다렸단 말이야?"

남편은 별 이상한 여자 다 보겠다는 투로 내뱉고는 그냥 픽 쓰러졌다.

그녀는 이튿날 남편의 와이셔츠를 빨려다 눈이 획 돌았다. 친구들한 테 말로만 듣던 일을 당한 것이다. 어깨 근처에 빨간 립스틱 같은 게 묻어 있었다. 그녀는 '친구의 말이 정말 맞구나' 하고 판단했다. 그러나 당장 남편에게 전화를 걸어볼까 하다 참았다. 괜히 자신이 초라해 보일 것 같 아서였다. 남편에 대한 별의별 억측이 꼬리에 꼬리를 물고 거세게 피어올 랐다.

'남편은 믿을 만한 사람이 아니었어.'

일단 신뢰가 깨지자 그때부터 남편의 일거수일투족을 요모조모 따져 보는 습관이 생겼다. 그러자 남편에 관한 것들이 마치 도미노처럼 모조리 부정적으로만 보이기 시작했다. 양말을 아무 데나 벗어놓는다거나 휴일 에 낮잠만 자며 빈둥거리는 등, 전에는 아무렇지 않게 받아들이던 면까지 밉고 가증스럽게 보였다. 부정적 생각이 부정적 생각만 끌어들이는 것이 었다.

그녀가 남편의 부정적인 면만 골라 바라보니 남편도 점점 그녀의 부 정적인 면만 바라보기 시작했다. 귀가 시간이 늦어지는 날도 점점 늘어 났다.

"오늘은 또 왜 늦었어?"

"일찍 오면 뭐해? 바가지만 긁어댈걸."

"늦으니까 바가지 긁지."

악순환이었다. 그러더니 남편은 아예 집에 안 들어오기 시작했다. 귀가하지 않는 날이 늘어나기 시작했다. 벌써 한 달째 안 들어오고 있었다. 새 애인을 만나 동거하고 있다는 소문이 흘러들어왔다. 어느 날 그녀는 화장실에서 거울을 들여다보다 정신이 번쩍 들었다. 벌써 양미간에는 가는 홈이 패어 있었다.

"남편 잘못 만나 내 인생이 이렇게…"

그녀는 욕조 가장자리에 의지한 채 엎드렸다. 가는 어깨가 심하게 들먹거리기 시작했다.

그녀의 사연을 들은 정신과 의사는 이런 처방을 내렸다.

"혹시 남편에게 연락이 오면 부정적인 말은 일절 하지 마세요. 오로지 남편의 긍정적인 면에 대해서만 말해야 합니다. 그리고 남편이 전화를 걸어오거나 집에 찾아오는 횟수를 꼼꼼하게 기록해둬요. 그래프로 표시하면 더욱 좋고."

그녀는 시키는 대로 스스로 남편에게 먼저 전화를 걸거나 접촉을 시도하지는 않았다. 다만 남편이 이따금 전화를 걸어오면 최대한 상냥하고 다정한 톤으로 대해주었다. 통화중 남편의 나쁜 점은 철저히 외면하고 좋은 점만 골라 칭찬해주었다. 의도적으로 긍정적인 면만 바라본 것이다.

초기엔 통화시간이 5~10분을 넘지 않도록 자제했다. 통화가 길어지면 감춰놓고 있던 갈등이 표출돼 말싸움으로 번질 소지가 컸기 때문이다. 그러다 보니 남편과의 짧은 통화는 점점 밝아졌다. 남편도 아내와의 통화가 즐거워지자 좀더 자주 전화를 걸게 됐고, 집에 들르는 횟수도 늘어났다. 그녀는 냉장고 벽에 붙여 놓은 그래프용지에 남편의 통화횟수와 방문횟수를 매일 체크해두었다. 마치 실험실 생쥐의 행동을 관찰하는 과학자처럼 정확하고 꼼꼼하게 남편의 행동변화를 기록해 나갔다.

어느 날 남편이 집에 들르자 그녀가 상냥하게 말했다.

"집에 들러서 참 반갑네요. 당신이 좋아하는 매실주를 담가두었어요."

그녀는 남편이 집에 들를 적마다 매실주를 한 잔씩 내놓을 계획이었다. 남편의 기호품을 미끼로 활용했던 것이다. 그녀는 남편이 언제, 무슨 이유로 들르든 변함없이 상냥하게 맞아주었다. 그러자 남편이 집에 들르는 횟수도 크게 늘기 시작했다. 얼마 후 남편은 아내를 찾아와 간절한 표정으로 말했다.

"그동안 못된 나 때문에 속 많이 상했지? 용서해줄 수 있어?"

남편은 집을 나간 지 6개월 만에 함께 살던 애인을 버리고 그녀의 품으로 스스로 되돌아왔다. 그녀가 남편의 결점만 바라보니 남편도 그녀를 점점 부정적으로 보게 됐고, 급기야 가출하기에 이르렀었다. 하지만 그녀가 생각을 돌려 거꾸로 남편의 장점에만 초점을 맞춰 바라보자 남편도 점점 긍정적으로 변했던 것이다.

장점만 바라보면 장점이 점점 더 커진다

내가 초등학교 5학년 때였다. 당시 우리를 몹시도 괴롭히던 못 말리는 문제아가 있었다. 그는 늘 칼을 갖고 다녔다. 그 칼은 칼집에 접어 넣으면 7~8센티미터 정도의 길이였지만, 펼치면 배로 늘어나 아이들에게는 섬뜩한 인상을 줄 만했다.

망나니 친구는 그 칼을 갖고 다니며 수시로 이리저리 던지곤 했다. 특히 아이들이 필기하려고 책상 위에 손을 올려놓고 있으면 불시에 나타나 손 주변에 칼을 휙 내리꽂았다. 그리고 기겁하는 아이들의 표정을 보며 자지러지게 웃어댔다.

공교롭게도 나는 그 친구와 5년 동안 줄곧 같은 반이었다. 등교할 때면 그 친구 얼굴이 떠올라 발길을 돌리고 싶었던 게 한두 번이 아니었다. 다른 아이들도 마찬가지였다. 우리는 그가 멀리 다른 학교로 전학 가버리거나 아예 이 세상에서 제발 싹 꺼져버렸으면 하고 간절히 바랐다.

선생님들도 그를 아예 내놓은 자식으로 취급했다. 교실 창문이 깨지거나 누군가 코피가 터지면 선생님들은 대뜸 이런 말부터 던졌다.

"또 네가 그랬지? 너 말고 그런 짓 할 사람이 누가 있겠니?"

그는 1학년 때부터 줄곧 그런 말을 들으며 자랐다. 그에게 관심을 갖는 사람은 아무도 없었다. 아이들이나 선생님들이나 그저 그가 말썽만 부리지 않으면 다행이라고 여겼다. 따라서 그가 매일 점심을 거르고 있다는 사실을 아무도 몰랐다. 그의 아버지가 알코올 중독자라는 사실도 아무도 몰랐다. 그의 얼굴이 시퍼렇게 멍든 채 나타나도 아무도 몰랐다. 그가 또 누군가와 싸움을 벌였으려니 했다.

그런데 5학년 담임선생님은 달랐다. 어떻게 알았는지 망나니 친구가 점심을 거른다는 걸 알고 도시락을 따로 챙겨왔다. 하루 이틀이 아니었다. 매일 챙겨왔다. 그렇게 6개월쯤 지나자 친구가 변하기 시작했다. 담임선생님을 좋아하기 시작한 것이었다.

하지만 세 살 적 버릇 여든까지 간다고. 어느 날 그가 또 창문을 깼다. 우리는 벌벌 떨었다. 선생님은 인자했지만 잘못에 대해선 몹시 엄했기 때문이다. 누군가 망나니 친구 대신 벌을 뒤집어써야 할 판이었다. 그렇지 않으면 전원이 단체기합을 받아야 할 게 뻔했다. 드디어 선생님이 교실에 나타났다.

"깨진 유리창 빨리 치워."

선생님은 아무 일도 없었던 것처럼 수업을 진행했다. 그리고 수업이 끝난 뒤 망나니 친구를 따로 불러 말했다.

"창문이 깨졌지?"

과거 선생님들은 으레 "또 네가 그랬지?"라고 했었다. 하지만 5학년 담임선생님은 "너"를 지칭하지 않고 "문제"만을 지적했다. 그리고 말없이 고개를 푹 수그린 그의 손을 슬며시 잡고는 미소만 짓는 것이었다. 잠시 후 선생님이 말했다.

"네가 이 세상에서 가장 바라는 게 뭐지?"

친구가 잠시 후 모기만 한 목소리로 대답했다.

"선생님이 제 아버지였으면 좋겠어요."

선생님은 친구의 다른 면을 찾아보기 시작했다. 그러다가 그가 땅바닥이나 종이쪽지에 그림을 끼적거리는 걸 보고 그림에 흥미를 갖고 있음을 알아차렸다. 우리는 미술시간에 선생님이 친구에게 "넌 미술에 소질이 있구나"라고 말하는 걸 자주 들었다.

선생님은 그의 재능을 꿰뚫어보았던 것일까? 아니면 선생님의 칭찬이 없던 재능을 만들어낸 것일까? 친구의 그림 실력은 정말 나날이 좋아졌다. 그림에 취미를 붙이자 서서히 다른 과목에도 관심을 갖기 시작했다. 그러면서 기적이 일어났다. 친구가 남을 괴롭히는 일이 싹 사라진 것이다. 5년 내내 우리를 공포에 몰아넣었던 칼도 자취를 감췄다. 나를 그토록 괴롭혔던 친구가 나의 가장 친한 친구가 됐다. 1년 후 졸업식 날, 그

친구는 최우등상을 받았다. 모든 선생님이 '이 아이는 구제불능이야' 하고 바라보자 그는 정말 구제불능의 망나니가 됐다. 하지만 그 담임선생님이 '이 아이에게도 숨겨진 재능이 있을 거야'라고 바라보자 정말 숨겨진 재능이 튀어나왔다.

잘하는 게 아무것도 없는 소년이 있었다. 공부도 못하고 친구들과 뛰어놀지도 못했다. 늘 교실 구석에 틀어박혀 어서 수업이 끝나기만 기다리는 게 하루 일과였다. 그런데 어느 날 그의 인생을 완전히 뒤바꿔놓는 일이 벌어졌다.

"야! 교실에 쥐가 나타났다!"

삽시간에 교실은 난장판이 됐다. 선생님과 학생들이 쥐를 잡기 위해 난리를 떨었지만 아무도 그 쥐가 어디 숨어 있는지 알아낼 재간이 없었다. 모두 체념하고 있을 때 조용히 앉아 있던 소년이 외쳤다.

"선생님, 그 쥐는 지금 벽장 속에 숨어 있어요."

모두가 단단히 준비를 갖춘 채 벽장문을 슬그머니 열었다. 쥐는 쉽게 잡혔다. 선생님이 그를 불러 칭찬했다.

"너에겐 참으로 놀라운 능력이 있구나. 네 귀는 정말 특별하구나!"

이 한 마디가 소년의 인생을 바꿔놓았다. 그때부터 그는 자신이 갖고 있는 그 유일한 강점을 키워나가는 데 초점을 맞췄다. 그리고 마침내 세계적인 팝 음악가로 성장했다. 앞이 안 보였던 스티비 원더 Stevie Wonder의 이야기다. 한 가지 강점만 파고들다 보니 그 강점이 점점 커져서 모든 약점을 완전히 뒤덮고도 남았던 것이다.

빌 게이츠는 직원들을 뽑을 때 학력을 보지 않고 가장 중요하게 여기는 한 가지만 본다고 한다. 그건 바로 창의력이다. 그리고 이렇게 선발된 직원들에게는 최고의 근무환경을 만들어주고, 능력보상제도인 스톡옵션도 전 직원들을 대상으로 시행한다. 실제로 마이크로소프트사에 입사한 사람들 중 2천 명 이상이 2년 만에 백만장자가 된다. 이 때문에 직원들은 주당 80시간 이상의 격무에 시달리지만 불평 한 마디 없이 근무한다고 한다. 빌 게이츠는 학력과 창의력과는 큰 관련성이 없다는 걸 알고 있다.

실제로 노벨상 수상자들은 하버드나 예일 등 명문대에서만 나오는 게 아니다. 평범한 대학에서 오히려 더 많이 배출된다. 2007년 이후 노벨의학상을 수상한 미국인 25명의 학력을 보면 하버드, 예일, 컬럼비아, MIT 등 알려진 명문대를 나온 사람들은 여덟 명뿐이다. 나머지는 안티오크 칼리지, 워싱턴, 드포우, 켄터키 유니온, 홀리크로스, 헌터 등 잘 알려지지 않은 대학 출신들이 많다. 노벨화학상은 어떨까? 역시 명문대 출신은 예닐곱 명 정도다. 나머지는 네브래스카, 베레아, 아우스버그, 호프 등을 졸업한 사람들이다. 사정은 일본도 마찬가지. 과학 분야 노벨상 수상자 열다섯 명 중 열 명이 홋카이도 대학 등의 지방대 출신이다.

창의성은 암기식 학교성적이 좌우하는 게 아니다. 가능성 역시 학벌에 의해 좌우되지 않는다. 10년 후, 20년 후 자신이 무엇이 되어 있을지는 아무도 모른다. 그러나 자신이 잘하는 단 한 가지 강점에 미친 듯이 파고드는 사람이 10년 후, 20년 후에 그 분야의 최고가 된다는 건 분명하다.

진실에 초점을 맞추면 독설은 들리지 않는다

나는 상보성의 원리에 대한 강의를 하면서 이런 말을 해준 적 있다.

"한밤중에 옆집 개가 요란하게 짖어대 잠을 설친 적 있죠? 아니면 도서관에서 누가 눈치 없이 계속 떠들어대 몹시 짜증 났던 일?"

모두들 "네" 하고 대답했다.

"그건 우리가 습관적으로 겉으로 드러나는 소리에만 귀를 기울여서 그래요. 개 짖는 소리나 떠드는 소리 배후에 깔려 있는 침묵의 소리에 조용히 귀를 기울여보세요. 개 짖는 소리나 떠드는 소리는 저절로 들리지 않게 됩니다."

남이 내게 독설을 쏟아 부을 때도 마찬가지다. 독설에만 귀를 기울이면 도저히 견디기 힘들고 나도 모르게 흥분해 같이 진흙탕에 뛰어들게 된다. 하지만 독설 대신 독설 속에 숨겨진 진실을 캐내겠다고 마음먹으면 독설은 시냇물처럼 그냥 흘러가 버려 들리지 않게 된다.

그 말을 유난히 주의 깊게 들었던 한 남학생이 몇 주 후 자진해서 입을 열었다. 시골 출신으로 평소 말수가 적고 발표하라면 뒤로 빼곤 하던 학생이었다.

그가 주말에 고향을 향해 고속도로를 달리던 중이었다. 중간에 가다 보니 바로 앞선 차가 어쩐 일인지 삐뚤빼뚤 차선을 넘나들고 있었다. 그러자 옆 차선에서 달리던 차가 갑자기 그 차 앞에 휙 끼어들더니 차를 멈춰 섰다.

"끼익—!"

그도 급브레이크를 밟았다. 위험천만한 순간이었다. 갑자기 세운 차

에서 20대 초반쯤의 운전자가 뛰어내렸다. 그러더니 삐뚤거렸던 그의 앞
차로 다가가 삿대질을 하는 것 아닌가?

"야, 이 XX야! 차선 똑바로 지켜!"

앞차에는 중년의 신사가 타고 있었다. 졸음이 쏟아졌었나 보다. 청년
은 한참 독설을 쏟아냈다. 신사보다 20년 이상 어려 보였다. 아무리 세상
이 막 돌아간다지만 저런 버르장머리 없는 녀석이 다 있나 하는 생각이
들었다. 하지만 어쩔 것인가? 그런 녀석과 맞섰다가는 도로 한복판에서
기막힌 이전투구가 벌어질 게 뻔했다. 봉변을 당할 수도 있다. 그런데 중
년 신사의 입에서는 뜻밖의 말이 나왔다.

"죄송합니다. 제가 차선을 좀 벗어났었나 보네요. 놀라게 해드려 죄송
합니다."

신사는 공손한 목소리로 사과했다. 욕설을 퍼붓던 청년은 흠칫 놀라
는 기색이었다. 마치 뭔가에 뒤통수를 얻어맞은 듯 말없이 자신의 차로
돌아갔다. 그 남학생도 다시 페달을 밟으면서 뿌듯한 깨달음을 느꼈다.

"수업시간에 배운 상보성의 원리가 퍼뜩 떠올랐어요. 신사는 청년의
욕설이 바가지로 쏟아졌지만 그걸 그냥 흘려보낸 거였어요. 대신 '차선
을 똑바로 지켜'라는 말에서 진실을 본 거죠. 그 진실을 캐내 자신을 가다
듬는 거울로 삼았던 겁니다."

그의 말이 끝나자 한쪽에서 "와!" 하는 소리가 들렸다. 상황을 꿰뚫어
보는 그의 날카로움에 대한 경탄이었다. 나도 그의 분석에 완전 동감이었
다. 신사는 쏟아지는 독설은 모두 흘려버리고 오로지 그 속에 숨어 있는
진실의 알갱이를 찾아내는 데 초점을 맞추었던 것이다.

'저 젊은이가 내게 저토록 독설을 쏟아내는 데는 분명히 이유가 있을

거야. 내가 잘못한 게 뭐지?'

그는 자신을 완전히 비웠다. 그리고 자신이 차선을 똑바로 지키지 않았다는 사실을 알고는 공손히 사과했다. 비굴하고 바보 같은 짓일까? 전혀 그렇지 않다. 그는 자신의 몸을 독으로 채우길 거부하는 현명한 길을 택했다. 대신 독설 속에서 자신의 잘못을 캐내 자기 발전을 위한 긍정적 거울로 삼았다. 독설은 독이 된 게 아니라 오히려 득이 됐다.

같은 원리로 악질상사가 퍼붓는 독설 속에서 살아남을 수도 있다. 졸업을 앞둔 학생들에게 이런 질문을 해보았다.

"여러분이 어느 회사에 취직했습니다. 그런데 공교롭게도 악질상사를 만났어요. 그 악질상사가 여러분에게 난데없이 부당한 독설을 퍼붓는다면 어떻게 하겠습니까?"

"아니꼽더라도 참아야죠. 회사를 그만둘 거 아니라면."

학생들은 대부분 참아야 한다는 의견이었다. 역시 생존문제가 걸리면 신중해진다.

"하지만 무조건 꾹 참고만 있으면 독이 됩니다. 어떻게 해야 할까요?"

학생들이 갸우뚱했다. 나는 미국 대학원 시절 한 교수가 소개했던 '악질상사 다루는 법'을 들려주었다.

"상사가 화를 낼 때 절대로 방어하려 들지 마세요. 화낼 때 방어하는 건 휩쓸려 드는 겁니다. 문제는 누구에게 있나요? 나에게 있는 게 아니라 무턱대고 화내는 그에게 문제가 있습니다. 따라서 나를 완전히 잊고 그에게 초점을 맞춰보세요. 그가 왜 화내는지 꼬치꼬치 묻고 또 물어서 진실의 알갱이가 뭔지 적극적으로 찾아보는 겁니다. 철저히 그의 눈으로 바라보세요. 철저하게 묻고, 듣기만 하는 겁니다. 그의 말 속에 과연 내가 건질 만한 진실의 알갱이가 들어 있는지 열심히 들어보는 겁니다."

이렇게 진실을 캐내는 데만 초점을 맞추면 자연히 나를 잊게 된다. 나를 잊으면 화에 휘말려 들지 않는다. 교수는 스스로 악질상사 역을 맡았다. 그리고 한 학생에게 앞으로 나오도록 하더니 말단직원 역을 맡도록 했다. 대화는 이런 식으로 진행됐다.

상사 : "자넨 영 엉터리야!"

직원 : "죄송합니다. 제가 어떤 면에서 엉터리인지 알려주십시오."

상사 : "일을 처리하는 것도 그렇고, 이기적이고. 한 마디로 무능해!"

직원 : "좀더 구체적으로 말씀해주시겠어요? 어떤 일처리가 잘못됐다고 생각하시는지요? 제가 왜 이기적으로 보였을까요? 무슨 일을 못해서 무능하다고 생각하시는지도 궁금합니다. 그걸 고치고 싶습니다."

상사 : "자넨 퇴근 시간이 너무 빨라. 일하는 속도도 느리다구."

직원 : "물론 제가 칼퇴근한 적도 있었습니다. 제가 고쳐야 할 또 다른 점들은 뭔가요?"

상사 : "여하튼 난 자네가 마음에 안 들어."

직원 : "제가 마음에 안 드는 점도 많을 겁니다. 일처리도 그렇고, 이기적으로 보일 때가 많을 겁니다. 저에 대한 불만이 있으시면 또 말씀해주세요. 최선을 다해 고쳐나가겠습니다."

목적이 분명한 사람에겐 누가 무슨 말을 던지더라도 귀에 들어오지 않는다. 직원은 오로지 한 가지 목적에만 초점을 맞춰놓았다.

"저 독설 속에 내가 건져낼 만한 가치 있는 게 들어 있을까?"

이렇게 초점이 맞춰지니 초점을 벗어난 독설은 그냥 허공에 흘러갈 뿐이었다. 악질상사 또한 품고 있던 불만들을 털어내니 금방 김이 빠져 제풀에 꺼져버렸다. 상황이 끝나자 직원은 큰 자부심을 느꼈다. 모든 말 싸움이 그렇다. 싸움이 끝나고 나면 화를 터뜨렸던 쪽이 되레 자괴감과 패배감을 갖는다.

아리스토텔레스는 말싸움이나 비난에 대처하는 방법에 대해 이런 말을 남겼다.

"비난은 아주 쉽게 피할 수 있는 것이다. 아무것도 말하지 않고, 아무런 행동도 하지 말고, 나 자신이 아무 존재도 아닌 것처럼 행동하면 된다."

남 탓은 스스로를 무력하게 만든다

그녀는 대학을 졸업한 뒤 직장에 잠깐 다니다 결혼했다. 결혼하자마자 남편이 직장을 그만두라고 했다. 그런데 아이를 낳자마자 남편의 잇따른 사업 실패로 평생 갚아도 절대 갚을 수 없는 엄청난 빚더미에 파묻혀버렸다. 밤이면 밤마다 사채업자들이 찾아와 행패를 부렸다. 갓난아기 딸에게 우유 살 돈조차 없었다. 하도 막막해 몇 번이나 자살을 결심하기도 했다. 자신이 사업하다 망했으면 억울하지나 않지. 그녀는 남편을 잘못 만나 인생을 완전히 망쳤다고 생각했다.

"시댁 식구, 남편 친구들…. 남편과 관련된 사람은 무조건 원수처럼 여겨졌어요. 모든 게 남편 탓이라고 생각했으니까요."

빚더미만 바라보며 남을 탓하다 보니 스스로는 피해자로 전락하고 말았다. 스스로는 아무것도 못하며 신세타령만 하는 무능력자가 돼버렸다. 하지만 갓 태어난 어린 딸은 어떻게든 당장 먹여 살려야 했다. 우윳값이라도 벌어볼 일념으로 그녀는 구인광고를 뒤적였다. 하지만 기가 막히게도 시내버스 토큰 하나 살 돈조차 없었다. 옆집 아줌마에게 토큰 세 개를 빌려 찾아간 곳이 바로 화장품 회사였다.

영업사원 교육시간에 사장은 정신교육부터 시켰다.

"내 생각이 머무는 곳에 내 인생이 있고 현재 내가 불행하다고 생각하는 모든 것은 내 탓입니다. 남을 탓하는 습관부터 버리세요!"

이 말이 어찌나 정곡을 찔렀던지 교육 도중 그녀는 화장실에 달려가 엉엉 소리 내어 울었다. 그리고 그 순간부터 세상을 전혀 다른 눈으로 보기 시작했다. 자나깨나 남만 탓하던 시각이 자신을 탓하는 시각으로 돌아섰다. 그러다 보니 스스로 할 수 있는 게 보이기 시작했다. 시각이 바뀌니 행동이 바뀌고, 행동이 바뀌니 숨어 있던 능력이 튀어나왔다. 마침내 스스로 운명의 주인이 됐던 것이다.

첫 보름 동안 단 한 건의 주문도 받지 못했지만 그녀는 남을 탓하지 않았다. 자신의 능력부족 탓으로 돌리고 때로는 음식점 종업원들을 상대로, 때로는 밤을 새가며 세일즈 연습을 했다. 뼈를 깎는 노력 끝에 그녀는 세일즈 여왕이 됐고, 입사 12년 만에 부회장 자리에 우뚝 설 수 있었다.

우리나라 화장품 업계의 신화로 통하는 박형미 씨가 29살에 겪었던 일이다. 내가 그녀를 만났던 건 2000년대 중반, 그녀가 연봉 12억 원의 화진화장품 부회장이었던 시절이다. 그런데도 그녀는 잠자는 시간이 아까워 겨우 두 시간밖에 자지 않는다고 말했다. 몇 년 후 그녀는 파코메리라는 화장품 회사를 설립해 단숨에 월매출 150억 원이 넘는 기업으로 키워냈다. 20년 전, 인생의 벼랑 끝에서 떨고 있던 그녀였다. 다른 비결은 없다. 단지 상황을 바라보는 시각을 돌린 것뿐이다.

한 여류작가의 이야기도 많이 알려져 있다. 작가가 되기 전 그녀는 군인이었던 남편을 따라 캘리포니아 주 모하비 사막 훈련소로 가게 되었다. 남편이 직장에 나가면 섭씨 45도를 오르내리는 지독한 무더위 속에 오두막집에 달랑 혼자 남았다. 시도 때도 없이 모래바람이 불어닥쳐 입안에서 모래알이 씹히고, 음식을 해두면 금방 쉬어버렸다. 뱀과 도마뱀이 집주변에 기어 다녔다. 몇 달만에 심한 우울증에 빠졌다. 마침내 고향 부모에게 이렇게 하소연했다.

"더 이상 못 견디겠어요. 차라리 감옥에 가는 게 나아요. 정말 지옥이에요."

그러나 아버지의 답장에는 다음과 같은 두 줄만 적혀 있었다.

"감옥 문창살 사이로 밖을 내다보는 두 죄수가 있다. 하나는 하늘의 별을 보고, 하나는 흙탕길을 본다."

이 두 줄의 글이 그녀의 인생을 바꿔놓았다. 그녀는 기피했던 인디언들과 친구가 되었고, 그들로부터 공예품 만드는 기술과 멍석 짜기를 배웠다. 사막의 식물들도 자세히 관찰해보았다. 선인장, 유카식물, 여호수아나무 등, 살펴보니 그것들은 너무나 매혹적이었다. 빨갛게 저무는 사막의 저녁노을에도 신비한 아름다움이 숨겨져 있었다. 그녀는 이 새로운 세계를 발견한 기쁨을 책으로 펴냈다. 사막을 배경으로 한 소설가로 변신한 것이었다.

"사막은 변하지 않았다. 내 생각만 변했다. 생각을 돌리면 비참한 경험이 가장 흥미로운 인생으로 변할 수 있다는 걸 깨달았다."

사막은 지옥이 아니라 온갖 경이로움과 평화가 가득한 천국이었다. 지옥은 스스로 세운 것이었다. 미국의 델마 톰슨Thelma Thomson의 이야기다.

3

나 이상의 나 바라보기

1 관찰자는 누구인가?

만일 당신이 이 책을 차근차근 읽어왔다면 머릿속 한켠에 몇 가지 의문들이 도사리고 있을 것이다.

"나를 남처럼 바라볼 수 있는 관찰자는 대체 누구인가?"

"넓게 바라볼수록 왜 지능도 점점 높아질까?"

"지능이 우주에서 무한하게 흘러나온다면 우주에 있는 '완벽한 지능'의 소유자는 대체 누구인가?"

짐작대로다. 관찰자는 바로 영혼이다.

하지만 당신은 영혼의 정체를 알고 있는가? 학기가 끝나갈 때쯤, 학생들에게 "영혼은 어디에 들어 있을까요?" 하고 물었더니 "당연히 제 머릿속에 들어 있겠죠"라는 식의 대답이 가장 많았다. 하지만 그건 착각이다. 영적 깨달음을 얻은 극소수를 빼놓고는 모두가 이런 착각 속에 살아간다. 지난 수천 년간 그랬다. 하지만 최근 불과 수십 년 사이에 눈부시게 발전한 양자물리학 덕분에 많은 사람들이 마침내 이런 착각에서 서서히 깨어나고 있다.

영혼은 두뇌의 밖에 있다. 관찰자가 나를 남처럼 바라볼 수 있는 것도, 넓게 바라볼수록 지능이 높아지는 것도, 지능이 우주에서 흘러나오는 것도 모두 완벽한 지능을 가진 영혼이 두뇌 밖의 우주에 퍼져 있기 때문이다.

"갈수록 황당한 소리를 늘어놓는군!"

육신 속에 갇혀 살아온 당신은 이렇게 반응할지도 모른다. 하지만 "영혼은 두뇌 밖의 우주에 퍼져 있다"는 사실을 분명히 깨닫는 순간 당신은 비좁은 육신의 한계에서 벗어나 더욱 폭넓은 변화를 겪게 된다. 그 한계로부터의 탈출을 시도해보자.

비좁은 나로부터의 탈출

한 청년이 깊은 계곡에서 등반을 하다가 끔찍한 사고를 당했다. 계곡 수십 미터 아래로 내려가고 있을 때 바위 덩어리가 굴러 내려와 오른손에 떨어진 것이다. 피범벅이 된 손을 빼내려 몇 차례 시도해보았지만, 바위는 꿈쩍도 하지 않았다. 아무리 머리를 굴려봐도 바위에 짓눌린 손을 빼낼 재간이 없었다. 외질 대로 외진 계곡 아래에 어떤 도움의 손길이 닿을 리도 만무했다.

'꼼짝없이 이렇게 죽게 됐구나!'

거센 죽음의 공포가 밀려왔다. 먹을 거라곤 작은 빵조각 두 개와 1리터의 물이 다였다. 그것도 닷새가 지나자 완전히 바닥나 버렸다. 닷새 동안 그는 손을 빼내기 위해 사투를 벌였다. 작은 휴대용 칼이 다 닳도록 바위 밑을 쪼아보기도 하고, 죽을힘을 다해 바위를 밀어보기도 했다. 손을 빼내지 못하면 그 자리서 꼼짝없이 죽게 될 판이었다.

"바위는 꿈쩍도 안 해. 이게 내 운명이야."

그는 점점 죽어가고 있었다. 죽음을 피할 수 없다는 걸 깨닫고는 계곡 모래벽에 무뎌진 칼로 자신의 생년월일과 죽는 날짜를 새겨 넣었다. 그러고는 가족에게 남길 유언을 비디오카메라에 담았다. 그런데 죽음을 받아들이기로 하자 뜻밖의 변화가 일어났다.

"처음엔 죽음의 공포에 떨었는데 모든 걸 체념하니 이상하게도 평화가 찾아왔어요."

죽음을 받아들이기로 마음먹으니 육신에 대한 모든 집착이 떨어져 나갔다. 자신을 텅 비우자 그제야 자신의 모습이 마치 남을 바라보듯 조용히 시야에 들어왔다. 자신을 바라보는 또 다른 자신은 누구인가?

"제 육신을 바라보는 또 다른 나, 그게 바로 제 영혼이었어요."

한쪽 팔이 사라진다고 해서 영혼도 줄어드는가? 영혼, 즉 '진정한 나'는 육신 속에 들어 있는 게 아니었다. '팔은 나'라고 바라보니, 팔이 바위에 깔려 꼼짝 못하자 '나'도 꼼짝 못했다. 그러나 이제 팔은 영혼을 담는 그릇의 한 작은 파편에 불과했다. 푸른 하늘, 푸른 숲, 푸른 바다를 바라보며 자유로이 살아갈 기쁨에 비하면 팔 하나쯤 없는 건 아무것도 아니었다.

"사랑하는 여자를 만나 결혼도 하고 아들을 낳아 행복하게 사는 제 미래의 모습들이 너무나도 생생하게 떠올랐어요. 세 살배기 아들을 한팔로 껴안은 장면도 현실처럼 눈앞에 펼쳐졌지요."

'나는 팔 이상의 존재'라고 자신을 바라보자 팔을 잘라낼 용기가 샘솟아 올랐다. 그는 일단 등반로프로 바위에 짓눌린 팔을 단단히 묶어 지혈시켰다. 그러고는 무뎌질 대로 무뎌진 칼로 지혈된 부위 아래 손목을 자

애런 롤스턴

"팔다리가 '진정한 나'가 아니라는 걸 깨닫고, 바위에 짓눌린 손을 절단한 뒤 자유의 몸이 됐다."

르기 시작했다. 이미 시퍼렇게 변한 터라 그리 아프진 않았다. 손목을 잘라내는데 한 시간 정도 걸렸다.

"저는 제 손목을 잘라내는 게 너무나 행복했습니다. 미래에 일어날 모든 기쁨과 행복의 순간들이 걷잡을 수 없이 밀려들었고, 손목만 잘라내면 그 모든 걸 누릴 수 있다는 생각 때문이었죠. 통증을 느낄 겨를도 없었어요."

그는 바위를 벗어나 몇 시간 동안 걸어가다가 구조 헬리콥터가 날아오는 걸 보았다. 미국에 사는 롤스턴(Aron Ralston) 씨의 실화이다.

얼마 전 나는 아침에 출근해 해외뉴스를 모니터하다가 그가 NBC TV와 인터뷰하는 모습을 보았다.

앵커가 그에게 물었다.

"만일 할 수 있다면 그때 상황을 되돌려놓고 싶지는 않은가요?"

"그런 생각은 눈곱만큼도 없어요. 그 상황이라면 나는 똑같이 할 겁니다."

"손을 잃는 것까지도요?"

"물론이죠!"

그건 진심이었다. 그 사고를 당하지 않았더라면 '육신 속에 든 게 바로 나'라는 착각 속에 일생을 살아갔을 터였다. 하지만 사고를 계기로 '나는 육신 이상의 존재'라는 사실을 발견했다. 그 결과 인생이 놀랍도록 행복해졌고, 사고의 폭도 경이롭도록 넓어졌다.

마비된 팔다리만 바라볼 것인가?

아예 양쪽 팔다리를 전혀 움직이지 못하는 여성도 있다. 그녀는 40여 년을 그렇게 살아왔다.

불행은 그녀가 막 꽃을 피기 시작하는 열일곱 살의 여고생 때 찾아왔다. 그녀는 언니와 강가에서 수영을 즐기고 있었다. 그러던 중 다이빙을 하겠다며 뛰어내렸다. 불행히도 바위에 머리를 부딪쳐 졸지에 사지마비 환자가 됐다. 목 아래쪽 모든 감각을 완전히 잃어버렸다. 평생 팔다리도 전혀 움직일 수 없게 됐다. 대학에 들어가려던 꿈은 산산조각 나버리고, 모든 걸 남의 손에 매달려 살아가야 했다. 침대에서 일어나고, 세수를 하고, 머리를 빗고, 밥을 먹고, 이를 닦는 것… 이 모든 사소한 일상의 것들을 말이다.

"이렇게 살 바에야 뭐 하러 산단 말인가. 차라리 죽는 게 백 번 낫지."

어쩌다 휠체어를 타고 외출이라도 하는 날이면 굴러떨어질 만한 높은 곳을 찾아 두리번거리곤 했다. 하지만 마음대로 죽지도 못했다. 그녀는 이 세상 그 누구보다 불행한 사람이었다.

지도교사가 처음 붓을 입에 물려주며 그림 그리는 법을 가르쳐줬을 때 그녀는 자신도 모르게 붓을 거칠게 내뱉었다.

"이런 건 장애인들이나 하는 거죠. 난 아니에요."

모든 걸 철저하게 불행의 눈으로 바라보았다. 완전히 마비돼 흐느적거리는 자신의 팔다리만 보고 살았다. 자신의 내면 깊숙한 곳에 무엇이 들어 있는지 거들떠보지도 않았다. 불행, 저주, 죽음만을 꿈꾸며 살았다. 그러던 어느 날, 그녀는 한 사지마비 환자가 연필을 입에 물고 알파벳을 힘겹게 써내려가는 걸 목격했다. 호흡기에 의존한 채 입조차 제대로 움직이지 못하는 남자였다. 그는 경건한 자세로 알파벳 세 글자를 천천히 그러나 또박또박 써나갔다. 평화와 감사에 가득한 얼굴이었다. 순간 그녀의 얼굴이 화끈 달아올랐다. 자신은 그동안 마비된 팔다리만 바라보며 살아왔지만, 그 남자의 얼굴에서는 육신의 한계를 뛰어넘는 찬란한 내면의 빛이 발산되고 있었다. 그제야 그녀는 자신을 남의 눈으로 보다 깊이 있게 바라볼 수 있었다.

"그 순간까지만 해도 저는 남들과 비교해 못 가진 것만 바라보며 살아왔었어요. 혼자서 일어날 수도 없고, 먹을 수도 없고, 이를 닦을 수도 없고… 그런 피상적인 것들만 바라보았죠. 그러다가 팔다리가 인생의 전부는 아니라는 걸 깨달았어요. 그러면서 제 내면에 감춰진 것들을 하나둘 꺼내 나가기 시작했죠."

'팔다리는 나'라고 생각하니, 팔다리가 마비되자 자연히 자신도 마비됐다. 인생은 끝장났다고 믿었다. 하지만 생각을 돌려보니 그게 아니었다. 팔다리는 인생의 수천 가지 면들 가운데 불과 한두 면에 불과했다. 한두 면에만 집착해 나머지 수천 가지 면들을 외면하며 살아왔던 것이다.

'나를 팔다리 이상의 존재'로 바라보자 마비된 팔다리를 뛰어넘는

나 이상의 나 바라보기

조니 타다
마비된 팔다리만 바라보자 인생도 마비됐지만,
무한한 내면의 잠재력을 바라보기로 하자 인생
이 극적으로 뒤바뀌었다.

숨어 있던 능력들이 꽃을 피우기 시작했다. 그녀가 붓을 입에 물고 그림 한 점을 그리는 데는 평균 6~8개월이 걸린다. 하지만 그녀는 행복하다. 내면의 무한한 가능성을 뽑아내는 일이 재미있기 때문이다.

"그림을 그릴 때마다 제 한계는 없다는 걸 느껴요. 팔다리가 할 수 있는 건 한계가 있지만, 마음으로 할 수 있는 건 한계가 없으니까요."

내가 맡고 있는 〈지구촌 리포트〉에서 소개한 바 있는 조니 타다Joni Tada라는 미국 여성의 이야기다. 마비된 팔다리의 철창 속에 갇혀 죽음만 생각하던 그녀가 지금은 베스트셀러 작가이자 세계적인 구족화가, 전 세계에 사랑과 희망을 전파하는 자선 사업가로 마음껏 날아오르고 있다. 한국도 방문해 희망의 메시지를 전한 바 있다.

이처럼 육신의 위기에 빠져 몸부림치다가 육신을 뛰어넘는 육신 밖의 또 다른 나를 발견한 예는 수없이 많다.

몸 밖의 나는 누구인가?

팔다리가 진정한 나가 아니라면 그럼 진정한 나는 두뇌 속에 들어 있을까?

뇌세포를 최대한 확대해보자. 초고성능 전자현미경은 상을 수백만 배까지 확대할 수 있다. 뇌세포의 섬유질을 확대해 살펴보면 분자가 보인다. 분자를 확대해보면 허공뿐이다. 분자를 구성하는 원자도 그렇다. 원자의 지름이 10미터가 되도록 원자를 1만 배 크기로 확대해보면 폭 1밀리미터에 불과한 핵이 가운데에 보인다. 원자를 미식축구장만 하게 더 부풀려놓으면 나머지는 온통 비어 있고, 0.001퍼센트도 안 되는 쌀알만 한 핵이 보인다.

그나마 핵도 더 확대해보면 텅 빈 공간이 나온다. 핵을 둘러싼 원자 궤도에서 돌고 있는 전자들도 확대할 수 없을 때까지 확대해보면 역시 빈 공간이다. 전자고 원자고 모두가 파동일 뿐이다. 모든 세포가 마찬가지다. 쪼개보면 빈 공간이다. 두뇌고 몸뚱이고 텅텅 비어 있다. 그래서 아인슈타인은 일찌감치 "우리는 시각적 착각 속에 살고 있다"고 했다. 스탠퍼드 대학의 양자물리학자인 틸러(William Tiller) 박사는 "인간의 99.9999 퍼센트는 빈 공간"이라고 말한다. 말 그대로 색즉시공色卽是空이다. 양자물리학자인 울프(Fred Wolf) 박사도 "영혼의 0.0001퍼센트만 육신 속에 들어 있고 나머지 99.9999퍼센트는 육신 밖의 우주에 퍼져 있다"고 말한다. 쉽게 말해 우주가 곧 영혼이며, 육신 속에는 육신의 부피에 해당하는 만큼의 영혼만 들어 있다는 뜻이다. 믿기지 않는가?

잠시 눈을 감고, 책을 덮어둔 채 당신의 지금 모습을 100미터 상공에서 가만히 내려다보라(이하의 장면들을 각각 5초 이상씩 상상하라). 다음으로, 시야를 더욱 넓혀 1,000미터 상공에서 내려다보라. 당신의 모습은 티끌만 하게 멀어지고, 당신이 들어 있는 건물도 성냥갑만 하게 작아진다. 이제 10,000미터 상공에서 내려다보라. 당신이 머물고 있는 도시가 훤히 내려다보인다. 시야를 점점 더 비약적으로 넓혀 한반도, 아시아, 지구가 차례로 멀어져가는 걸 바라보라. 이제 지구가 아득하게 멀어져가면서 무한한 별들이 반짝이는 은하수를 그려보라. 시야를 더욱 넓혀 은하수가 사라져가고 다른 무수한 은하들이 명멸하며 멀어져가는 우주를 그려보라. 그 우주가 어마어마하게 큰 투명풍선에 담겨 점점 멀어져간다고 상상해보라.

투명풍선은 멀어져가면서 차츰차츰 축구공만 하게, 야구공만 하게, 콩알만 하게 작아진다. 마침내 먼지만 하게 작아져 깜빡깜빡 명멸한다. 그걸 바라보는 건 누구인가? 바로 당신이다. 이처럼 당신은 우주보다 더 큰 것도 바라볼 수 있다. 하지만 그게 육신 속에 들어 있는 당신인가? 육신 속의 당신은 육안이 볼 수 있는 것밖에 보지 못한다. 하지만 우주에 퍼져 있는 당신, 즉 당신의 영혼은 모든 걸 다 볼 수 있다. 당신의 육신을 10,000미터 상공에서도, 우주 저 끝에서도 훤히 내려다볼 수 있다. 상상을 깊이 하면 할수록 이미지는 더욱 선명해진다. 이런 명상을 깊이 하면 할수록 당신은 영혼의 존재를 그만큼 깊이 깨닫게 된다.

"눈 감고 상상 속에서 보는 우주가 무슨 진짜 우주야?"

당신은 이렇게 반문할 것이다. 하지만 무한한 상상력도 우주에 퍼진 영혼이 존재하기 때문에 가능한 것이다. 영혼이 그리는 이미지가 점점 선명해지면 당신은 실제로 볼 수 있다. 그걸 보지 못하는 건 뿌리 깊은 의심과 잡념 때문이다. 선명하게 그려지는 이미지가 실제라는 사실은 다음 장에서 자세히 알게 될 것이다.

그럼 우주에 퍼져 있는 영혼의 존재를 과학적으로도 확인할 수 있을까? 방법은 의외로 간단하다. 사후 세계를 만들어보는 것이다. 그럼 육신은 죽고 영혼만 남는다. MIT, 프린스턴, 스탠퍼드 대학의 양자물리학자들은 실제로 여러 차례 완벽한 사후세계를 만들어보았다. 큰 방 크기의 초강력 냉동실에 완벽한 죽음의 세계를 만들어놓고 거기서 살아남는 게 있는지 살펴보는 것이다.

"사후 세계에서도 영혼이 정말 존재할까?"

완벽한 죽음을 만드는 방법은 두 가지다. 첫째, 모든 생명체가 완전히 얼어 죽도록 기온을 어마어마하게 차갑게 떨어뜨리는 것이다. 둘째, 모든 물질이 도저히 생존하지 못하는 완전진공 상태로 만드는 것이다.

과학자들은 먼저 기온을 떨어뜨리는 방법을 생각해보았다. 기온은 분자나 원자의 진동으로 생기는 열이다. 기온을 떨어뜨리면 열도 떨어진다. 기온을 떨어뜨리고 또 떨어뜨려 섭씨 영하 273.15도까지 떨어뜨리면 열은 완벽한 제로(0) 상태가 돼버린다. 그 이하의 기온은 존재하지 않는다. 이보다 더 차가울 수는 없다. 그래서 과학자들은 273.15도를 절대영도(absolute zero)라 부른다.

모든 생명체는 열을 발산한다. 그러나 죽고 나면 아무런 열도 발산하지 않는다. 절대 영도에서는 오로지 고요한 죽음만 존재할 뿐이다. 온 세상 모든 것들이 죽어버린다. 남는 거라곤 얼어붙은 공기밖에 없다.

"이런 완벽한 죽음 속에서도 과연 살아남는 게 있을까?"

섭씨 영하 273.15도라? 지구 역사상 가장 추웠던 기온은 영하 89.2도가 기록이었다. 1983년 러시아의 보스톡 남극기지의 기온이었다. 그 기온에서는 침을 뱉기조차 어려웠다. 뱉자마자 입술에 얼음이 달라붙어 입술이 쩍쩍 갈라졌기 때문이다. 말 한 마디 할 때마다 입김도 공중에서 얼어붙었다.

"내 입김이 얼음덩어리가 돼버렸어!"

얼음덩어리는 땅바닥에 떨어져 쨍그랑하고 깨져버렸다. 날아가던 새도 얼음조각이 돼 떨어졌다. 우주에서 가장 차가운 해왕성의 달인 트리톤Triton도 영하 270도이다. 상상을 초월할 정도로 추워 티끌만 한 생명도 존재하지 못한다. 그런데 그보다 더 차가운 영하 273도로 기온을 떨어뜨린다? 그 죽음 속에서 과연 살아남는 게 있을까?

모든 게 죽어 있을 것으로 생각했던 과학자들은 깜짝 놀랐다. 뭔가 빛을 내며 움직이는 게 보였기 때문이다.

"도대체 뭐지? 완벽한 죽음 속에서도 꿋꿋이 살아남는 게?"

그건 광자나 전자, 양자 등의 미립자들이었다. 그들은 절대영도에서도 여전히 왕성하게 진동하며 빛을 발하고 있었다. 과학자들은 입을 다물지 못했다.

"절대영도라는 완벽한 죽음 세계 속에서도 살아남는 게 있다니. 이 빛들이 정말 영혼들일까?"

그들은 분명히 알고 싶었다. 그래서 절대영도에서 완전진공 상태를 만들어버리기로 했다. 모든 생명체를 한 번 더 완벽하게 죽여버리려는 시도였다.

완전진공 상태를 만들려면 철저한 조건이 충족돼야 한다. 첫째, 눈에 보이는 모든 물질을 깡그리 제거한다. 둘째, 눈에 안 보이는 가스와 공기도 제거한다. 셋째, 모든 전자기파도 제거한다. 절대영도의 완전 죽음 상태에 이처럼 완전진공이라는 또 다른 죽음 상태를 이중으로 만들어놓았다. 그보다 더 철저한 죽음이 존재할까?

하지만 이런 이중의 죽음 상태에서도 미립자들은 끄떡없었다. '완전진공'이란 말 자체가 허구였다. 미립자들은 그 안에서도 끄떡없이 빛을 발산하고 있었다.

이처럼 영혼은 육신이 죽어도 끄떡없이 살아 있는 미립자인 게 틀림없다. 이 우주의 모든 생명체가 꽁꽁 얼어 죽는 절대영도 섭씨 영하 273.15도에서도, 완벽한 진공 상태에서도 영혼은 절대로 죽지 않는 불멸의 존재인 것이다. 미립자로 만들어진 영혼이 영원히 죽지 않는다는 사실은 더 쉬운 방법으로 확인할 수 있다. 별들이 총총한 밤하늘을 보라. 수십억, 수백억 개가 넘는 무수한 별빛이 밤하늘을 수놓는다. 별빛이 내 눈에 도달하는 데는 수백만 년씩 걸리기도 한다. 상상을 초월하는 먼 거리를 수백만 년간 날아오면서 소멸하지 않고 살아 있다는 얘기다. 그 빛은 나를 통과한 뒤에도 수백만 년, 수억 년간 소멸되지 않고 반짝거리며 우주여행을 계속할 것이다. 빛은 무엇인가? 빛을 구성하는 미립자(광자)나 영혼을 구성하는 미립자나 다 같은 미립자다. 미립자는 아무리 세월이 흘러도 죽지 않는 것이다.

아인슈타인은 양자물리학이 본격 궤도에 오르기 훨씬 전인 반 세기 전 이미 이런 사실을 깨닫고 있었다. 언젠가 한 랍비가 16살 동생의 죽음에 파묻혀 삶의 의욕을 완전히 상실한 열아홉 살의 딸을 도대체 어떻게

아인슈타인

"인간은 우주와 분리된 개체가 아니라 우주의 일부이다."

달래야 하느냐고 묻는 편지를 그에게 보냈다. 그때 아인슈타인의 답신이 뉴욕타임스에 실렸다.

"인간은 우주라 불리는 전체의 티끌에 불과합니다. 인간은 자신을 우주와 분리된 개체로 보며 살아가지만 그건 시각적 착각일 뿐이지요. 이런 착각이 인간을 고통의 감옥에 빠트립니다. 이 비좁은 감옥에서 벗어나 모든 생명체를 연민의 감정으로 껴안고 살아야 합니다. 물론 그런 완전한 경지에 이를 사람은 아무도 없겠지만, 비좁은 감옥에서 벗어나려는 노력 자체만으로 고통에서 해방될 수 있습니다."

아인슈타인은 육신이 죽어 사라지더라도 영혼은 미립자 에너지 형태로 여전히 존재함을 상기시키고 있었다. 그의 눈엔 육신이 스쳐 가는 껍데기에 불과했다. 그런데 그토록 슬퍼할 이유가 있느냐고 완곡하게 지적하고 있었다. 물론 사랑하는 동생을 잃은 19세 소녀에게는 다소 현학적인 답변이었을 것이다.

영혼은 모든 정보를 갖고 있다

미립자 차원의 우주를 양자물리학자들은 영점공간(영점장, ^{zero-point} field)이라 부른다. 미립자들은 절대영도에서도 살아남기 때문에 붙여진 이름이다. 아인슈타인 역시 절대영도에서도 진동에너지가 가득히 존재한다는 사실을 간파하고 이를 독일어로 영점에너지^(Nullpunktsenergie)라고 표현한 바 있다.

미립자들은 모든 정보, 지혜, 사랑, 에너지를 다 갖고 있다. 모르는 것도, 불가능한 것도 없는 전지전능한 존재이다. 그래서 물리학자인 라즐로^(Ervin Laszlo) 박사는 미립자들이 가득한 영점공간을 "무한한 가능성의 바다"라고 정의한다. 무한한 정보창고, 영혼의 공간, 신의 마음, 신의 공간 등으로 불리기도 한다. 주요 종교들이 말하는 영생, 구원, 해탈 등을 얻을 수 있는 곳도 바로 여기다.

노벨물리학상 수상자이자 양자물리학의 아버지격인 막스 플랑크는 "영점공간은 적어도 형체를 지닌 모든 것에 대한 설계도^(blueprint)를 갖고 있는 것으로 보인다"고 분석했다. 내 키는 얼마나 클 것인지, 얼굴 형태

라즐로 박사

"영점공간은 무한한 가능성의 바다이다."

는 어떻게 변화할 것인지 등이 이미 그려져 있다는 얘기다. 또 내가 언제 어디서 누구를 만나 어떤 일을 하고, 어떤 직업을 갖고 일하다 몇 세에 죽을 것인지도 몽땅 담겨 있다.

집단적 정보가 영점공간에 저장돼 있다는 사실은 1920년대에 하버드 대학의 맥두걸(William McDougall) 교수에 의해 처음 발견됐다. 그는 쥐들이 미로를 어떻게 헤쳐나가는지 유심히 관찰해보았다. 어미 쥐들은 무려 165번의 실패를 거친 뒤에야 헤매지 않고 미로를 완벽히 찾아갈 수 있었다. 그러다가 어미 쥐들이 새끼를 낳았고, 새끼들이 자라 어미 쥐만큼 커졌다. 그 새끼 쥐들은 몇 번 만에 미로를 찾아갔을까?

"어, 이럴 수가! 120번 만에 찾아가네."

새끼 쥐들이 성장해 또 새끼를 낳았다. 그 새끼 쥐들은 더 빨라졌다. 몇 세대를 거치자 쥐들은 불과 20번의 시행착오만 거친 뒤 미로를 찾아갔다. 놀라운 사실은 아무도 새로 태어난 쥐들에게 미로를 찾는 법을 가르쳐주지 않았다는 것이다. 오로지 스스로의 시행착오만으로 미로를 찾아가도록 했다. 그런데도 새끼 쥐들은 세대를 거치면서 어떻게 선조들보다 점점 더 빨리 미로를 찾아갈 수 있었을까? 그 답은, 선조들이 터득한 미로 찾기 정보와 지혜가 영점공간에 저장돼 있었기 때문이다.

사람은 안 그럴까?

미시간 대학의 심리학자 니스벳(Richard Nisbett) 박사가 실험을 해보았다. 그는 학생들로 하여금 한 사람씩 비좁은 복도를 지나가도록 했다. 그런데 복도 중간에서 한 뚱뚱한 남자가 캐비닛 서랍을 열어놓고 뭔가 하는 척하도록 했다. 그러다 보니 비좁은 복도는 더욱 비좁아져 통과하기가 몹

니스벳 박사

"옛 선조들의 정보가 시공간을
뛰어넘어 현대인들에게까지
대물림된다."

lsa.umich.edu

시 불편해질 수밖에 없었다. 그것만으로도 짜증 나는 일이었다. 그런데 그 뚱뚱한 남자는 한술 더 떴다. 학생들이 그처럼 비좁아진 지점을 간신히 통과할 때마다 학생들이 심한 모욕감을 느끼도록 자극했다. 즉 서랍을 느닷없이 쾅 닫고는 학생을 어깨로 툭 밀친 뒤 나지막한 목소리로 이렇게 외쳤다.

"병신새끼, 꼴값하고 있군!"

이런 말을 들은 학생들은 어떤 반응을 보였을까? 니스벳은 실험 전후로 학생들의 타액을 채취해 남성호르몬 테스토스테론과 스트레스 호르몬 코르티솔의 수치를 측정해보았다. 또 평소보다 손아귀에 얼마나 더 힘이 들어가 있는지 파악하기 위해 악수도 해보았다. 즉 심한 모욕을 받은 뒤 얼마나 공격성을 띠게 되는지 살펴보는 실험이었다. 결과는 판이하게 갈렸다.

북부출신 학생들은 별 변화가 없었다. 하지만 남부출신 학생들은 테스토스테론과 코르티솔 수치가 훌쩍 뛰어올랐다. 손아귀에도 바짝 힘이 들어가 있었다. 더 건드리면 누구든 박살 내고 말겠다는 태세였다. 남부

학생들은 왜 하나같이 이런 공격성을 띠고 있을까? 그건 200년 전 그들의 선조들이 공격적이었기 때문이다. 그들의 선조들은 18세기에 남부에 정착한 카우보이들이었다. 논리적으로는 도저히 이해가 가지 않는다. 후손들은 지금 북부의 미시간 대학에 다니고 있다. 그들은 카우보이를 본 적도 없다. 부모들도 카우보이가 아니었다. 대개 중산층인데다가 대도시에서 자라난 세대였다. 그런데도 왜 200년 전 카우보이 선조들의 공격성을 띠고 있을까?

니스벳은 이렇게 말한다.

"문화적 유산은 수세대가 지나도 지속됩니다. 참 이상한 일이죠? 유전자가 달라진 것도 아니고, 옛 환경에 노출되는 것도 아닌데."

양자물리학자들은 영점공간에 저장된 선조들의 문화적 정보가 시공간을 뛰어넘어 후손들에게 대대로 전달되는 것으로 분석한다. 쥐들이 영점공간에 저장된 집단정보를 자자손손 물려받듯이 말이다. 내 영혼은 이 모든 걸 갖고 있다.

이런 사실을 알고 살아가는 것과 모른 채 살아가는 건 하늘과 땅의 차이다. 관찰자 효과 때문이다.

* "내 영혼은 내 육신 속에 들어 있다고" 바라본다.
    → 관찰자 효과에 따라 비좁은 내 육신이 내 능력의 한계가 된다.
* "내 영혼은 육신 밖의 전지전능한 존재"라고 바라본다.
    → 관찰자 효과에 따라 육신의 한계를 벗어난다.

우리가 타고난 천재라고 생각하는 아인슈타인도 자신의 실체를 깨닫기 전까지는 인생의 낙오자였다. 어린 시절엔 바보로 낙인 찍혔다. 만으로 네 살이 될 때까지도 말도 못 했고, 일곱 살이 돼서야 겨우 글을 깨우쳤다. 아홉 살이 돼서도 말이 어눌하고 너무 느렸다. 같은 문장을 여러 번 되풀이하는 말더듬 증세까지 있었다. 초등학교에 들어가서도 다른 아이들을 따라가지 못했다. 참다못한 교장이 부모를 불러 선언했다.

"이 아이는 아무리 가르쳐도 소용없습니다. 차라리 노동일을 시키는 게 나아요."

그는 취리히의 폴리테크닉 공과대학을 졸업한 뒤에도 취직을 못해 백수생활을 해야 했다. 생활비가 바닥나 자신의 전공과는 동떨어진 보험회사에 간신히 취직했으나 거기서도 곧 해고당했다. 어린 시절 아들이 저능아가 아닌가 걱정했던 아버지도 "내 아들은 인생의 낙오자"라고 한탄하며 돌연 세상을 떠났다. 당시 아인슈타인이 친구에게 보냈던 편지에는 그가 자살충동까지 느꼈다고 적혀 있다.

"나는 지금 백수건달로 가족들에게 부담만 되고 있어. 이렇게 사느니 차라리 죽는 게 낫겠어."

그를 절망의 벼랑 끝에서 구해준 건 또 다른 대학친구였다. 친구가 그를 스위스 특허청 하급직원으로 추천해준 거였다. 그게 돌파구였다. 그는 거기서 특허관련 업무를 일찌감치 해치운 뒤 어린 시절부터 꿈꿔오던 자신만의 시간을 갖게 됐다. 그러면서 빛과 우주에 대한 상상에 빠져들었다. 빛을 연구하면서 자연히 영혼의 실체도 알게 됐다. 그러면서 사고의 폭도 폭발적으로 넓어지기 시작했다.

2 육신과 영혼의 숨바꼭질

양심을 지키면 손해일까?

당신이 신출내기 회사원이라고 상상해보자. 당신은 아침에 일어나자마자 목이 바짝바짝 타들어간다. 아침 8시 회의에 적어도 10분은 지각할 게 뻔하다. 조금 늦어도 괜찮은 여느 회의가 아니다. 출장을 앞두고 사장이 긴급 소집한 특별회의다. 출장자들은 전원 빠짐없이 참석하라는 엄명도 내려졌다.

'이럴 때 지각하면 이 직장에서는 끝장인데⋯.'

당신은 입사하자마자 인물 좋고 실력 좋은 재원으로 일찌감치 주목받아왔다. 당신을 대하는 선배들의 눈길부터 달랐다. '출세가도를 보장받은 사람'으로 바라보는 눈길이었다. 그런데 애써 쌓은 그런 이미지가 일순간 와르르 무너질 위기에 처한 것이다.

"대체 이렇게 늦게 나타나면 어떡합니까?"

당신은 30분이나 늦게 도착한 냉장고 기술자에게 분통을 터뜨린다. 전날부터 냉장고 냉동칸 밑에서 물이 흘러나왔다. 밤사이 부엌 바닥엔 물이 흥건했다.

256

"저는 일단 출근할게요. 냉장고 고치고 나서 문 꼭 닫아놓고 가세요."

낯선 기술자를 집 안에 놔두고 출장 가는 게 꺼림칙하지만 어쩌겠는가? 차 열쇠와 출장용 트렁크를 홱 집어 들고 5층 계단을 부리나케 뛰어 내려간다. 자동차 시동을 걸면서도 숨이 턱턱 막힌다. 평균 잡아 40분 거리지만 남은 시간은 겨우 30분. 무슨 짓을 해서라도 지각해서는 안 된다며 어금니를 꽉 문다.

"에잇! 굼벵이 같은 차들!"

다른 운전자들에게 욕설을 퍼붓는다. 빨간 신호를 무시하고 달리기도 한다. 문득 뭔가 깜빡한 것 같다는 느낌이 든다. 손을 뻗어 뒷좌석을 더듬어본다. 출장가방은 있다. 전날 저녁 미리 짐을 꾸려놓은 게 참 다행이다. 그럼 뭐지? 바로 그 순간이다.

"아차! 강아지!"

강아지가 먹을 밥과 물을 깜빡한 것이다. 얼굴이 화끈 달아오르면서 이마엔 진땀이 송글송글 맺힌다.

당신은 어릴 때부터 강아지를 무척 갖고 싶어했다. 하지만 어머니는 말도 못 붙이게 했다. 그래서 전세 아파트를 얻어 분가하자마자 가장 먼저 산 게 강아지다. 강아지는 역시 당신과 죽이 잘 맞는다. 아무리 짜증스런 얼굴로 귀가해도 변함없이 늘 꼬리를 쳐댄다. 이 세상에서 당신을 무조건적으로 사랑해주는 건 강아지밖에 없다는 생각도 든다. 강아지 눈을 가만히 들여다보면서 이런 생각도 했다.

'개에게도 영혼이 들어 있는 게 분명해.'

그런 강아지를 깜빡하다니…. 출장기간 사흘 내내 꼬박 굶겨야 할 판이다. 그날 회의가 끝나자마자 출장자 전원이 곧바로 비행기를 타고 부산까지 가야 하기 때문이다. 거기서 만날 사람들이 줄줄이 약속돼 있다. 회의를 마치고 집에 들러 강아지 먹이를 준다는 건 불가능하다.

'열쇠를 내가 가지고 있으니 누구한테 부탁할 수도 없고…'

이러지도 저러지도 못하는 상황이다. 강아지는 사흘 동안 굶어도 생존할 수 있을까? 배고픔에 지쳐 마구 짖어대는 강아지가 떠오른다. 그러다가 굶어죽기라도 하면?

당신은 운전대를 더욱 단단히 움켜잡는다. 일단 어떻게든 회의에 참석하는 게 급선무다. 이제까지 잘 쌓아온 공든 탑을 와르르 무너지게 할 순 없는 일이다. 잘하면 지각을 안 할 수도 있을 거란 생각도 든다. 하지만 강아지는 어떻게 하나? 먹이가 아니면 물이라도 마셔야 할 것 아닌가? 강아지가 물 한 모금 못 마신 채 며칠이나 생존할 수 있을까? 당신은 페달을 더욱 거세게 밟으며 어떤 선택이 가능한지 다시 한 번 점검해 본다.

8시 회의 참석 후 집에 들렀다가 비행기를 탄다는 건 불가능하다. 그럼 회의 중간에 갑자기 나온다? 그럼 회사 간부들에게 찍혀버리는 거다. 그게 안 되면 회의에만 참석한 뒤 출장은 포기한다? 그럼 이 직장은 끝장이다. 이제 회사건물이 몇 블록 앞이다. 어떻게 할까?

'강아지 때문에 내 인생을 망칠 순 없지.'

당신의 머릿속은 육신의 생존에 관한 생각으로 가득하지만, 그래도 마음 한구석이 켕긴다.

'그러면 안 돼. 강아지가 죽을지 몰라.'

이것은 영혼의 목소리다. 만일 당신이 영혼의 목소리를 외면한다면?

그래서 강아지가 끝내 굶어죽는다면?

"양심을 지켜서 무슨 짝에 쓸모 있어? 손해만 볼 뿐이지—."

당신은 정말 아무 일도 일어나지 않은 것처럼 살아갈 수 있을까? 직장에서는 계속 탄탄대로를 달릴 수 있을까? 당신은 마음부터 불편하다. 영혼은 당신으로 하여금 죄책감을 느끼도록 한다. 속이 켕기는 건 그래서다. 당신의 속이 켕기는 순간, 놀랍게도 우주도 속이 켕긴다. 특히 당신과 옷깃만이라도 스쳐 간 사람들은 무의식적으로, 혹은 직감적으로 당신이 어떤 행동을 했는지 컴퓨터처럼 알아차린다.

'저 친구는 뭔가 나쁜 짓을 한 거 같아. 대체 무슨 미심쩍은 짓을 한 거지?'

당신은 즉각 펄쩍 뛸 것이다.

'설마! 내 아파트 안에서 일어난 일을 남들이 어떻게 알아?'

아인슈타인도 설마라고 생각했다. 하지만 직접 실험해보고는 혀를 내둘렀다.

그는 초면인 두 사람에게 몇 분간 서로 가볍게 대면할 시간을 주었다. 말하자면 옷깃만 스칠 정도의 인연을 맺도록 한 것이다. 그런 다음 서로 50발짝 정도 떨어진 패러데이 상자(Faraday cage)에 각기 들어가 있도록 했다(패러데이 상자란 전자기파가 통하지 않도록 차단한 상자다). 그러고는 두 사람의 머리에 두뇌활동을 그려내는 뇌파계(EEG)를 각각 연결시켰다.

"이쪽 사람의 양 눈에 펜라이트를 비추면? 저쪽 사람의 눈에도 어떤 신호가 갈까?"

펜라이트(penlight)란 펜 모양의 아주 작은 손전등을 말한다. 펜라이트를 눈에 비추면 동공이 좁아지면서 뇌파계에 미세한 두뇌 활동이 감지된다. 그런데 뜻밖의 일이 일어났다.

"어? 이쪽 사람 눈에만 펜라이트를 비췄을 뿐인데, 저쪽 사람의 뇌파계도 똑같이 움직이네?"

정말 귀신이 곡할 노릇 아닌가? 이쪽 패러데이 상자에 들어 있는 사람의 동공과 뇌파가 움직이자 50발짝이나 떨어진 저쪽 패러데이 상자에 들어 있는 사람의 동공과 뇌파도 역시 똑같이 움직이는 거였다! 그래서 이번엔 두 사람을 훨씬 더 멀리 떨어뜨려 놓아보았다. 하지만 아무리 멀리 분리시켜놓아도 결과는 마찬가지였다. 그래서 실험대상자들을 바꿔서 실험해보았다. 그래도 똑같은 결과였다.

이것은 아인슈타인이 동료 물리학자인 포돌스키 Podolsky, 로젠 Rosen 과 함께 실시한 실험이다(흔히 E-P-R 실험이라 일컫는다). 이 실험이 뜻하는 건 자명했다. 나와 단 한 번이라도 인연을 맺었던 사람들은 나도 모르게 나와 끊임없이 정보를 주고받는다. 내가 무슨 생각을 하고 무슨 짓을 하는지 무의식적으로 훤히 알고 있는 것이다. 그렇다고 인연을 맺지 않았다고 해서 전혀 영향이 없는 것은 아니다. 앞서 관찰자 효과를 설명할 때 언급했듯, 나의 모든 생각과 행동은 몽땅 우주에 기록된다.

그럼 조물주는 왜 모든 게 낱낱이 기록되도록 창조해놓았을까?

"그건 영혼을 갈고 닦도록 하기 위해서죠. 인과응보의 법칙이 존재하는 것도 그래서입니다. 남에게 가한 심신의 상처는 반드시 내게 되돌아와요."

이는 영혼여행을 경험한 전 세계의 임사체험자들, 최면치료를 받다가 영계를 본 수많은 사람들, 깊은 영적 깨달음을 얻어 영계와 물질계를 드나드는 사람들, 수십 년간 영혼을 연구해온 정신의학자들이 이구동성으로 하는 말이다. 악한 마음을 품고 사느냐, 선한 마음을 품고 사느냐에 따라 자신도 모르게 눈빛과 인상이 달라지는 것도 우리의 속마음이 시나브로 얼굴에 낱낱이 기록돼나가기 때문이다. 따라서 양심을 지켜서, 혹은 남을 돕다가 손해를 보게 되는 일은 결코 일어나지 않는다. 어느 순간 어떻게 내게 이득으로 되돌아올지는 아무도 모른다. 10년 후일 수도, 100년 후의 내세일 수도, 영계일 수도 있다. 우주엔 시공간의 개념이 없기 때문이다.

창조주가 누구는 늘 이득만 보고, 누구는 늘 손해만 보도록 엉성하게 우주를 만들어놓았을 리 만무하지 않은가? 우주의 질서는 톱니바퀴보다 더 정교하게 돌아간다. 우주를 구성하는 미립자들이 사람의 속마음을 속속들이 읽어내지 않는가? 따라서 만일 내가 선행을 한다면 그 보답도 반드시 되돌아온다. 미립자들에 저장된 선행의 정보는 영구히 지워지지 않기 때문이다.

선 행 은 몇 곱 절 로 되 돌 아 온 다

오래전, 첫째 아이가 태어나기 전의 일이다. 나는 점심식사 후 머리도 식힐 겸 산책을 마치고 사무실로 돌아오던 참이었다. 한 남자가 새파랗게 질린 얼굴로 안절부절못한 채 허둥대고 있었다.

"애가 어디 갔지? 금방 여기 있었는데?"

아이를 잃어버린 것이었다. 나도 모르게 가슴이 방망이질을 해댔다.

"몇 살이죠?"

"다섯 살요."

"옷 색깔은?"

"파란색요."

"그럼 저쪽을 찾아보세요. 이쪽은 제가 찾아볼 테니까."

우리는 서로 반대 방향으로 내달으며 좌우를 훑어나갔다. 가게 주인들이나 아파트 경비원 등 도움이 될 만한 사람들이면 무조건 "혹시 이런 아이 보셨어요?"를 연발하며 헤집고 다녔다. 10여 분쯤 지났을까? 아무리 찾아도 그런 아이는 없었다. 다시 발길을 되돌려 그 남자를 찾아갔다. 그 남자는 사색이 돼 있었다.

"지금 아이가 길을 잃고 쩔쩔매는 모습을 생각하고 계시죠? 그러지 말고 머릿속으로 활짝 웃는 아이 얼굴을 떠올려보세요! 아빠를 찾아서 활짝 웃는 얼굴!"

내가 왜 그때 그런 말을 외쳤는지는 나도 모른다. 다시 얼마나 더 지났을까? 내가 공원 중간쯤 훑고 있는데 뒤쪽에서 밝게 외치는 소리가 들렸다.

"찾았어요! 아저씨, 찾았어요!"

온몸에 기쁨의 전류가 흘러 퍼졌다. 아이는 남자 팔에 안겨 멋쩍은 듯 싱긋거리고 있었다. 그가 아이를 슬쩍 쥐어박았다.

"임마! 말도 안 하고 거기로 가버리면 어떻게 찾니?"

그가 그렁그렁한 눈으로 아이를 바라보았다.

그로부터 10여 년의 세월이 흐른 뒤의 일이다. 첫째 아이가 여섯 살 때쯤, 나는 워싱턴에 특파원으로 나가 있었다. 그때 아이를 데리고 플로리다 주 디즈니월드에 갔었다. 여름 휴가철 성수기라 사람들이 바글바글했다. 한 가지를 구경하려면 30분 이상 줄을 서야 했다. 그런데 줄을 서서 기다리는 동안 카메라로 뭔가를 찍다 보니 아이가 안 보였다.

'어, 어디 갔지?'

순간적으로 얼굴이 확 달아오르면서 진땀이 주르륵 흘렀다. 번개처럼 달려가며 인파를 차례로 훑어나가기 시작했다. 얼마나 지났을까? 끝도 없이 흘러가는 인파 속에서 나는 눈앞이 캄캄해지기 시작했다. 심장은 사정없이 쾅쾅 뛰었다. 제발 꿈이었으면 하는 절박감으로 온몸이 흠뻑 젖었다. 그때 돌연 등 뒤에서 나를 부르는 소리가 들렸다.

"Daddy! Daddy! Daddy!"

정말 우리 아이였다! 한 미국인 부인의 손을 잡고 나를 부르고 있었다. 와락 달려가 아이를 껴안고 부인을 향해 울부짖듯 외쳤다.

"너무 고맙습니다! 너무 고맙습니다!"

생면부지의 그 부인도 내 모습을 바라보더니 눈가를 훔치며 제 갈 길로 걸어갔다. 10여 년 전, 나는 아이를 잃은 낯선 남자에게 작은 도움을 주었을 뿐이다. 하지만 우주는 그 작은 선행을 기억하고 있다가 몇 곱절로 내게 되돌려주었다. 꼭 선행이 아니라도 그렇다. 두꺼운 '나'의 벽을 열고 설사 말 못하는 미물에게 아주 작은 사랑을 베풀기만 해도, 그 사랑의 기운은 몇 곱절로 내게 되돌아온다. 그리고 나를 건강하고 행복하게 한다.

베풂은 건강으로 되돌아온다

한 요양원에 65세가 넘는 노인들이 입주해 있었다. 그런데 요양원에서 편안하게 여생을 즐기던 노인들이 어느 날 술렁대기 시작했다. 원장이 새로운 생활지침을 발표했기 때문이다. 그는 우선 1층 노인들을 불러 모아 이렇게 말했다.

"오늘부터 여러분께서는 모든 걸 스스로 하셔야 합니다. 먼저 일주일에 한 번씩 보여드리는 영화관람 시간을 스스로 결정하십시오. 또 정원의 식물 돌보는 일도 여러분이 알아서 책임져주십시오. 물을 주고, 풀을 뽑고, 가지를 치는 일도 여러분이 하셔야 합니다. 저희는 손을 떼겠습니다."

이번엔 2층에 사는 노인들을 불러 말했다.

"여러분께서 원하시는 것이 있으면 서슴지 말고 말씀해주십시오. 저희가 다 해드리겠습니다. 영화 관람도 가장 편안한 시간으로 저희가 정해드리겠습니다. 정원 관리도 신경 쓰실 것 없습니다. 여러분께선 그저 각자의 몸만 잘 챙기시면 됩니다."

그때부터 1층 노인들은 정원을 돌보랴, 영화관람 시간을 서로 맞추랴, 바쁜 하루를 보내야 했다. 반면 2층 노인들은 아무 걱정 없이 오로지 '나'에 대해서만 신경 쓰면 그만이었다.

그로부터 18개월 후 노인들의 건강상태를 검사해보니, 1층 노인들과 2층 노인들 사이엔 놀라운 차이가 나타났다. 매일 정원에 나가 일했던 1층 노인들의 몸에선 스트레스 호르몬이 줄어들고 복용하던 약도 크게 줄었다. 얼굴엔 화색이 돌고 몸의 움직임도 기민해졌다. 1층 노인의 93퍼센트는 건강이 더 좋아졌다.

그렇다면 손가락 하나 까딱할 필요 없이 오로지 '나'만 챙기며 지냈던 2층 노인들은 어땠을까? 그들의 얼굴에선 생기가 사라졌다. 검진 결과, 71퍼센트가 전보다 더 허약해진 것으로 나타났다. 그 사이 세상을 등진 이도 있었다. 더욱 놀라운 사실은 2층 노인들의 사망률이 1층 노인들의 두 배나 됐다는 것이다. 그 실험을 주도한 예일대학의 로딘(Judith Rodin) 교수는 이렇게 말한다.

"내 몸뚱이 하나만 편하면 된다는 생각으로 살면 모든 게 나 하나로 좁혀집니다. 나의 벽을 세우는 거죠. 반면 나무 한 그루라도 키우면 벽이 열리게 됩니다."

'나'의 벽이 세워지면 우주로부터 아무것도 흘러들어오지 못한다. 반면 벽이 허물어지면 우주로부터 사랑과 지혜, 에너지가 가득 흘러나온다.

캘리포니아 대학의 셔비츠(Larry Scherwitz) 교수는 나에 집착하며 사는 게 얼마나 해로운지 알아보기 위해 600명의 대화를 녹음해봤다. 그리고 녹음테이프를 들으면서 어떤 사람들이 "나", "나의", "나를", "내 것" 등의 말을 얼마나 자주 쓰는지 세어보았다.

"아니, 이럴 수가! '나'에 관한 말수와 심장병 위험성이 정확하게 일치하네!"

말끝마다 "나"를 가장 많이 반복하는 사람들의 심장병 확률이 가장 높은 것이었다. 그들은 '나'에 집착한 나머지 남에게 귀를 기울일 줄 몰랐고 '내 것'만을 최고로 여겼다.

"나를 열고 남에게 베푸세요. 그게 무병장수의 비결입니다."

셔비츠 교수의 결론이다.

미시간 대학 연구진은 노인 부부 423쌍을 대상으로 남을 돕는 습관과 수명 사이에 어떤 관계가 있는지 지켜봤다. 여기서 돕는 일이란 거창한 게 아니었다. 친구, 이웃, 가족들의 집안일이나 아이 돌보기, 시장보기, 차량 제공 등 일상의 자잘한 일들이었다.

조사기간 5년 동안 134명이 숨졌다. 숨진 노인들은 대부분 남을 돕는 데 인색한 사람들이었다. 평소 남들을 잘 도와주지 않는 노인들의 사망률은 잘 돕는 노인들보다 두 배 이상 높았다. 특이한 것은 남들로부터 도움만 받고 '나'만 챙기며 지내는 노인들의 건강은 전혀 좋아지지 않았다는 것이다.

미시간 대학의 브라운(Stephanie Brown) 교수의 분석은 이렇다.

"남한테 받기만 하는 사람 치고 건강하게 오래 사는 사람은 드물죠. 남에게 주기만 하는 사람들이 물질적으로는 손해 보는 것 같지만, 사실은 득을 보는 겁니다."

놀라운 사실은 남들을 위해 봉사활동을 하는 것이 규칙적인 운동을 하는 것보다 건강에 더 이로운 효과를 갖는다는 것이다.

과학자들이 캘리포니아 주 마린 카운티(Marin County)의 55세 이상 주민 2,025명을 5년간 조사해보니 두 곳 이상에서 봉사활동을 하는 사람들은 사망률이 보통사람들보다 63퍼센트나 낮았다. 규칙적으로 운동하는 사람들은 44퍼센트, 매주 교회 등에 나가는 사람들은 29퍼센트 순으로 사망률이 떨어졌다.

영혼이 육신을 떠나 영계에 올라가면 오로지 사랑을 얼마나 베풀었느냐로 심판을 받는다고 한다. 사랑을 베푸는 사람들은 지상에서도 건강하게 오래 산다.

진공묘유 眞空妙有 :
나를 텅 비우면 오묘한 일들이 일어난다

이 책 앞부분 제1부 3장에서 생각을 잠재우는 방법을 소개한 바 있다. 그때 사용한 그림을 다시 보자.

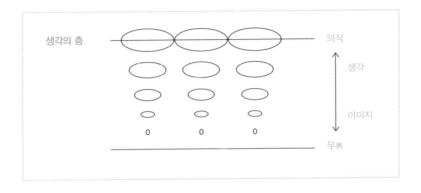

우리 의식의 표면은 시도 때도 없이 피어오르는 생각들로 늘 뒤덮여 있다. 주로 '나'와 관련된 생각들이다. 하지만 우리가 조용히 바라보면 그 생각들은 저절로 사라진다. 그러면서 아무 생각도 없는 텅 빈 무한한 공간, 무無가 드러난다. 그 공간은 생각들이 싹트기 전부터 존재해왔고, 생각들이 사라진 후에도 영원히 존재한다. 즉, 나는 늘 생각에 가득 차 있는 게 아니라 원래부터 텅 빈 무한한 공간이다. 양자물리학자들의 말대로 나는 텅 비어 있다. 그런데 텅 빈 나를 바라보는 또 다른 나는 또 누구인가? 몸속의 '나'가 나를 바라볼 수 있는가? 그건 몸 밖의 나이다. 몸 밖에 있는 나도 텅 비어 있다. 어떤 방법으로 보든, 진정한 나는 텅 비어 있다

헌트 박사

"자신을 텅 비우는 순간 천리안,
원격치료, 원격대화 등 숨어 있
던 능력들이 깨어난다."

valerievhunt.com

는 사실이 다시 한 번 생생하게 입증된다.

그런데 만일 당신이 많은 연습을 통해 텅 비어 있는 상태를 마음대로 장시간 유지할 수 있다면? 그때 당신에겐 신기한 능력이 생긴다! 별의별 오묘한 일들이 꼬리를 물고 일어난다. 왜 그러냐고? 그 텅 빈 공간, 즉 영점공간에는 당신이 원하는 정보가 다 들어 있기 때문이다. 거기서 원하는 바를 그리면 곧바로 현실로 나타난다. 앞서 몇 차례 언급한 UCLA의 생리학 교수인 헌트(Valerie Hunt) 박사의 예를 들어보자. 그녀는 지난 50여 년간 기(氣) 에너지 연구에 몰입해온 세계 최고의 권위자이다. 그녀는 자신을 텅 비우는 방법을 완전히 몸에 익히면서 저절로 신비한 힘을 얻었다. 95세의 나이에도 불구하고 방 한복판 바닥에 손을 짚고 거꾸로 설 수 있으며 사람의 마음을 손바닥 들여다보듯 훤히 읽을 수 있다. 지구 반대편에 떨어진 사람의 질병도 치료할 수 있다.

"우리가 자신을 완전히 텅 비우는 순간 어마어마한 변화가 일어납니다. 천 리 밖을 내다보는 능력, 마음으로 질병을 치유하는 능력, 만 리 밖에서 마음으로 대화하는 능력, 숨어 있던 이 모든 능력이 깨어나게 되죠."

268

그녀는 천리안이나 도술, 혹은 명상법을 따로 배운 적이 없는 순수한 학자이다. 오로지 우주의 원리를 깨닫고 자신의 잠재력을 완전히 이해하게 된 것뿐이다. 단지 자신을 제대로 바라보는 것만으로 그런 신비한 능력이 저절로 생긴 것이다. 스탠퍼드 대학의 푸토프(Harold Puthoff) 박사 역시 그런 원리를 이해하고 나서 천리안을 갖게 됐다. 그는 지난 1970년대부터 물리학자인 타그(Russell Targ) 박사와 함께 미중앙정보국 CIA 요원들에게 천리안을 가르쳐왔다. 그가 한번은 탁월한 투시력을 지닌 두 사람에게 각기 유럽 한 도시의 뒷골목을 묘사해보도록 했다. 박사 자신은 직접 가보았지만 그들에게는 진혀 깜깜한 곳이었다. 놀랍게도 그들은 자세하게 그곳을 묘사했고, 박사는 그들의 투시력이 어디까지 미치는지 궁금해졌다.

그래서 이번에는 목성을 묘사해보도록 했다. 미국의 우주왕복선 파이어니어 10호가 목성을 촬영한 사진을 보내오기 전의 일이었다.

스윈이라는 투시력자는 당황하는 듯한 표정으로 이렇게 대답했다.

"거참, 목성에도 고리가 보이네요. 아마 제가 실수로 토성을 잘못 본 건 아닌지 모르겠네요."

그의 말에 귀를 기울이는 사람은 아무도 없었다. 하지만 한참이 지난 후 미항공우주국 NASA가 공개한 목성 촬영 사진을 보고는 모두들 입이 딱 벌어졌다. 목성에도 정말 고리가 있다는 사실이 처음으로 확인됐던 것이다!

미 중앙정보국 CIA는 푸토프 박사의 실험결과에 큰 호기심을 보였다. 러시아 등의 적대 국가들 내에서 어떤 일들이 벌어지고 있는지 투시력을 이용해 정탐해낼 수 있다면 굳이 첩보원들을 보내지 않아도 될 것이기 때문이었다. 그래서 CIA가 프라이스라는 이름의 투시력자를 직접 시험해보았다. CIA는 한 요원으로 하여금 세 가지 숫자가 적힌 종이쪽지를 호주머니에 넣고 비행기를 타도록 한 다음, 프라이스에게 물었다.

"지금 비행중인 우리 요원의 호주머니에 들어 있는 종이쪽지에 어떤 숫자가 적혀 있는지 말해보시오."

프라이스는 식은 죽 먹기라는 듯 즉시 세 숫자를 나열했다. 순서까지 정확하게 일치했다. 하지만 숫자를 맞히고는 괜히 구역질이 난다고 말했다. 곧 구역질이 나는 이유가 밝혀졌다. CIA 요원이 탔던 비행기가 난류를 만나 심하게 요동쳤던 것이다.

푸토프 박사는 이번엔 실험보조원 몇 명을 각기 멀리 떨어진 다른 곳에 보내 15분 내에 그곳을 촬영하고 서면으로 묘사하도록 했다. 그런 다음 투시력자들에게 실험보조원들이 가 있는 곳을 알아맞춰보라고 했다. 그들은 완벽하게 그곳의 모습들을 묘사해냈다.

투시력자들은 미래도 예측해낼 수 있을까? 푸토프 박사는 여행자들을 특정한 몇 곳에 보내기에 앞서 투시력자들에게 거기서 앞으로 일어날 일들을 묘사해보라고 했다. 여행자들이 각기 30분~5일 후 실제로 현지에 가서 겪게 될 일들과 대조해보니 투시력자들이 미리 묘사한 것과 딱 맞아떨어졌다. 여행자들이 채 도착하기도 훨씬 전에 투시력자들은 거기서 벌어질 일들을 훤히 내다보고 있었던 것이다.

푸토프 박사는 투시력자들을 대상으로 모두 336차례에 걸친 실험을 실시했지만, 시간과 공간에 상관없이 결과는 거의 예외 없이 일치했다.

프린스턴 대학 교수였던 라딘(Dean Radin) 박사나 캘리포니아 대학의

푸토프 박사

"누구나 마음을 텅 비우면
시공간을 초월해 모든 걸 보게 되죠."

arlingtoninstitute.org

타그(Elisabeth Targ) 박사 등도 역시 사람의 마음을 읽거나 만 리 밖을 내다보는 능력을 갖고 있다. 이들이 산속에 들어가 수십 년간 도를 닦아서가 아니다. 육신의 생각을 완전히 비우고 관찰자의 깊은 눈으로 바라보면 반드시 모든 게 훤히 보이게 된다는 원리를 꿰고 있기 때문이다. 불교의 고승들은 이미 수천 년 전, 생각을 텅 비우면 오묘한 현상들이 일어난다는 사실을 깨닫고 진공묘유眞空妙有라고 불렀다. 수천 년 전 인도의 파탄잘리도 "마음속의 잔물결을 잠재우면 모든 기적이 일어난다"고 했다. 또, 예수가 "마음이 가난한 자는 복이 있나니 천국이 저희 것임이요."라고 했던 것도 마음을 완전히 비우면 실제로 천국이 보인다는 뜻이었다. 그 천국이란 먼 곳에 있지 않다. 바로 내 안에 있다. 누구나 마음을 비우는 연습만 충분히 하면 신비한 경험을 할 수 있다. 이번엔 보통 사람들의 사례를 들어보자.

한 여중생이 안대로 눈을 가린 채 당신 앞에 서 있다. 당신은 종이에 아무도 모르게 어떤 글자를 적어 봉투에 집어넣은 뒤 그 여중생에게 건네준다.

"봉투 안에 어떤 글자가 들어 있는지 알아맞혀 보세요."

그 여학생은 과연 육안을 가린 채 글자를 읽어낼 수 있을까?

몇 분이 지난 뒤 여학생이 말한다.

"이 봉투엔 M 자가 들어 있네요."

당신은 깜짝 놀란다. 당신이 종이에 써서 봉투에 집어넣은 글자가 정말 M 자이기 때문이다.

몇 년 전 한국뇌과학연구원이 취재진에게 공개했던 투시력 시연장면이다. 당시 학생들과 직장인 등 보통 사람 다섯 명이 투시력을 선보였다. 조선일보와 SBS, YTN 등 언론매체들이 이를 보도했다. 일어난 대로 그대로 보도한 신문도 있었지만, 뭔가 의심스러워 믿지 못하겠다는 식으로 묘사한 매체와 심리학 교수들도 있었다.

"사람이 어떻게 눈을 가린 채 앞을 볼 수 있어? 뭔가 속임수가 있었을 거야."

오감에 길든 생각들로 가득 찬 사람들은 직접 보고도 믿지 못하는 게 당연하다. 하지만 그런 생각들을 몽땅 잠재우면 장애물을 뚫고 마음의 눈으로 볼 수 있다.

"무슨 도 닦는 소리 같은 말만 늘어놓는군."

아마 이렇게 생각하는 독자도 있을 것이다. 하지만, 오해하지 말라. 내가 주제넘게 당신에게 당장 천리안이나 투시력 등 불가사의한 능력을 배워보라고 하는 게 절대 아니다. 단지 무한한 가능성을 열어놓으라는 것이다. 앞서 누차 언급했듯 가능성을 열어놓고 사는 것 자체만으로도 관찰자 효과에 따라 능력의 크기가 저절로 달라진다. 내가 이 책을 쓰는 것도 그렇다. 만일 내가 예전처럼 '비좁은 나'의 감옥에 갇혀 '난 뜬구름 같은 얘기는 안 믿어' 하고 가능성의 문을 철컥 닫아버렸다면 이런 책을 쓰기는커녕, 여전히 고통 속에 허우적거리며 살고 있을 것이다. 하지만 가능성의 문을 활짝 열어젖히는 순간 나도 모르던 것들이 조금씩 스며들기 시작했다.

사람들의 99.9퍼센트는 지능이나 능력, 한계가 대개 엇비슷하다. 그런데 0.1퍼센트도 안 되는 사람들은 보통사람들보다 저 멀리 앞서 있다. 선천적으로 능력을 타고난 게 아니다. 과학자들이 아인슈타인의 두뇌를 이리저리 분석해봤지만 그것은 보통사람들과 똑같은 뇌세포 덩어리였다.

능력의 크기는 단지 '나'를 어떻게 정의하느냐가 결정짓는다. 내 모든 능력은 내 육신 속에 들어 있다고 믿는 사람은 육신의 한계를 벗어날 수 없다. 반면 '나는 우주만큼 무한한 존재'라고 바라보면 능력도 무한하게 쏟아져 나온다. 단순한 시각의 차이로 인생이 갈린다.

육신과 영혼은 늘 숨바꼭질한다. 육신이 눈을 뜨면 영혼이 잠들고, 영혼이 눈을 뜨면 육신이 잠든다. 그래서 돈과 권력, 명예 등 육신의 욕망에 집착하면 영혼이 눈멀고, 영혼의 실체를 깨달으면 그런 욕망에서 저절로 멀어진다. 동시에 두 가지로 바라볼 수는 없다. 상보성의 원리 때문이다.

"인생을 사는 방법은 두 가지다. 하나는 아무 기적도 없는 것처럼 사는 것이요, 다른 하나는 모든 게 기적인 것처럼 사는 것이다."

아인슈타인의 말 속에 진리가 담겨 있다. 영혼에 눈뜨고 살면 기적 같은 나날이 꼬리를 문다.

나를 타인처럼 바라보며 살아라

영혼에 눈뜨는 가장 쉬운 방법은 나를 남의 눈으로 깊이 바라보는 것이다. 육신의 눈은 나를 남처럼 바라보지 못한다. 하지만 텅 빈 무한한 공간, 우주에 퍼진 영혼은 나를 남처럼 바라볼 수 있다. 나를 남처럼 바라보는 순간 영혼은 저절로 눈뜨기 시작한다. 영혼을 거대한 우주 거울로 삼아 나를 남처럼 비춰가며 살면 영혼이 지닌 양심, 사랑, 평화, 연민, 지능, 에너지가 저절로 흘러들어온다.

우리가 매일 사용하는 흔한 유리 거울로 자신을 비춰도 영혼이 삐쭉 고개를 든다. 나를 남으로 객관화시켜 바라보도록 하기 때문이다.

일리노이 대학의 디너(Ed Diener) 교수는 어떤 학생들에게는 거울을 마주 본 채 문제를 풀도록 하고, 다른 학생들에게는 거울을 등지고 풀도록 해보았다.

이윽고 시험 종료를 알리는 "따르릉" 소리가 울렸다. "따르릉" 소리가 났는데도 계속 문제를 푸는 건 부정행위다. 하지만 거울을 등진 학생들은 한 문제라도 더 풀려고 낑낑거리고 있었다. 반면 거울을 마주 본 학생들은 순순히 펜을 놓았다.

또 다른 심리학자도 이와 비슷한 실험을 했다. 교실로 어린이들을 모이게 한 다음, 커다란 사탕 그릇을 보여주며 "한 사람당 사탕 하나씩만 가져가거라"고 했다. 그리고 자리를 떴다. 어린이들은 시키는 대로 하나씩만 가져갔을까? 아니다. 전체의 34퍼센트가 두 개 이상 집어갔다. 그래서 이번에는 사탕 그릇 옆에 큰 거울을 비스듬히 세워놓고 다른 아이들에게 똑같이 "한 사람당 하나씩만"이라고 말했다. 두 개 이상 집어간 어린이는 몇 명이나 됐을까? 두 개 이상 집어간 비율이 4분의 1로 뚝 떨어졌다.

같은 이치로, 폐쇄회로 TV에 자신의 모습이 비치기만 해도 양심은 되살아난다. 행동과학자 캘그린(Carl Kallgren)은 폐쇄회로 TV 이미지가 대학생들의 쓰레기 무단투기에 어떤 영향을 미치는지 실험해보았다. 그는 먼저 대학생 절반에게 폐쇄회로 TV에 찍힌 자신의 이미지를 보여주었다. 나머지 절반에게는 도형 이미지를 보여주었다. 그런 다음 이렇게 말했다.

"자, 이제 실험의 끝 순서로 맥박을 재야 하니까 손에 젤을 발라주지."

그리고 젤을 닦아내라고 휴지를 나눠준 후에, 학생들이 나가면서 휴지를 어디에 버리는지 관찰해보았다.

폐쇄회로 화면에서 도형을 본 학생들은 46퍼센트가 나가면서 계단에다 휴지를 버렸다. 반면 자신의 이미지를 본 학생들의 경우 24퍼센트만이 거기에 휴지를 버렸다.

캘그린은 이런 궁금증이 들었다. "휴지를 아무렇게나 버린 학생들은 과연 거울로 매일 자신의 모습을 바라볼까?" 조사해보니 그들은 예상대로 거울을 보지 않았다. 거울에 자신을 자주 비춰보는 사람일수록 더 양심껏 행동하게 된다.

이런 원리를 이용해 살을 뺄 수도 있다. 부엌에 거울을 놓아두는 것이다. 그럼 훨씬 덜 먹게 된다. 이처럼 자신을 거울로 비춰보듯 남으로 바라보는 순간, 영혼과 육신 간의 숨바꼭질에서 영혼이 이기게 된다.

온종일 걷다 보니 배가 몹시 고프다. 길가의 한 작은 가판 위에 먹음직

한 사과 하나가 놓여 있다. 먹을까 말까? 주변을 둘러보니 아무도 없다. 내 머릿속에서는 두 목소리가 싸운다.

"아무도 안 보는데 먹으면 어때?"

"안 돼. 남의 물건에 손대면 안 돼."

행인 열 명 중 여덟아홉 명은 슬쩍 집어먹는다. 하지만 만일 사과 위에 사람의 눈을 그려 붙여놓는다면? 거의 아무도 집어먹지 않는다.

영국 뉴캐슬대학 연구진이 사무실 앞에 무인판매대를 세워놓고 유사한 실험을 해봤다. 판매대에는 커피, 차, 우유가 놓여 있었다. 판매대 위쪽 벽에 붙어 있는 포스터엔 예쁜 꽃 그림과 함께 다음과 같은 안내문을 적어놓았다.

〈커피, 차, 우유 중 필요한 것을 골라 드십시오. 가격은 각기 50펜스입니다. 돈은 판매대 옆에 있는 돈 박스에 넣어주십시오.〉

직원들 가운데 정직하게 꼬박꼬박 50펜스를 내고 커피나 우유를 마시는 사람은 몇이나 됐을까? 몇 푼 안 되는 돈이었는데도 그리 많지 않았다.

그래서 이번에는 다른 포스터를 붙여 보았다. 꽃 그림 대신 사람의 눈 한 쌍이 흑백으로 크게 그려져 있는 안내 포스터였다. 그러자 직원들의 행동이 확 달라졌다. 정직하게 돈 박스에 동전을 떨어뜨리는 직원들이 급증한 것이다.

10주간에 걸쳐 지켜보니 눈이 그려진 포스터가 붙어 있을 때 낸 돈이 꽃 포스터가 붙어 있을 때 낸 돈보다 무려 세 배나 더 많았다. 직원들은

베이트슨 교수

"누군가가 나를 지켜보고 있다는 암시만으로
도 커다란 변화가 일어난다."

포스터에 그려진 눈이 진짜라고 생각했던 것일까? 물론 그건 아니다. 실
험을 이끈 베이트슨(Melissa Bateson) 교수의 설명은 이렇다.

"비록 사람의 눈이 포스터에 그려진 그림에 불과할지라도 사람들은
무의식적으로 영향을 받게 됩니다. '누군가 날 지켜보고 있을지 모른다'
고 생각하게 되는 거죠."

'누군가 날 지켜볼지 모른다'는 생각이 드는 순간, 나도 모르게 나 자
신을 남의 눈으로 바라보게 된다. 작은 유리 거울이나 눈 포스터조차 이
런 효과를 갖는다. 하물며 우주라는 무한한 거울에 비춰가며 산다면 우리
영혼은 얼마나 맑아질까? 이처럼 우주가 늘 나를 지켜보고 있다는 마음
가짐으로 살아가는 것, 그게 바로 맑은 영혼을 지키는 길이자 최고의 인
생을 사는 길이다.

자신을 남의 눈으로 좀더 깊이 바라보는 방법도 있다. 자신의 묘비명
을 써놓고 사는 것이다. 이를테면 이런 것이다.

"여기 자신의 가족을 온 마음으로 사랑했던 (   )가 고이 잠들다."

당신이라면 당신의 묘비에 어떤 글이 쓰여지길 원하는가?

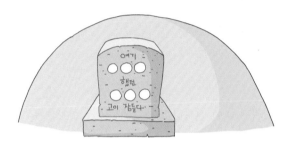

네바다 대학의 심리학 교수인 헤이즈(Steven Hayes)가 삶의 의욕을 잃고 방황하는 젊은이들로 하여금 묘비명을 쓰도록 했더니 놀라운 변화가 일어났다. 묘비명을 쓰는 간단한 행위만으로 술과 마약, 섹스에 중독됐거나 우울증으로 삶의 의욕을 완전히 상실했던 청소년들이 돌연 새 삶을 찾기 시작했던 것이다.

자신의 죽음을 바라보며 묘비명을 쓸 수 있는 건 누구인가? 바로 자신의 영혼이다. 영혼에 눈을 뜨면서 자신도 모르게 자기집착적 삶의 늪에서 벗어나게 되는 것이다.

더 나아가, 미시간 대학의 피터슨(Christopher Peterson) 교수는 자신의 묘비명에 인생 목표를 쓰도록 유도하면 목표 달성도가 부쩍 높아진다는 사실을 발견했다. 또한 사람들에게 장의사 건물 앞이나 공동묘지가 보이는 곳에서 자선단체에 기부하도록 하면 기부금이 훨씬 더 많이 걷힌다는 연

278

구결과도 나온 바 있다. 인생의 종착역을 연상하는 순간 자신을 타인의 눈으로 바라보게 되기 때문에 일어나는 현상이다.

아인슈타인은 늘 자신을 영혼의 거울에 비춰가며 살았다. 그래서 잡념이 없었고, 오로지 과학에만 몰입할 수 있었다. 그는 이런 말을 한 적 있다.

"화는 바보들의 가슴속에나 존재한다."

화를 못 다스리는 사람들을 비웃는 말이 아니었다. 화는 거울처럼 비춰주기만 하면 사라지는 건데, 거기에 파묻혀버리는 행위가 바보스럽다는 얘기였다. 그는 자신을 우주 거울에 완전히 열어놓고 우주와 하나가 됐다. 그래서 죽음을 두려워하지 않았다.

그는 76세 되던 해인 1955년 어느 날 갑자기 쓰러졌다. 복부 동맥류가 터져 심한 출혈이 일어난 것이었다. 내로라하는 의사들이 긴급히 달려와 수술하자고 했지만 그는 뜻밖에도 단호히 손을 내저었다.

"제가 가고 싶을 때 가고 싶습니다. 인위적으로 생명을 연장하고 싶지 않아요. 제 몫을 살았고, 갈 때가 됐으니 조용히 가고 싶습니다."

수술만 하면 더 살 수 있었는데도 거부한 것이었다. 그가 남긴 유언도 이례적이었다. 시신을 화장해 연구실 주변에 뿌릴 것, 묘지나 묘비는 절대 만들지 말 것, 장례식도 치르지 말 것, 두뇌를 제거해 과학발전에 이용토록 할 것 등이었다.

그는 어떻게 자신의 죽음을 그토록 초연하게 바라볼 수 있었을까?

보통 사람들은 육신이 자신의 전부라고 믿는다. 육신 속에 자신의 모든 게 들어 있다고 생각한다. 그래서 죽음은 '나의 영원한 끝장'이라고 여긴다. 자신의 모든 걸 걸었던 인생이 끝장나게 되니 한이 맺혀 도저히 눈을 감을 수 없다. 어쩔 수 없이 눈을 감으면서도 후손들이 장례식을 성대히 치러주고, 묘지도 근사하게 세워놓기를 기대한다.

하지만 아인슈타인에게 육신은 영혼이 잠시 발을 걸치고 사는 껍데기일 뿐이었다. 그는 대지로부터 잠시 껍데기를 빌려 쓰다가 되돌려줄 뿐이라 생각했다. 영혼은 늘 존재해왔고, 앞으로도 영원히 존재할 것이었다. 그렇게 바라보니 생명을 인위적으로 연장할 필요도 없었고, 장례식도, 묘지도, 묘비도 다 부질없고 헛될 뿐이었다.

한 설문조사 결과, 80세 이상 노인들의 90퍼센트 이상이 자신의 인생을 후회한다고 대답했다. 그리고 뭘 가장 후회하느냐는 물음에 "내가 꼭하고 싶었던 걸 못 했어요"라고 응답했다. "꼭 하고 싶었던 게 뭡니까?"라고 물으니 대답은 뜻밖에도 세계 여행이나 많은 돈, 출세 등 거창한 게 전혀 아니었다.

"내 아이가 소원했던 걸 해줄 수 있었더라면…"

"가족에게 좀더 따뜻한 말을 건네며 살았더라면…"

"돌아가신 어머니께 좀더 친절하게 대해 드렸더라면…"

쉽게 말해 사랑을 베풀지 못하고 살았던 걸 가장 후회했다. 사랑은 영혼의 본질이다. 나를 비우고 남에게 베풀면 영혼이 열린다. 하지만 영혼에 눈을 못 뜨고 살다 보니 사랑은 뒷전이 되어버렸다. 겨우 죽음에 이르러서야 다급하게 영혼을 찾고 사랑을 찾는다. 한 세상 다 살고 나서야 "내가 누구지?" 하고 두리번거린다.

아인슈타인은 자신이 진심으로 사랑하는 게 뭔지 알고 살다 죽었다.

우주를 사랑했고, 인생을 사랑했다. 누구에게나 똑같은 선택이 주어진다. 아인슈타인처럼 내가 누군지 분명히 알고 살다 죽을 것인지, 아니면 누군지도 모른 채 허둥지둥 바삐 살다 후회 속에 죽을 것인지….

내가 입사 2년 차쯤 됐을 때의 일이다.

어느 날 출근해보니 무척 깐깐해 보이고 뚱뚱한 사람이 새 부장으로 왔다. 권위의식으로 꽉 들어찬 사람이었다. 나는 첫눈에 불편함을 느꼈다. 그는 오자마자 내게 이런 지시를 내렸다.

"우리 부서가 앞으로 추진하거나 개선해야 할 점들이 있을 거야. 그걸 묶어 보고서로 만들어오게. 사흘간의 시간을 주지."

나는 선배들에게 이것저것 물어가며 열심히 보고서를 만들었다. 하지만 부장은 보고서를 받더니 홱 내던지는 것 아닌가?

"어이, 저런 것도 보고서라고 만들었나? 도대체 2년간 뭘 배웠나?"

그 말을 듣는 순간 목구멍으로 뭔가 울컥 올라왔다. 구체적인 이유도 제시하지 않은 채 남들 앞에서 나를 그토록 깡그리 무시하다니. 하지만 꾹 참았다. 홧김에 상사에게 대들었다간 화만 자초할 게 뻔했다.

"네, 알겠습니다. 다시 써보겠습니다."

하지만 부장은 또 얼굴을 찌푸렸다.

"그만둬. 자네는 싹수가 이미 글러 먹은 거 알고 있어."

동료직원들이 무안한 듯 흘끗거렸다.

그날부터 생지옥이었다. 부장은 내가 인사해도 못 본 척했고, 어떤 일도 시키지 않았다. 다른 직원들은 다 퇴근시켜놓고도 유독 나한테만큼은 퇴근하란 말이 없었다. 철저한 무시 작전이었다. 온갖 부정적 생각이 꼬리에 꼬리를 물고 피어올랐다.

그러다가 어느 회식 날. 다 함께 식사를 마친 뒤 2차로 노래방에 갔다. 부장은 일일이 순서를 정해가며 노래시켰다. 다른 직원들은 차례로 다 노래를 마쳤는데 유독 나한테만큼은 노래하란 말이 없었다. 그의 눈에 나는 존재하지 않았다. 동료직원들이 안 됐다는 듯 내 얼굴을 자꾸만 흘끗거렸다. 하지만 부장 눈치 보느라 누구도 내게 감히 말 한 마디 건네지 못했다. 왕따를 당하는 거였다. 얼굴이 확확 달아오르고 목구멍으로 뭔가 자꾸만 치밀어 올랐다. 집에 돌아가서도 잠이 오지 않았다.

'난 이 회사에서 잘 되기는 틀렸어.'

'동료들도 날 무능하게 생각할 거야.'

그런 나날이 계속 이어졌다. 어느 날 밤 뒤척이다가 간신히 잠이 들었지만 새벽에 돌연 엄청난 통증이 복부에 밀려왔다. 부장 얼굴이 다시 떠올랐다. 다음날 점심시간에 부랴부랴 병원에 달려갔다.

"스트레스예요. 젊은이가 웬 스트레스를 그렇게…"

의사가 혀를 끌끌 차며 약을 처방해줬다.

'병을 얻으면서까지 이 직장을 다녀야 하나?'

하지만 당장 직장을 바꾸기도 어려웠다. 아들이 쉽게 취직했다고 대견해하시던 부모님 얼굴도 어른거렸다.

얼마 후 더욱 이상한 증세가 나타나기 시작했다. 출근 버스에서 내려 회사가 가까워지면 심장이 사정없이 두근두근하는 거였다. 의사가 또 혀를 찼다.

"불안증세가 심하군요. 무슨 억눌린 감정이 있나요?"

나는 그 사람의 그림자만 봐도 가슴이 두근거렸다. 혹시나 그의 목소리라도 들릴까 봐 멀찌감치 돌아갔다. 그의 얼굴만 떠올라도 내 머릿속은 과거의 고통으로 가득 차올랐다. 고통에서 벗어나기 위해 나는 그 고통을 억누르려 들었다. 그럴수록 그것은 마치 호리병 램프에서 빠져나온 지니처럼 더욱 기승을 부리며 피어올랐다. 나는 거기에 파묻혀 버렸다.

만일 그때 내 마음을 비춰주는 속 깊은 친구가 딱 한 명이라도 있었다면? 고통은 쉽게 사라졌을 것이다. 학교에서 왕따를 당하는 경우도 그렇다. 방관하는 다수의 학생들 가운데 단 한 명만이라도 진정한 친구가 돼주면 고통은 사라진다.

정신분석가인 코헛(Heinz Kohut)은 "인간은 누구나 자신을 거울처럼 비춰주는 타인이 필요하다"고 말했다. 열등감이 심하고 쉽게 상처를 받고 쉽게 절망하는 사람들을 분석해보니 하나같이 어릴 때 자신의 마음을 거울처럼 비춰주는 부모가 없던 사람들이었기 때문이다.

아이가 상처를 받을 때 상처받은 마음을 비춰주어 바라보도록 하면 그 상처는 사라진다. 화날 때 화난 마음을 비춰주어 바라보도록 하면 그 화는 사라진다. 누구나 자신의 마음을 비춰주는 거울이 필요하다. 어릴 땐 부모가 이 역할을 해준다. 하지만 어른이 되면 이 역할을 해줄 사람이 없다. 그래서 사람들은 고통의 바다에서 살아간다.

고통은 고통을 통해 영혼을 갈고 닦으라는 우주의 신호다. 그래서 고통은 외면하려 들면 더욱 심해진다. 하지만 거꾸로 "이 고통을 통해 뭘 깨달을 수 있지?"하고 받아들여 깊이 바라보면 거짓말처럼 고통은 저절로 사라지고, 값진 깨달음이 찾아온다. 그래서 양자물리학자들은 왓칭을 "신이 부리는 요술"이라고 부르는 것이다.

미 국립과학재단(National Science Foundation)에 따르면, 사람들은 하루에 최고 5만 가지 생각을 한다고 한다. 그런데 그 가운데 10퍼센트만 쓸모 있는 것이고, 나머지 90퍼센트 이상은 부정적인 것이라 한다. 교토 대학의 연구팀은 사람들에게 "20대에 고민했던 생각들이 정말 가치가 있었습니까?" 하고 물어보았다. 사람들은 "5퍼센트 정도만 가치 있는 생각이었고, 나머지 95퍼센트는 삶에 아무런 영향도 미치지 못하는 부정적인 생각들이었다"고 응답했다. 즉 우리는 깨어 있는 인생의 90~95퍼센트를 아무 쓸모도 없는 부정적인 생각에 허비하는 것이다. 자신의 마음을 거울처럼 바라보지 못하고 그 속에 파묻혀 버리기 때문이다. 얼마나 소모적이고 불행한 일인가?

　내 마음을 비춰주는 거울은 내 안에 들어 있다. 내 마음속의 관찰자가 바로 그 거울이다. 세상이 나를 버려도 관찰자는 변함없이 따뜻한 어머니처럼 언제나 미소 지으며 나를 감싸주고 위로해준다. 유혹에 흔들리고 있을 때 바라보면 그 유혹이 떨어져 나간다. 끙끙 앓던 문제도 실마리가 풀린다. 무엇보다도 우주만큼 넓고 깊게 바라보게 해준다. 나만의 이득에 집착하기보다 나보다 못한 사람을 연민과 사랑의 눈으로 바라보게 해준다. 삶도 그만큼 넓고 깊고 풍성해진다. 우리가 이 세상에 태어나 짊어지는 모든 고통과 고민은 바라봄으로써 해결된다. 단지 이 왓칭 요술은 바라보는 만큼만 일어난다. 깊이 바라보면 깊이 일어나고, 얕게 바라보면 얕게 일어난다. 나는 우주의 가장 깊은 원리와 진실이 거울처럼 고스란히 이 책에 투영되도록 간절히 기도하며 원고를 썼다. 관찰자의 눈으로 바라보고 또 바라보려고 애썼다. 생각이 막힐 땐 어느새 관찰자가 고요히 나타나 생각을 풀어주었다.

　부디 이 책을 통해 신이 부리는 요술이 여러분의 머릿속을 거울처럼 비춰 깊은 변화가 일어나길 기도한다.

참고문헌

Amit Goswami, *Physics of the Soul: The Quantum Book of Living, Dying, Reincarnation and Immortality*, Hampton Roads Publishing, 2001

Brian Greene, *The Hidden Reality: Parallel Universes and the Deep Laws of the Cosmos*, Knopf, 2011

Bruce H. Lipton, *The Biology Of Belief: The Power Of Consciousness, Matter And Miracles*, Unleashing Mountain of Love, 2005

Bruce Rosenblum, *Quantum Enigma : Physics Encounters Consciousness*, Oxford University Press, 2008

David D. Burns, *Feeling Good, the New Mood Therapy*, Avon Books, 1980

Dean Radin, *Entangled Minds: Extrasensory Experiences in a Quantum Reality*, Paraview Pocket Books, 2006

Dean Radin, *The Conscious Universe: The Scientific Truth of Psychic Phenomena*, HarperOne, 2009

Dennis Greenberger, Christine Padestky, *Mind over Mood*, Guilford Press, 1995

Frank Joseph Kinslow, *Beyond Happiness: How You Can Fulfill Your Deepest Desire*, Lucid Sea, 2008

Frank Joseph Kinslow, *The Secret of Instant Healing*, Lucid Sea, 2008

Gary E. Schwartz, *The Living Energy Universe*, Hampton Roads Publishing, 2006

Gary E. Schwartz, *The G.O.D. Experiments: How Science Is Discovering God In Everything, Including Us*, Atria, 2007

Jon Kabat-Zinn, *Full Catastrophe Living*, Delta Book, 1989

Lynne McTaggart, *The Field: The Quest for the Secret Force of the Universe*, Free Press, 2008

Mark G. Williams, John D. Teasdale, Zindel V. Segal, Jon Kabat-Zinn, *Mindful Way through Depression*, The Guilford Press, 2007

Michio Kaku, *Physics of the Impossible*, Anchor, 2008

Richard Bartlett, *Matrix Energetics: The Science and Art of Transformation*, Atria Books / Beyond Words, 2007

Richard Bartlett, *The Physics of Miracles: Tapping in to the Field of Consciousness Potential*, Atria Books / Beyond Words, 2009

Robert Schwartz, *Your Soul's Plan: Discovering the Real Meaning of the Life You Planned Before You Were Born*, Frog Books, 2009

Russell Targ, *Limitless Mind: A Guide to Remote Viewing and Transformation of Consciousness*, New World Library, 2004

Russell Targ, *Miracles of Mind: Exploring Nonlocal Consciousness and Spritual Healing*, New World Library, 1999